A HISTORY OF THE AFRICAN PEOPLE OF SOUTH AFRICA

Generations of South Africans, white and black, have been conditioned to perceive Africans as peripheral actors outside the main theatre of South African history, appearing rarely on the central stage – and even then only as hindrances obstructing the progress of European civilisation.

In the past fifteen years extensive new research into the history of African societies in South Africa has been published. Much of this writing, however, has reached a relatively small readership of academics and senior students. A primary aim of this book, which ranges over the subcontinent, including present-day Botswana, Lesotho and Swaziland, is to compress and synthesise the findings of this research in the hope that it will be filtered through to a wider audience.

The book tries to look inside these African societies, examining their internal dynamics, regional variations, and processes of change over time. Two broad phases are covered: firstly, the precolonial, precapitalist era, beginning some 1 700 years ago with the Early Iron Age; and secondly, the period from the mid-nineteenth century when colonial subjugation gradually evolved into the modern apartheid system.

In dealing with the first phase the book highlights the material base of Iron Age society, and considers some of the dominant power structures that emerged within African states and chiefdoms. In the second phase the emphasis is on the varying African responses to white domination. These responses have ranged between, on the one hand, quiescence or cooptation into the structures of domination, and on the other, various forms of resistance and protest: violent confrontation; peaceful, constitutional organisation and opposition; community-based popular struggles; and working-class organisation and action.

Dr Paul Maylam, who is the author of *Rhodes, the Tswana and the British*, is Senior Lecturer in the Department of History, University of Natal.

A HISTORY OF THE AFRICAN PEOPLE OF SOUTH AFRICA: FROM THE EARLY IRON AGE TO THE 1970s

Paul Maylam

Croom Helm: London

David Philip: Cape Town & Johannesburg

FIRST PUBLISHED 1986 IN PAPERBACK IN SOUTHERN AFRICA AND AUSTRALASIA BY DAVID PHILIP, PUBLISHER (PTY) LTD, 217 WERD-MULLER CENTRE, CLAREMONT 7700, SOUTH AFRICA

PUBLISHED 1986 IN HARDBACK IN THE UNITED KINGDOM BY CROOM HELM LTD, PROVIDENT HOUSE, BURRELL ROW, BECKENHAM, KENT BR3 1AT; AND IN THE UNITED STATES OF AMERICA BY ST. MARTIN'S PRESS INC., 175 FIFTH AVENUE, NEW YORK, N.Y. 10010

ISBN 0-86486-041-2 (PAPERBACK, SOUTHERN AFRICA)
ISBN 0-7099-4653-8 (HARDBACK, UNITED KINGDOM)

BRITISH LIBRARY CATALOGUING IN PUBLICATION DATA:

MAYLAM, PAUL
A HISTORY OF THE AFRICAN PEOPLE OF SOUTH AFRICA
1. SOUTH AFRICA—HISTORY
I. TITLE
968 DT 766
ISBN 0-7099-4653-8

THIRD IMPRESSION 1989

PRINTED AND BOUND BY CREDA PRESS, SOLAN ROAD, CAPE TOWN, SOUTH AFRICA

CONTENTS

Preface vii

PART ONE: AFRICAN SOCIETY IN THE PRECOLONIAL ERA: FROM THE THIRD CENTURY TO c. 1830 1
1 The South African Iron Age 2
2 Nguni Communities until c. 1830 20
3 Sotho, Venda and Lemba Communities until c. 1830 42
4 The Difaqane 54
5 Problems of Conceptualisation and Interpretation 64

PART TWO: AN ERA OF TRANSITION c. 1830–1900 69
6 The Nguni: The Path to Colonial Subjugation 70
7 The Sotho and Venda: Peasantisation, Resistance and Incorporation 111

PART THREE: THE TWENTIETH CENTURY: PROLETARIANISATION, PARTITION AND PROTEST 135
8 Land, Labour and African Politics 1900–1936 136
9 Control and Confrontation 1936–1976 166
10 Colonialism, Decolonisation and Neo-colonialism : The BLS Countries 196
11 Conclusion 216

References 225
Bibliography 239
Index 249

PREFACE

The purpose of this book is to offer an outline of the history of the African people of South Africa. The term 'African' is itself problematic, as many would argue that all the inhabitants of the region, regardless of their race, are 'African'. In this book, however, the label is applied to those people who belong to the Nguni or Sotho language families, as well as to the Venda and Lemba, who fall outside those families.

Some might argue that the very conception of this book rests on a classificatory framework based on race and ethnicity — that the writing of an African history of South Africa represents, albeit unwittingly, a form of academic apartheid. In defence of this enterprise I would argue that there are legitimate reasons for adopting a specifically African focus. Firstly, any study of the South African Iron Age is concerned essentially with the ancestors of the present African population. Secondly, over the centuries there emerged a number of African states and chiefdoms. Although these were never exclusive, isolated entities, they do constitute appropriate units of analysis. Thirdly, while one has to recognise that major problems are encountered in trying to continue this African history into the twentieth century, yet even in the twentieth century there are some grounds for differentiation: Africans have been subjected to numerous laws, restrictions and an overall system of repression to which no other racial group in the country has been subjected on the same scale.

In many histories of South Africa, with some recent exceptions, Africans have appeared as shadowy figures in the background of the white historical experience. Africans have tended to come into the picture only when they have blocked the path of white expansion or rejected white authority. For the readers of such histories, their perception and knowledge of African history would probably amount to little more than a series of conflicts and confrontations — the Cape eastern frontier wars, the rise of Shaka, the Battle of Blood River, and the Anglo–Zulu War.

In this history it is the whites who appear as the shadowy background figures. For instance, the South African War is viewed from the perspective of the African experience rather than from that of the two main protagonists. This is not because whites are deemed to have played an insignificant role in South African history, but simply because they fall outside the scope of the study. The present book does not purport to be a history of South Africa.

An underlying assumption of this history is that there exists a constant interplay between the past and present. People's views about the present state of affairs in South Africa must inevitably contain in-built assumptions about South African history. Similarly, present preoccupations and concerns determine to a considerable extent the way in which the past is approached and studied. For instance, the South African government's present homelands policy rests upon an assumed historical model of a static, exclusivist tribalism. Furthermore, implicit notions of a static past have permeated some explanations of South African economic history. It is easy today to draw a sharp contrast between a white-dominated, developed capitalist economic sector and an impoverished African rural sector. On this score many are tempted to read the present back into the past, and assume that this current disparity is a product of a static, long-standing, racial differential in levels of skill, ingenuity, inventiveness and energy. Part of the aim of this book is to test and challenge some of these assumptions.

The geographical scope of this study is largely restricted to South Africa's eastern half, which has always been the main area of Nguni and Sotho occupation. South Africa is a vague label. For the purpose of this book it is taken to include Swaziland, Lesotho and Botswana (even though, of course, these territories have never formed part of South Africa in a formal political sense), as well as South Africa and the homelands, and to exclude Namibia, Zimbabwe and Mozambique. This means, of course, that there will be no coverage of Nguni and Sotho peoples who migrated north of the Limpopo during the *difaqane* — namely the Ndebele, Ngoni and Kololo.

A wider objective of this book is to attempt to synthesise and popularise the findings of recent research on the African history of southern Africa. In the past dozen years or so, massive advances have been made in our knowledge and understanding of this history. Perhaps the most spectacular advances have been achieved by archaeologists in their examination of the southern African Iron Age. Other scholars have probed a variety of themes in the history of Nguni and Sotho societies. Studies of the precolonial or precapitalist era have highlighted socio-political and economic structures and the ways in which these have varied over space and changed over time. For the nineteenth century there has been a special emphasis on several processes: frontier interaction, colonial subjugation, primary resistance, capitalist penetration, peasantisation and proletarianisation. Some of these themes carry over into the twentieth century, where we also find that significant work has been done on rural impoverishment, underdevelopment, urbanisation, class stratification, and the growth of African political organisations, protest movements and trade unions.

None of the empirical data in this book is original. It is all material that has been gleaned from secondary sources, mainly from books and articles written during this recent period of prolific and innovative scholarship. It would be an invidious task to name specific individuals; my consolidated footnotes show who they are. To those who are familiar with their works, my own reliance on them in writing this book will be readily apparent. The task of compressing their analytical insights and their wealth of data has been utterly daunting. During the course of this exercise in compression and synthesis much of their best material will necessarily have been lost; and perhaps some of my emphases were not intended by the authors whose work I have drawn upon. Such omissions and distortions are, of course, mine and not theirs.

I am especially grateful to a number of individuals who have helped with the production of this book. Christopher Saunders and Colin Bundy carefully scrutinised my original manuscript; and Tim Maggs cast the expert eye of an archaeologist over this layman's view of the South African Iron Age. Russell Martin has been a thorough and careful editor; Connie Munro typed the two drafts of this manuscript; Jenny McDowell drew the maps. I thank them for their assistance. My wife Gill has been very supportive of this enterprise, helping with proof-reading, offering encouragement, and bearing some of the indirect burdens that the project entailed.

For Gill, John and Genevieve

Part One

AFRICAN SOCIETY IN THE PRECOLONIAL ERA: FROM THE THIRD CENTURY TO c. 1830

1
THE SOUTH AFRICAN IRON AGE

The name Van Riebeeck and the associated date of 1652 are familiar to almost every student of South African history. As much as they are familiar, so are the name Silver Leaves and the date A.D. 270 likely to evoke an utterly blank response, even from the most experienced of South Africanist historians. That this should be so is hardly surprising. The disembarking of Van Riebeeck at the Cape in 1652 is a long-known, verifiable fact; and it marks the origins of permanent white settlement in South Africa. Silver Leaves, on the other hand, is a seemingly unimportant farm near Tzaneen in the northern Transvaal and has only taken on significance in the last ten years; and no single, identifiable historical event occurred at Silver Leaves in the year 270. But in a loose sense this date can be paralleled with 1652. For 270 is the earliest possible approximate date, as yet recorded by archaeologists, for the occupation of South Africa by Iron Age people; and Silver Leaves is the site of that occupation.

In the past fifteen years there has been a dramatic breakthrough in archaeological investigation of the southern African Iron Age. Archaeologists have uncovered an increasing number of important sites. Their approach has been interdisciplinary, drawing particularly upon history, oral tradition, linguistics and anthropology. Their dicoveries have, on occasions, been made possible by strokes of good fortune. At least two important archaeological sites, Silver Leaves and Mzonjani, were first uncovered during road-working operations. And enthusiastic amateurs have made their own contribution. Not the least of these was Dr L. von Bezing, who in 1964, when still a schoolboy, discovered some important terracotta heads near Lydenburg. But it is to the archaeologists that the greatest credit must go for the recent dramatic advances in our understanding of the early societies of South Africa. They have long since laid to rest the well-worn myth that Bantu-speaking Africans arrived south of the Limpopo at much the same time as whites were first settling in the western Cape. Now they are asking important new questions, and providing us with fascinating insights into the nature of South Africa's Iron Age societies.

The Early Iron Age

The distinction between the Early Iron Age and the Late Iron Age in southern Africa has now been drawn for several years. Archaeologists have discerned a noticeable break in the Iron Age sequence occurring at about the end of the first millennium A.D. The evidence indicates changes in ceramic style, new patterns of land occupation, and perhaps a slight shift of emphasis from cultivation to herding. Important questions as to how and why these changes occurred remain largely unanswered, still in the realm of speculation. But as research progresses new clues are coming to light.

There are over two hundred known Early Iron Age sites in Africa south of the Limpopo River. Many of these have been identified as a result of surface finds of pottery; only a few have as yet been professionally excavated. Those that have been investigated by archaeologists have yielded a number of radiocarbon dates covering a broad time-span.

The dating of charcoal found at Silver Leaves near Tzaneen in the northern Transvaal suggests that the site was occupied in the late third century A.D. Similar dates have come from Klein Afrika and Eiland, also in the northern Transvaal. Two other Transvaal sites, Broederstroom, on the south bank of the Hartbeespoort Dam, and Sterkspruit, near Lydenburg in the eastern Transvaal, have been dated to the fifth–sixth century, as has Castle Cavern in Swaziland. Similar early dates have been found for sites in Natal and Zululand. The earliest comes from Mzonjani, a site located about 15 kilometres north of Durban and discovered during bulldozing for the North Coast freeway in 1977. A charcoal sample from Mzonjani has been dated to around the third century A.D. Further north up the coast a site at Enkwazini, near Lake St Lucia, has been dated to the fourth–fifth century A.D. In this Natal–Zululand region almost no sites have yet been discovered for the period 400–550 A.D. Msuluzi Confluence, a site on the Tugela River, has yielded a seventh-century date; and the Ntshekane site, also in the Tugela Basin, has been dated to the ninth century.[1]

A growing number of Early Iron Age sites have thus brought forth a relatively wide range of dates. A similarly wide range is discernible in the geographical distribution of Early Iron Age sites. They are to be found as far north as the Klein Afrika site in the Soutpansberg, and as far south as the Chalumna River, near East London. At one time the state of archaeological research placed the most westerly Early Iron Age site at Broederstroom in the Magaliesberg Valley, north-west of modern Johannesburg. More recent research has, however, produced evidence of Early Iron Age settlements in eastern Botswana. It would, nevertheless, be misleading to suggest that the most dense areas of Early Iron Age occupation extended to these limits. Evidence of Early Iron Age settlement in the Transkei, for instance, is rather limited, although once again recent research has uncovered new sites in the Mbashe River valley.

The vast majority of South African Early Iron Age sites are to be found in the eastern lowland valley and coastal regions of present-day Transvaal, Swaziland, Zululand and Natal. There is known to have been, for instance, a widespread Early Iron Age culture in the eastern Transvaal. Maggs has depicted the Natal–Zululand valley region: 'By A.D. 600 if not earlier the lower-lying areas of the Tugela Basin, below an altitude of about 1 000 m, were dotted with EIA [Early Iron Age] settlements. These were quite large villages, separated from one another by several kilometres and situated on the best arable land.' And it is highly probable that the coastal region was extensively occupied during Early Iron Age times. The greater Durban region may not have been a local 'metropolis' only in the nineteenth and twentieth centuries. A number of sites in the area, in addition to Mzonjani, have yielded Early Iron Age pottery; this has been found at Durban North Reservoir, Glenwood High School, Mdloti Dune, Tongaat Monastery, Merebank, the Bluff and Whitfield Drive. Another cluster of similar sites has been discovered on the eastern shores of Lake St Lucia. It is likely that Early Iron Age occupation stretched along the coast between the two foci of research around Durban and St Lucia, but evidence for such continuous settlement is still to be discovered.[2]

As new sites are uncovered and new materials found so are archaeologists gradually managing to piece together the jigsaw puzzle. The implications of the chronological spread of Early Iron Age sites are as yet unclear. But the geographical distribution of the sites has been more revealing, and archaeologists have been able to analyse this distribution pattern, along with material remains, in order to probe more deeply into the nature of Early Iron Age society.

Probably the most significant criterion for distinguishing the Early Iron Age has been ceramic typology. The divide between the Early and Late Iron Ages was initially drawn by archaeologists almost entirely upon the basis of a discerned change in pottery styles, occurring at the end of the first millennium A.D. Recently the analysis of pottery types has been further advanced, bringing out the more subtle variations that have occurred over time and space.

The contrast between Early and Late Iron Age pottery has been summarised by Inskeep:

> In general terms Early Iron Age pottery tends to be thick, pale (pink, buff, or reddish) in colour, and freely and boldly decorated. By contrast the Later Iron Age pottery is generally thinner and almost invariably grey (sometimes very dark) and whilst decoration may occasionally be extensive it has a more formal, less 'free' appearance than the earlier pottery.

This typological division is strongly substantiated by the radiocarbon dating of organic matter that is stratigraphically associated with particular pottery pieces.

Within the Early Iron Age it is now recognised that there are two broad divisions of pottery type. The distinction is clarified by Inskeep and Maggs:

> There is ... some justification for contrasting an eastern ceramic zone, extending from Kenya in the north to Natal or Ciskei in the south ..., in which comb-stamping as a decorative technique is either absent or markedly subordinate to grooving (or incision), with an inland region, incorporating most of Zambia, Rhodesia [Zimbabwe] and parts of the Transvaal, in which comb-stamping is important, if not dominant.

There are very few Early Iron Age sites south of the Limpopo that fall in the inland zone. Klein Afrika in the Soutpansberg is one; its pottery is similar to that found at the Early Iron Age site at Gokomere near the famous Great Zimbabwe site. Similar pottery has been found at Matokomo, near Louis Trichardt, and dated to the ninth century.

The vast majority of South Africa's Early Iron Age sites belong to the eastern zone. There seems to be a broad resemblance between the styles of pottery found at these sites. There are a number of common stylistic features among pottery found at Transvaal sites such as Broederstroom, Eiland, Lydenburg and Plaston, and that unearthed at more southerly sites, such as Msuluzi Confluence and Ndondondwana in the Tugela Valley, and Mpame in the southern Transkei. These ceramic assemblages in turn reveal affinities with pottery from other East African countries, notably Mozambique (Matola ware), Malawi (Nkope ware), and Kenya (Kwale ware).

It would, however, be a mistake to suggest there was uniformity of ceramic style. Evers has grouped Early Iron Age pottery found only at eastern Transvaal sites into twelve different classes. Silver Leaves pottery does not bear a close resemblance to other South African Early Iron Age wares. There are differences between eastern Transvaal Early Iron Age pottery and that found in Natal. And Maggs has shown that within the latter region ceramic styles evolved and changed over the several centuries that comprise the Early Iron Age. So the task of ceramic analysis is just one of the many complex undertakings being carried through by South Africanist archaeologists. Just as potsherds have to be pieced together to discover individual styles, so different assemblages have to be compared in order to discern regional similarities and variations. And still there remains the hazardous task of interpreting the evidence.[3]

It has already been mentioned that the case for characterising distinctive Early Iron Age pottery styles is considerably substantiated by radiocarbon dating. There is a similar correspondence between the ceramic evidence and another distinctive feature of South Africa's Early Iron Age societies — their settlement patterns. These societies showed a marked preference for occupying the low-lying regions east of the great Drakensberg escarpment. Some sites are exceptional, notably Klein Afrika in the Soutpansberg, and Broederstroom. But the vast majority fall in lowland areas, particularly along the coast and the river valleys. Maggs has recently observed that no Early Iron Age sites south of the Pongola River have yet been found above an altitude of 1 000 metres. All sites in this region occur in the coastal lowlands or the inland river valleys. Most of the coastal sites are situated less than 3 kilometres from the sea, in high rainfall areas. And most inland sites are in valley bottoms close to rivers or major streams.

This preference for lowland settlement can tell us something about the economies of Early Iron Age societies. The coastal region from Mozambique down to Natal is an area of high rainfall and lush vegetation, highly suitable for shifting agriculture. It is possible that this land was once covered with forest or thick bush, and thus had to be cleared by the Early Iron Age farmers. The inland valley sites also seem to have been located on fertile soil, albeit in areas of lower rainfall. All this suggests that these Early Iron Age people were cultivators. There is some further evidence to support this view. Numerous grindstones have been found at Early Iron Age sites, as have a number of pits, which have been identified as probable grain stores. More direct evidence of cultivation is extremely limited, but impressions of millet seed have been discovered on the third-century site at Silver Leaves. Furthermore, it seems that Early Iron Age communities occupied large villages for relatively long periods of time. This suggests that agricultural production was an important means of subsistence.[4]

Cultivation was probably a primary economic activity, but one should not ignore other Early Iron Age branches of production. The teeth of domestic cattle, sheep and goats were found at the fifth-century site of Broederstroom. Remains of cattle and sheep have also been found at Msuluzi Confluence, a sixth–seventh century site in the Tugela Valley, and at Ntshekane, a ninth-century site near Greytown. Cattle remains are more abundant at the later Early Iron Age sites, suggesting that herding may have become a more important branch of production as time progressed. Hunting and gathering were other means of subsistence, although of less importance, for Early Iron Age communities. Faunal remains from a number of sites are an indication that hunting was engaged in; the presence of hare remains at Msuluzi Confluence suggest snaring; and shellfish were collected at coastal settlements.

More recent archaeological work has tended to focus not just on the study of material remains but also, more and more, on man's interaction with his environment and on the ecological constraints operating on economic activity. This approach enables us to see regional variations in economic behaviour and to understand the basis for selective land occupation. It certainly helps to explain the limits of occupation in the Early Iron Age. In this respect the Chalumna River site in the southern Transkei takes on significance. Maggs has shown how this site, which represents the most south-westerly point at which Early Iron Age pottery has been found, 'corresponds almost exactly' with the limits of summer rainfall adequate for growing the most common tropical African cultigens of the Early Iron Age, sorghum, cowpeas and millet.[5]

A more detailed picture of Early Iron Age technology is also emerging gradually. The working or mining of iron, or both, are evident from many sites. The earliest evidence as yet comes from Mzonjani, a third-century site where two pieces of slag have been found. Iron-smelting took place on a considerable scale at Msuluzi Confluence; and other Early Iron Age sites in the Tugela Basin show evidence of smelting. The earliest Transvaal evidence comes from Broederstroom, where two large accumulations of iron slag and furnace debris have been discovered. The most famous South African Iron Age mining complex was located at Phalaborwa in the north-eastern Transvaal. It is uncertain when mining first began at Phalaborwa, but a heavy deposit of charcoal found in one mine has yielded an eighth-century date.

Evidence of art and symbolism is limited for Early Iron Age communities. But the terracotta heads found at Sterkspruit near Lydenburg represent a famous exception. The finds comprise five smaller heads, which were probably attached to a static object, and two larger ones, which could have been worn as masks. It has been speculated that the masks probably carried some vital significance. Apart from the Lydenburg heads, ceramic sculpture, mainly in the form of animal figurines, has been discovered at an increasing number of recently investigated Early Iron Age sites. And evidence of ivory production, particularly of bangles, has been found at Ndondondwana.

The culture of South Africa's Early Iron Age communities can, in many ways, be sharply distinguished from that of their Late Stone Age counterparts. But it would be a mistake to infer from this that the two societies existed in isolation from each other. Broederstroom, for instance, has been shown to be an Early Iron Age site; but archaeologists have found there hundreds of stone implements used for making shell beads of Stone Age style. This suggests a measure of interaction between the two cultures. At Msuluzi Confluence and other sites, Late Stone Age implements have been similarly found in association with Early Iron Age material. Maggs has speculated that a client relationship may have developed between the two cultures. San may have acted as hunters and herders for the Iron Age villagers, in exchange for food and other items. At Msuluzi Confluence the stone assemblage shows a bias towards small scrapers, which are regarded as skin-dressing equipment. This has suggested to Maggs that hunting and the processing of the resultant produce were part of this interaction. Material traces of such client relationships have rarely been found on Late Iron Age sites, indicating that these forms of peaceful interaction were perhaps more common in earlier times.[6]

As archaeological research progresses, our understanding of the Early Iron Age in South Africa is becoming clearer. More and more is being learnt about ceramic styles, land occupation, patterns of settlement, economic activities, and levels of technology. But crucial questions still remain largely unanswered. For instance, one might well be led to ask about the identity of these Early Iron Age farmers. Were they the ancestors of the present African population? Were they immigrants and, if so, where did they come from? Were they perhaps in the forefront of the great migration of Bantu-speakers through Africa? These questions tend to offer a particular fascination to laymen particularly concerned about origins and identity. They are also questions with which archaeologists and linguists have for long been grappling. As yet no clear-cut answers have emerged, but a few tentative suggestions can be put forward.

One might expect human skeletal material to provide the answer to the identity problem. Such material, however, is rarely found at Early Iron Age sites. Skeletal remains found at Broederstroom and at the sixth-century site of the Lydenburg heads in the eastern Transvaal have been identified as probably representing the 'negro' physical type. But we also have to take heed of the warning recently issued by Hall and Morris that one should not draw too ready a correlation or connection between physical type and cultural practice.

The presence of these farmers must have resulted from an original south-

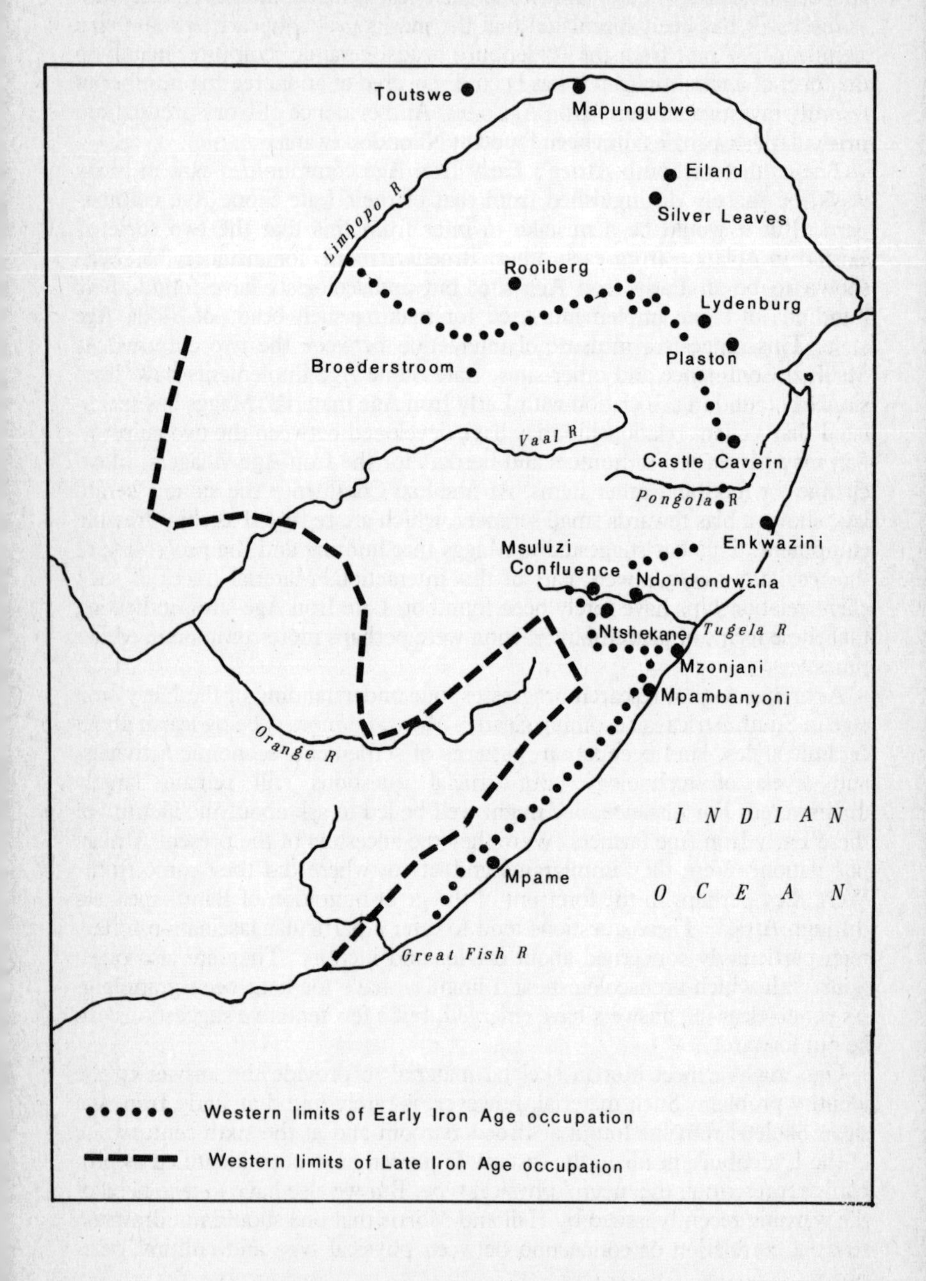

Some major Iron Age sites, and the main areas of Iron Age occupation in southern Africa.

ward migration or series of migrations. And the evidence of numerous radiocarbon dates gives us a hint as to how this might have occurred. As Hall has observed, 'the initial dispersal of the first farming communities does seem to have been a rapid process, as radiocarbon dates for sites with very similar pottery suggest movement along 3 500 kilometres of coastland in a couple of centuries — perhaps the equivalent of 400 kilometres in a generation.' It seems likely that this dispersal followed a route down the east coast of Africa. This hypothesis is largely based on a comparative analysis of ceramic styles. There seem to be clear typological links between the Early Iron Age pottery of south-east Africa and that of Mozambique, Malawi, Tanzania and Kenya. This pottery is found on the Kenya coast by the second century A.D., and south of the Limpopo by the third–fourth century. So the possibility has been suggested by Maggs that 'a movement from the Kenya–north Tanzania coastal region as far as the south coast of Natal, a distance of some 3 200 km, may have taken place in as little as 150 years.' This central zone would, at least initially, have provided rich agricultural land, making possible such rapid expansion. The fact that the earliest of the Early Iron Age sites — those dated around A.D. 300 — are all located east of the Great Escarpment lends further weight to this hypothesis. All the more westerly Early Iron Age sites have later dates. The Transvaal plateau was probably first settled in the fifth century, and eastern Botswana as late as the eighth century.

We are still, though, left with the problem of continuity. What are the links between the Early Iron Age farming communities and the present African population of South Africa? The trend of recent research favours continuity. According to Hall, this research 'lends greater support to the view that, in southern Africa as a whole, there is a direct line of continuity from the earliest phases of the Early Iron Age to the present day and that the Bantu languages in the sub-continent date back to the second century A.D.' However, the question of continuity very much involves the Late Iron Age, and it is to an examination of this that we must now turn our attention.[7]

The Late Iron Age

Archaeologists seem to be widely agreed that a major break in the Iron Age sequence occurred approximately at the end of the first millennium. As Inskeep puts it, 'All the way from Lake Victoria to the Transkei coast the same general picture emerges of an Early Iron Age superseded roughly 1 000 years ago by a Later Iron Age.' Although this transition is not clear-cut in all regions, the evidence for a break is extensive and will be discussed below. But first it is necessary to obtain a broad picture of the chronological pattern and the distribution of Late Iron Age sites south of the Limpopo.

The first few centuries of the Late Iron Age present a somewhat hazy picture. This is particularly true for the eastern seaboard and hinterland south of the Pongola River, a region in which there are at present only two excavated sites that have been dated between 900 and 1400. More evidence is available for the Transvaal. Mason writes of a 'Middle Iron Age' covering the period from the eleventh century until the sixteenth century. Sites belonging to this period are to be found in widely separated parts of the Transvaal. New dates from the famous Mapungubwe site in the far northern Transvaal fall between the late eleventh and early twelfth centuries. The 'Middle Iron Age' seems to have been widely distributed in the Witwatersrand–Magaliesberg region of the southern and western Transvaal. The Melville Koppies site occurs within this area, as do the sites belonging to what Mason calls the Uitkomst and Buispoort Cultures. In the eastern Transvaal, pre-1400 Late Iron Age sites are to be found in the lowveld area, notably at Harmony, Eiland and Phalaborwa.

From about 1400 the picture of the Late Iron Age in South Africa is much clearer, and, in Evers's words, 'the amount of evidence becomes overwhelming.' The southern highveld was to be extensively occupied from this time. Expansion into the upland areas of Natal and into the grasslands of the Transkei and Ciskei hinterland also took place. And numerous settlements in the eastern Transvaal escarpment area can also be attributed to this post-1400 era. Thus by the middle of the present millennium most of the fertile regions in the eastern half of southern Africa had come to be occupied by Iron Age farmers. But crucial questions still need to be considered: how do we explain the changing distribution of Iron Age societies in the second millennium? And what distinguishes the Late Iron Age from the Early Iron Age?[8]

In delineating the distinctive character of the Late Iron Age it will be necessary to draw upon much the same criteria that have already been applied to the Early Iron Age. So once again, ceramic styles, patterns of land occupation and settlement, and economic behaviour will feature prominently. The end of the first millennium marks a break in the ceramic sequence in some areas, where the pottery undergoes changes in both structure and style of decoration. This change in style is described by Phillipson:

> The majority of later Iron Age pottery vessels had undifferentiated or tapered rims. Undecorated vessels, particularly at the beginning of the later Iron Age, were more frequent than they had been in earlier times. Decoration tended to be more areal, rather than banded, and was concentrated on the body of the vessel instead of on the rim.

The reasons for this change of style are not at all clear. Phillipson suggests that Early Iron Age pottery may have been made by men, while in Late Iron Age society potters have generally been women. He points out that in parts of central Africa there is a continuity of ceramic style from the Early Iron Age to the present, and in these areas men still make pottery. In most, if not all, African societies of southern Africa the potting is today the work of women; and it is interesting to note that in many parts of southern Africa there is a distinct continuity of ceramic style throughout the Late Iron Age up to the present day.[9]

The Late Iron Age also brought a significant change in patterns of land occupation and settlement. As we have seen, Early Iron Age societies preferred to settle in the low-lying coastal regions and river valleys. Occupation of these areas continued during the Late Iron Age, but at the same time higher ground came to be settled on an extensive scale. There are known to be many

Late Iron Age upland sites in Natal and Zululand. But the most dramatic manifestation of this trend towards high-lying settlement appears in the highveld of the Transvaal and Orange Free State. Maggs has shown how the southern highveld was occupied on an increasingly extensive scale from the fifteenth century onwards. And Evers has identified, by aerial survey, the remains of thousands of enclosure units in the eastern Transvaal escarpment area.

Settlement patterns in the Late Iron Age tend to display less uniformity and more regional diversity than those of the Early Iron Age. In Natal and Zululand the trend of the Late Iron Age was towards smaller, more dispersed settlements, suggesting that the family homestead rather than the village was the basic unit — a pattern that has persisted into more recent times. In the southern highveld Maggs has distinguished between the large, compact, densely populated settlements in the westerly region, and the smaller, more dispersed, village-type settlements to the east.

Architectural styles and building techniques also change in the Late Iron Age. The contrast with the Early Iron Age is particularly marked by the extensive use of stone for building. The numerous remains of Late Iron Age stone huts and enclosures are widespread through large areas of the Orange Free State and Transvaal highveld; they are also to be found in the grasslands of the Tugela Basin. Mason has identified intermittent stone-walled structures covering the flat summit of Klipriviersberg in the southern highveld. The settlements run for several miles, and each comprises an outer wall, about eighty yards in diameter, surrounding a group of inner walls, about forty yards in diameter. Mason notes that considerable effort must have gone into the building of these wall systems, 'many thousands of tons of loose rock being collected and carried for the purpose'. And, Mason goes on to say, 'The building could only have been done under relatively tranquil social conditions, with an orderly social system to control the builders and an efficient economy to support them.' It would, however, be a mistake to attribute the development of stone-building to the emergence of a 'superior' culture. Building methods seem to have been determined largely by the availability of materials. In the treeless zones of the interior, stone was an obvious alternative to timber; but where timber was available this would be used. Maggs tries to play down the difference between stone-building and non-stone-building societies. He argues that settlement patterns, rather than building materials, represent the most important factor in cultural comparison.[10]

Just as ecological considerations assist our understanding of changing settlement patterns and building techniques, so they also help us to explain shifts in economic behaviour. It is now being recognised that a greater emphasis on cattle-keeping is another distinguishing characteristic of the Late Iron Age. This changing emphasis can be linked to the more extensive settlement on higher ground. The link is explained by Hall:

> Although rainfall is often higher and more dependable [in the higher regions], soils are in consequence more leached and poorer for agricultural purposes. In addition, the lack of tree cover severely restricts swidden cultivation, which is dependent on the

cutting and burning of trees and bush for enriching cleared plots. On the other hand, the higher areas offer far more potential for stock rearing, particularly if territories are large or are linked by seasonal transhumance with a winter-rich grazing on fertile river valley soils. Consequently, it may be implied that the early second millennium saw a shift in economic emphasis, with livestock increasing in importance against the products of cultivation.

This view is supported by Maggs's research in the southern highveld. There the grazing is sufficiently nutritious to maintain stock throughout the year, in contrast to the sour grazing which predominates in most of the coastal lowland areas of Early Iron Age occupation. Maggs also notes the central position of stock-pens in all southern highveld settlement patterns; this further attests the importance of livestock in the Late Iron Age economy of this region.

Although cattle-keeping took on greater importance, agriculture continued to be a major economic activity in the Later Iron Age. Direct evidence exists in the shape of carbonised cereal seeds, or seed impressions, found at several sites. Hunting and gathering likewise continued to be an important branch of production. Spear-heads were found on most of the southern highveld sites investigated by Maggs. And at Mpambanyoni, on the Natal south coast, evidence of numerous freshwater and oceanic fishes was found in the middens. This is of particular interest because many of the coastal Nguni people observed a fish taboo.[11]

The Late Iron Age also seems to have been marked by a more intensified exploitation of mineral resources. As is the case today, this activity was mainly concentrated in the Transvaal. It has been claimed that ancient mine-workings extend through the northern Transvaal down to the edge of the highveld, about the latitude of Pretoria. They are especially plentiful in the Soutpansberg, Waterberg, Rustenburg and Middelburg districts. Trevor notes that 120 separate mines have been found in the Messina area alone. Wagner has listed 60 other important mines in the Transvaal, of which 6 are gold mines, 20 copper, 3 tin and 31 iron. Mason believes it 'possible that the number of probable Iron Age mines runs into hundreds'.

What is possibly the most famous site of ancient mining in South Africa is located at Phalaborwa in the north-eastern Transvaal lowveld. Phalaborwa is an important mining centre today, and probably has been for over a thousand years. Much of this present and past activity has been concentrated around vast copper and iron deposits at Lolwe hill. A general picture is provided by Van der Merwe and Scully:

> Lolwe ... was the site of mineshafts, galleries and adits, which were uncovered in the course of blasting. A rough estimate by mining engineers indicates that well over 10,000 tons of rock containing secondary copper ore deposits ... had been removed from the hill before the start of recent mining activities.... Low, grass-covered mounds of slag and the occasional remains of a smelting furnace are scattered in the surrounding plain and attest to an iron and copper industry which is now only dimly remembered by the oldest members of the BaPhalaborwa tribe.

There is evidence that at Lolwe vertical shafts were sunk to depths of up to seventy feet, some of the shafts branching off into horizontal galleries. It appears that the ore was removed by cracking the rock with fire, and chipping away at it with gads and chisels. A large number of these implements have been found at the site.

Smelting occurred within a 15-mile radius from the source. About fifty smelting sites in the area have been located by archaeologists; several hundred more probably existed. Van der Merwe and Scully provide a description:

A typical smelting site consists of several tons of slag in a circular heap, with a furnace at the centre. Copper furnaces are shaped like beehives, about 2-3 ft in height and in diameter at the base, tapering to a 'chimney' hole at the top of about 1-1½ ft in diameter. A single entrance, about 9 in. in height and in the shape of a gothic arch, occurs at one side.

Further items of smelting equipment included clay tuyères and bellows. Iron seems to have been produced more extensively than copper. Iron objects were much more numerous at the site than copper items, which were relatively scarce.

Evidence of mining and metal production also comes from other areas. In the southern Transvaal, Mason has identified Olifantspoort as a metal-producing centre. A few dozen smelting furnaces have been found there, in addition to numerous whetstones which may have been used for sharpening newly made blades and points. Tin was mined at Rooiberg in the western Transvaal. When the Rooiberg Minerals Development Company began mining operations early in the twentieth century it did so only after three years had been spent examining the ancient workings in the area. It is estimated that about 18 000 tons of ore were extracted by ancient miners at Rooiberg; more recent mining has simply been an extension in depth of the ancient workings. Extensive copper working was carried out in the Messina district of the northern Transvaal. Apparently, several thousand tons of copper were removed from the numerous stopes and shafts in the area. It has been observed that these shafts were narrow and the stopes extremely small, suggesting that the work may have been performed by women and children. In the eastern highveld and escarpment area of the Transvaal there are some ancient goldmines, notably at Roossenekal, Middelburg, Pilgrim's Rest and Waterval-Onder.[12]

It now seems clear that thousands of tons of different metals, primarily iron and copper, were mined and smelted in South Africa for several centuries before extensive mineral exploitation was begun by whites. There can be no doubt that these metal producers were the ancestors of the present Bantu-speaking population of South Africa. This is attested by archaeological, skeletal and ethnohistorical evidence. Production was carried out on a small-scale basis. Tools were simple, mainly comprising iron gads and stone hammers. Mining techniques were also rudimentary, but they were sufficient for shafts to be sunk to depths of up to eighty feet. Water seems to have posed a major problem. Iron Age miners had no means of removing water from the bottom of workings; this deficiency may often have led to the closing of mines. However, the overall achievement is impressive. As Evers and Van den Berg remark, 'Technically, the ancient miners are to be greatly respected.' This is particularly true in the field of prospecting, where it is 'staggering to realize' that ancient miners in Zimbabwe failed to detect only one occurrence of gold.

For what purpose were these metals produced? It is clear that iron was worked for domestic consumption — to produce iron tools and implements. A proportion of these would have been traded to areas where iron was scarce, such as the southern highveld. Copper and gold seem to have been produced almost entirely for export. Almost no gold items have been found at Iron Age sites, except at Mapungubwe in the northern Transvaal. Gold was neither mined nor smelted at Mapungubwe, so the gold beads, pieces of gold foil, and occasional fragments of coiled wire that have been found there must almost certainly have been imported from Zimbabwe. It seems that when copper and tin were smelted they were converted into ingots. Copper ornaments have been found at many sites, but much of the copper was almost certainly exported. Historical evidence suggests that both the Messina and Phalaborwa mines were supplying copper to Delagoa Bay at least by the eighteenth century and probably as early as the sixteenth century. Tin was also reported at Delagoa Bay in the early eighteenth century.[13]

Trade was just one form of interaction linking different Late Iron Age communities. Like their Early Iron Age predecessors, Late Iron Age societies continued to interact with the Late Stone Age peoples of southern Africa. The exact forms of this interchange are problematic. Some of the skeletal evidence, for instance, tends to be confusing. Two burials at Phalaborwa have been analysed recently. One skeleton seemed to be of negro type, the other showed Khoisan affinities. Such skeletal evidence is limited and difficult to interpret, but it does serve as a warning against drawing too ready an equation between race, language and culture in the study of southern African society and history.

The discovery at Late Iron Age sites of typical Stone Age items, such as ostrich egg-shell beads, bone arrow-points and link-shafts, strongly suggests that the two cultures continued to interact. This is substantiated by cultural and linguistic evidence. For instance, some Nguni peoples have adopted the San custom of cutting off the final joint of the little finger. The presence of clicks in Nguni languages gives a clearer indication of interaction. On grounds such as these, the probability of peaceful interaction, in the form of economic and cultural exchange, is therefore strong. It is a theme that will be further explored later.[14]

It now seems to be well established among scholars that a break in the Iron Age occurred at about the end of the first millennium A.D. But this gives rise to a crucial question which is still largely unanswered: why did the break occur? Did the Late Iron Age represent a migration of new peoples into southern Africa? Or was it simply the expansion of Early Iron Age people into new territory?

Until recent decades the conventional wisdom tended to see African history in terms of the wanderings of migratory hordes, or Trevor-Roper's 'gyrations of barbarous tribes'. Evidence for migrations can often be found in

African oral tradition, but obviously such traditions do not stretch back as far as the eleventh century when the break in the Iron Age occurred. So it seems that our understanding of the divide between the Early and Late Iron Age must be largely based on speculation.

One hypothesis posits an expansion of Early Iron Age communities into new territory. The explanation combines ecological considerations with an analysis of changing economic patterns. It has already been shown that Early Iron Age communities preferred to occupy the coastal lowland areas and river valleys. This preference was probably determined partly by a need for timber for building, but largely by soil fertility, which was a crucial consideration for a society that relied to a great extent on agriculture for subsistence. These considerations seem to define the limits of Early Iron Age settlement. Maggs suggests that those communities living close to these limits may gradually have ventured westwards into the high-lying grasslands. In this new environment, where soils are less fertile but grazing is good, cattle take on a new significance — hence the greater emphasis on cattle-keeping in Late Iron Age society. It is debatable, however, whether cattle were the cause or consequence of this expansion. Inskeep, in an interesting hypothesis, suggests a causal connection:

> If we assume that Early Iron Age cattle were kept in small numbers primarily as a source of meat, the introduction of milking may be seen as a powerful new factor in the economy. Milk and its by-products would constitute a new and highly nourishing element in the diet, and new attitudes to cattle could be speculated to develop. Given favourable conditions herds in Africa can show an annual increase of from 4 to 10 per cent, an increase rate greater than that of their owners. Even at the lower rate of increase it has been said that the need for new land would grow alarmingly. Here we have the kind of mechanism needed to explain the rapid dispersals required by the linguistic evidence and suggested by that of archaeology.

These interpretations appear promising. They fail, however, to explain the change in ceramic style. And they do not take account of changes that occurred in existing Early Iron Age areas during the transition to the Late Iron Age. So if one is going to argue for a degree of continuity between the Early and Late Iron Age these problems will have to be tackled.[15]

Scholars may differ on the question of continuity between the Early and Late Iron Age, but there is considerable agreement that a strong thread of continuity runs between the Late Iron Age and the present. Here the availability of other types of evidence places one on safer ground. There is, first of all, a remarkable continuity of pottery styles throughout the Late Iron Age. Although styles may vary from region to region they tend to remain fairly uniform over time within any particular region. Mason, for instance, has observed the close resemblance between pottery of the Late Iron Age Uitkomst Culture and the pottery made by the present Sotho–Tswana inhabitants of the area. Pottery found at Badfontein, a site on the eastern Transvaal highveld, is in Evers's words, 'indistinguishable from modern Pedi ware and the lay-out both of homesteads and settlements is equally Pedi in design'. Maggs has succeeded in drawing similar parallels between southern highveld settlement patterns discerned from the archaeological record and those documented in the historical or anthropological record. He has convincingly linked the remains of large, compact settlements with the Tswana people, who have been known in historical and recent times to live in densely populated 'towns'. Similarly the remains of the easterly, more scattered settlements can be readily identified as Sotho on the basis of comparison with more recent Sotho settlement patterns.[16]

The evidence for continuity through the Late Iron Age to more recent times is overwhelming. The results of archaeological investigation and the information derived from oral or documentary sources neatly dovetail or correspond with each other. Through this interdisciplinary approach we are gradually obtaining a clearer picture of the Late Iron Age, particularly for the past 500 years of African history south of the Limpopo.

Although our knowledge and understanding of South Africa's distant past is growing all the time, we should not forget that huge gaps still exist. There are, after all, severe limits to what archaeological evidence can tell us. One can, for instance, do little more than speculate about the political, social and ideological character of South Africa's Iron Age societies in the era before documentary sources become available. Archaeology can give an idea of the distribution of peoples, but one has to be wary of the possibility that such conclusions are perhaps simply a reflection of archaeological sampling, telling us where archaeologists have concentrated their investigations rather than how settlements were distributed. One also has to be careful in the handling of cultural remains. Can it be assumed, for instance, that there is a correlation between different pottery styles and different peoples? A warning against this has been issued by Hall: 'The ... assumption that a discontinuity in ceramic tradition reflects a change in human population, however, is not nearly as sound, for we know little of what artefact traditions reflect in sociological terms.'

Finally, archaeologists may encounter the difficulty of not being able to find any material remains at all. Until recently this was the case in the Transkei and Ciskei. One would have expected these areas to have been occupied from a relatively early stage of the Iron Age, and the evidence from the Chalumna River site indicates that this was probably the case. Early archaeological investigations were marked by a striking failure to find Iron Age materials in the region. There appeared to be no signs of iron-working; rubbish was dispersed, so middens were absent; there seemed to have been no building in stone; and homestead structures, usually built of reeds, were burnt on abandonment. However, even in this region the picture is beginning to change as new archaeological research proceeds. Recent excavations have produced evidence of iron production at some Transkei sites, where slag and tuyère fragments have been found.

In spite of these limitations one must recognise that the recent archaeological breakthrough in South African Iron Age studies has been of enormous value, not only to the archaeologists, historians and anthropologists, but also to any person who is interested in South African society. Perhaps the greatest value of this archaeological work has been the way it has contributed to the correction or destruction of certain well-worn myths and stereotypes that are associated with past and present African societies in South Africa.

Firstly, archaeologists have been able, once and for all, to lay to rest what Marks calls 'the myth of the empty land'. This myth claims that the ancestors of the present African people of South Africa migrated southwards across the Limpopo at much the same time as whites were first settling in the western Cape in the mid-seventeenth century. Marks says of this myth that it

> may no longer be proclaimed in quite such unambiguous simplicity. Nevertheless, more sophisticated variants of those myths still permeate the history textbooks used in South African schools and the propaganda put forward sedulously by the South African Department of Information. They have even crept into textbooks used in British schools and on to British television.

For the defenders of white supremacy in South Africa the question, 'who got here first?', is a loaded one. Those who cling to this myth should be told that the issue is basically irrelevant to current politics, and, moreover, that they have their chronology wrong by about 1 400 years.

Another stereotype that has featured prominently in the conventional wisdom is that of the static African past. In its crudest form this assumes that Africans lived in isolated, self-sufficient communities, whose existence was essentially stagnant and unremarkable but for tribal wanderings and inter-ethnic conflicts. The archaeological evidence alone can break this stereotype at several levels. Although it is true that Iron Age economies were essentially self-sufficient in character, they were not entirely so. It seems clear that some communities specialised in the production of commodities that were elsewhere scarce and thus in demand as trade goods. Many Sotho–Tswana communities, for instance, must have acquired their iron hardware from external sources. We know that the Letaba district of the north-eastern Transvaal was a centre of salt production; the presence of imported trade items at the site suggests that the salt was exported. Copper was traded by producers at Messina and Phalaborwa. And there was, undoubtedly, extensive trade at a local and regional level, involving the exchange of more basic products like grain and cattle.

The evidence for interaction between Iron Age and Late Stone Age societies serves to expose the myth of ethnic isolationism. The main ideological pillar of the South African government's divide-and-rule Bantustan policy is the notion that the country's African societies display wide ethnic differences. This notion also rests on an interpretation of history, because it has to be shown that these differences have deep roots in the past. But Iron Age sites have yielded material which substantiates the view, already supported by linguistic and documentary evidence, that African farmers and Khoisan hunter-gatherers interacted in a number of peaceful ways. This is not to ignore the reality of the many cultural differences that existed both between Iron Age and Stone Age societies, and between various Iron Age communities. Nor is it to suggest that the African Iron Age was a golden age of peace

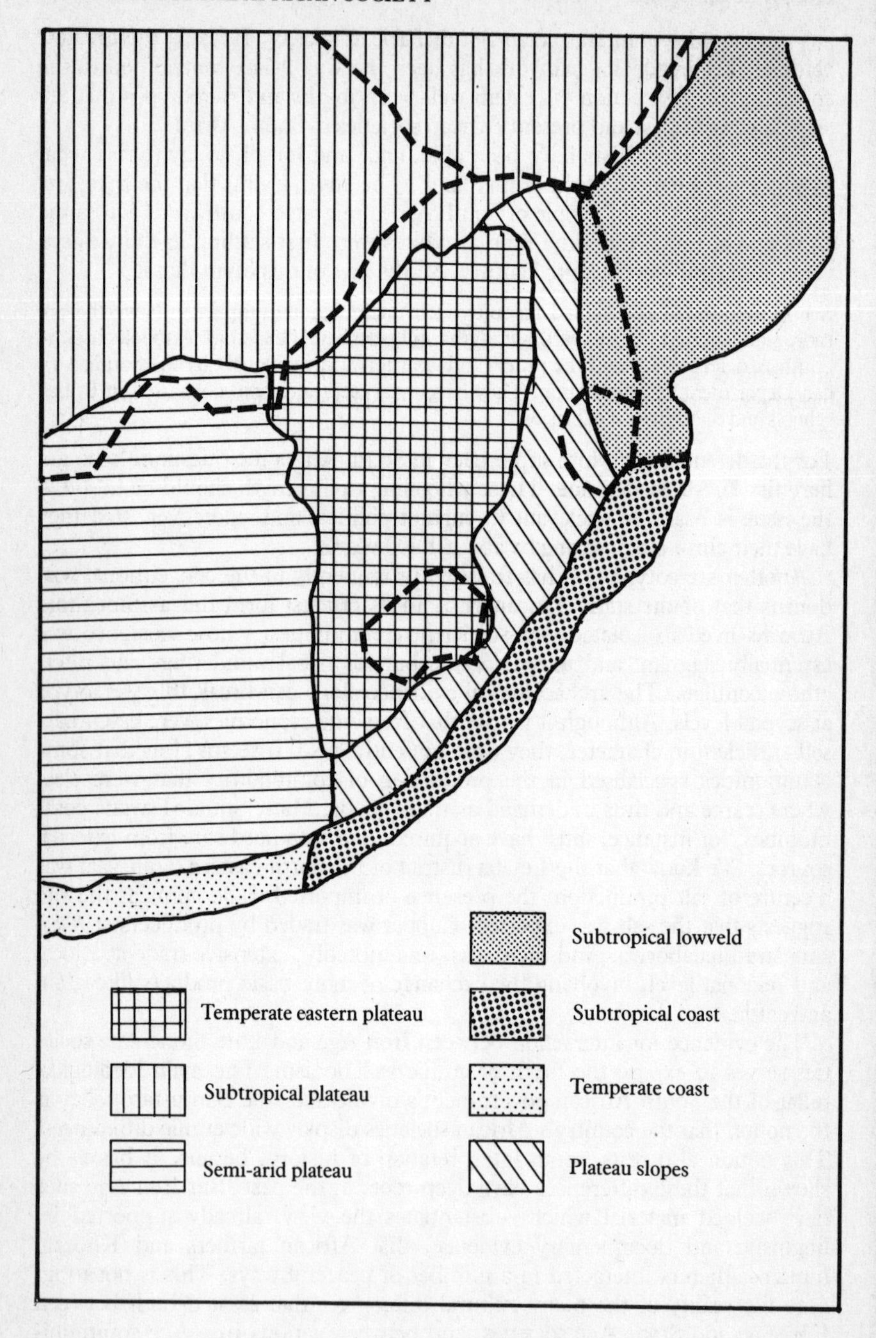

Climatic regions of South Africa.

and tranquillity. But it does confirm the need to escape from simplistic notions of ethnicity and to subject the whole concept of ethnicity to careful historical examination.

Finally, archaeological research tells us that the South African Iron Age was dynamic. The past was not static, but ever changing. One gains the impression of peoples engaged in a dynamic interaction with their environment. Without slipping into a determinist view, one can see how the possibilities offered by different environments were utilised by Iron Age societies. Minerals were exploited with a simple technology but with a level of expertise that would astound those who associate South African mining solely with developments that have occured over the past 120 years. But one must beware of highlighting precolonial mineral exploitation simply because it appears to have been a spectacular achievement. Iron Age people were essentially farmers. Here again the findings of archaeologists lead us to believe that efforts were made to maximise the environmental potential. The cultivators of the Early Iron Age were concentrated in those areas where rainfall and soil were most conducive to agriculture. When cattle seem to take on a new importance in the Late Iron Age the grasslands of the highveld become extensively occupied. Iron Age societies were perhaps unable to manipulate and control their environment, but there were able to interact with it in a dynamic and productive way.[17]

2
NGUNI COMMUNITIES UNTIL c. 1830

Problems of classification

The rigid classification and demarcation of ethnic groups has been a major obsession of successive white governments in South Africa. While the approach of government may be crude and political, scholars of various disciplines still have to grapple with the problem of classifying human groups in southern Africa, and establishing criteria for such classification. Race, physical type, language, and culture represent the most convenient means of labelling. However, the common tendency in southern Africa is for at least one of these criteria to overlap between 'different' societies so that it becomes virtually impossible to use all the major criteria at the same time to define neatly differing, self-contained entities. Reification is another dangerous consequence of classification, because in the process southern African societies become not only mutually exclusive ethnic entities, but also static, timeless units. Wary of these dangers, historians are now striving to draw out the essential dynamics of southern African societies, highlighting change and variation over time and space.

In the twentieth century the vast majority of African people south of the Limpopo have come to be classified under one of two broad generic labels — Nguni or Sotho. Both labels are of recent origin. As Marks and Atmore have pointed out:

> the latter-day terms Nguni and Sotho are flags of convenience to describe the post-*Mfecane* situation and ... their wide-ranging use is due to white intervention or invention, not least on the part of Bryant. In pre-*Mfecane* times they were either group names of local or at least limited application, or terms referring somewhat vaguely to foreign groups in general.

Similar doubts about the 'Nguni' label are shared by Wright, who has recently subjected the term to a careful critical examination. He has thoroughly investigated the different usages of the term through to the early twentieth century, and highlighted its 'appropriation' by academics in the 1930s in the context of the South African state's shift towards a policy of retribalisation. Wright concludes that the 'Nguni' label serves 'to impose a spurious primordial ethnic unity on the African peoples of the eastern seaboard of South Africa' – and he recommends that it be discarded. In spite of Wright's misgivings, the term will still be used as a label of convenience and as an organising category in this book. It stands essentially as a linguistic term. Although the Nguni people share some common cultural traits, their classification as

Nguni is based on a broad linguistic uniformity. There are many local differences of dialect, but the dialects are closely related. The historical heartland of southern Africa's Nguni people has been the south-eastern region between the interior plateau and the Indian Ocean, stretching from present-day Ciskei to Swaziland. For purposes of convenience the Nguni can be divided into a northern group — basically the Zulu and the Swazi — and a southern group, including the Xhosa, the Thembu, the Mfengu, the Mpondo and the Mpondomise.

'Sotho' is another broad generic term. It designates a large group of people who display linguistic and some cultural similarities. They occupy the interior plateau of South Africa, and they can be distinguished from the Nguni in a number of ways. The Sotho can conveniently be subdivided into three main groups: firstly, the western Sotho, or Tswana; secondly, the northern Sotho, who comprise the Pedi and Lobedu; and thirdly, the southern Sotho, or Basotho, who occupy present-day Lesotho and adjacent areas. Although related linguistically and culturally the three groups are not homogeneous. There are differences between and within the groups, and the historical experience of each has varied. But the term 'Sotho' remains a convenient label, one which is widely accepted by the Sotho people themselves.

Both the Nguni and Sotho peoples speak a Bantu language. Both have lived in patrilineal societies in which the chiefdom has been an important social and political unit. And the economy of each society has centred around cultivation, herding and hunting. If we attempt to distinguish between the Nguni and the Sotho, three major differences stand out. Firstly, although both are Bantu-speakers, their respective languages are distinctly separate components of the greater Bantu language group. Secondly, their settlement patterns have differed enormously. Nguni settlement has tended to be widely dispersed in scattered homesteads and villages — a pattern that Sansom has called a 'chequerboard realm'. The Sotho have lived in more concentrated settlements or towns. According to this pattern, which Sansom has called the 'tribal estate', the people themselves may have been far removed from their agricultural, pastoral and hunting grounds. The third major difference centres on kinship. While Nguni clans have been exogamous, the Sotho have practised a system of preferred cousin marriage.

It has often been asked why, how and when this divergence and these distinctions between the Nguni and Sotho occurred. Over ten years ago Monica Wilson wrote:

> As we peer back into South Africa's past one question obtrudes. It is this: is the division between Sotho and Nguni ancient or not? Looking as an anthropologist at different sorts of societies and how they change, I think that Sotho and Nguni have diverged not merely during the past two centuries when we can document divergence, but perhaps even for ten centuries.

In an earlier piece of speculation Wilson had linked the Nguni, who placed a greater emphasis on cattle than the Sotho, with pastoral peoples of East Africa. She suggested that these pastoralists may have fused with Bantu-speaking cultivators spreading out from the southern savannah.

Magema Fuze, the first Zulu to write a major work in his native language, begins his historical account, *The Black People*, with a statement about African origins:

Our forbears tell us that all we black people originally came from the north. When we make close enquiry as to where this north may be, they point in an upward direction; but because no written records were left by those who came before us, all they can do is to point in that northerly direction upward of the country ..., which we hear referred to as the Horn of Africa near where the sea almost meets [Suez Canal].

The vagueness of this statement suggests that the whole question of African origins is beset with problems. It is an issue that stands at that awkward interface between archaeology and history. There is a great scarcity of verifiable data that can supply us with answers.

Much of the writing on Nguni and Sotho origins has been based on the work of A. T. Bryant, a missionary and writer who collected a vast body of Zulu oral traditions in a fifty-year period from 1883. The value of Bryant's data is inestimable, but his conclusions have to be treated with great caution. Having carefully examined Bryant's work, Marks argued that his general theory of the peopling of south-east Africa was a mixture of 'fact and fantasy'. Bryant's basic theory reads like this:

The baKoni Sutus (now populating the north-western Transvaal and Bechuanaland) and the abaNguni Zulu–Xosas (now populating Zululand and the Cape) are but two divisions of what was originally one single Bantu family or tribe. The first or baKoni section of that tribe we might distinguish as the Western (or Sutu) Ngunis, and the latter or abaNguni section as the Eastern Ngunis (in Zululand) and the Southern Ngunis (in the Cape).

According to Bryant this 'whole family of Nguni Bantu' was settled around the upper Vaal River in the early sixteenth century. There 'the family' broke into two parts. One moved away to the north-west, eventually to be 'swamped' by Sotho migrants coming down from the north. The other section, the 'purer' Nguni, moved eastwards towards the coast in four main parties (Ntungwa, Xhosa, Mbo, and Lala); these parties 'probably corresponded with four closely related clan-groups already existent within the all-containing Nguni family'. Bryant suggests that the Mbo and Lala were the first parties to migrate. The Mbo settled among Sotho people in the region of present-day Swaziland, while the Lala reached the Delagoa Bay area and intermingled with the Tsonga. The other two Nguni parties moved in a south-easterly direction, avoiding Sotho and Tsonga communities. The Xhosa party took a more southerly route, while the Ntungwa settled further to the north in the modern Zulu heartland.

Thus, for Bryant, the ancestors of some present-day Sotho–Tswana peoples were originally Nguni. They became 'Sotho-ised' under the influence or domination of later Sotho immigrants. The original 'purer' Sotho had probably been occupying the north-eastern region of the modern Transvaal; and it was they whom the Mbo encountered in their migration. Bryant also reckoned that the Basotho, or southern Sotho, were the descendants of these original 'purer' Sotho. The Tswana, while still speaking a Sotho language, have a closer linguistic affinity with Nguni dialects than do the Basotho. This led Bryant to conclude that the Tswana were descendants of the original Nguni inhabitants.

Bryant's version is almost certainly flawed both in detail and in its larger conception. His chronology does not correspond to the archaeological record. As we have seen, there is firm evidence of an African presence south of the Limpopo centuries before Bryant's dating of the African arrival. Moreover, Bryant's notion of the peopling of southern Africa as occurring in great migratory waves is now widely rejected. As Marks has pointed out, 'there is little record in the traditions of such large movements.' Legassick, too, has commented, '"Migations", defined as a large body of people moving a considerable distance over a short period of time, are a relatively rare phenomenon, and cannot be used to explain each change of culture or structure. All cultures and populations are mixed, absorbing new elements and evolving *in situ*.' It is in fact more likely that migrations occurred over relatively short distances. So, as Marks again conjectures, 'it may be that Bryant was only tapping the top layers of Bantu-speaking migration into the area.' The traditions that Bryant collected were probably referring to more recent, small-scale movements, rather than to any original great migration. Moreover, Bryant's nomenclature and division of groups are dubious. As Wright and Hamilton have shown, there was in all likelihood no such people designated as 'Lala' in pre-Shakan times: the term 'Lala' was an 'invention of the Shakan period' when it emerged as a term of contempt for people of lowly status.

The whole question of African origins remains extremely problematic. The rapid advances in archaeological research over the past ten years may provide further suggestions. But the problem is to bridge the gap between archaeology, with its emphasis on material culture, and oral tradition, which has much to say about genealogies and migrations. Ultimately a greater understanding may be derived from further linguistic investigation. A careful but imaginative analysis and synthesis of archaeological and linguistic evidence and oral tradition will be necessary before we can come closer to solving this problem.

It has already been stated that the term 'Nguni' is a label of convenience. The Nguni people do not see themselves as Nguni. Similarly the division between southern and northern Nguni is one that has been created by scholars. The use of this generic term can carry with it dangerous implications of timeless homogeneity, but it does serve to encapsulate the language, material culture, and socio-political structure which have been broadly, but not universally, characteristic of Nguni peoples.

The economic base of the Nguni centred on herding, cultivation and hunting. They made skilful use of the different types of pasture, moving their cattle where possible from sourveld to sweetveld at the appropriate time of year. They practised shifting cultivation based on the 'slash-and-burn' technique. Hunting was also an important branch of the economy, producing extra food for subsistence, materials for clothing, and trade items — notably

The distribution of African chiefdoms
at the beginning of the nineteenth century.

ivory. Cultivation and hunting depended on the availability of satisfactory iron implements. These were made locally by the Nguni, whose other crafts included pottery, the making of clothing, and the manufacture of ornaments.

The fundamental unit of Nguni society was the lineage, which had its territorial base in the homestead. Lineages comprised all the descendants of a common male ancestor, but their tendency to segment, with men hiving off to form their own lineages, prevented their ever becoming too large. A number of lineages claiming descent from a common ancestor, mythical or real, made up a clan. The exogamy rule applied with respect to clans.

The chiefdom represented the main political unit. The chief was a pivotal figure whose prerogative was wide, ranging through executive, military, judicial and religious powers. But even this great authority was subject to checks; and a chief's practical exercise of power depended very much on his ability to maintain his following and to control key material resources. As we shall see, these factors were also to play an important part in the consolidation of northern Nguni chiefdoms into larger power blocs from the late eighteenth century.[17]

The northern Nguni

Up until the eighteenth century the territory of both the northern and the southern Nguni was almost certainly occupied by numerous relatively small chiefdoms. The more centralised socio-political structure that later came to differentiate the northern from the southern Nguni was not apparent at that time. However, by the late eighteenth century a process of political consolidation among the northern Nguni was well under way, and a number of power blocs had emerged.

The Ngwane represented the most northerly of these blocs. According to Bryant they were an offshoot of the Mbo. The genealogies of the Dlamini, the Ngwane royal line, can be traced back for several generations, perhaps even as far as the tenth century, although there is no reliable time depth. For a long time the Dlamini were based in the coastal region around Delagoa Bay. In the second half of the eighteenth century they came under pressure from the Tembe, the dominant power in the Delagoa Bay hinterland. So during the reign of Dlamini III the Ngwane migrated southwards, eventually settling north of the Pongola River in the southern region of modern Swaziland, an area ideally suited to their mixed arable and pastoral economy.

It was also an area that was already populated by a number of chiefdoms. These were gradually conquered or subjugated, as the Ngwane expanded their power and territorial control. Some of these chiefdoms were Sotho, and it is interesting to note how elements of Sotho culture were assimilated by the Ngwane. Today the Swazi are generally classified as Nguni, but as Bonner has observed, 'their culture is literally cluttered with Sotho borrowings'. Whereas the Nguni have normally practised exogamy, the Swazi adopted the Sotho custom of preferred cross-cousin marriage. Moreover the special position assigned to the Swazi queen mother is not typical of the Nguni, and may also represent a Sotho influence.

The main area of Ndwandwe power lay between the Pongola and Black Mfolosi Rivers. During the late eighteenth century the Ndwandwe ruling lineage was able to subordinate other neighbouring lineages, as the Ndwandwe chief, Yaka, and his son and successor, Zwide, conquered local chiefdoms. A possible source of Ndwandwe dominance was their control of the east–west trade between the coast and the uplands. But the degree of this dominance should not be exaggerated. Although Zwide was able to establish overall political hegemony, many of the subordinated lineages, notably the Gaza under Soshangane and the Ncwangeni–Jere under Zwangendaba, remained semi-autonomous.

The Qwabe comprised the southernmost power bloc. Their area of dominance, established in the eighteenth century, lay in the region of the Ngoye hills between the Mhlatuze and Tugela Rivers. In the sixteenth and seventeenth centuries the Qwabe were one among a number of independent lineages in the area. Early in the eighteenth century, during the reign of Kuzwayo, the Qwabe became increasingly powerful. They gradually gained control of the Ngoye and forced their main rival lineages, the Cele and Thuli, to move south of the Tugela. At the height of their power the Qwabe were also able to dominate the region west of the Ngoye.

North-east of the Qwabe lay the region of Mthethwa power, extending between the Mhlatuze and Mfolosi Rivers. It is uncertain how Mthethwa dominance of this region was established, but it seems to have dated from the mid-eighteenth century. Control of crossing-points over the lower Mfolosi, and hence control also of local trade, may have been a factor; and the Mthethwa domain offered good agricultural land and hunting grounds.

A key figure in the expansion of Mthethwa power was Dingiswayo. According to oral traditions, Dingiswayo was forced into exile in the 1790s, during the reign of his father, Jobe. When Jobe died at the beginning of the nineteenth century he was succeeded by a younger son, Mawewe. Soon after this Dingiswayo returned from exile, riding a horse and carrying a gun — so the tradition goes. He then proceeded to wrest the Mthethwa chiefship from Mawewe.

There has long been debate about the place of Dingiswayo's exile. Some have said that he went to the Cape, others that he stayed among the Hlubi. More recently Argyle has suggested that the traditions have disguised Dingiswayo's true position, that of a non-Mthethwa impostor, while Koopman argues that he spent his exile among the Langeni clan.

More important than this issue is the whole question of the role of Dingiswayo and the Mthethwa in the larger process of centralisation among the northern Nguni at this time. Under Dingiswayo, Mthethwa power grew rapidly. He secured greater control over the northern trade. This was facilitated by a commercial alliance that Dingiswayo contracted with the kingdom of Maputo at Delagoa Bay. And he extended Mthethwa control westwards, bringing the Zulu and Buthelezi lineages inland under his sway.

The process of consolidation among the northern Nguni did not cease with the emergence of the four power blocs. Tensions developed between them, and conflicts arose. In the south the Mthethwa and Qwabe clashed. The Qwabe had harboured Mawewe, a rival claimant to Dingiswayo's chiefship; and the Qwabe resented Mthethwa encroachment into their spheres of power and influence. In the ensuing conflict the Mthethwa conquered and incorporated the Qwabe.

In the north the Ngwane and the Ndwandwe had been uneasy neighbours. A clash between the two was sparked off by a dispute over grain fields on the south side of the Pongola River. Zwide launched an invasion, which, in Bonner's words, 'very nearly obliterated the Ngwane state'. Sobhuza, the Ngwane chief, fled to the north with a remnant of his followers, most of whom had been abandoned to Zwide. A series of Ndwandwe attacks forced Sobhuza to take refuge in a succession of mountain strongholds. He obtained some respite when Zwide's attentions shifted towards the Mthethwa and the Zulu. Although this enabled Sobhuza to regroup his followers and even launch attacks on neighbouring chiefdoms, his position remained precarious throughout the late 1810s and early 1820s.

A third clash developed between the Ndwandwe and the Mthethwa. In 1818 Zwide ordered the murder of Malusi, the husband of Dingiswayo's sister. Dingiswayo challenged Zwide to produce the murdered man, only to be lured to his own death. Deprived of their leader the Mthethwa were driven by the Ndwandwe across the Mfolosi River almost as far as the Tugela.[19]

The death of Dingiswayo created an opening for Shaka to rise to power. Shaka was the son of Senzangakhona, head of the small Zulu chiefdom, one of a number of chiefdoms that had acknowledged Dingiswayo's paramountcy and so had fallen under the sway of the Mthethwa. As a child Shaka had left the Zulu chiefdom with his mother, Nandi, who had been driven out of Senzangakhona's household. In his youth Shaka served in Dingiswayo's regiments. Around 1816 Senzangakhona died, and was succeeded by his son Sigujana. But Shaka, backed by Dingiswayo, wrested the Zulu chiefship from Sigujana, his half-brother, and put him to death. For about two years thereafter Shaka remained loyal to Dingiswayo. But after the latter's death the Mthethwa power bloc began to disintegrate, and Shaka exploited the vacuum by bringing Mthethwa-linked chiefdoms under his sway.

The Shakan state expanded as other chiefdoms were conquered or incorporated. In 1819 the Zulu decisively defeated the Ndwandwe in a battle at the Mhlatuze River. Shaka followed up this victory by razing large areas of Ndwandwe territory. Zwide fled with the remnant of his followers, eventually settling in the upper Nkomati valley in the present-day eastern Transvaal. In 1826 Zwide's successor, Sikunyana, led an Ndwandwe force back to attack the Zulu, only for it to be utterly decimated in a short engagement. Ndwandwe survivors fled northwards to attach themselves to other chiefdoms.

In the meantime the Zulu state had been expanding in other directions, particularly in the fertile Tugela valley and in the coastal region. Both the Mbo and Ngcolosi chiefdoms soon submitted to Shaka. The ruling lineage of the Ngcobo chiefdom, also situated in the Tugela valley, was forcibly incorporated into the loyal Mbo chiefdom. In the southern coastal region Shaka installed a subservient chief over the Cele chiefdom; and he destroyed the ruling lineage of the Thuli and replaced it with a pliant junior section. More powerful lineages were also made subservient. Shaka secured the allegiance of the Qwabe; and in 1821 Mlandela, an ally of Shaka, gained control of the Mthethwa ruling lineage. At the height of his power Shaka could claim to hold sway over a vast area bounded by the Indian Ocean, the Pongola in the north, the Drakensberg, and the Tugela in the south.

As we have seen, the expansion of the Zulu kingdom was partly achieved through military conquest. And conquest in turn rested on the use of a strictly disciplined, mobile army whose warriors, well-protected by large shields, engaged in effective hand-to-hand fighting, using a short stabbing spear. The army grew in size as it incorporated young men from conquered chiefdoms. But Shaka did not just depend on military might. As Hedges has noted, Shaka expanded his power 'by the use of existing ruling lineages, the exploitation of rivalries within them, and between them and their subordinates'.

Subjugated lineages came under Zulu hegemony in varying degrees and forms. Those lineages based close to the Zulu heartland were fully incorporated into the kingdom. Other lineages were treated rather differently, as Hamilton and Wright have pointed out:

> On the peripheries of the kingdom by contrast, members of existing lineages tended to be incorporated less as exploited 'subjects' of the king than as super-exploited 'tributaries'.... Altogether, members of these lineages seem to have had fewer rights and heavier obligations than members of the lineages of the heartland.

Transcending these differential forms of incorporation was a loose sense of Zulu nationhood. This was fostered by Shaka's emphasis on national ceremonies, and by the use of national symbols, notably the *inkatha*, a woven grass coil.

Statehood was further reinforced by the strong centralised authority vested in the Zulu king. Shaka made the key decisions of state, wielding enormous executive, judicial and military power. As Slater has observed, Shaka's position became 'something approaching divine kingship'. Religious systems were reorganised to focus on the king at the apex. An independent group of rainmakers was destroyed by Shaka immediately on his accession to power. Moreover, central intervention in the economy enabled Shaka to accumulate abundant material resources. The bulk of income derived from the exchange of ivory, for instance, fell to the Zulu state.

Nevertheless the degree of centralisation in the Zulu state should not be exaggerated. The size of the state necessitated the delegation of authority. Heads of pre-existing chiefdoms, although ultimately subject to Shaka, retained a degree of autonomy. Some of these were allocated land and cattle by Shaka to ensure their loyalty. Shaka entrusted key advisory and executive roles to senior members of the ruling lineage, both men and women. And he appointed a large number of *izinduna*, state officials who performed various administrative functions.

One of the fundamental elements of northern Nguni society, the homestead, continued to operate as a productive unit under Shaka's rule. But its productive capacity was to some extent drained by the enforced service of young males in age-regiments (*amabutho*). The homesteads would be deprived of the labour of these men for the length of their *amabutho* service, which could last up to twenty years. The primary function of the *amabutho*, which were commanded by *izinduna*, was military, but they also served the state in other ways, forming hunting parties or labour-gangs for public works.

Shaka's exercise of power seems to have rested heavily on the use of force. Under his reign of terror political opponents were ruthlessly killed. After the death of Shaka's mother in 1827 the terror escalated, as more and more of his subjects were executed for various offences. This terror bred fear and discontent, which in turn made Shaka's own position vulnerable. It could hardly have been a surprise, therefore, when in 1828 Shaka was assassinated, in a plot organised by his half-brother Dingane.[20]

The process of social and political consolidation among the northern Nguni raises a number of questions. As we shall soon see, attempts to explain the dynamics of this consolidation have aroused considerable historical debate. Some historians have also been concerned with the timing and tempo of the process. The orthodox view has tended to emphasise the sudden, cataclysmic nature of the northern Nguni political revolution. As Wright has stated, the conventional view places emphasis on 'developments in the Mthethwa and Zulu kingdoms, and on the military functions of the male *amabutho*. The initial stages of these developments are associated with the rise of Dingiswayo and the Mthethwa kingdom, and its later stages with the rise of Shaka and the Zulu kingdom.' Dingiswayo is said to have abolished the circumcision schools and developed the age-regiments, while Shaka is thought to have introduced full-time military service, imposed a ban on marriage during the performance of that service, and conscripted females into separate age-regiments. More recently it has been argued that the process of transformation was less sudden than is usually thought. Wright has found evidence to support 'the argument that Shaka's *amabutho* can be seen as the products of a process of social and political change that had begun in northern Nguniland decades before he came to power.' And according to Hedges, Mthethwa traditions record the existence of *amabutho* before Dingiswayo, indicating that the process of centralisation had an even earlier origin.

The reasons for this transformation in northern Nguni society and politics have been the subject of more intense debate. Essentially four broad types of explanation have been put forward: the theory of white influence, the individualist approach, the trade hypothesis, and interpretations rooted in demography and ecology. The first of these views derives from the assumption that in general the history of African societies has been essentially static and timeless, unless those societies have fallen under some dynamic external influence. Thus the story goes that Dingiswayo, while wandering in exile, met a white traveller called Cowan from whom he learnt of white techniques of military organisation; and during a visit to Grahamstown Dingiswayo was supposedly inspired by what he saw at military barracks. It was from these influences that Dingiswayo derived the idea of implementing a regimental system among the Mthethwa. This white inspiration theory is now widely discredited. Apart from being based on faulty assumptions it is factually implausible. Both Cowan's travels and the establishment of Grahamstown post-date the rise of Dingiswayo; and it is doubtful that such a major socio-political transformation could have been brought about as a result of these random occurrences.

A second set of interpretations draws upon the individualist tradition of historiography. In the case of Zulu state formation this tradition has a number of variants. One places an exaggerated emphasis on the roles of great men and heroes. Thus Dingiswayo and Shaka emerge as great innovators, as men with vision and political skill who could shape the course of history. Gluckman has offered another variation of the individualist approach. Instead of stressing the heroism of Shaka, Gluckman has rather highlighted the disturbed personality of the Zulu king. Particular attention is given to the abnormal sexual, or asexual, behaviour of Shaka. Thus Gluckman sees the prohibition on marriage, a crucial element of the Zulu military system, as a product of Shaka's psychosexually disturbed personality. A third variation of the individualist approach can be found in Walter's interpretation. Walter places special emphasis on Shaka's systematic use of violence in his reign of terror. Whereas Gluckman sees this violence as a product of madness, Walter regards it as a calculated act of policy on Shaka's part: 'Shaka was able to utilize violence on such a scale as to create what some social scientists have called a proto-totalitarian system.' And there is no doubting the individualist strand in Walter's interpretation: under Shaka the Zulu state 'was to be a vast predatory organism directed by a single will'.

Attempts to explain historical change in terms of the roles of key individuals are generally unsatisfactory. Such explanations tend to separate individuals from their broader context, failing to account for the circumstances in which they operate. Thus, while not minimising the significance of Shaka's reign of terror, one has to dismiss Walter's interpretation as having little analytical value. It says nothing about the reasons for Shaka's rise, or about the conditions that made Shaka's despotism possible or necessary. Gluckman's hypothesis is also flawed. The successful pursuit of psychohistory requires a large body of information about the individual subject of analysis. In the case of Shaka the available data is minimal.

More convincing is the trade hypothesis; variants of this have been propounded by Smith, and more recently by Hedges. Both have highlighted the importance of trade through Delagoa Bay. There is evidence that trade was conducted between the northern Nguni and the Portuguese as early as the mid-sixteenth century. In 1554 a Portuguese party observed ivory at the Mfolosi River being carried northwards for trading. From the late seventeenth century the English and the Dutch also began to participate in the Delagoa Bay trade, thereby increasing the demand for ivory. A more dramatic increase in the Delagoa Bay trade occurred from the mid-eighteenth century. The Portuguese were no longer able to control the trade, and competition between European traders forced up the ivory price. Ivory was the commodity most sought after by European traders at Delagoa Bay, and it seems likely that the northern Nguni region was a major source of this product. Contemporary European observers stated that the hinterland to the south of Delagoa Bay was the best area for trade. Moreover, beads and brass, two of the main commodities to be imported through Delagoa Bay, were known to be common among the northern Nguni.

Smith argues that this trade contributed significantly to the processes of both consolidation and conflict among the northern Nguni. He points out that the Hlubi, Ngwane and Ndwandwe were among the first northern Nguni chiefdoms to consolidate into larger polities. Each of these chiefdoms also had a long history of trade; and the Ngwane and Ndwandwe settled along the Pongola, 'a major artery of commerce to Delagoa Bay'. Trade may not only have motivated consolidation but also facilitated it: 'By distributing goods obtained from the long-distance trade, a chief could command increased loyalty from both within and without the normal lineage structure.' Dingiswayo, for instance, exercised a personal monopoly over trade — a sure sign that he was aware of its political importance.

Hedges also stresses that control of the ivory trade was important to a ruling lineage. Management of the exchange system enabled ruling lineages to reproduce their domination by controlling the reproduction of subordinate lineages. Access to the ivory trade allowed some lineages to expand at the expense of others. Hedges adds a further dimension by relating the development of *amabutho* to the ivory trade. The growing demand for ivory in the eighteenth century gave an added importance to hunting. *Amabutho* were raised not just for military purposes, but also to mobilise the manpower required for hunting parties, thereby increasing the supply of ivory. At the same time, the *amabutho* ensured that the control of hunting, and therefore control of ivory too, was more centralised in the chief's hands. However, Hedges continues, at the end of the eighteenth century there was a sharp decline in the ivory trade. Centralisation now had to be maintained mainly by the export of cattle, a commodity that, unlike ivory, had a high local value. The new role of the *amabutho* thus becamc the acquisition of cattle from outside the chiefdom to replace exported cattle. According to Hedges, it was these changes in productive forces that underlay the conflicts of the early nineteenth century and the emergence of the Zulu state.

The connection between trade and state formation seems to be a prominent and widespread feature of precolonial African history. Both Smith and Hedges have marshalled sound evidence to support their related, but differing, interpretations. It seems likely that trade was a source of both conflict and centralisation among the northern Nguni. However, trade alone was probably an insufficient factor; it is necessary as well to examine the demographic and ecological background.

The possibility of a link between environment and state formation among the northern Nguni was first explored by Daniel and Webb. They showed that the respective heartlands of the Ngwane, Ndwandwe and Mthethwa in the late eighteenth century all enjoyed access to key natural resources. They were close to watersheds; average rainfall levels were high; the soil was generally fertile; and their proximity to both sweetveld and sourveld facilitated all-year grazing. However those particular combinations of resources in close proximity to each other were scarce. So Daniel and Webb have suggested that it was competition for these resources that set off the process of state formation. Daniel, for instance, notes that the Ngwane–Ndwandwe conflict, one of the earliest of the clashes that were to develop among the four power blocs, arose out of a dispute over arable land in the Pongola valley.

About forty years ago Gluckman suggested that population pressure was probably the key factor in the process of socio-political consolidation among the northern Nguni. In his view the land shortage arising out of population pressure made it more difficult for chiefdoms to segment and for dissident groups to break away into new areas. Like Gluckman, Daniel and Webb also argued that competition for resources was aggravated by mounting population pressure and by the devastating drought and famine that afflicted the northern Nguni at the end of the eighteenth century.

In a similar way Guy builds his interpretation around the ecological crisis of the late eighteenth century. This crisis, he argues, intensified competition for scarce resources, particularly pasture land, among the northern Nguni; and political consolidation may well have been a response to this crisis. Greater centralisation of authority facilitated a more rational exploitation of different pasture types — sweetveld and sourveld — at the appropriate times of year. Furthermore, Shaka's marriage prohibition imposed on members of *amabutho* may have been intended to alleviate population pressure. Guy's interpretation is a subtle piece of speculation. But the hypothesis also contains a strong individualist strand, assuming great power of foresight and calculation on the part of Shaka. As Guy himself admits, 'We can neither assert that environmental changes "caused" the Shakan revolution, nor that Shaka necessarily realised that there was a population crisis and solved it by slaughter abroad and contraception at home.'

This more recent research and analysis has successfully brought about a shift of focus. Earlier writers tended to emphasise the military features of the northern Nguni 'revolution'. *Amabutho* were seen as essentially military units; and changes in military technique and strategy were deemed to be central to the dynamic of change. But the work of Guy, Hedges, Wright, Slater and others has shown that the 'revolution' was perhaps more of a socio-economic transformation than a military one. *Amabutho* were not just military units; they also performed important labour functions for the state, thereby enhancing the king's power. 'From this standpoint', states Wright, 'state formation among the northern Nguni cannot be explained simply in terms of military conquest, but must also be understood as encompassing a major social transformation, central to which was the forming of these multi-functional *amabutho*.'[21]

The southern Nguni

Our knowledge and understanding of early southern Nguni history are somewhat limited. The archaeological record for the region is scanty in comparison to the relative wealth of archaeological material for the northern Nguni. Moreover, the southern Nguni remained an essentially stateless society (although this is debated), and did not undergo the process of state formation experienced by the Zulu in the early nineteenth century. Given the longstanding tendency of historians to concentrate their attention on large-scale, centralised, more spectacular political entities, the early history of the southern Nguni was neglected until more recently. Their place in South African historical writing has generally been confined to that of protagonists in the wars on the eastern Cape frontier from the late eighteenth century. Only in recent years has there been any serious effort to try to understand the internal development and dynamics of southern Nguni history.

Little is known about the exact manner and date of the arrival of the southern Nguni in the region of present-day Transkei and Ciskei. But there is evidence to show that by the mid-sixteenth century the Transkei was occupied by Nguni-speakers practising mixed farming. The accounts of shipwrecked travellers inform us that there were Xhosa-speaking peoples as far south as the Mthatha River in 1593. According to Derricourt the Transkei coast was probably occupied by Nguni people from the sixteenth century. While this represents the earliest *evidence* of Nguni southward expansion, their actual occupation of this region may have begun earlier.

By the early nineteenth century the southern Nguni comprised five main groupings: the Xhosa, Thembu, Mpondo, Mpondomise and Bomvana. The existence of these groupings has posed problems of conceptualisation and interpretation, which will be discussed later. If socio-political structure is a problematic area, it is possible to provide a fuller picture of southern Nguni economic behaviour in the two centuries before the *difaqane*. The accounts of shipwrecked travellers from the sixteenth century show that this economy was firmly based on cultivation and herding. The evidence suggests that a wide range of agricultural products were grown in various parts of southern Nguni territory at different times. The basic crop was sorghum, and its cultivation seems to have been widespread. Maize was known to be grown in the mid-Transkei by 1635. This was not an indigenous crop, probably spreading into Nguni territory from the east coast of Africa.

Further fragments of evidence reveal that other products were cultivated during this era in a few or more areas occupied by the southern Nguni. These products included calabashes, watermelons, gourds, beans, pumpkins, potatoes, bananas, sugar, tobacco and dagga. Cattle-keeping was general practice. There is also evidence that some groups domesticated sheep, goats, dogs or poultry in limited numbers. However, the southern Nguni did not generate a food supply only by domesticating plants and animals. Like the San and Khoikhoi they also resorted to hunting and the gathering of wild plants.

It is customary to classify African precapitalist economies as 'self-sufficient'. This can be misleading as it fails to take acount of trading networks that often developed across the subcontinent. Both the archaeological and the historical record attest to the relative scarcity of metal in the Transkei and Ciskei. So iron and copper were imported into the region, usually from the north-east along a trade route that ran parallel to the sea. Such was the demand for metal that it could fetch a high price. The survivors of the wreck of the *Santo Alberto* in 1593 were able to negotiate deals involving the exchange of 6 cattle for one gimlet and one piece of copper, 2 cows and 2 sheep for three handsized copper pieces, and 1 lamb for one piece of copper. Beads represented the other major import. They too came mainly from the north-east, this source being supplemented later by a developing trade with the Cape Colony. There is evidence that from the late eighteenth century the Xhosa were trading with the white settlers, exchanging cattle for iron, copper and beads.[22]

Just as it is necessary to repudiate the myth that African precapitalist economies were purely self-sufficient, so must the myth of ethnic exclusivism be rejected. There are various indications, for instance, that the southern Nguni and Khoisan interacted in diverse ways. The archaeological evidence, in the shape of skeletal remains, is 'sparse and confusing' for the Transkei coastal region, although it does suggest, according to Derricourt, an 'admixture of Khoisanoid, Negroid and Caucasoid'. More significant are the clues provided by linguistics. As Harinck argues, 'Comparative analyses of Khoi and Xhosa linguistic interrelationships indicate that interaction between Khoi and Xhosa peoples was intimate and of long duration.' He observes, 'Of some fifty-five consonants ... of the Xhosa phonemic stock, twenty-one are primarily traceable to the Khoi sound system. Fifteen of these twenty-one are so-called "click consonants".' While Xhosa is a Bantu language, clicks are not general features of Bantu languages. There must, therefore, have been significant interaction between the Xhosa and Khoi peoples. The details of Xhosa linguistic borrowing offer further clues to the nature of Xhosa–Khoi interaction: 'Khoi word roots and phonetic elements exist in Xhosa nomenclature denoting aspects of the socio-economic and ritual spheres.' There is correspondence between the two languages in several words relating to cattle and to religion. Moreover, the word 'Xhosa' is derived from the Khoi verb stem meaning 'to destroy'.

These linguistic links need to be interpreted carefully. Peires rejects the idea that because of the similarity of the cattle vocabulary the Xhosa must have obtained their cattle from the Khoi. He points to the different social practices associated with cattle-herding in the two societies. In Xhosa society, for instance, women were excluded from activities relating to cattle, while in Khoi society women did the milking. It is more likely that the linguistic similarities are indicators of a trading connection and other forms of interrelationship. Certainly the existence of trade between Xhosa and Khoi is confirmed by documentary evidence. As Harinck observes:

> This evidence suggests that there existed in the mid-seventeenth century a trade connection coupled with a political alliance between the Xhosa and the Chainouqua Cape

Khoi chiefdom. This reciprocal relationship reflects attempts by Khoi and Xhosa to regulate the flow of goods in their trading system.

Xhosa-grown dagga would flow westwards and Dutch-imported metal and beads would move eastwards from Table Bay, with the Khoi playing a key intermediary role in this trading network.

Oral traditions provide further information of Xhosa–Khoi interaction. One tradition reveals that a Xhosa paramount chief, Togu, took as a minor wife the daughter of a Khoi chief, probably in the early seventeenth century. There also seems to have occurred a process of mutual assimilation. There were times when Xhosa refugees attached themselves to Khoi chiefdoms and became assimilated. Over time, however, the assimilation process came to work in the other direction. By the mid-seventeenth century the Xhosa had built up a local ascendancy over large sections of the Cape Khoi. Initially the Xhosa seem to have exploited local Khoi rivalries to establish their influence. Later the pressure of an expanding white colonial society, disease, and the depletion of cattle herds further weakened the Khoi. And so in various ways numerous Khoi came to be absorbed into Xhosa society during the course of the eighteenth century. For instance, the Inqua chiefdom of Hinsati disintegrated around 1700, and its people were assimilated into the Xhosa polity. But absorption did not always mean full assimilation. Many Khoi attached themselves to the Xhosa as clients, offering labour or military service in return for protection and security. Others resisted any form of Xhosa domination, preferring to enter the service of white colonists.

Similarly diverse forms of interaction, violent and peaceful, occurred between the Xhosa and the San. There is evidence of great Xhosa brutality towards the San. But, as Peires has observed, there was also peaceful contact:

San were renowned rainmakers and useful trading partners, exchanging ivory for cattle and dagga. Intermarriage was rare, but not unknown. San became tributary to Xhosa chiefs and according to one report, there were more San than Gona Khoi living among the Gcaleka. At least one Xhosa clan, the isiThathu, was partly San in origin. Conversely, Xhosa sometimes joined San bands.[23]

It is clear that the kinds of interrelationship that developed between the southern Nguni and the Khoisan were complex and varied. Equally complex is the problem of defining and distinguishing between southern Nguni polities. The southern Nguni have been separated by scholars into two broad categories. The first includes the earliest immigrants into the region, namely the Mpondo, Mpondomise, Thembu, Bomvana and Xhosa. The second group comprises more recent immigrants who moved southwards during the *difaqane*. At this stage it is necessary to consider the early history of the first of these two groups.

The Mpondo may have migrated southwards from the region of present-day Swaziland around the mid-sixteenth century or earlier. Burial sites suggest that Ncindise was the first Mpondo chief to rule south of the Mzimkhulu River. He reigned in the ninth generation before Faku, who ruled from 1824 till 1867. Under Tahle, three generations before Faku, the Mpondo first settled south of the Mzimvubu.

Traditions claim that the Mpondo and Mpondomise were descended from a common ancestor, Njanya. It is possible, therefore, that the two groups migrated southwards at much the same time. And the chronology of the Mpondomise genealogy ties up with Wilson's estimation of a mid-sixteenth century arrival in southern Nguni territory. Allowing for a 30-year generation one is able to deduce from the genealogy and the burial sites of chiefs that the Mpondomise were south of the Mzimkhulu during the reign of Ncwini, who ruled in the mid-sixteenth century and was buried at Lotana in the Qumbu district.

The Thembu and Bomvana came to be situated south of the Mpondo and Mpondomise. It is difficult to estimate the date of their arrival. The Thembu are reputed to have a particularly ancient lineage. One early Thembu chief, Nxego, who probably reigned in the first half of the seventeenth century, was buried at Msana on the Mbashe River. But the Thembu almost certainly migrated southwards before Nxego's time. The survivors of the shipwrecked *Santo Alberto* may well have encountered Thembu at the mouth of the Mbashe River in 1593.

Their relative proximity to the Xhosa came to pose problems for the Thembu. From the mid-eighteenth century they seem to have fallen under Xhosa sway. Towards the end of the eighteenth century the Xhosa were reported to be devastating Thembu homes, stealing cattle and exploiting their labour. Later the Xhosa chief, Hintsa, claimed some authority over the Thembu. Less is known about Thembu relations with their other eastern neighbours, the Bomvana, or about the actual history of the Bomvana themselves. Their founding chief, Bomva, probably held sway in the early sixteenth century; but the arrival date of the Bomvana is uncertain. Some sources suggest that they arrived among the Mpondo as refugees from the north in the late seventeenth or early eighteenth centuries.[24]

The fifth and most southerly group among these earliest southern Nguni immigrants were the Xhosa. Their exact origins are also uncertain. Xhosa people today claim descent from a great common ancestor called Xhosa. According to J. H. Soga, Xhosa must have been ruling around 1535. This date is derived on the basis of a 25-year generation taken back from the reign of Togu, who was ruling in 1686 when the *Stavenisse* was shipwrecked. The key figure in the emergence of a more centralised Xhosa polity seems to have been Tshawe. Soga places his reign in the early seventeenth century, but Peires, wary of the faulty genealogy, more cautiously sets the 'story of Tshawe' at 'some time before 1675'. This 'story' involved Tshawe's usurpation of the chiefship and his destruction of the independence of the various clans that then existed. From that time the Tshawe lineage came to be established as the royal lineage among the Xhosa.

Following upon Tshawe there reigned a succession of chiefs, about whom little is known. For about forty years in the mid-eighteenth century, from the 1730s to 1775, Phalo held the Xhosa chiefship. Again, little is known about the nature of his rule, but a significant development did occur in his reign —

a major division within the Xhosa polity. This arose out of a quarrel between two of Phalo's sons, Gcaleka and Rharhabe, both of whom claimed to be Phalo's legitimate successor. The dispute degenerated into a war in which Gcaleka was successful and Rharhabe was captured. Upon his release Rharhabe moved across the Kei, taking Phalo with him. And so originated the split between the Gcaleka of the Transkei and the Rharhabe of the Ciskei.

Phalo died in 1775, and Gcaleka in 1778. Gcaleka's successor, Khawuta, reigned ineffectually from 1778 to 1794. He placed people of low birth in positions of authority, thereby weakening royal power and prestige. In the meantime Rharhabe was building up his power west of the Kei. He subjugated Khoi and San groups; he attacked Khawuta; but he finally met his death in a clash with the Thembu in about 1782. Rharhabe's heir, Mlawu, was also killed in the same clash. The succession therefore fell to Mlawu's son, Ngqika; but since Ngqika was still a minor, power was vested in Ndlambe, Mlawu's brother, as regent.

It was Ndlambe who consolidated and strengthened the position of the Rharhabe. He subjugated neighbouring chiefdoms by subtly playing them off against the Dutch frontiersmen. He drove the imiDange, another autonomous Xhosa chiefdom, into a conflict with the white colonists who were expanding from the west. In the First Frontier War of 1779–81, the imiDange were defeated by the boers. Ndlambe also gradually wore down the Gqunukhwebe, a mixed Xhosa–Khoi chiefdom. Ndlambe defeated the Gqunukhwebe in a series of battles, but finally he had to rely on boer support to deliver the crushing blow in 1793.

While Ndlambe succeeded in establishing Rharhabe power west of the Kei, his own position became insecure as Ngqika came to the end of his minority. It may have been that Ndlambe tried to cling on to power; or Ngqika may have wanted his own chiefly authority to be undisputed. Whatever the case Ndlambe and Ngqika clashed in 1795. Although Ndlambe sought Gcaleka assistance across the Kei, Ngqika was able to repel their joint invasion. Ndlambe was taken prisoner and deprived of any power, but was allowed to carry on his life at Ngqika's great place.

Ngqika was an ambitious ruler who had pretensions to becoming paramount over all the Xhosa. This ambition was in the event to go unrealised, but he was able, at least, to concentrate greater power in his hands within the Rharhabe chiefdom, and to develop a network of external alliances. He won the support of the imiDange; the Gqunukhwebe paid him tribute; among his other supporters were groups of Khoi and some boer adventurers. These boers were led by Coenraad de Buys, who became the lover of Ngqika's mother.

By the end of the eighteenth century Ngqika seemed to be in a powerful position. But from 1800 he began to come up against problems. In 1800 Ndlambe escaped from his semi-captivity at Ngqika's great place and fled into the Cape Colony. East of the Kei the Gcaleka were recovering from previous defeats and internal divisions. At some time in the first decade of the nineteenth century Hintsa assumed the chiefship and proceeded to rebuild Gcaleka power and prestige. Facing danger from two sides, Ngqika was compelled to look towards the colonial authorities for aid. In the Fourth Frontier War of 1811–12 imperial troops, joined by the boer militia, drove Ndlambe and his followers back beyond the Fish River. And so there developed an alliance of mutual convenience between Ngqika and the Colony. The colonial government, successfully playing on Ngqika's ambitions and pretensions, recognised him as paramount over all the Xhosa. At the same time Ngqika was to be used as a colonial agent in suppressing cattle-raiding.

These internal Xhosa divisions and conflicts soon came to a head. At the battle of Amalinde in 1818, Ndlambe's forces gained an overwhelming victory over Ngqika. This drew the intervention of colonial forces. By the end of 1819 Ndlambe had been defeated in the Fifth Frontier War. This victory seemed to establish Ngqika's supremacy over Ndlambe and Hintsa, who had put his weight behind Ndlambe. But colonial collaboration was to have its price for Ngqika. Soon after the war the Cape Governor, Somerset, announced the colonial expropriation of approximately 4 000 square miles of Ngqika's lands. Ngqika protested, but to no avail; and in the 1820s he slipped into a rapid decline, becoming increasingly attached to brandy. As Peires writes, 'He purchased it, danced for it, sold his wives for it, begged for it, and ultimately died for it.' Ngqika's death in 1829 followed a year after the death of Ndlambe. Just as they had been divided against each other so their successors became embroiled in internal conflicts.[25]

These internal divisions raise larger issues concerning the nature of the Xhosa socio-political structure. Certain fundamental questions have been the subject of debate among historians and anthropologists. Firstly, how does one define or conceptualise the Xhosa polity? Did it posssess the characteristics of statehood or statelessness? Secondly, how can one explain the relative absence of centralised authority among the Xhosa, or indeed among the southern Nguni in general, compared to the northern Nguni?

Hammond-Tooke has tried to tackle the problem of definition by developing the notion of a 'tribal cluster'. While all the chiefdoms within a tribal cluster were related and ranked, they were essentially independent of each other and enjoyed equal status:

> Taking the Cape Nguni as a whole, then, we get the picture of a series of independent chiefdoms, some of which are organized into larger hierarchical structures which I have called the tribal clusters. In some respects a tribal cluster resembles what Southall has called a segmentary state, by which he means a political unit with some centralization of authority and a hierarchy of offices but which lacks the high degree of integration characteristic of true unitary states.

For Hammond-Tooke the Xhosa polity would have represented a tribal cluster. In other words, that polity comprised a series of related but independent chiefdoms.

Peires is inclined to ascribe a greater degree of unity to the Xhosa socio-political structure. He uses terms such as 'king', 'kingdom', 'nation', in relation to the Xhosa: 'The king had the right to mobilise the entire nation for war,' and he was 'the ultimate arbiter in all judicial and ritual disputes'. Furthermore, 'the kingship possessed symbolic and emotional associations which transcended its narrow political functions. The king was the "very personification of government" and the symbol of national unity.' Peires, however, does recognise a gradual decline in the power of the 'king' during the course of Xhosa history.

The processes by which divisions developed within the Xhosa polity have been a source of further debate between Hammond-Tooke and Peires. Hammond-Tooke has emphasised the inherent 'instability' of southern Nguni political units: 'the chiefdoms were inherently segmentary and there was a strong tendency to split up into two independent contraposed groups of co-ordinate status.' Internal division could arise out of dissatisfaction with a chief. More significant, though, was a fissiparous tendency that was built into the socio-political structure. This derived from the inherent tension between the chief's great house and his right-hand house. After marrying a number of wives a chief would choose his great wife, who would be senior wife and the mother of the chief's heir. Following upon this choice the chief would then nominate a right-hand wife; all remaining wives would be allocated either to the great house or to the right-hand house. According to Hammond-Tooke, this structural division led to political fission among the southern Nguni. By way of illustration he claims that from the end of the seventeenth century the original Xhosa tribe split into ten separate chiefdoms over six generations. Four of these divisions originated in the secession of the right-hand house, and two involved supporting houses hiving off from the great house. Among the southern Nguni as a whole, Hammond-Tooke was able to identify fifteen instances of a right-hand house seceding, and three cases of a minor house seceding.

Peires takes a different view from Hammond-Tooke. What the latter terms fission, the former prefers to call segmentation. Through this process of segmentation sons of chiefs would move with their followers into new territory and eventually establish themselves as chiefs in their own right. Peires thus argues:

> Xhosa history is best viewed not as a series of schisms destroying a previously unified people, but as the on-going expansion of the Xhosa polity brought about by the dispersion of the Xhosa royal lineage and its conquest of new lands and independent groups of Khoi, San and Nguni.

For Peires, the segmentation process, rather than fostering internal conflict, actually eased political tensions by providing for the dispersion of young chiefs and their followers.

Although Hammond-Tooke and Peires disagree on the nature of this process and on the degree of Xhosa political unity, they would ultimately agree that the Xhosa (and, of course, the southern Nguni in general) failed to come near to the degree of statehood achieved by the Zulu. However, in contrasting northern Nguni statehood with southern Nguni statelessness, one must not forget the broad similarity between their respective socio-political structures. Perhaps the similarities and differences are best encapsulated in a three-tiered model of Nguni society. This model incorporates three units of authority: the homestead, the chiefdom and the state. The first two of these are common to the southern and northern Nguni; the third represents the important point of differentiation.

At the lowest level the homestead was a fundamental unit of Nguni society. It was the 'matrix of Xhosa political and social organisation', as Peires puts it. The same could be said of the Zulu homestead. However, homesteads could not function in total isolation. They belonged to a larger unit, the chiefdom; and this belonging was vital to their survival. A single homestead was not a viable defensive unit. So, in times of war the homestead depended upon the protective cloak of the chiefdom, which took on the responsibility of mobilising forces. All land within the tribal domain was vested in the chief, who could therefore control the access of each homestead to land. And the chiefship carried with it an aura and mystique that provided an ideological reinforcement to chiefly authority.[26]

The homestead and chiefdom were crucial units among both the southern and northern Nguni. But the third tier, that of statehood, was clearly more developed among the northern than the southern Nguni. Among the latter there occurred no equivalent of the Shakan revolution. Scholars have pondered the reasons for this difference, and a few suggestions can be ventured here. At a simplistic level one could say that there was no Shakan-type revolution among the southern Nguni because they did not produce a Shaka. But this view suffers from the pitfalls of a narrow methodological individualism. Wilson suggests that whereas the chiefly monopoly of trade was a clue to political centralisation among the northern Nguni, the absence of such a monopoly among the southern Nguni may explain their lack of centralisation. Perhaps, though, ecology can again provide us with stronger clues to this problem. It has already been argued that the Zulu state may well have been formed in response to an ecological crisis in the early nineteenth century. The greater centralisation of authority made possible a more rational exploitation of declining economic resources. One can reasonably argue that the situation among the southern Nguni may have been different. It is true that they were encountering the pressure of an expanding colonial society. But excess land was still available, so that local crises could resolve themselves through the mechanism of the segmentary lineage system. As long as land was available sons could break away from their lineages and colonise new lands. Among the northern Nguni it seems that population pressure and the limited availability of land was obstructing this process, leading rather towards consolidation and centralisation.

It would be a mistake to overemphasise the contrast between the sociopolitical structures of the northern and southern Nguni. It would be equally erroneous to suggest that the Zulu state represented a more advanced or developed form of political organisation than its southern Nguni counterpart. This is a faulty assumption that has crept into Western historiography over the years: that precolonial political structures that approximate most closely to Western models somehow represent a higher level of civilisation. Essentially the Zulu state was superimposed upon a pre-existing structure that was firmly rooted in the homestead. And the homestead was the common denominator of Nguni socio-political organisation. It was also a particular feature that enables us to distinguish between the Nguni and Sotho peoples of southern Africa.

3
SOTHO, VENDA AND LEMBA COMMUNITIES UNTIL c. 1830

The problem of Sotho origins

As with the Nguni, one cannot talk of a single, homogeneous Sotho people in southern Africa; the term 'Sotho' is essentially a label of convenience. Its usage rests essentially upon the broad linguistic homogeneity of the Sotho peoples and upon certain generalised practices, such as preferred cross-cousin marriage. At the same time, however, it must be recognised that this generic label blurs differences of dialect, varying settlement patterns, and differing forms of socio-political organisation within the greater Sotho 'family'. In particular, we can distinguish between three major sub-groups: firstly, the Tswana or western Sotho; secondly, the Basotho or southern Sotho; and thirdly, the northern Sotho. These distinctions are based primarily on differing political structures that developed during the *difaqane*.

Our knowledge of Sotho origins is somewhat hazy. The known Iron Age occupation of the southern highveld does not date back much further than the fifteenth century. But there are earlier dates for the northern highveld, reaching back to the eleventh century, and for eastern Botswana going as far back as the Early Iron Age. Moreover, Maggs believes that 'it would not be surprising if future research were to extend the known Iron Age occupation of the southern Highveld back well into the first millennium A.D....'

Given the limitations of the archaeological evidence we are compelled to seek further clues from oral traditions. These traditions suggest that the earliest Sotho inhabitants of the highveld were the Kgalagadi and Fokeng peoples. Neither of these groups was to feature prominently in later Sotho history. The Kgalagadi were eventually forced westwards into the desert where they adopted a hunter-gatherer lifestyle, or attached themselves as clients to neighbouring chiefdoms; the Fokeng were to experience severe dislocation during the *difaqane*. The Hurutshe represent another of the most ancient of Sotho–Tswana lineages. They probably generated two other senior lineages, the Kwena and the Kgatla, both of which became dominant in the sixteenth century. Most of the later Sotho–Tswana chiefdoms can trace their origins back to the Kwena or Kgatla.

By the end of the eighteenth century Sotho communities had expanded throughout large areas of the interior plateau. There were also signs that certain communities were adapting to different environments in varying ways. Settlement patterns differentiated the western Sotho, or Tswana, from the southern Sotho. While the southern Sotho have tended to live in small, loosely arranged villages, the Tswana have occupied much larger, more compact and more densely populated settlements. Moreover, among the southern Sotho the ward has been a geographical unit, including residential, agricultural and pastoral areas; the Tswana ward, on the other hand, has been geographically fragmented, with its residential area being some distance away from its farm lands.

These divergent patterns of settlement are confirmed by archaeological evidence. The earliest form of settlement in the archaeological record has been labelled Type N by Maggs. He links this form with an early stage in the expansion of Sotho lineages and associates it particularly with the early Fokeng, Kwena and Kgatla lineages. A fifteenth-century date for one such Type N settlement at Ntsuanatsatsi, in the north-eastern Orange Free State, accords well with the evidence of oral tradition, which suggests that the Fokeng and Kwena were among the first Sotho groups to move across the Vaal. It seems probable that this area, where numerous remains of other similar settlements have survived, was a major population centre during the early Sotho occupation of the highveld.

Two other settlement patterns, which developed later, have been labelled Type V and Type Z by Maggs. The Type V settlements were more densely populated than the Type N equivalents; and they were mainly located to the south-west. Maggs identifies the Taung as the Type V builders. In the north-western region of the present-day Orange Free State and the south-western Transvaal Maggs found the Type Z settlements. These were even larger and more complex, resembling the Tswana towns described by early nineteenth century travellers. These Type Z settlements are linked with particular Tswana chiefdoms, the Rolong and Tlhaping. For Maggs this difference of settlement pattern represents 'a major cleavage within the Sotho–Tswana as a whole'. The westerly, more densely populated Type Z settlements are clearly identified with the Tswana; the more easterly Type N settlements are ascribed to the southern Sotho.

Maggs's typological study of Sotho settlements offers clues as to how this cleavage may have occcurred. It seems likely that the more easterly Type N settlements represent the earliest Sotho occupation of the highveld. The later Type V and Type Z settlements, therefore, may well have been a manifestation of Sotho expansion westwards. This expansion would have carried Sotho communities into areas of ever-increasing aridity until the limit of human occupation was reached on the edge of the desert.

Sansom has argued that it was the ecological constraints of this arid region that may well explain the denser settlement patterns of the Tswana. The Nguni inhabitants of the eastern coastland and river valleys have been able to subsist within relatively small, scattered communities because each of those communities has tended to enjoy a beneficial configuration of natural resources within its domain. Tswana communities, on the other hand, occupied a very different kind of terrain. In particular, water sources were scarce and far afield. The choice of sites for settlements was therefore seriously constrained according to the availability of water. This in turn meant that there was a smaller number of settlements and they tended to be very much more densely populated than their Nguni counterparts.

In spite of these ecological constraints there are signs that the economic life of Sotho–Tswana communities was no less vigorous than that of the Nguni. Like the Nguni, Sotho–Tswana economies rested on the twin pillars of cultivation and herding, supplemented by hunting, certain forms of manufacturing, and trade. Maggs has shown that hoe agriculture was a fundamental branch of production for these communities from the time of their initial occupation of the highveld. The earliest staples included sorghum, as well as a variety of pumpkins and melons. The Hurutshe were renowned tobacco cultivators. According to Stow, the Tswana were 'characterized by intense love of agricultural pursuits'; and 'the early travellers were filled with admiration and astonishment at the wonderful proofs of industry which the extent of the cultivated land surrounding their great towns exhibited.' The archaeological evidence also attests to the considerable importance attached to herding and hunting by these highveld communities. While domestic animals seem to have been the main source of meat, the product of the hunt represented an important supplement. The use of pitfall traps and circular game drives is described in the writings of early travellers.

There is almost no evidence of mining being practised by early Sotho–Tswana communities, although at Sebilong in southern Tlhaping territory specular iron, called *sebilo*, was mined in small flakes. Metal-working was carried on by local smiths. This is confirmed by finds of tuyères and sandstone crucibles. Another form of local industry was the manufacture of leather and skin goods.

The Sotho–Tswana people participated in extensive internal and external trade networks. Metals would probably have been obtained from north of the Vaal; and there is evidence that iron goods were imported across the Drakensberg from the Zizi of the Tugela basin. The main exports would have been surplus grain, ivory, and skins. In 1801 the first white traders arrived in the region, bringing beads to exchange for cattle and ivory. There also existed more localised trade networks, reflecting a degree of economic interdependence among Sotho–Tswana communities. Before the *difaqane* this network embraced a series of largely autonomous chiefdoms. As we have seen, most of these could trace their origins to a few common ancestral lineages. But largely as a result of social and political developments that occurred during the nineteenth century, it became possible to distinguish three main branches of the Sotho people. It is to a more detailed examination of these branches that we must now turn.[27]

The Tswana

Unlike the Nguni, the Tswana regard themselves as Tswana, but probably have not always done so. The label 'Bechuana' was developed by whites in the nineteenth century and was often applied very loosely to cover all the African peoples of the interior. As a classificatory term, 'Tswana' is convenient. But while it denotes a degree of cultural homogeneity, it in no way represents any kind of socio-political entity. Indeed, Tswana history is characterised by internal fission and division resulting in the creation of numerous independent chiefdoms.

For our knowledge of Tswana origins we have to rely largely on oral traditions. These have been probed by Parsons, who has presented a clear general picture of Tswana beginnings:

> All Tswana ruling lineages are traced to one of three founding ancestors, named Morolong, Masilo and Mokgatla. Morolong appears to have lived in the western Witwatersrand area around the 13th–14th centuries; Masilo appears to have lived in the northern Witwatersrand area around the 14–15th centuries; Mokgatla appears to have lived in the north-eastern Witwatersrand area around the 15th–16th centuries.

The history of each of these lineages was marked by processes of fission, giving rise to the numerous chiefdoms that appear in later Tswana history.

Around the end of the fifteenth century Masilo's lineage divided into two, and from this split arose the Hurutshe and Kwena chiefdoms. The Hurutshe, originally based at Tshwenyane near modern Zeerust, was one of the most powerful Tswana chiefdoms by the early eighteenth century, its territory stretching from the area of modern Rustenburg to the Pilanesberg. Later in the eighteenth century it came into conflict with other groups, particularly the Kwena.

The Kwena were another of the most powerful Tswana chiefdoms in the seventeenth and eighteenth centuries. Many Tswana and southern Sotho lineages claim descent from the Kwena, who were originally based north-east of the Hurutshe in the present south-western Transvaal region. In the eighteenth century two new important Tswana chiefdoms were founded after breaking away from the Kwena. First the Ngwaketse broke away. They became a powerful chiefdom under Moleta, who ruled from about 1770 to 1790. They were based in two successive stone-walled capitals, initially at Seoke, and later at Kanye. By the late eighteenth century their power rivalled that of the Hurutshe, with whom they were engaged in constant conflict.

The Ngwato were the second chiefdom to break away from the Kwena in the late eighteenth century. Mathiba, the first ruler of the newly independent Ngwato chiefdom, soon came to offend his former Kwena overlords. This tension escalated into war. The Ngwato were defeated and fled northwards, establishing themselves at Shoshong, their first capital, around the 1770s or 1780s. Within a few years the Ngwato themselves were subject to a breakaway when the Tawana seceded in the 1790s and migrated even further north to establish a new chiefdom in Ngamiland.

The Kgatla lineage, whose founding father was Mokgatla, also divided on numerous occasions. The Pedi state, which we shall be examining later, was an offshoot of the Kgatla. So was the Tlokwa chiefdom, which broke away from Mokgatla's lineage during the late sixteenth century. The Tlokwa themselves then proceeded to split, and in the seventeenth and eighteenth centuries Tlokwa chiefdoms could be found in various areas of the southern and western highveld.

The third main Tswana founding lineage, the Rolong, developed a powerful state in the seventeenth and eighteenth centuries in the region of the modern north-western Cape and south-western Transvaal. The Rolong built large stone-walled towns, notably Taung, their capital, and Dithakong. They probably reached the height of their power under Tau, a ruthless chief who reigned in the early eighteenth century. A number of dissident groups fled to escape Tau's rule. Many of these dissidents came to form the Tlhaping chiefdom, whose independence was firmly established by the late eighteenth century. By that time the Rolong themselves had also undergone the common Tswana process of fission. They had divided into four chiefdoms, named after four sons of Tau — the Rratlou-Rolong, the Seleka-Rolong, the Tshidi-Rolong and the Rrapulana-Rolong.

Tswana communities were not self-contained ethnic entities. There is much evidence of Tswana interaction with neighbouring Khoisan hunter-gatherers. The Rolong ruler, Tau, for instance, came into conflict with the Kora, a Khoi community whose territory was threatened by Rolong expansion. The Tlhaping, on the other hand, sharing with the Kora a common enmity against the Rolong, developed more peaceful forms of interaction. In the mid-eighteenth century the dominant Tlhaping lineage formed marriage alliances with leading Kora families. And later the Tlhaping were known to have taken into clientage Balala hunter-gatherers. The Balala were expected to supply labour for the Tlhaping, who in turn gave the Balala a chance to create their own herds by supplying them with cattle.

Some early Nguni offshoots also moved into the Tswana heartland. These later came to be known as Transvaal Ndebele (and must not be confused with Mzilikazi's Ndebele who broke away from Shaka and to-day live in Zimbabwe — there is no direct connection between the two). Parsons has noted how the early Ndebele 'settled among Tswana and Pedi as mercenaries or mine-workers, and became metal-workers, traders and rain-makers. In time they adopted Tswana or Pedi language and culture, but kept their separate identity as independent chiefdoms.' But some Transvaal Ndebele have continued to speak a Nguni dialect.

During the late eighteenth and early nineteenth centuries there seems to have been a state of endemic warfare among Tswana chiefdoms. As Parsons has remarked: 'By 1820 warfare was so widespread among the western Tswana that hardly a chiefdom had not seen its chief recently killed in battle.' Parsons suggests two general reasons 'why competition between the Tswana states turned to warfare — shortage of agricultural land or pasture, and a growing volume of trade between states and with the east and south coasts.' Competition for key resources would have been exacerbated during the drought years betwen 1790 and 1810.[28]

Any analysis of Tswana socio-political structures raises major problems of definition, conceptualisation and interpretation. It is clearly impossible to speak historically of a single Tswana polity. Over the centuries the Tswana have tended to proliferate into several autonomous entities. Tlou refers to these entities as 'states', and to their rulers as 'kings'. But they can be more adequately labelled as 'chiefdoms'. The Tswana chiefdom was a unit of fundamental importance in both the socio-political and the economic realms. Great authority was vested in the chief, who possessed supreme executive, legislative and judicial power; and he regulated the allocation of land, the annual cycle of agricultural tasks, external trade, and other economic activities.

A number of components comprised a chiefdom. The smallest of these was the family household, consisting of a man, his wife or wives, dependent children and other dependants. Several different households, linked patrilineally through a common male ancestor and situated close together in the same village, made up a family group. An elder, the senior male descendant of the common ancestor, exercised some authority over this group. A number of family groups together made up a ward, which came under the control of a hereditary headman. Each ward was a distinct administrative unit, occupying its own separate part of the village or town, or forming a separate village itself. But a ward was generally not a geographical unit, as its residential, agricultural and grazing areas tended not to adjoin each other. Within a ward the headman's authority was considerable; and collectively the headmen represented a kind of nobility, the *dikgosana*. Ultimately, however, power lay with the chief. The subservience of local units was maintained through the payment of tribute, and the recognition of the chief as repository of supreme executive, legislative, and judicial power.

Sansom has likened the Tswana chiefdom to a 'Tribal Estate'; the whole chiefdom could be regarded as 'an integral unit made up of three sections — residential, arable and grazing lands'. Because the headman's area of jurisdiction was rarely a territorial entity, the 'Tribal Estate' had to be administered as a unit, with the chief as its central overseer. 'Rulers of Tribal Estates were manipulators of bounds and grants. The bias in their power was toward governance exercised over access to territory and over seasonal regulation of work.' They were estate managers, not unlike the manorial lord, regulating the local economy.

In Sansom's view, Tswana chiefdoms took on this centralised character because of environmental constraints. He contrasts the Tswana domain with that of the Nguni:

> In the West, several factors militate against concentration of subsistence activities within small areas. The first is the nature of the terrain: a variety of resources is less frequently contained in small configurations such as those provided by the convolutions of Zulu hill country. On the inland plateaux one is often confronted with large expanses of relatively uniform country. To move from one type of plant cover to another, or to find different soil types, one must travel over larger distances. There is a general problem of finding a constant water supply and water resources are often far apart. Because people need to exploit variations of terrain, they must range over an extensive area.

The whole chiefdom thus became the smallest self-contained unit of economic exploitation. The people were necessarily concentrated in villages and towns because there were few areas that could cater for a small-scale subsistence community.

Environmental forces seem to have played a significant role in both Nguni and Sotho history in southern Africa. Among the Zulu, ecological factors may have contributed to the process of state formation. Among the Tswana, they seem to have led to a strengthening of chiefly authority. Clearly, though, different environmental conditions have exerted diverse forces in different regions. The process of state formation, for instance, was undergone by the Zulu, but not by the Tswana.

Schapera, in a similar vein to Hammond-Tooke's analysis of the southern Nguni, has attributed the absence of statehood among the Tswana to fissiparous tendencies within their chiefdoms. Dynastic quarrels were common, usually arising either out of succession disputes or out of dissatisfaction with the chief's exercise of power. Many of these quarrels resulted in secession, with a section of the chiefdom breaking away under a leader and moving into a hitherto unoccupied area to establish a new chiefdom. While these secessionist movements may have relieved internal tension, they certainly blocked any possible process of Tswana state formation. What is perhaps significant is that unoccupied land must have been almost continually available to allow secession to occur. Had avenues for expansion been blocked, as seems to have been the case with the northern Nguni early in the nineteenth century, then the Tswana would have found themselves in a major crisis situation which might have required a different kind of solution. This solution could perhaps have involved the amalgamation of political units and a greater centralisation of authority above the level of the chiefship. Instead the Tswana continued to fragment, and, as we shall see, their lack of overall unity and cohesion made them extremely vulnerable during the *difaqane*.[29]

The southern and northern Sotho

There have been various historical and social links and similarities between the Tswana and southern Sotho. Firstly, there is the linguistic connection. Secondly, certain ancestral lineages, notably the Kwena and Kgatla, were common to both. And thirdly, both Tswana and southern Sotho chiefdoms have displayed the similar propensity to divide and segment. At the same time there have also been differences. The more mountainous terrain of the southern Sotho offered a contrast to the flatter savannah country of the Tswana. As a result their respective settlement patterns tended to differ, those of the southern Sotho lacking the density of Tswana towns. And the more easterly location of the southern Sotho tended at times to bring them into the orbit of Nguni history.

Most southern Sotho are descended from certain dominant Sotho lineages. Foremost among these were the Fokeng and Kwena; the Fokeng may have been the earliest Bantu-speaking immigrants into the area, perhaps arriving in the sixteenth century. It appears that they were forced to move southwards by Kwena expansion over the Witwatersrand area. Both the Fokeng and Kwena were susceptible to fission. The Fokeng, whose main area of occupation lay south-east of the Caledon River, fragmented into many groups. The Kwena, who settled mainly along the upper Caledon valley, divided into numerous chiefdoms, many of which, although autonomous, retained the common name Kwena. Other Sotho chiefdoms, notably the Sia, Tlokwa and Phuthing, were descended from the Kgatla lineage. These came to be based north-east of the Caledon, near the Elands and Wilge Rivers.

All the Sotho immigrants came into contact with Khoisan hunter-gatherers, who had long since been living in this southern highveld region. There is evidence of Sotho–Khoisan intermarriage; and the Sotho language incorporated Khoisan words and click-sounds. It also appears that some Nguni lineages crossed the Drakensberg to settle in the area of modern Lesotho before the arrival of the Sotho. One such lineage was the Zizi.

It seems likely that the occupation of Lesotho by Iron Age Bantu-speakers may have been relatively late, compared to other regions of south-eastern Africa. Oral traditions tend to point to the sixteenth century as the period of earliest occupation. Archaeological evidence does not reveal Iron Age settlement much before the seventeenth century; and, as Maggs points out, 'although this may merely reflect the paucity of research, the seventeenth century may prove to be the earliest, as this area is approaching the southern limit of Iron Age expansion on the Highveld.'

The pre-*difaqane* social and political structure of the southern Sotho is striking for its fragmentary character. In the Caledon valley there was a general pattern of small groups arriving and establishing settlements, then subdividing with segments moving to new sites. Various types and sizes of communities emerged, ranging from a near autonomous village to a larger chiefdom. The problem is to define and conceptualise these units. For Sanders the village, normally comprising fifty to one hundred inhabitants, was the 'basic community' of the southern Sotho. But he goes further and terms this community a chiefdom, in that 'its nucleus would be formed by the chief and his relatives' and it would include people who had no family links with the chief. Some chiefdoms were independent; some might be in relations of overlordship or subordination to other chiefdoms; others might be acknowledged as overlord by one chiefdom, at the same time as being subordinate themselves to another. 'Thus there were independent chiefdoms and subordinate chiefdoms, and there were various grades of subordination.'

Chiefdoms varied in size. The Tlokwa, in the north-east, comprised several thousand people. But most southern Sotho chiefdoms were small, largely, it seems, because of their tendency to split and segment. Occasionally a member of a ruling lineage would break away with his age-mates and other followers to form his own chiefdom. It seems that at times ecological factors may have lain beneath this fissiparous tendency. Owing to the poor quality of grazing, cattle-posts were often established in far-flung areas. Younger chiefs would from time to time be commissioned to set up and maintain these cattle-posts. Eventually they might come to establish new villages in these distant areas; their remoteness from the centre would enable them to take on the status of independent or quasi-independent chiefs.

The process of fission could continue as long as surplus land was available for cultivation and pasture. By the first quarter of the nineteenth century this surplus was increasingly being occupied, and population density among the southern Sotho seems to have been growing. An ecological crisis may have been setting in. On top of this, the fragmentary character of their polities would seem to have made the southern Sotho highly vulnerable to any external threat. Given this apparent vulnerability, their eventual response to the *difaqane* (which we shall discuss later) must be regarded as surprising.[30]

The 'core group' among the northern Sotho has for long been the Pedi. On the edge of the escarpment there were three peripheral Sotho chiefdoms — the Pulana, Kutswe and Pai. The Pulana and Pai came to be largely subjugated or displaced by the emergent Swazi state. The Kutswe were Kwena who had migrated from the west. Other groups to have occupied the northern Sotho territorial area were the Roka, Koni and Tau. The Lobedu chiefdom also falls within the northern Sotho area. The origins of the Lobedu are uncertain, but it seems likely that their founding dynasty may have been Shona. After 1800 the Lobedu were ruled by 'rain queens', who attracted Pedi into their domains through their rain-making abilities. Gradually the Pedi language came to predominate among the Lobedu. The cultural and linguistic diversity of this north-easterly region underlines the futility of rigid ethnic classification. The Pedi polity, the largest and most significant among the northern Sotho, was a fluid entity whose subject population was not ethnically homogeneous.

The Pedi seem to be the only Sotho society to have experienced a process of state formation before the *difaqane*. In their case the typical Sotho tendency to segment and divide was reversed in the eighteenth century. The particular chiefdom responsible for this reversal was the Maroteng. According to their traditions the Maroteng were an offshoot of the Kgatla and had once been settled in the region of present-day Pretoria. Around the mid-seventeenth century they seem to have migrated eastwards, crossing the Lulu mountains and settling in the Steelpoort River valley. A century or so later, at some time in the second half of the eighteenth century, the Maroteng and the Tau took the lead in establishing a more centralised and more powerful Pedi polity.

Delius has provided a convincing explanation for this process. He notes that the Tau were relatively strong in numbers and cattle when they settled near the Oliphants River; and the Maroteng played a crucial role as metal-workers. This wealth in cattle and control of metal production may have enabled the Tau and Maroteng to enlarge their followings by securing women from less well-endowed groups, particularly as iron hoes, in addition to cattle, were probably used for the payment of bridewealth.

During the second half of the eighteenth century a series of conflicts developed in the region, culminating in the extension of Maroteng control over the area. The Tau and other groups retained a degree of local autonomy, but were also brought under Maroteng paramountcy. Subordinate chiefdoms had military obligations; and their chiefs were compelled to take their main wives from the paramountcy. During the reign of Thulare, from the late eighteenth century till about 1820, the zenith of Pedi power was reached. Large areas of the Transvaal were conquered in Maroteng-led military campaigns. These campaigns ranged as far south as the Vaal River, and as far west as the Fokeng, near modern Rustenburg; to the east, societies in the lowveld were also attacked by the Pedi.

Delius offers a twofold explanation for these conflicts. Firstly, he suggests, as Guy does for the northern Nguni, that by the mid-eighteenth century a growing human and stock population had brought about a social and economic crisis. A period of drought may have exacerbated this crisis, which in turn generated competition for scarce resources. Secondly, the Pedi occupied a crucial position in various trade networks. They could have been intermediaries in the exchange of metal goods, produced in the Phalaborwa region of the lowveld, for pastoral and agricultural commodities produced on the highveld. And the Pedi may have been in trading contact with Delagoa Bay. Maroteng traditions suggest that direct links with Delagoa Bay were built during the reign of Thulare. The need to secure control over trade, together with the accumulation of wealth and prestige goods derived from this trade, may have stimulated the trend towards a greater centralisation of authority. Delius also takes up the lead offered by Hedges, by speculating that the contraction of the Delagoa Bay trade from the late eighteenth century may have further generated conflict. As the trade declined, so it may have become necessary to assert an even stronger control over what remained of it; or else raiding could have developed as an alternative source of wealth as trade declined.

By the end of the eighteenth century, therefore, certain forces had been working towards the greater centralisation of the Pedi polity. But it seems that this centralisation stopped short of statehood, and that a looser type of confederal structure came into being. The Pedi polity comprised a number of chiefdoms that became subordinate to the Maroteng paramountcy. The population of a chiefdom was generally concentrated in a single village that could range in size from fifty to five thousand inhabitants. Villages were divided into *kgoro*. These were not unlike Tswana wards, but it seems that the *kgoro* had more autonomy than their Tswana counterparts.

The socio-political organisation of the Pedi was characterised by a number of typical Sotho elements. Endogamy, for instance, was preferred to exogamy. But in other ways the Pedi polity differed from southern Sotho and Tswana chiefdoms. The Pedi were the only Sotho society to develop before the *difaqane* an umbrella authority that embraced a number of chiefdoms. The Pedi paramount had wide power over subordinate chiefdoms. His was the final court of appeal; he regulated access to land; and he created bonds of dependence and clientage by giving his sisters and daughters in marriage to subordinate chiefs, or by loaning cattle to displaced and impoverished communities.

The building of these links created a greater potential solidarity among the Pedi, and therefore a stronger defensive capability as well. The fissiparous tendency of the southern Sotho and Tswana made those societies vulnerable to external threats. The Tswana, in particular, suffered enormous devastation during the *difaqane* because of their inability to weld alliances between chiefdoms. On the other hand, the Pedi, with their more unified structure, appeared better able to withstand the ravages which the *difaqane* inflicted.[31]

The Venda and Lemba

The Venda and Lemba, whose heartland lies in the far north of the modern Transvaal, have generally been viewed as falling outside the greater Nguni and Sotho 'families'. It is certainly true that the Lemba have displayed distinctive cultural and physical characteristics that seem to set them apart; and the Venda have had strong historical links with the Shona of Zimbabwe. However, elements of Sotho language and culture can also be found among the Venda — another reminder of the dangers of rigid ethnic classification.

The main area of Venda habitation has been the fertile Soutpansberg mountains; and it seems that they rarely ventured far south of this region. Until recently it was commonly held that the 'true' Venda were Shona immigrants who established themselves over the original non-Venda inhabitants, the Mbedzi and Ngona. But recent archaeological and linguistic research has altered this view. As Beach has noted, 'we now know that the basic Venda-speaking people have been present in the Zoutpansberg from very early times, and that they have absorbed a number of groups of Shona immigrants.'

As we have seen, there is archaeological evidence of Early Iron Age occupation in the northern Transvaal. It seems likely that the Ngona and Mbedzi were descended from these Early Iron Age inhabitants, and so they may have occupied Venda territory for centuries. It is known that a Venda state existed around the early eighteenth century and before. This state was known as Thovela. Its ruler lived in a Shona-style *zimbabwe* (stone-walled enclosure). The state was a producer of minerals and ivory, and was in trading contact with the Shona to the north.

In the second half of the eighteenth century a new dynasty, the Singo, took control of the Venda state. The Singo were Shona immigrants, and they were probably an offshoot of the Changamire Rozvi dynasty, which had come to dominate large areas of Shona territory in modern Zimbabwe since the late seventeenth century. The Singo conquered the Venda and established themselves as the ruling dynasty. They built a state modelled on the Changamire state, and seem to have received tribute from the entire Venda population. Although Shona traits were transmitted, the Singo in time came to assimilate Venda culture and language. They adopted, for instance, the Venda custom of initiation, and worship of the Venda god.

Early in the nineteenth century the Singo were riven by a dynastic quarrel. A civil war, waged among members of the Singo ruling family, broke the state in two. The southern and western regions of Venda territory came to be controlled by the house of Ramabulana. The eastern region came under the house of Tshivhase. Each became an independent dynasty.

As we saw earlier, archaeological evidence indicates that mining was carried on extensively in the northern Transvaal centuries ago. The Venda were heavily involved in these mining operations. The copper mines at Messina on the Limpopo were worked by the Venda, who also mined iron ore south of the Soutpansberg. Much of the business of working and trading these metals was carried on by the Lemba. They were skilled craftsmen who were masters at smelting and working iron, copper and gold; and Lemba women were renowned as potters. Moreover, the Lemba often travelled far afield to trade their products, which they might exchange for grain or livestock.

The Lemba have displayed certain 'peculiar' characteristics that have led scholars to set them apart from all Nguni and Sotho peoples. They have been marked by a distinctive physical appearance. Their economic base was unusual, resting more on manufacturing and trading, rather than on cultivation and herding. They have not constituted any particular kind of socio-political entity, preferring to live in dispersed groups among the Shona, Venda and Pedi. Although they generally spoke the language of those among whom they were residing, they tended otherwise to keep apart from the local inhabitants, practising strict endogamy.

These 'peculiarities' have caused scholars to puzzle over the origins of the Lemba. It has for long been held that the Lemba were descended from early Muslim traders. This was the view of Stayt in the 1930s and, more recently, of Van Warmelo. The Lemba followed the Muslim practices of male circumcision and not eating pork; and texts of Lemba prayers have revealed a Muslim influence. Parsons has doubted the Muslim origins, pointing out that male circumcision and the pork taboo are also to be found among neighbouring peoples. The most likely explanation has been put forward by Beach. He notes that the Shona-speaking Muslim traders of the interior plateau were in decline in the seventeenth century. And so, he continues: 'The Muslim community was gradually becoming more and more absorbed into the Shona world, to become the Lemba groups scattered across the Plateau, groups that retained little more than fragments of the Islamic faith and culture.'[32]

4
THE DIFAQANE

The present demographic structure of South Africa owes much to events that occurred in the two crucial decades between 1820 and 1840. The arrival of British settlers and boer migrations within the subcontinent considerably altered and expanded the distribution of the white population. But more dramatic were the cataclysmic changes in Nguni and Sotho society wrought by the *difaqane*. The overall impact of the *difaqane* was varied: some societies were severely devastated; some were forced to migrate and establish themselves in other parts of Africa; others withstood the traumas and even consolidated their position.

The chain reaction of attack, counter-attack, devastation and dispersal that constituted the *difaqane* had its origins in Dingiswayo's time. Both Dingiswayo, head of the Mthethwa power bloc, and Zwide, the Ndwandwe leader, had successively attacked Matiwane, chief of the Ngwane, who lived in the area of present-day north-western Natal. The Ndwandwe attack forced Matiwane to flee westwards towards the Hlubi, who occupied an area in the foothills of the Drakensberg. The Hlubi had been looking after a large quantity of Ngwane cattle; and they tried to capitalise upon Zwide's defeat of Matiwane by expropriating the entrusted cattle. In their westward retreat, the Ngwane, in about 1821, attacked and defeated the Hlubi, killing their chief, Mtimkhulu, and breaking up their chiefdom. One group of Hlubi fled southwards into southern Nguni territory where they joined those refugee bands that came to be known collectively as the Mfengu; a remnant group stayed in the Drakensberg foothills and was for a while incorporated into the Zulu state before moving to the western border of Natal; a third section of the Hlubi, led by Mpangazita, fled across the Drakensberg into the highveld. Mpangazita was followed about a year later in 1822 by the Ngwane. The Ngwane had briefly occupied the territory of the conquered Hlubi, until they found themselves on the receiving end of a Zulu attack which drove them, too, across the Drakensberg into the highveld.

In the meantime a third Nguni group, the Ndebele, was in the process of breaking away from Shaka and migrating across the Drakensberg. The Ndebele were led by Mzilikazi, a grandson of Zwide and a member of the Khumalo clan. During the Zulu–Ndwandwe conflict Mzilikazi had switched his allegiance from Zwide to Shaka, whom he came to serve as a military commander. But after conducting a successful military campaign Mzilikazi incurred Shaka's wrath by refusing to hand over to him a sufficient proportion of captured cattle. To escape punishment by Shaka, Mzilikazi in 1821 led a band of refugees across the Drakensberg into the eastern Transvaal.

While some refugees from Shaka were moving westwards, others were taking off to the north. After Shaka's defeat of the Ndwandwe, three chiefs who had formerly been subordinate to Zwide led their respective followings into Mozambique in the early 1820s. For some years southern Mozambique was disrupted by their presence, both the Portuguese and local Tsonga peoples bearing the brunt of the devastation. In time the three bands of refugees came to clash among themselves. One leader, Soshangane, emerged out of these conflicts with sufficient dominance to enable him to establish the Gaza state in southern Mozambique. The other two leaders, Zwangendaba and Nxaba, moved even further north early in the 1830s, cutting a way across the Zambezi. From there they spread out into various parts of present-day Zambia, Malawi and Tanzania, where they established a number of chiefdoms that came to be known collectively as Ngoni.

The impact of the *difaqane* was thus felt far into eastern and central Africa. But as the main focus of this survey is upon southern Africa, we must return to the highveld where in the early 1820s Sotho communities were coming under pressure from three bands of Nguni refugees — the Hlubi, Ngwane and Ndebele. The Tlokwa, located near a key mountain pass, were the first Sotho chiefdom to bear the brunt of this pressure. At this time the Tlokwa were ruled by MaNthatisi, who was acting as regent during the minority of her son, Sekonyela, the heir to the chiefship. The invading Hlubi, under Mpangazita, soon drove the Tlokwa from their villages, forcing MaNthatisi and her followers to flee westward on their own path of conquest and destruction. For two years the Hlubi and Tlokwa, in addition to engaging each other in violent clashes, preyed upon and pillaged Sotho communities along the upper Caledon River.

The Hlubi were soon followed across the Drakensberg by Matiwane's Ngwane. The Tlokwa were again the first victims of the initial Ngwane thrust. In 1825 the Ngwane fell upon the Hlubi. A five-day battle ended with the Hlubi defeated and Mpangazita killed. Once again the Hlubi broke up, some attaching themselves to their Ngwane conquerors, others to the Ndebele, and yet others to Moshoeshoe. For the next two years Matiwane was able to maintain his dominance over the Caledon area, until in 1827 he was attacked by a Zulu force and driven south. The Ngwane then became embroiled in two further unsuccessful engagements against Moshoeshoe and against the Ndebele. So in 1828 Matiwane led his followers south into southern Nguni territory. Feeling the threat of this incursion the Thembu appealed to the Cape colonial authorities for aid, and the Ngwane were crushed by a combined force of Africans and colonists. Some Ngwane remnants proceeded to attach themselves to Moshoeshoe's burgeoning state; others made their way back to Zululand where Matiwane was murdered by Dingane, who had recently usurped the Zulu kingship from Shaka.[33]

The *difaqane* wrought severe dislocation and devastation on the southern highveld. The small size and autonomous character of southern Sotho communities made them especially vulnerable to piecemeal attack. As an early missionary to the southern Sotho observed, Mpangazita 'ruined them one after another, without their ever dreaming of combining to oppose the common foe'. The ruin was extensive. Thompson has painted the general picture in this way:

nearly every Sotho community between the Vaal and the Orange rivers had been utterly disrupted. Thousands of the inhabitants had fled — some to the north, where they caused destruction beyond the Vaal ...; others to the south-west, where they obtained a footing among the Griqua, or took service with white farmers in the Cape Colony, or joined southern Nguni chiefdoms. In most of the Vaal–Orange area itself the old settlements were abandoned, the stock was destroyed, the fields ceased to be cultivated, and in several places the landscape was littered with human bones. Demoralized survivors wandered round singly or in small groups, contriving to live on game or veld plants. Even cannibalism was widespread.

One southern Sotho group to migrate to the north was a Fokeng community led by Sebetwane. This particular branch of the Fokeng had been attacked and defeated by MaNthatisi in 1822. Thereafter Sebetwane led his people north of the Vaal. Assuming the name Kololo, they became embroiled in a series of clashes with the Tswana and Ndebele during the 1820s. The Kololo moved even further north during the 1830s and established the Lozi state in the western region of present-day Zambia.

The Taung were another southern Sotho community to gain prominence during the *difaqane*. Their ruler, Moletsane, emerged as one of the most powerful Sotho leaders during the early 1820s; and he strengthened his position by allying with Sebetwane. In the early years of the *difaqane* the Taung moved across the Vaal and became engaged in attacks on various Tswana chiefdoms, notably the Seleka-Rolong. But late in the 1820s Moletsane's foolhardiness led the Taung into tussles with the Ndebele. Suffering successive setbacks at the hands of the Ndebele and Griqua in 1829, Moletsane and his followers obtained temporary refuge at Philippolis before returning to their home territory.

Many small autonomous Sotho communities, unable to withstand the impact of marauding bands, were broken up during the *difaqane*. For the members of these communities there were two options open to them. One was to flee from the areas of conflict. Some, like the Kololo, maintained a considerable degree of cohesion during their flight. Others made their way in disorganised bands of refugees. Large numbers of Sotho refugees, for instance, flocked into the Cape Colony to find employment with white colonists.

A second option for Sotho refugees was to attach themselves in some way to a stronger polity for protection and security. It seems that the *difaqane* set off two widely differing socio-political processes. On the one hand, as we have seen, it had the disintegrative effect of dislocating and disrupting numerous autonomous chiefdoms. On the other hand it also had the result in some areas of stimulating social and political consolidation. Two groups in particular, the Tlokwa and Moshoeshoe's Basotho, were given this stimulus by the *difaqane*.

The Tlokwa had been the first victims of the Nguni invasions across the Drakensberg. Forced to abandon their territorial base after the Hlubi attack, the Tlokwa led a semi-nomadic existence during the turmoil of the *difaqane*. But in spite of this they were able to retain a remarkable degree of cohesion under the leadership of MaNthatisi. During their wandering the Tlokwa were loosely organised in bands, comprising not only original members of the chiefdom but also other refugees and stragglers. They could carry cattle and a few possessions with them, but they depended for survival upon frequent raiding.

After a period of migration the Tlokwa were able to lead a more settled existence when, around 1824, they based themselves on two mountain fortresses at Joalaboholo and Marabeng near the Caledon River. The security of these positions attracted new adherents to the chiefdom, which expanded as it incorporated immigrant refugees from broken communities. By the mid-1830s it was estimated that the Tlokwa comprised about 14 000 Sotho and between 2 000 and 3 000 Nguni. MaNthatisi had built up a strong sphere of Tlokwa influence, radiating from her mountain bases. When Sekonyela came of age and acceded to the chiefship early in the 1830s his lands extended to the north and east as far as the Caledon.[34]

The Tlokwa not only withstood the *difaqane* but even exploited the situation of turmoil to expand and consolidate their chiefdom. In a similar way but on an even larger scale, Moshoeshoe built up the Basotho state. Moshoeshoe was a man who rose to prominence from small beginnings. Before the *difaqane* he was a village headman of the Mokoteli, a junior Kwena lineage. In 1820 or 1821 he established his village on the slopes of Botha Bothe mountain. From there he withstood the initial invasions of the *difaqane*.

Moshoeshoe used a subtle blend of diplomacy and military defence to ward off the invaders. The first threat he faced was posed by the Hlubi. Moshoeshoe bought them off with a peace-offering of cattle. In 1822 his community came under pressure from a Ngwane raiding party. Moshoeshoe ordered his followers to beat a hasty retreat to evade the attack. Then he again resorted to the strategy of deferential diplomacy to secure peaceful relations with the Ngwane. His payment of cattle was accepted by Matiwane, who thereafter temporarily refrained from attacking. After a brief lull Moshoeshoe and his followers became embroiled in a clash with the Tlokwa. Forced into retreat, Moshoeshoe was able to avoid defeat by allying with a group of refugees who were fleeing from the conquering Ngwane. The Tlokwa themselves retreated in the face of this combination. A year later, in 1824, the Tlokwa reappeared for another contest. This time Moshoeshoe held out in his mountain fortress at Botha Bothe.

Effective defence was crucial for Moshoeshoe's survival. In 1824 he moved his followers to an even more impregnable mountain stronghold, Thaba Bosiu. It was an ideal fortress. Its spacious summit was well watered and well grassed; and its sheer cliffs provided a formidable defence against attackers. Thaba Bosiu was dangerously close to Matiwane's headquarters. So Moshoeshoe continued to adopt a deferential stance towards the Ngwane chief. But in 1827 events again left Moshoeshoe vulnerable to a Ngwane assault. In that year a Zulu force crossed the Drakensberg and captured a large quantity of Ngwane cattle. Seeking to replenish his herds Matiwane looked towards his Sotho neighbours, and in 1828 launched an assault against Moshoeshoe. The attack was repelled and the Ngwane retreated southwards in disarray. A considerable area of territory, formerly controlled by the Ngwane, now came under Moshoeshoe's sway. And when Matiwane was finally crushed by a Cape colonial force many Ngwane refugees returned to the southern highveld to seek protection under Moshoeshoe.

External pressures did not cease with the removal of the Ngwane threat. Moshoeshoe continued to live in an uneasy peace with his main Sotho rivals, the Tlokwa. His community soon came under attack from marauding bands of Kora. And in 1831 he successfully repulsed a Ndebele assault after a fierce battle. But all the while that Moshoeshoe was warding off attackers, he was continuing to consolidate and expand his chiefdom. As his reputation as a successful defensive strategist spread far and wide, so refugees and other threatened communities gravitated towards his orbit of control. Moshoeshoe offered a welcoming hand to these newcomers. He had been building up his own herds by cattle-raiding; and he was able to loan cattle to these destitute refugees who sought his protection. Moshoeshoe established a loose overlordship over these protected communities, but he further earned their goodwill by allowing them a considerable degree of autonomy. Their chiefs, for instance, could continue to enjoy chiefly status. But this was not all altruism and benevolence on Moshoeshoe's part. While he granted protection to refugees, he also expected them in turn to protect him. He allocated land to these communities on the periphery of his emergent state so that they could serve as buffers against external invaders. In this way Moshoeshoe was able not only to consolidate his own defensive position but also to expand his following and enlarge his state. It is estimated that by 1840 the number of people under his authority had trebled to about forty thousand in 15 years. To have welded these diverse groups into a single, albeit loosely organised, polity during a time of great turmoil and upheaval, as Moshoeshoe had, was one of the most remarkable achievements of the *difaqane*.[35]

Among the Tswana the *difaqane* does not appear to have stimulated any parallel process of state formation. Indeed, the Tswana were probably the *difaqane*'s worst-hit victims, suffering severe devastation and dislocation. Their first depredations were suffered at the hands of marauding southern Sotho groups who had themselves been displaced and forced northwards by the Hlubi and Ngwane. Two such bands were the Phuthing, led initially by Tshwane and then by Ratsebe, and the Hlakwana, under Nkharahanye. Both had been early victims of the Hlubi, and had then crossed the Vaal to raid the Tswana. The Phuthing attacked the Seleka-Rolong, Kgatla, Kwena, Hurutshe and Ngwaketse in turn. The Hlakwana also cut a path of destruction through Tswana territory, following in the footsteps of the Phuthing. In 1823 the Phuthing and Hlakwana launched a combined assault on Dithakong, the capital of the Tlhaping, a southern Tswana chiefdom. But the assault was beaten off with the aid of Griqua horsemen whose help had been summoned by local missionaries. Both the Phuthing and the Hlakwana were put to flight. Many Hlakwana drowned trying to cross the Vaal River, and thereafter their chiefdom disappears from the historical record. The Phuthing did manage to retreat further north, only to be defeated by the Ndebele.

Various Tswana chiefdoms also suffered at the hands of the Taung and Kololo (Fokeng) during the 1820s. The Taung had been forced to abandon their homeland on the eastern highveld after being displaced by the Hlubi and Ngwane. Under Moletsane's leadership the Taung organised themselves for raiding, attracting ruffians into their ranks: Kinsman describes the Taung at this time as 'a mixed bag of brigands'. Late in 1823 they were raiding in the present-day Orange Free State. For a while the Taung joined with Sebetwane's Kololo in attacks on Kwena, Hurutshe and Ngwaketse settlements. Then the Taung and Kololo embarked on their own separate forays. In 1824 the Taung attacked the Rolong, only to be repulsed in a battle on the Molopo River. Thereafter Moletsane continued raiding north of the Molopo. Both the Taung and the Kololo eventually came into conflict with the Ndebele. In 1829 the Ndebele defeated the Taung, who ceased thereafter to be a military force. The Kololo, awed by one encounter with the Ndebele, migrated northwards, raiding the Ngwato and Tawana on their way, before eventually reaching their new home north of the Zambezi.

Although the Tswana may have been relieved by the departure or decline of the Hlakwana, Phuthing, Taung and Kololo, they themselves continued to be victims of Ndebele marauding. In 1823 the Ndebele had reached the Vaal River where they established their base for the next five years. They were soon raiding the Kwena and other Tswana communities, forcing them to flee westwards. By 1825 or early 1826 they were raiding as far north-west as the Molopo River, where Rolong chiefdoms bore the brunt of their attacks. In 1827 the Ndebele abandoned their Vaal River base and moved to the Magaliesberg mountains, near the Kgatla and Kwena. There they remained for another five years, attacking Tswana chiefdoms to the west. By 1830 the Hurutshe had been reduced to tributary status; some of them had been directly absorbed into Ndebele society. This five-year pattern of migration and settlement continued when the Ndebele moved to the Marico valley in the western Transvaal in 1832, remaining there until 1837. From this new base they sustained their attacks on the Tswana; the Kwena, Ngwaketse and Rolong all succumbed to Ndebele assaults at this time. During 1836 and 1837 the Ndebele themselves came under pressure from various quarters — from the Voortrekkers, the Zulu and the Griqua. And in 1837 they migrated north of the Limpopo to establish a more permanent, territorially based Ndebele state.

The *difaqane* had had a particularly devastating impact on the Tswana. Chiefdoms had been dislocated and communities had been scattered. As Kinsman shows for the southern Tswana, the material base of life nearly collapsed: 'it was a period of dramatic transformation, when communities were stripped of their agricultural base — the source of their subsistence — and were forced to seek alternative means of survival.' Thousands died of starvation. Many were forced to abandon cultivation and lead a semi-nomadic existence. Some gravitated towards mission stations, notably the Kuruman station. Some accepted Ndebele overlordship, paying taxes or tending Ndebele cattle, while others became fully incorporated into Ndebele society.

The existence of numerous autonomous chiefdoms had made the Tswana vulnerable to external attack. There seems to have been little effort to form military alliances between chiefdoms. Nor did the *difaqane* throw up a Moshoeshoe among the Tswana. No dominant Tswana state emerged from the conflagration. But, although battered, most Tswana chiefdoms survived the *difaqane*; and when, later in the century, they became subjected to the pressures of colonialism, they developed new methods of coping and were able to escape some of the more immediate and traumatic consequences of colonial subjugation.[36]

The *difaqane* also brought disruption and dislocation to northern Sotho society. During the last decade of the eighteenth century and the first two decades of the nineteenth, the Pedi had formed themselves into a powerful polity through the energetic leadership of Thulare, the Maroteng chief. Military campaigning over wide areas of the Transvaal greatly expanded the orbit of Pedi power. One might therefore have expected the Pedi to withstand the ravages of the *difaqane*. That they did not do so, at least in the short term, was partly due to an internal political crisis. The death of Thulare around 1820 set off a series of succession disputes among his sons, leaving the Pedi ill-equipped to withstand any severe external pressures.

Such pressures were to come from two main quarters. In 1822 the Ndebele, soon after their escape from Zululand, attacked and defeated the Pedi. Although the Ndebele only remained in Pedi territory for about a year, their presence severely depleted local supplies of food and stock. Most historians have seen the Ndebele invasion as a decisive setback to the Pedi. Recently Delius has revised this view, suggesting that Zwide and the Ndwandwe were the chief destroyers of Pedi power at this time. Ndwandwe raids for cattle and grain wrecked the economic basis of Pedi society. Competition between chiefdoms for increasingly scarce resources further exacerbated the political disintegration of the Pedi. But this political and economic breakdown in time gave way to a process of regeneration. The key figure in this process was Sekwati, a junior son of Thulare. Having witnessed the ravages of the Ndwandwe, Sekwati and his followers fled from their homeland in 1826. For the next two years Sekwati enlarged his following by attacking neighbouring settlements and by forging alliances. Through cattle-raiding he re-stocked his herds. This in turn enabled him to distribute cattle among groups recently incorporated in the chiefdom, thereby ensuring their subordination and loyalty. Like Moshoeshoe, Sekwati refrained from engaging in futile military confrontations, preferring to exploit the defensive advantages offered by mountain fortresses. In 1828 he returned to the Pedi homeland in the Steelpoort River area and steadily proceeded to gain recognition for himself as the paramount authority in the region.[37]

The *difaqane* probably had its most significant impact on the highveld where the two processes of social and political disintegration and regeneration were most far-reaching. But the rise of Shaka also had important consequences that ramified through large areas of the region south of the Tugela and east of the Drakensberg. Serious devastation was experienced in the early 1820s in the territory that came to be Natal. The agents of destruction were either refugees from Shaka or Zulu impis themselves. The basic economic activities of cultivation and herding were brought to a standstill. Those who survived the devastation had two options open to them: to accept incorporation into the Zulu state, or to flee southwards.

Thousands chose the latter, moving south of the Mzimkhulu River and creating further upheavals among the southern Nguni. The northern Thembu, for instance, displaced by Shaka, cut their way through Natal before reaching Mpondo territory. There they were attacked and defeated by Faku, the Mpondo chief. The Thembu then broke up, some migrating back to Zululand, others accepting absorption into Mpondo society. Other refugee groups coalesced under the leadership of Madikane; out of this fusion emerged the Bhaca chiefdom, which established itself close to the Mpondo.

The Mpondo themselves came under severe pressure during this upheaval. They were twice raided by the Zulu. The second raid in 1828 was particularly devastating, as the Zulu razed Mpondo settlements on both sides of the Mzimvubu River. But the chiefdom recovered under Faku. Cattle herds were replenished through raiding; closer settlement patterns tightened Mpondo defences; and a number of captives and refugee groups were incorporated into the chiefdom. So Faku, in Beinart's words, 'emerged as the dominant power on the southern periphery of the Zulu state'.

The most well-known northern Nguni refugees to migrate southwards were the Mfengu. They were a heterogeneous group, comprising people of diverse origins. One section of the Mfengu was made up of those Hlubi who fled to the south after being defeated by the Ngwane in the early 1820s. Remnant groups from the Bhele and Zizi chiefdoms also joined the ranks of the Mfengu. The Mfengu arrived in southern Nguni territory not as a cohesive community, but as small groups or individuals. Initially they came to Gcalekaland where they approached petty chiefs or headmen and requested food and shelter. The Mfengu attached themselves to the Xhosa in various ways. Some became incorporated into Xhosa society, perhaps by intermarriage. Other Mfengu groups became Xhosa clients, performing services and paying tribute in return for the use of land and the loan of cattle. However, the inferior, dependent status associated with clientage soon rankled with many Mfengu, and they increasingly looked towards Cape colonial society as an avenue for their advancement. Thus mission stations came to attract Mfengu adherents; and the colonial authorities were in time able to make military and political use of a class of African collaborators.

For the Mfengu the *difaqane* brought severe tribulation in the short term. Homeless and without visible means of support, they became dependent on the goodwill of others for their survival. It could be argued, however, that in the long term the *difaqane* had very different consequences for the Mfengu. It broke their ties with particular chiefdoms and set them loose in an insecure world in which the bonds of collective social organisation had been undermined. Their response to this challenge was to adopt a more individualist mode of existence. Many Mfengu were to become prominent in the ranks of the African peasantry at the Cape; and from the later nineteenth century, members of the Mfengu educated elite could be found in the forefront of early African opposition movements.

There can be little doubt that the *difaqane* represented a cataclysmic and devastating upheaval in the lives of many African communities in southern Africa. Thousands must have died during the upheaval, either in warfare or from starvation and disease. Whole communities were uprooted. Some of these migrated to new lands away from the turmoil; others broke up into groups of refugees who sought protection inside stronger, surviving chiefdoms.

The *difaqane* also had longer-term consequences. The combined effect of white migration into the interior and the emergence of African states created a new set of frontier zones which were to become significant arenas of black–white cooperation and conflict. Kinsman emphasises the significance of the *difaqane's* disruptive impact on subsistence production, disruption that brought on a shift to new means of acquiring resources: 'Thus, these decades saw the onset of migrant labour and commodity production.' Marks and Atmore see links between the *mfecane* (an oft-used alternative term to *difaqane*) and later African responses to colonial penetration:

On the one hand, the more powerful of the Mfecane-created military states, such as the Zulu, the Ndebele or the Swazi, and to a lesser extent the Pedi, were able to prevent this encroachment until well into the nineteenth century; on the other, the experiences other African societies had had of the Mfecane/Difaqane led to an acquiescence and indeed at times an alliance with the newly arrived Trekkers on the Highveld.

It has also been suggested that there are links between the *difaqane* and the present geo-political and demographic configuration of South Africa. Thus, Omer-Cooper writes that 'the battles and massacres of the Mfecane have left a permanent mark. Not only do they account for the existence of the enclave African states, Basutoland, Swaziland and Bechuanaland, but also for the general distribution of white and Bantu landownership.' In a recent paper Cobbing has rejected this view. He argues that the enclave states were not the creation of the *difaqane*, but of later white expansion. 'Equally untenable', Cobbing contends, 'are the allied claims that the *mfecane* pushed African peoples into a peripheral horse-shoe shaped ring that enclosed a fertile empty arena which thereby lay fortuitously open just in time to receive white migrants.' Such claims were based on an exaggerated estimate of the extent of depopulation wrought by the *difaqane*. These claims also conceal the real reasons for South Africa's present geo-political structure — colonial conquest and the white seizure of African land, which reach back to the nineteenth century. Cobbing puts it neatly: 'The 1913 Natives Land Act and the *mfecane* were close companions, the latter describing as self-inflicted what the former took by force.'

If Cobbing's essay is brilliantly suggestive, it also leaves something of a void. Clearly the *difaqane/mfecane* concept needs to be treated with caution and used in a clearly defined sense, given its various usages that Cobbing has pointed to. One also has to be careful to prevent the *difaqane* from constituting part of the present South African regime's historical legitimation. However, the *difaqane* must remain a highly significant, dramatic series of events in the history of southern and central Africa. As a descriptive label to denote these events, the term *difaqane* seems to be adequate. What is needed perhaps is not a change of terminology, but further research into the demographic consequences of the *difaqane*.[38]

5
PROBLEMS OF CONCEPTUALISATION AND INTERPRETATION

Our survey of African societies has thrown up numerous problems of definition, conceptualisation and interpretation. Several questions spring to mind. How, for instance, does one best label and conceptualise the various forms of African polity? Can one distinguish between states and chiefdoms, or between states and stateless societies? How valuable is mode of production analysis for precolonial African history? What was the internal dynamic of pre-capitalist African economies? Or, as Meillassoux asks more specifically, 'who is working with whom and for whom? Where does the product of the labourer go? Who controls the product? How does the economic system reproduce itself...?' One also has to go beyond these essentially static questions, and examine the dynamic of change over time. Why did some societies undergo the process of state formation, and others not? How can one explain this process?

During the 1960s, in the afterglow of liberation from formal colonialism, the spirit of African nationalism permeated historical writing about Africa. As former African colonies were granted independence, so was African history decolonised. Special emphasis came to be placed on the African achievement in the precolonial era; what it tended to highlight were precolonial African states. This emphasis supposedly refuted the idea that all Africans had once lived in 'tribes'; and it showed that Africans had long since been capable of building structures that approximated to the model of the Western nation-state. A concomitant of this glorification of states was a tendency to distinguish between states and stateless societies, the latter being acephalous, smaller, decentralised polities.

In the 1970s, as the afterglow faded under the dark clouds of poverty and dependency, African nationalist historiography came to be seriously questioned. The glorification of states was shown to be misguided, and the state–stateless dichotomy to be misplaced. As Lonsdale has remarked, 'The first African histories after the colonial era tended to be ... studies in state-formation as achievement. In more recent years, it has been objected that these were really chronicles of injury, not, as was thought, of pride; for states were and are engines of oppression, not civilization.' In the Marxist analysis the state contains the coercive apparatus required to secure and sustain the dominance of a class of non-producers over an exploited class of producers.

The distinction drawn between states and stateless societies has also come under criticism. The dividing line between the two is in fact not always as clear as was thought. The state may have been the lineage or chiefdom writ large. Or, as Hedges and Bonner have suggested, the lineage may have represented a latent state. States, chiefdoms and stateless societies could each, in varying degrees, fulfil many of the possible criteria of statehood, such as territoriality, longevity, and the incorporation of outsiders. Moreover, so-called stateless societies also contained social strata and forms of domination and exploitation characteristic of more centralised structures. However, to discard the state–stateless dichotomy altogether is to leave an uncomfortable void. However inadequate the categories may be, they still retain some value. And in this survey of southern African societies the notion of statehood has been constantly present.

Those who have been most concerned to break away from the state–stateless dichotomy have been the Marxist historians. They have drawn upon the work of French Marxist anthropologists and have tried to identify various modes of production in precolonial Africa. But in this attempt it has been discovered that Marx's schemata are not readily applicable to Africa. No African society was as simply self-sufficient for it to be classified as a 'primitive community' in the Marxist sense. Some years ago there were flirtations with the feudal mode, but this too has come to be seen as inappropriate. Thereafter the concept of the Asiatic mode seemed to offer analytical leverage. This mode presupposes the existence of semi-autonomous village communities which are exploited economically through the agency of a superimposed state structure. This too has been rejected by Coquery-Vidrovitch and others as inapplicable to Africa, although it might be seen to bear some resemblance to the nineteenth-century Zulu state: while the Zulu state hierarchy imposed demands on local communities, notably for tribute and labour service, the homestead survived intact as a fundamental unit of Zulu society.

The concept of a lineage mode of production has gained wider acceptance among Marxist Africanists. Bonner has described its identifying characteristics as 'communal appropriation of the social product and its extended or "complex" redistribution among the lineage members'. Implicit in this conceptualisation is the notion of surplus extraction by a dominant group, generally elders, at the expense of exploited direct producers. Furthermore, these relations of production are legitimated in the ideology of kinship.

The application of mode of production analysis to precolonial Africa has been widely criticised. It has been charged that the analysis has been carried out at too high a level of abstraction with insufficient empirical evidence. Inappropriate, or 'foreign', concepts are being imposed on African societies. The analytical models are considered to be too static, akin to those of the structural-functionalist anthropologists of whom Marxists are so critical. And the search for 'modes' has tended towards an absurd atomisation. Crush has aptly summarised this tendency:

> Researchers have moved rapidly from Coquery-Vidrovitch's single African mode of production, through Cliffe's five modes in East Africa, to Clarence-Smith's multiplicity of modes in southern Angola.... Cooper's cynicism is painfully apposite when he notes that 'if every way of catching an antelope or growing a banana is a mode of production, the concept blends into ... empiricism.'

So African mode of production analysis may have been inconclusive. But it has been valuable in opening up new lines of inquiry and forcing us to look at African societies in new ways. The shift of focus away from kinship systems and socio-political structures towards the material base has been particularly useful. The foundation of authority and power has been shown to have rested not just on ideological forms but on the regulation of access to key resources or on the extraction of tribute and labour. The organisation of production has been seen to be fundamental. As Marks and Atmore point out:

> Although agricultural production for subsistence needs was undertaken largely within individual homesteads, grouped in lineage-based villages, co-operation in the production of the socially necessary surplus was also crucial. Some forms of agricultural production based on work-parties, cattle-keeping, hunting and defence cut across homestead boundaries, and had important structural ramifications for consumption, exchange and distribution.

And once one begins to look at relations of production one also starts to identify forms of exploitation and internal divisions and tensions within African communities. At the same time clues that explain the dynamic of historical change, may also be discovered.

One form of change that has preoccupied us in this survey has been that of state formation. As we have seen, the era of state-worship in African historiography is largely past, and doubts have been expressed about the applicability of the 'state' concept to precolonial Africa. But there still remains a concern, even among radical scholars, to explain why it was that some African societies developed more centralised institutions and forms of control. Attempts at such explanation have taken various forms.

Until the last two decades historians had tended to operate within a dominant paradigm which stressed politics, ideology and individual agency as the chief motors of history. The explanation of state formation in precolonial Africa for a long time remained the captive of this paradigm. As Lonsdale has commented, 'Africa's pre-colonial past was similarly invoked with the drum-and-trumpet history of kingdoms, autonomous actors endowed with a political will, midwives apparently at their own birth, whose "genius was for integration".'

One of the first shifts away from what Lonsdale calls this 'autonomist paradigm' towards a more materialist emphasis came in the 1960s when some scholars began to stress the links between trade and state formation. Trade may well have provided both the motive and the means. The need to protect trade routes and the sources of trade commodities could have stimulated political centralisation and military expansion. And a chief or ruler could enlarge his own power by securing for himself a sizeable share in the profits of trade. In this way he could enhance his own prestige and accumulate wealth, which could be redistributed in order to expand his following or ensure its loyalty. We have seen how Smith and others have developed a trade hypothesis to explain Zulu state formation. And if one looks elsewhere in Africa there seems to be a strong case for linking the growth of early states in the western Sudan to the trans-Saharan trade, and the growth of West African coastal states to the slave trade.

In more recent years doubts have been expressed about the trade hypothesis. To some it seemed to be just another variant of the 'external influence' hypothesis: that is to say, that small-scale 'tribal' formations were 'natural' in Africa, and any departure from these formations must have been the product of outside influences — the intrusion of external invaders, the diffusion of new ideas, or, perhaps, long-distance trade. 'The point of all these hypotheses', to use Lonsdale's words again, 'was that something rather exceptional was needed to explain any concentration of power in a logically tribal Africa.' Coquery-Vidrovitch has also questioned the value of the trade hypothesis. She argues that long-distance trade influenced the most diverse societies, and it thus 'transcends the traditional contrast between states and stateless societies'. In some cases, too, doubts have been voiced about the lack of firm empirical evidence to support a trade hypothesis. This is particularly so for the Zulu case-study.

A more recent trend has been to analyse precolonial African polities in terms of ecological factors. In some instances ideal environmental conditions may have strengthened certain polities, as was the case with the Ngwane in the fertile region of southern Swaziland. In other cases demographic pressures and ecological imbalances could create the conditions for state formation, as Guy argues in the Zulu case. And Sansom has shown how the sociopolitical structure of Tswana chiefdoms has to some extent been shaped by ecological constraints.

All this goes to illustrate the fluid state of the current historiography of precolonial Africa. Old assumptions are being questioned and rejected; new models, concepts and approaches are being tested, and often, too, discarded. A major concern of scholars is to escape from static, mechanistic models and to come to grips with the dynamics of change. In the study of precolonial or precapitalist societies this concern has often floundered because of the scarcity of empirical evidence. But once these societies came to be penetrated by an encroaching capitalist order, as happened throughout southern Africa in the nineteenth century, the data becomes more substantial, and likewise it becomes easier to grapple with the task of explaining the dynamics of change.[39]

Part Two

AN ERA OF TRANSITION
c. 1830–1900

6
THE NGUNI: THE PATH TO COLONIAL SUBJUGATION

Around 1830 almost all the African people of southern Africa lay outside the orbit of formal colonial domination. By the end of the nineteenth century Nguni, Sotho and Venda communities south and west of the Limpopo had all been subjugated in one way or another. Formal African political independence was effectively at an end. But the process of subjugation had been long and complex. The boer trek into the interior created from the 1830s a number of new frontier zones in which various forms of black–white interaction were to occur. Competition for land and cattle could produce conflict situations; these were generally aggravated by the absence of defined boundaries. However, it is grossly misleading to characterise these frontiers in terms of two monolithic race groups constantly clashing over scarce resources. In the past twelve or so years re-interpretations of the nineteenth-century southern African frontier have shown that, conflict apart, various forms of interracial cooperation often took place in these zones. Patterns of trade, military alliance, and social and sexual interaction could cut across racial differences.

This era, covering approximately the last seven decades of the nineteenth century, can be viewed as transitional in a number of different ways. Not only did it encompass the colonial subjugation of formerly independent African societies. It also saw a number of changes occurring within these societies. There emerged a class of independent African producers who operated outside the domain of the 'traditional' communal economy, producing for a growing market as well as for subsistence. This economic individualism was particularly fostered by Christian missionaries, and many African peasant communities were to be found in and around mission stations. The discovery of diamonds and gold in the short term enlarged the opportunities for African peasants. In the longer term, however, these discoveries stimulated in South Africa a rapid process of capitalist development that would soon undermine the position of the small-scale independent African producer.

Extensive African resistance to colonial conquest and colonial rule was another feature of this period. This resistance was generally inspired by a desire to retain or regain independence from colonial domination. And the leadership and organisation of this resistance was firmly rooted in the traditional authority structure of the chiefdom or state. By the end of the nineteenth century however, African opposition to colonialism was beginning to take on new forms and different kinds of leadership. Once again Christian missionary activity proved to be a catalyst in this respect. Ethiopianism —the African independent church movement — not only was directed against white domination of the church in southern Africa, but also took shape as an expression of protest against colonialism. Moreover, mission education was steadily producing an emergent African middle-class elite. It was the members of this elite who were to constitute the leadership of early African opposition movements.

This era was thus both a transitional and a formative one in the African history of southern Africa. Colonial conquest largely destroyed African political independence and severely curtailed African access to land, a disability that was to be aggravated by subsequent legislation and government policy. Within African societies one can detect a process of incipient class formation. This manifested itself in economic terms with the growth of the peasantry, and in political terms, with the emergence, somewhat later, of African opposition movements. Both of these processes were to be severely stunted by the repressive policies of the state in the twentieth century. But that story belongs to a later chapter. It remains for us to examine more closely how these transitions occurred in the various African societies of southern Africa.

The Zulu state

In 1830 the Zulu kingdom was the most powerful independent African state in southern Africa. By the end of the century, however, Zululand had been annexed to the Colony of Natal. Why had this downfall occurred? Although powerful, the Zulu state structure contained inherent strains and tensions that weakened the kingdom's capacity to cope with external pressures. From the late 1830s such pressures were to mount. Boer trekkers, missionaries and traders were in the forefront of those who impinged upon the kingdom. Ultimately though, it was the full weight of British imperialism that was to destroy the independence of the Zulu state.

One source of instability in the state was the uncertain basis of royal power. Just as a Zulu king depended on military force to retain his position, so he was vulnerable to violent usurpation. In 1828 Shaka was assassinated by his brother Dingane, who thereupon acceded to the kingship. Dingane seems to have set out with the intention of minimising the use of terror as a basis of royal power. He promised to moderate the harsh practices of his predecessor; military discipline was relaxed; and he pledged to restore some authority to the council of chiefs. Dingane's intentions, however, could not match the realities of the situation, and he was soon embarking upon a more ruthless course of action. In 1829 the Qwabe chief, Nqetho, led his people in an unsuccessful rebellion against Dingane. Nqetho and many of his followers were killed in the suppression of the rebellion. Soon afterwards Chief Magaye of the Cele, suspected of being in league with Nqetho, was put to death; and in 1831 the Cele chiefdom was decimated by a royal purge. Members of the Zulu royal family who posed a potential threat to Dingane were also purged. All of Dingane's half-brothers, except Gqugqu and Mpande, were killed. And in 1837 most members of the Qadi chiefdom were massacred.

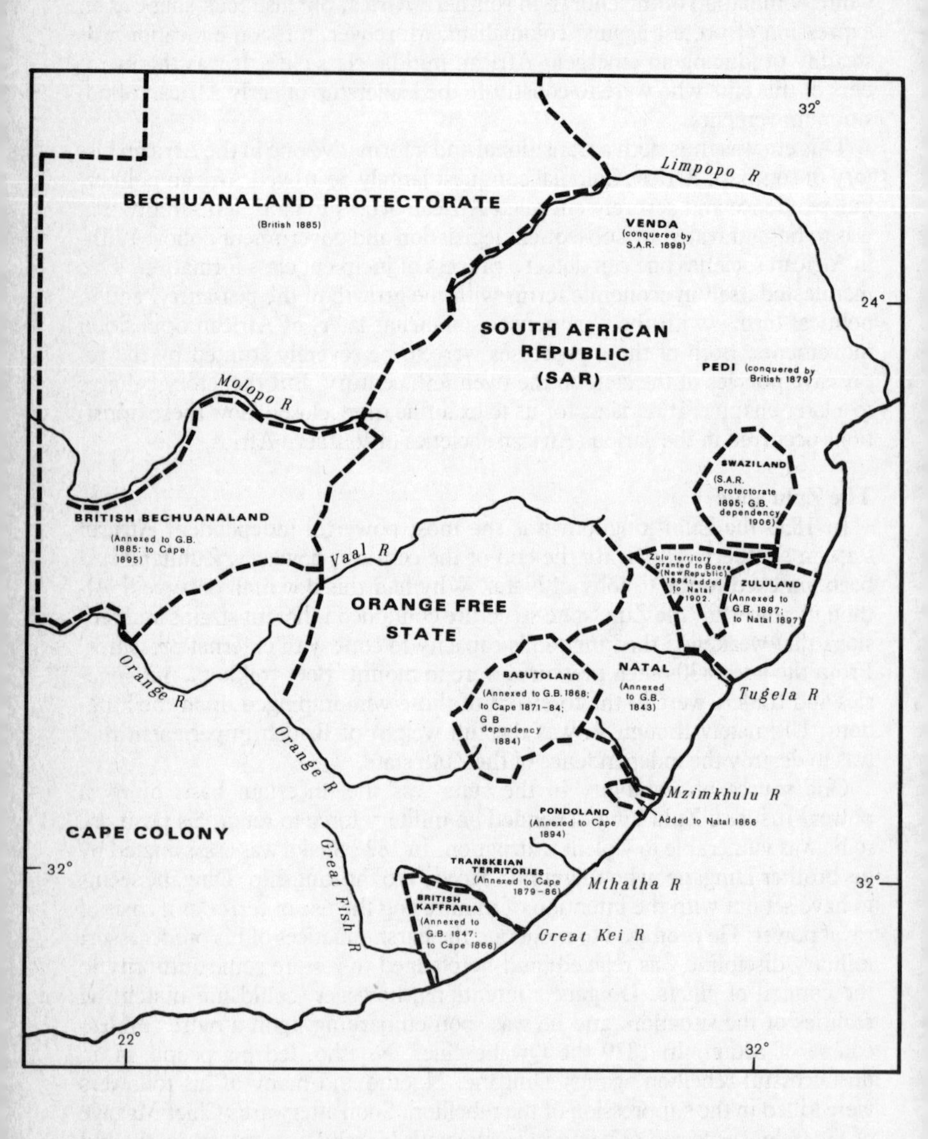

The colonial conquest and subjugation of African chiefdoms and states in the nineteenth century.

Dingane's purges led to discontented and intimidated groups fleeing from Zululand. Many of these took refuge in and around Port Natal, where a few white traders had recently made their base. Dingane himself tried to build up friendly relations with these traders, even though dissident groups were gravitating towards them. In 1831 he sent messengers to the traders to assure them of his goodwill; and soon after this he hospitably received a group of traders at his royal kraal. Dingane wanted trade goods, especially firearms. The king's relaxation of military discipline seems to have weakened Zulu military power. He hoped therefore that an accumulation of firearms might serve to restore the state's fighting capacity.

From about 1835 Dingane's relations with his white neighbours apparently deteriorated, especially after the traders discontinued the sale of firearms. In 1834 a Zulu regiment fled into Natal; this and other cases of desertion may have convinced Dingane that his position was being undermined by the white presence. And shortly thereafter Dingane was having to cope with a much larger body of whites impinging on his domain — the Voortrekkers. The leader of one trekker party, Piet Retief, realised that trekker aspirations depended on reaching some accommodation with the Zulu state. Late in 1837 he therefore visited Dingane at his royal kraal, where it appears that the two concluded a deal. Dingane would grant the trekkers land in Natal on condition that Retief organised the recovery of Zulu cattle stolen by the Tlokwa chief, Sekonyela. Retief proceeded to lead a successful expedition that not only regained the Zulu cattle, but also acquired a number of guns and horses from Sekonyela. Early in February 1838 Retief and his party of about one hundred men returned to Dingane's kraal at Mgungundlovu to hand over the cattle. On Dingane's orders the whole party was massacred.

Some historians have suggested that Dingane ordered the massacre because he felt threatened by the presence of the Voortrekkers. Others argue that it was Retief's refusal to hand over to Dingane the guns and horses taken from the Tlokwa that provoked the Zulu king. Okoye examines this refusal in the light of Dingane's desperate quest for firearms consequent upon the traders' decision to discontinue supply. 'Had the European traders not discontinued the sale of fire-arms', concludes Okoye, 'Dingane would not have had cause to obtain these weapons by means of murder.'

Whatever Dingane's motive, his action ultimately led to his own downfall. In December 1838 the Voortrekkers gained their revenge. Taking advantage of their vastly superior fire-power and their strong defensive *laager*, they won a decisive victory over the Zulu army at the Battle of Blood (Ncome) River. After fighting one more successful engagement the Voortrekkers withdrew beyond the Zulu kingdom into Natal where they received overtures from Mpande, Dingane's half-brother. Mpande's antipathy towards the Zulu king had been growing; it culminated in his refusal to support Dingane's efforts to regain lost prestige through a military campaign against the Swazi. Instead Mpande led about 17 000 followers into Natal where he made an alliance with the Voortrekkers. Early in 1840 the two forces invaded Zululand. Dingane's resistance collapsed; and Dingane himself, fleeing northwards, was captured and killed by the Swazi.[1]

It is uncertain why Dingane had spared Mpande during his purges. While most of his other half-brothers and potential rivals were killed, Mpande was allowed to live at his homestead in southern Zululand.

Although not prominent in public affairs during Dingane's reign, Mpande had gradually built up a substantial personal following. It seems that Dingane had come to feel increasingly threatened by his half-brother, and he had made two vain attempts, in 1832 and 1838, to have Mpande assassinated. This serious danger to his position had led to Mpande's flight into Natal and his alliance with the boers.

Many historical accounts have portrayed Mpande as a lazy, incompetent and ineffectual Zulu king. It has been suggested, for instance, that his alliance with the Voortrekkers turned him into a boer puppet. In recent years Mpande has been reassessed by historians. It has been pointed out that his reign lasted over thirty years and that he himself, unlike some other Zulu kings, died a peaceful death.

Far from being a boer puppet, Mpande was in fact a skilful diplomat. His treaty with the Voortrekkers merely required that a boundary between Natal and Zululand be observed, and included a few other vague pledges. Mpande was to seek boer permission before going to war; and he was to provide military support to the boers should they come under attack. It seems, though, that Mpande did little to abide by these terms, for in 1842 he was offering to assist the British in taking over Natal from the Voortrekkers. Artfully he continued to play off one group of white neighbours against another. In 1847, for instance, he encouraged the attempt of some boers in the Klip River district to secede from Natal and form a republic. As Kennedy has observed,

> He [Mpande] pretended to be loyal to several white settler groups at the same time .... He also ceded the same territory to different white governments and the resulting tensions which seemed to have nothing to do with the Zulu were really the fruits of his careful calculations. At the least, he manipulated Voortrekker groups and the British against their better interests, while instilling the erroneous impression that the Zulu kingdom survived only through their specific support.

While Mpande was able with considerable skill to withstand external pressures on the Zulu state, he also had to confront the familiar problem of consolidating his internal power base, a problem which had troubled his predecessors. Although his exercise of power was generally more moderate than that of his two predecessors, he still had to resort to autocratic and violent methods to secure his position. Dingane's leading supporters were purged. Mpande's only surviving half-brother, Gqugqu, a potential rival, was put to death along with his entire household in 1843. This massacre induced Mawa, a sister of Senzangakhona and an ally of Gqugqu, to lead a following of two to three thousand dissidents into Natal.

Mpande used methods of terror to curb the secessionist tendencies of subordinate chiefdoms. This exercise of force required the retention of the Zulu regimental system. Regimental residences (*amakhanda*) were concentrated around the royal capital; and royal control over marriage was maintained. By utilising the Shakan system of control, albeit in a somewhat less despotic manner, Mpande was able to sustain his centralised authority more or less intact for a large part of his reign. In the late 1840s and early 1850s Mpande was at the peak of his power. But thereafter his authority began to weaken. The ostensible cause of this decline was a succession crisis which degenerated into a civil war. The underlying cause was a fundamental contradiction inherent in the social and political structure of the Zulu state.

There were two main contenders for the succession to the kingship. Mpande's eldest son, Cetshwayo, had many influential supporters, while Mpande himself favoured his second eldest son, Mbuyazi. In 1856 the conflict escalated into a civil war. At the battle of Ndondakusuka Cetshwayo's Usuthu army inflicted a crushing defeat on Mbuyazi and his isiGqoza followers. Thousands of Zulu were killed, including Mbuyazi and five other sons of Mpande. Thereafter Mpande remained *de jure* ruler in Zululand, but his actual authority was considerably weakened by Cetshwayo's rise to prominence.

One effect of the civil war was to involve the Colony of Natal more in the ambit of Zulu politics. Thousands of Mbuyazi's followers fled into the Colony after Cetshwayo's victory; and in mid-1857 many of Mpande's followers took refuge in Natal, fearing retribution from Cetshwayo. The aftermath of the civil war also saw Mpande and Cetshwayo vying for supremacy. Each tried to strengthen his respective position by winning the support of the Natal government. In 1861 Natal's Secretary for Native Affairs, Theophilus Shepstone, visited Zululand to mediate in the power struggle. Shepstone ceremonially proclaimed Cetshwayo as Mpande's successor; and Cetshwayo himself expressed his loyalty to Mpande as king. This compromise served to ease rather than resolve the tension between the two. In the 1860s Cetshwayo's power was greater than that normally exercised by an heir apparent; and he bolstered that power by accumulating firearms with the help of John Dunn, a white trader in Zululand who had acquired chiefly status by gaining Cetshwayo's favour and by marrying into leading Zulu families. Equally, Mpande's role was more substantial than that of a mere figurehead. Both, though, seemed determined that the kingdom should not be torn apart, and the Zulu state was still intact at the time of Mpande's death in 1872.

'To all appearances the career of Mpande was one of the great paradoxes of southern African history.' Kennedy's assessment is highly appropriate. Mpande displayed unmistakable 'signs of weakness and vacillation' and yet 'he was the most enduring of the Zulu kings.' He ruled during a period that was relatively free of trauma. The great upheavals wrought by the *difaqane* had largely subsided by the time of his accession; and he died before the Zulu state came under the full weight of the forces of colonialism. As Edgecombe and Wright have observed, Mpande's 'ability to grasp the changing realities of his position as head of the Zulu nation qualified him to lead it through times which demanded the skills of the politician and diplomat rather than of the fighter.' It was left to Mpande's son and successor, Cetshwayo, to confront a number of internal and external pressures that threatened the Zulu state from the 1870s.[2]

At the outset of his reign Cetshwayo stood in an advantageous position. Cetshwayo himself, as Guy has remarked, 'possessed many of the qualities of a successful leader, being shrewd, politically astute, and having a commanding physical presence'. Shepstone's return to Zululand in 1873 to give his formal recognition to Cetshwayo's accession seemed to offer the prospect of friendly relations between Natal and the Zulu state. Even if relations between the Zulu and their white neighbours were to deteriorate, Zulu military might would seemingly have deterred any potential aggressor. And Cetshwayo himself appeared to be in secure control of the kingship, manipulating key resources such as cattle and firearms to maintain his authority.

If, it must be asked, the prospects looked so promising for Cetshwayo in 1873, why was the Zulu state invaded in 1879? Beneath its aura of power and might there were signs in the 1870s that the kingdom was becoming increasingly vulnerable. Inherent tensions in its political structure, depletion of resources, and external pressures all combined to make for this vulnerability.

The potential for internal conflict and disintegration was built into the Zulu political structure. The Shakan state system had been superimposed upon a pre-existing structure of autonomous communities. As Guy has written,

> The Zulu kingdom can be seen as the social integration of two systems, which although they must be analysed separately can only be understood in their interaction. On the one hand there was social power based on production, coming from the production units — the homesteads ... — and expressed in terms of kinship and the clan: on the other hand there was the power of the state coming from above, and based on the extraction of surplus, mainly in labour through the military system.

Shaka had striven to build a centralised state, but he lacked both adequate administrative machinery and an effective communications system to be able to maintain centralised authority throughout the realm. This deficiency carried two implications. Firstly, the relative weakness at the centre enabled local chiefs to exercise considerable autonomy. Secondly, in an effort to offset this decentralising tendency, Zulu kings were compelled to delegate authority to members of the royal family. While it was intended that these should become instruments of royal power throughout the state, in practice they could become rivals to the king by building up power bases in their own areas and challenging royal authority. Mael, Colenbrander and Kennedy see these disintegrative tendencies at work during Mpande's reign and the early years of Cetshwayo's rule. Guy, on the other hand, prefers to stress the cohesion of the Zulu state on the eve of the war of 1879. This, he argues, was highlighted by the ability of the Zulu to offer concerted resistance to the British invasion.

While its political structure was inherently unstable, the Zulu state was being further threatened in the 1870s, argues Colenbrander, by a crisis of resources. In particular, disease, pasture degeneration and drought had severely depleted cattle herds by the late 1870s. It also seems probable that the Zulu population was growing rapidly, thereby exacerbating the ecological crisis. All this suggests that the Zulu political economy was under strain in the decade before the Anglo–Zulu war. And internal stress would clearly have undermined the state's ability to cope with growing external pressures.

Missionaries and traders were often in the forefront of the European penetration of Africa. In the nineteenth century traders from Delagoa Bay and Natal imported various commodities — hardware, textiles and firearms — into Zululand in exchange for hides and cattle. But this trade had a minimal impact, as the traders did not introduce any products that the Zulu deemed essential or that they could not manufacture themselves. Similarly the missionary impact on the kingdom was slight. Mpande and Cetshwayo permitted a certain amount of missionary activity in Zululand, and even welcomed some missionaries who might serve royal interests. Mpande, for instance, allowed Schreuder, known for his medical skill, to establish a mission station in Zululand at a time when Mpande himself was ill. Cetshwayo believed that missionaries might help him stave off boer encroachment into Zululand. But generally both kings saw missionary teaching as a threat to the Zulu state, and accordingly restricted missionary activities. By the mid-1870s the restrictive policy of the Zulu royal house had virtually brought missionary operations to a standstill. And when on account of their involvement in a campaign to secure British intervention, Cetshwayo's hostility towards the missionaries intensified, most were forced to leave Zululand by 1877.[3]

Much more threatening to the Zulu state than the activities of missionaries and traders were the forces of colonial expansion. From the mid-nineteenth century land-hungry Transvalers, exploiting the absence of a defined boundary, had been steadily encroaching into the north-western region of Zululand. In the 1860s and 1870s Mpande and Cetshwayo issued numerous complaints to the Natal government about boer encroachment. Although Shepstone was generally sympathetic to the Zulu cause, the dispute lingered on. Shepstone's sympathy was only apparent, as he himself had his eyes on the disputed territory. For Shepstone this disputed territory straddled a vital corridor to the north. The corridor was not only a route along which his grand vision of Natal expansion was directed; it was also a key artery for the supply of migrant labour from the north into the expanding capitalist economy south of the Limpopo. Given Shepstone's own visions of expansion it is hardly surprising that, after the British annexed the Transvaal in 1877 and he himself became chief administrator of the new Colony, he soon adopted the Transvaal cause in the boundary dispute with the Zulu.

The growing pressures on the Zulu state did not only emanate directly from land-hungry neighbours. The critical position of the kingdom also needs to be viewed within the broader context of British imperialism and the political economy of southern Africa. At the Colonial Office in London the Zulu kingdom had few admirers. Etherington argues that Lord Carnarvon, Colonial Secretary from 1874 to 1878, shared Shepstone's expansionary vision:

> Once he [Carnarvon] ... understood the logic of the developing economy, saw Durban as the bottom of an imperial funnel, it was easy enough for him to see why autonomous republics and independent kingdoms which threatened vital supply lines could no longer be tolerated.

Accordingly, in 1877, Sir Bartle Frere was sent to South Africa as British High Commissioner. His task was to achieve confederation — to tidy up the geo-political map of southern Africa. The confederation scheme was, however, incompatible with the survival of the Zulu state. One of Frere's tasks, therefore, was to eliminate that state, not only to facilitate confederation, but also to create political structures that were more in tune with the emerging capitalist economy of southern Africa.

To Frere it was clear that the Zulu state could only be destroyed by war. Such a war required justification. So Frere proceeded to bombard the Colonial Office with lengthy despatches that highlighted the supposed dangers posed by the Zulu kingdom. The Zulu state was represented as highly militarised, with 'a frightfully efficient manslaying war-machine' at its disposal. Cetshwayo himself was depicted as a barbaric despot who, in the late 1870s, was not only planning an attack on neighbouring white settlements, but was at the centre of a pan-Africanist conspiracy to overthrow white authority throughout south Africa.

Frere took advantage of certain incidents to fuel this alarmism. A small Zulu party crossed into Natal to capture the two adulterous wives of Chief Sihayo and took them back to Zululand to be killed; Frere viewed this as a serious border violation. He also made political capital out of alleged Zulu persecution of Christian missionaries and converts. It was less easy, however, for Frere to make such gains out of the Zulu–Transvaal boundary dispute. In June 1878, a commission, appointed by the Lieutenant-Governor of Natal to investigate the dispute, had issued an equivocal report that largely supported the Zulu claim but also recognised boer rights in areas where their occupation was firmly established. This conclusion did not suit Frere, who accordingly delayed his own decision on the dispute. In December 1878 Frere did finally announce to Zulu representatives the decision of the boundary commission. But the announcement was accompanied by the issue of an ultimatum, the terms of which included the abolition of the Zulu military system and the payment of cattle fines for certain border infringements. Cetshwayo tried to meet some of the terms by collecting cattle to pay the fines; but it would have been impossible for him to have abided by other more far-reaching demands, which in effect amounted to the destruction of Zulu independence. Later, after the war, Cetshwayo reflected bitterly on Britain's treatment of the Zulu:

> Mpande did you no wrong, and I have done you no wrong, therefore you must have some other object in view in invading my land. It cannot be because of Usirayo's sons [who had been involved in kidnapping the chief's adulterous wives]. The English have just crowned me. How is it that they crown me in the morning and dethrone me in the afternoon?

Cetshwayo was thus unable to abide fully by the terms of the ultimatum. So on 11 January 1879 British forces invaded Zululand. Eleven days later the Zulu inflicted a crushing defeat on the British at the battle of Isandhlwana. But thereafter the British recovered and after regrouping in Natal their renewed thrust took them further into the heart of Zululand, culminating in a successful attack on Ulundi, the Zulu capital, in July. Although it marked the end of hostilities, the battle of Ulundi was not the crushing military victory that has often been represented. The Zulu might have opted to carry on a guerrilla war against the British had it not been for a promise made by Sir Garnet Wolseley, the new High Commissioner, that the Zulu kingdom would be spared.[4]

The Zulu state was not destroyed by the war, but it came to be mutilated by the post-war settlement. After Ulundi Cetshwayo had been captured and exiled to Cape Town Castle. Early in September 1879 Wolseley announced the terms of the settlement to be imposed on the Zulu. The Zulu kingship was to be removed, and the kingdom was to be divided into thirteen chiefdoms, each ruled by a British-appointed chief. The chiefs were forbidden to maintain an army or impose marriage restrictions. Furthermore, a British Resident would be stationed in Zululand, ostensibly to exercise a diplomatic and advisory role.

In theory the demarcation of thirteen chiefdoms was supposed to restore the pre-Shakan structure of the northern Nguni. In practice it was a calculated British strategy of divide-and-rule. The strategy also involved the appointment of several chiefs who were no more than puppets. The largest chiefdom was granted to John Dunn, an alien figure with no roots whatsoever in the pre-Shakan structure. Dunn was a white trader who had gained the favour of Cetshwayo after 1857; and by accumulating wives and material resources he had established a sphere of influence in the Zulu kingdom. During the war he switched to the British side, his opportunism being duly rewarded with his appointment to a chiefship. Another appointed chief, Hlubi, was a Tlokwa. The Tlokwa were a Sotho group who had collaborated with the Natal government before and after the war. Hamu, a member of the Zulu clan, was another collaborator to be rewarded with a chiefship.

Guy has described Wolseley's settlement as 'hurried and ignorant':

> Its basic weakness was not so much that it failed to establish 'effective authority' (as was argued at the time by critics of the settlement, and later by historians), but that it failed to recognize that the war had not fundamentally altered the distribution of power in Zululand. Although the king had been exiled, new authorities created, and high-sounding pronouncements made about the end of the Zulu system, the *izikhulu* (great men) of the nation, and members of the royal family, had survived the war with large followings and substantial material power.

The settlement thus created a potential conflict between the surviving, but suppressed, old Zulu royal order and the new order of appointed chiefs.

The aggressive, self-seeking behaviour of three of these particular chiefs brought this conflict closer to realisation. Zibhebhu, Hamu and John Dunn all saw that the post-war settlement offered them opportunities for self-enrichment. Wolseley had ordered the appointed chiefs to collect royal cattle and firearms. Zibhebhu, Hamu and Dunn carried out this order vigorously, harassing members of the royal family in the process. Royal cattle were seized; and people suspected of concealing royal herds were fined. These aggressive actions heightened the internal tensions in Zululand and sowed the seeds of civil war.

Cetshwayo's supporters began to organise a campaign in defence of the royal cause. They were led by Ndabuko and Mnyamana, the exiled king's brother and former chief minister respectively. In May 1880 Ndabuko led an Usuthu deputation to Natal. The deputation complained to the colonial government about Hamu's and Zibhebhu's maltreatment of the Usuthu, and asked for the return of Cetshwayo to Zululand. The deputation also used the occasion of its Natal visit to mobilise the support of Bishop Colenso.

Over the next two years the restoration of Cetshwayo became the central focus of a broad-based campaign. Cetshwayo himself, although restricted by his detention in Cape Town, was still able to publicise his cause. In November 1880 Cetshwayo was visited by Bishop Colenso and his daughter Harriette; it was they who advised the exiled king to visit England to petition the British government and gain publicity for his cause. Cetshwayo himself proceeded to write petitions and letters which were distributed in southern Africa and England. In April 1882 a deputation of two thousand Zulu converged on Pietermaritzburg. The deputation comprised a large body of Usuthu supporters and other disaffected elements. The restoration of Cetshwayo was the deputation's main demand; but beneath this demand lay extreme discontent with the new order of appointed chiefs, whose rule was threatening the very survival of many people in Zululand.

In July 1882 Cetshwayo, temporarily released from detention, arrived in England to bring his case before the imperial authorities. He had discussions at the Colonial Office; and he was granted an audience with the Queen. The government's decision on his future was not made known to Cetshwayo before his departure from England in September. Upon his arrival back in Cape Town Cetshwayo was dismayed to learn of the official decision to partition Zululand. Cetshwayo was to be allowed to return to Zululand, but only on condition that he accepted a curtailment of his authority and a reduction of territory. Two substantial areas were to be excised to accommodate Zulu who opposed Cetshwayo. One portion in the north was to remain under Zibhebhu; and a southern reserve was to be created that would fall under white authority. Realising that acceptance of the partition was a precondition for his return to Zululand, Cetshwayo reluctantly agreed to the terms. In January 1883 he returned to Zululand, and was installed by Shepstone as chief of his truncated territory.

The partition of Zululand was a recipe for violence. The excision of two portions of territory failed to separate effectively the Usuthu from Cetshwayo's opponents. Violent clashes soon occurred. Zibhebhu tried to expel a group of Usuthu from his territory. The Usuthu responded by launching a retaliatory invasion, but suffered a crushing defeat at the hands of Zibhebhu's army in March 1883. Many northern Usuthu homesteads were devastated in subsequent follow-up operations carried out by Zibhebhu and Hamu. In July Zibhebhu's Mandlakazi army attacked Ulundi, Cetshwayo's capital. The Usuthu could offer little resistance and fled in disarray. Cetshwayo escaped just before the royal homestead was razed to the ground. Numerous Usuthu leaders were killed. Cetshwayo, having placed himself under the protection of the British Resident Commissioner, died at Eshowe in February 1884.

At the time of Cetshwayo's death the Usuthu were in desperate straits. The rampant armies of Zibhebhu and Hamu had forced many to take refuge in defensive strongholds, particularly in the northern districts. Cut off from their arable lands these refugees were threatened with disaster. In this situation a group of Usuthu, early in 1884, made overtures to some Transvaal boers. In return for their military assistance and recognition of Cetshwayo's son, Dinuzulu, as Zulu king, the boers were to be granted a large tract of Zulu land. Late in May 1884 a combined Usuthu–boer force advanced into Zibhebhu's territory. With the British imperial authorities refusing to intervene, the Mandlakazi suffered a devastating defeat at the battle of Etshaneni, on the Mkhuze River.

The consequences of this battle were costly for both victor and vanquished. Zibhebhu and the remnants of his Mandlakazi faction could do no more than take refuge in Zululand's southern reserve under the nominal protection of the British Resident, Melmoth Osborn. Eight of Wolseley's original thirteen appointed chiefs found their way into this reserve. For the conquering Usuthu the cost of victory was also enormous. They were forced to abide by the terms of their treaty with the boers, and in August 1884 Dinuzulu signed away 4 000 square miles of land. Out of this grant emerged an independent boer mini-state, the New Republic, comprising more than one-third of Zululand.

Having sat aside for eight years and watched the disintegration of the Zulu state, the British imperial authorities finally annexed what remained of Zululand in June 1887. Under the new administrative structure the Governor of Natal was vested with the authority of Supreme Chief over the Zulu people; and he was to be assisted by the Resident Commissioner and Chief Magistrate, Osborn, who was placed over six resident magistrates.

Britain's imperial administration of Zululand depended much on the continuing collaboration of a group of puppet chiefs. By 1887 most of the leading chiefs of the old independent Zulu state were dead, in gaol or in exile. The last were soon to be joined by Dinuzulu. The British decision to allow Zibhebhu to return to his former territory in the north aroused the indignation of the Usuthu. In 1888 Dinuzulu led a successful Usuthu attack on the Mandlakazi, only to meet with British retaliation. Dinuzulu was captured, tried, and exiled to St Helena in 1889.

From 1893 Sir Marshal Clarke, Osborn's successor as Resident Commissioner, tried to depart from the previous policy of divide-and-rule based on undermining the power of the hereditary chiefs. Clarke proposed to administer Zululand through a smaller number of chiefs whose authority would have a firmer, more legitimate basis in Zulu society. But Clarke did not have enough time to make his strategy effective. Natal colonists, particularly sugar interests, had been casting longing eyes on land north of the Tugela. A change of government in Britain brought Chamberlain to the Colonial Office in 1895. He was sympathetic to Natal's ambitions, and in 1897 the British accordingly disannexed Zululand, offloading the administrative responsibility for the territory onto Natal.

British policy in the two decades after 1879 had aimed, at least in part, at preserving some of the elements of the old Zulu social and political order. At the same time, however, there were forces set in motion that were to have a disintegrative impact on the political economy of Zululand. One was the hut-tax. This was imposed on the whole of Zululand from 1888, and it soon became the major source of revenue for the territory. Many Zulu were forced to sell cattle to pay the tax. Even more began to enter wage labour to raise the necessary cash. Large-scale labour migration from Zululand can be dated from 1888. There were employment opportunities on railway construction in northern Natal, but gradually more and more Zulu migrants headed for the Rand.

The impact of labour migrancy on Zulu society was generally disruptive. The exodus of able-bodied male labour undermined the productive capacity of the homestead. Familial ties and obligations were broken as young men cut their links with their rural homes. Often the workers did return, but not always with beneficial consequences. During 1892–3 there were outbreaks of smallpox in the Nquthu district of Zululand. The disease had been introduced from Johannesburg by returning workers.

These years of social change coincided with a series of natural disasters that further weakened the material base of Zulu society. The crops failed in the drought of 1889. Locusts devastated the 1894–5 grain crop. In 1897 rinderpest entered Zululand and killed 85 per cent of the cattle in the territory within a year. These setbacks seriously affected homestead production and forced more men into wage labour. But Guy argues that one cannot interpret these natural disasters 'as the major force in the subordination of Zulu society to the demands of capitalist production.... [The] pattern was already being established before 1894.' Earlier in the century the independent Zulu state had been able to withstand such natural disasters. The imposition of colonial rule, however, so weakened the Zulu social structure that ecological stress became far more devastating in its impact.

For a period of over sixty years the Zulu state had endured a series of external pressures and internal strains. These external and internal forces had often become closely intertwined, sometimes offsetting each other, but mostly combining to undermine the stability of the kingdom. The Zulu survived the initial pressure from the Voortrekkers in the 1830s, albeit not without tribulation. There followed a fifteen-year period of remarkable stability under the rule of Mpande, one of the less conspicuous Zulu kings. The state was also able to survive the internal strain of civil war in the mid-1850s; and in the 1870s Cetshwayo's rule was marked by apparent Zulu unity.

This unity was not strong enough, however, to withstand the wider pressures that were increasingly bearing down upon the kingdom. In the north-west land-hungry Transvalers were steadily encroaching further into Zulu territory. From the south Shepstone was devising ways in which the Zulu state could be made to serve the needs of Natal. He looked upon Zululand both as a potential outlet for the colony's surplus African population, and as a gateway to the interior — an avenue along which Natal could expand to the north. These expansionary tendencies of the Transvaal and Natal must also be viewed within the broader context of British imperialism and the changing political economy of southern Africa. The British quest for geo-political symmetry in southern Africa, in the shape of confederation, would necessarily involve the subjugation of the powerful independent Zulu state. And the emerging capitalist economy of southern Africa, stimulated by the diamond discoveries, would increasingly find the precapitalist Zulu social formation incompatible with its needs.

These accumulating pressures culminated in the Anglo–Zulu War. But it was not this war that provided the deathblow to the Zulu state. As Guy argues, it was the second battle of Ulundi in July 1883, fought four years after the first, that marked the end of the Zulu kingdom: 'In 1879 Wolseley persuaded the Zulu to lay down their arms by offering them their land; in 1883 the Usuthu's enemies drove them into the forest and denied them access to their land.' After the 1879 war the British left the Zulu state to bleed to death. Whether it was a calculated, machiavellian divide-and-rule strategy or not, the post-war settlement had the effect of creating bitter internecine strife within Zululand. Not only did this strife bring about serious political instability, but it also caused catastrophic disruption to the whole productive process in Zululand. Faced with the prospect of mass starvation the Usuthu were forced to seek unnatural allies in a group of Transvaal boers. The ogre of Transvaal expansion in turn aroused the slumbering British, who formally annexed Zululand in 1887. Ten years later the process of colonial subjugation was completed when the British abandoned Zululand to the acquisitive Colony of Natal.[5]

The Natal Nguni

There seems to be little doubt that between 1817 and 1820 established African communities south of the Tugela River were severely devastated by Shaka's wars. So when the first white traders, and later the Voortrekkers, moved into Natal from the 1820s they found a depleted population in the territory. But over the next decade Natal was to be repopulated in a variety of ways, mostly as a result of the reconstitution or reappearance of local communities who had earlier fled to escape the impact of the Shakan wars. It is necessary for us to examine how the nineteenth-century experience of Natal's African population differed from that of the members of the Zulu kingdom.

From 1824 a small group of white traders began to settle at Port Natal. Within a few months northern Nguni refugees began to gravitate towards the white settlers, seeking either protection or economic opportunity. Some of these refugees were able to cultivate crops for sale to the growing settlement; others assisted the settlers in their hunting and trading expeditions. The number of Zulu immigrants into Natal grew rapidly; in 1834 an entire Zulu regiment defected across the Tugela from Dingane's rule. And previously displaced African communities continued to return to their former homes in

Natal. By 1838 estimates of Natal's African population ranged between 5 000 and 11 000. The next five years saw a further massive influx resulting from the Zulu–boer conflict and Mpande's revolt against Dingane. In 1843 Mpande had his brother, Gqugqu, put to death. This prompted a reported exodus of about 50 000 Zulu, so that the estimated African population of Natal in that year rose to between 80 000 and 100 000.

In 1844 Natal was formally annexed to the Cape (and therefore to Britain). A top priority of the new colonial administration was to devise a policy for governing the Colony's large African population. In 1846 Lieutenant-Governor West appointed a commission to arrange a system of reserves for Natal's Africans. By 1849 seven such reserves, or locations as they were called, had been demarcated. Land was also later set aside for African occupation in the form of mission reserves. By 1864 Natal had forty-two locations, covering over 2 000 000 acres, and twenty-one mission reserves, covering almost 175 000 acres. But it was one thing to create the reserves, quite another to ensure that all Africans moved into them. In 1851 Theophilus Shepstone, Natal's Diplomatic Agent to the Native Tribes and later the Colony's Secretary for Native Affairs, estimated that two-thirds of Natal's Africans lived outside the reserves on Crown and private lands; and the proportion was not much less thirty years later.

In addition to the allocation of land another prime concern of the colonial government was the establishment of an administrative system for Africans. The formulators of policy assumed that in the course of the Shakan wars the socio-political cohesion of Natal's African population had largely broken down. In their view, to fill this vacuum new authorities had to be created. So Ordinance 3 of 1849 vested in the Lieutenant-Governor the powers of a supreme chief. But in practice it was to be Shepstone who for about thirty years was to function, in Etherington's words, 'as uncrowned king of Africans in Natal'. Shepstone's own ideal would have been to implement a direct rule approach to African administration. But as it happened financial constraints forced him to resort to indirect rule methods. These in turn involved the creation of synthetic 'tribal' units and artificial chiefs, because, according to Shepstone's own estimate, between one-third and one-half of the African population were without chiefs. The new appointed chiefs were essentially intended to serve as agents of the colonial administration. Traditional chiefly powers were severely circumscribed; and recalcitrant chiefs could be punished under the Shepstonian system. Africans were to fall under a dual legal system, which Welsh has described: 'Customary law and the judicial powers of chiefs was recognised in the reserves in cases involving Africans, and in civil cases between Africans outside the reserves. Criminal cases involving Africans outside the reserves were heard under Roman-Dutch law.'

The underlying purpose of Shepstonism was to control Natal's African population by ensuring their access to land and by establishing an effective administrative system that had a veneer of traditionalism. But in time this veneer gradually wore thinner. At the outset the impact of the Shakan wars, for some, and emigration from the Zulu state, for others, had tended to break down cohesion and undermine traditional authorities and structures. And once they had arrived or resettled in Natal further processes and pressures were to operate to bring about significant transformations in African communities. Some of these processes were to manifest themselves most strongly at mission stations.

In southern Africa missionaries generally had great difficulty in penetrating cohesive centralised precapitalist societies. Their operations tended to be more successful among communities that had been disrupted or were under strain. Thus the relatively disjointed Nguni communities of Natal proved to be a more fertile ground for missionary enterprise than the Zulu state. In Natal the African response to the first American Board missionaries was initially enthusiastic. By 1851 the American Board had eleven mission stations and six out-stations in Natal; and other missionary societies were beginning to establish themselves at about the same time.

In time African enthusiasm for missionaries in Natal began to wane, and the survival of their enterprise increasingly came to depend on their ability to offer secular benefits. Missionaries were seen as potential intermediaries in dealings with the colonial authorities, and as providers of welfare services. Some chiefs looked to missionaries for assistance in buying land. Missionaries with medical skills were particularly popular. And from the 1860s the education offered at mission stations proved increasingly attractive to many blacks. But even in Natal there was widespread African resistance to Christian conversion. The ethical and doctrinal requirements of Christianity were considered too far-reaching. What is more, missionaries were often deemed to be in league with the colonial government.

In spite of this resistance there did emerge in Natal a substantial community of African converts (*kholwa*). Many of these converts were, to use Etherington's words, the 'flotsam and jetsam' of African society — the aged and decrepit, outcasts and rebels. But the ranks of the *kholwa* also produced resourceful, enterprising people. In the last three decades of the nineteenth century *kholwa* aspired to positions of leadership in the church; and they displayed a growing sense of political awareness. Perhaps even more significant was their economic contribution, for *kholwa* were to take a prominent place in Natal's emerging African peasantry.[6]

For the refugees who left Zululand, as well as for those individuals and communities returning to Natal after the Shakan wars, the events of the 1820s and 1830s must have been highly disruptive and traumatic. At the same time, though, their incorporation into the political economy of colonial Natal created new opportunities and stimulated changing patterns of economic activity. A crucial determinant of this change was access to land.

During the middle decades of the nineteenth century large areas of land in Natal were not utilised by direct producers. So opportunities for landholding existed for those thousands of Africans who did not reside in the locations. It seems that neither the Voortrekkers from the 1830s nor the early English settlers from the early 1850s engaged in direct exploitation of their land claims on any large scale. Instead both groups tended to sell off large tracts of land to speculators. These speculators, in turn, refrained from direct productive activity on their estates: as Slater points out, 'with their capital resources extended by the costs of acquiring and maintaining their lands, commercial farming activities were not seriously considered.' One way, therefore, of making a return on this investment was for these absentee proprietors to rent out land to African tenants. In 1874 it was estimated that about five million acres of Natal land owned by colonists and companies were in practice occupied by Africans, most of whom paid some form of rent, whether in cash or in kind, to their landlords.

Land was also accessible to Africans in other ways. Mission stations were allocated areas of land, often amounting to between six and eight thousand acres for each station, for African occupation. It was in the mission reserves that the practice of African land purchase originated. Some mission stations encouraged Africans to acquire individual freehold title. This practice soon spread outside the mission reserves. In 1880 new regulations were introduced for the sale of rural lands, and from that time land purchase by Africans became more widely reported. Some African buyers operated as individuals; others formed themselves into syndicates. By 1905, some 238 473 acres of land in Natal were owned or were in the process of being purchased by Africans. Herein lay the origin of the 'black spots' which have been a prime target for government resettlement policy in recent decades.

Access to land was thus open to Africans in various ways. As Bundy has remarked, 'African cultivators could choose between occupation of Crown Lands, or land owned by absentee landlords, or mission lands, or land provided in return for labour services or rent by white farmers or graziers, or they could reside in the locations.' This access to land made possible the emergence of an African peasantry in Natal. The relative failure of white farming in the Colony in the nineteenth century meant that considerable opportunities were open for Africans to produce and market an agricultural surplus. In 1849 it was reported that African-grown maize was being exported to Cape Town in large quantities, and that African peasants were selling wool on the Natal market. In 1853 the Natal 'Kafir' Commission observed that Africans were 'rapidly becoming rich and independent'. To use Bundy's words again, by 1870

> the involvement by a black peasantry in the wider economy was well under way. Numbers of mission-based and peri-urban peasants, and very many more small peasants and squatter-peasants on locations and privately owned lands, were cultivating more widely and seeking to dispose of a surplus. The colonial sector of Natal's rural economy continued to stagnate, especially during the commercial depression of the mid-1860s. Local farmers complained long and loud about the shortage of labour and the 'independence' of Africans living about them.

One of the most prosperous African peasant communities in Natal grew up at Edendale, near Pietermaritzburg. Edendale's origins can be traced to the late 1840s when the Methodist missionary, James Allison, led a multi-ethnic following of refugees, numbering about 450, from Swaziland into Natal. In

1851 Allison bought a 6 000-acre farm, which came to be named Edendale, and soon subdivided it into plots that could be purchased for £5 on a freehold basis. The members of the Edendale community seem to have been enterprising and resourceful; and their mission education encouraged them to participate in a simple commodity economy. Thus African peasants were soon exploiting Edendale's proximity to Pietermaritzburg by supplying vegetables and maize to the local market. By 1860 a thousand acres were under cultivation, and the more successful peasant farmers were beginning to use their profits to buy more land elsewhere. In 1867 a group of thirty to forty families paid £1 100 for a farm near Ladysmith; and Kleinfontein, another farm in this vicinity, was purchased by Africans in 1870. For about three decades from the 1850s an incipient tendency towards capitalist relations was emerging at Edendale and other mission communities.

One of these other mission communities was based at the American Board station at Mvoti. By 1871 the Groutville community (as it had come to be called, after the missionary Aldin Grout) had built up a small-scale sugar industry. In that year 47 African planters cultivated 300 acres of cane and milled 140 tons of sugar. Evidence of African sugar cultivation or milling at this time also comes from Ifumi, Amanzimtoti, and Verulam. There is also evidence that Africans ventured into cotton production. At the first public sale of Natal-grown cotton in 1863, the bales put up for auction were produced entirely by Africans.[7]

Mission stations were not the only arenas of African peasant activity in Natal. Research on the political economy of the colony's locations in the nineteenth century is at present limited. But a picture for one particular African community, the Hlubi, is emerging. The first half of the nineteenth century had been a traumatic period for the Hlubi. They had suffered severe disruption during the *difaqane*. And in 1847 an attack against them by Mpande prompted their chief, Langalibalele, to seek permission to move into Natal. The Hlubi were eventually settled by the Natal government in a location on the slopes of the Drakensberg.

Their movement into Natal brought the Hlubi into the nexus of the colonial economy. From 1849 those who lived in locations had to pay a hut-tax of 7*s*. a year. Moreover, those Hlubi who lived on privately owned lands outside the location would have to pay rent in the form of cash or labour. The Hlubi responded in varying ways to this new situation. Some voluntarily took up employment with white colonists in the late 1850s and 1860s. And after the discovery of diamonds in Griqualand West the Hlubi, more than any other group of Natal Africans, went to work on the diamond fields. But apart from discretionary participation in the labour market, the Hlubi also displayed signs of peasant activity. Their cattle herds were known to be considerable in size in the 1860s and early 1870s. And their widespread substitution of ploughs for hoes had raised the level of agricultural production.

It seems that their relative economic independence earned the Hlubi the resentment of local white farmers. As Etherington puts it, 'Fear of economic competition, shortage of labour at the old cheap rates and the swagger of

Hlubi boys back from the mines were making Weenen county farmers very jumpy by 1873.' The resilience of the Hlubi economy not only deprived the colonists of labour but also created competitive conditions at a time when, in the latter half of the 1860s, the colonial economy was in a slump.

In these tense circumstances it was hardly surprising that in 1873 white resentment should escalate into a confrontation with the Hlubi. Langalibalele's so-called rebellion of 1873 was occasioned by his failure to ensure the registration of guns in the possession of his followers, as ordered by the local magistrate, Macfarlane. Langalibalele was twice ordered to report to Pietermaritzburg to account for this apparent disobedience. The Hlubi chief failed to respond to the order on both occasions. It was decided therefore to coerce Langalibalele into submission. In October 1873 a colonial force was sent to the Hlubi location. Langalibalele fled across the Drakensberg into Basutoland, but not before his rearguard had become involved in a skirmish with the pursuing troops. In the ensuing operations pockets of resistance in the Hlubi location were broken up; and the neighbouring Ngwe people, accused of collaborating with the Hlubi, were forced to yield to a show of colonial force. Langalibalele himself was captured in Basutoland. The colonial authorities then proceeded to break up the Hlubi chiefdom. Its key resources, land and cattle, were expropriated. Langalibalele was tried, found guilty and sentenced to banishment for life. In 1874 he was imprisoned on Robben Island, where he remained till 1887 when he was allowed to return to Natal to live in the Zwartkops location.

Recent studies have significantly reinterpreted the Langalibalele affair. The extent of Langalibalele's defiance has been shown to have been exaggerated. And the colonial response has come to be examined in the context of Natal's political economy. Firstly, evidence has been produced to suggest that Langalibalele was not the fractious and recalcitrant chief that he had previously been made out to be. The quantity of unregistered guns in the hands of his followers was minimal. He refused to answer the summons to Pietermaritzburg partly because an old injury made travel uncomfortable for him, and partly out of fear that the summons was a trap to arrest him — he remembered the case of Matshana, a petty chief who had been called to Pietermaritzburg in 1857, only to be assaulted by John Shepstone.

It thus seems that one needs to look beyond Langalibalele's apparent defiance for an explanation of Natal's handling of the affair. As Manson argues, 'a relatively trivial issue such as the refusal to register guns became complicated by mutual fears and panic, allowing the settlers and some white officials an opportunity to give expression to their resentment, jealousy and ambitions.' This view becomes credible when one examines the supposedly punitive measures that were taken against the Hlubi. Large areas of land in the Hlubi and Ngwe locations were opened up for settler occupation in 1874. By early 1875 over £24 500 had been added to government funds through the sale of captured Hlubi and Ngwe cattle. And Hlubi and Ngwe captives were eagerly looked upon by colonists as potential labourers.[8]

While the Hlubi peasantry was crushed by a sudden, devastating blow, most of Natal's African peasants became subjected to more gradual pressures, which were, in time, to undermine their prosperity. Peasants had for long been a target for the anger and resentment of white farmers. These farmers had two main complaints. Firstly, they were unable to compete successfully with African peasants, whose production costs were kept relatively low through their access to family labour. Secondly, the existence of an African peasantry and the resilience of the African subsistence economy seriously impeded the flow of labour to white farms.

These complaints did not result in immediate pressures being brought to bear on the African peasantry. Such pressures, when they did materialise, arose more from broad structural changes within the political economy of the region. Bundy, Slater and others have pointed to two fundamental alterations that were occurring, particularly from around 1890. The first was the development of the mining industry, most notably gold-mining on the Rand and coal-mining in the Natal interior. This, in turn, created a large new market that served as a stimulus for mercantile enterprise, commercial farming, secondary industry, and railway construction. The second change was Britain's grant of responsible government to Natal in 1893. As Bundy comments, 'those interests which gained politically by the grant of responsible government stood to gain economically by a rise in the value of land, the commercialization of agriculture, and a diminution in the competitiveness of a (culturally and ethnically distinct) rival agricultural class, the black peasantry.'

A significant feature of this changing political economy was the growing commercialisation of white agriculture in Natal. The growth of urban markets stimulated a shift away from renting towards direct productive activity on the part of white farmers. The number of colonists engaged in agriculture rose from about 2 000 to over 3 000 between 1875 and 1895; and the colonists' combined agricultural output grew from approximately 130 000 tons in 1893 to over 850 000 tons by 1904.

Some African peasants were also able to exploit the opportunities offered by the expanding market in the last decade of the nineteenth century. This was particularly true of peasants who either owned land or had managed to accumulate capital over the years. Generally, though, the changes in the colonial political economy worked to the disadvantage of African peasants in Natal. The shift away from renting to direct production on the part of white farmers deprived many peasants of access to land. Lands previously rented to African tenants were sold to white farmers; and, as land values rose, so did rents, making it more difficult for tenants to remain on the land. African peasants were further disadvantaged by the policies of the colonial state. These were very much geared to the interests of white farmers, who received favoured treatment when it came to railway construction and government aid.

By the end of the nineteenth century Natal's African peasantry was under severe stress. Not only had the terms of a changing political economy been loaded against it, but it had also been subjected to ecological catastrophe. In 1897 the rinderpest epidemic hit Natal, following upon a number of dry years, and severely decimated cattle herds. It is estimated that six-sevenths of African-owned cattle died in the outbreak. This, of course, had a devastating effect on both the peasantry and the subsistence economy. Indeed, it would be true to say that almost the whole of Natal's African population was under strain at the turn of the century. Their fundamental problem was curtailed access to the means of production. Cattle losses resulting from rinderpest were catastrophic at a time when the reserves were becoming increasingly overcrowded and opportunities for tenant-farming were being reduced. On top of this the Natal government was about to increase the tax burden on Africans. It was thus hardly surprising that in 1906 this situation should give rise to an African rebellion.[9]

The Swazi state

The widespread turmoil that followed the rise of the Zulu state created the conditions for the consolidation and expansion of the Swazi state. The invasions of Zwide's Ndwandwe had forced Sobhuza and his Ngwane followers to flee northwards beyond the Pongola. But Shaka's defeat of Zwide in 1819 had brought some relief and enabled Sobhuza to consolidate his position in the central and northern region of modern Swaziland. A series of expansionist campaigns then brought a number of Sotho, Tsonga and Nguni chiefdoms under Sobhuza's suzerainty. But Sobhuza's hold over this expanding Swazi state was precarious. Some of the subjugated chiefdoms clung to their autonomy; and it took time for the ruling Dlamini clan to establish their control. It was only towards the end of his reign that Sobhuza's rule rested on firmer foundations.

The vulnerability of the Swazi state arose not only from internal instability but also from external threats. The Ndwandwe remained a danger; and Sobhuza had to be especially wary of his powerful southern neighbour, the Zulu kingdom. So, when Shaka displayed any signs of aggressive intent towards the Swazi, Sobhuza adopted a submissive stance. But for most of his reign Shaka's preoccupations lay elsewhere. The death of Shaka in 1828 and Dingane's subsequent relaxation of Zulu militarism brought further relief to the Swazi, enabling Sobhuza to consolidate and expand his own position. When Dingane did eventually launch two major invasions of Swaziland in 1836 and 1839, the Swazi were sufficiently strong to repulse them.

It was around this time, in the late 1830s, that Sobhuza died. Like Moshoeshoe, Sobhuza, in Bonner's words, 'showed himself to be one of the *Mfecane's* great survivors'. At the time of his death the Swazi state was still troubled by internal division and external dangers. But in Bonner's view, Sobhuza had succeeded in establishing the basic structure that formed the foundation of the Swazi state: 'In the end, then, modern Swaziland must be seen as Sobhuza's creation, and one need look no further than this for a lasting monument to his reign.'

When Sobhuza died his heir, Mswati, was still a young boy. During his minority, power rested with his mother, Thandile, his uncle, Malunge, and his eldest brother, Malambule. It was only from about 1845 that Mswati began to assume power — and then not without difficulty. Mswati's accession seems to have aroused the resentment of some of his brothers, who themselves entertained hopes of power. One of these brothers was Malambule, the former regent, who was soon gaining support for his cause from Mpande, Dingane's successor as Zulu king. Mswati, in his turn, looked to the support of a boer community at Ohrigstad in the eastern Transvaal; in 1846 an 'alliance' between the two parties was formed when Mswati ceded an area of land to the boers.

At this point there was beginning to take shape a pattern that was to form an integral feature of Swazi history for the rest of the nineteenth century. This pattern was to be characterised by a complex set of interactions and interrelationships between the Swazi state and its neighbours, particularly the Transvaal boers and the Zulu, and eventually also involving Natal and Mozambique. Internal divisions in one society had ramifications in another; and over time there were formed numerous cross-cutting alliances or attachments that transcended local or ethnic ties.

This pattern was best exemplified in the events of the late 1840s. The boer community at Ohrigstad was divided into two factions: those who supported the autocratic commandant-general, Potgieter, were opposed by a democratic group who wanted authority vested in an elected volksraad. It was the latter camp that concluded the 1846 agreement with the Swazi; and it was they who helped Mswati to stave off a Zulu invasion of Swaziland in 1847, at a time when Mpande was collaborating with Malambule, Mswati's rival. The complexity of the situation was further underlined when Potgieter, threatened by hostilities from the volksraad group, made an effort to align with the Zulu.

No sooner had the threat to Mswati's authority posed by Malambule been removed, when a new threat appeared in the person of Somcuba, another of Mswati's brothers. In 1846 Mswati tried unsuccessfully to bring Somcuba into line by force, prompting the latter to take refuge with the Ohrigstad boers. Other brothers were also believed to be conspiring against the king at this time; and the loyalty of many chiefdoms was in doubt.

Facing both internal strains and external pressures the Swazi ruling family took steps to build up royal authority. Thandile, Mswati's mother, had initiated this process when acting as regent during Mswati's minority. She strove to reinforce the pillars of royal authority. She created nation-wide age-regiments as a framework for the state's military organisation; and she established a network of royal villages as instruments of royal control in outlying areas. On his accession Mswati himself continued the centralising process. The autonomy of local chiefdoms was further undermined, often as a result of Mswati's forcible intervention in their affairs. Dlamini princes were deployed throughout the state as agents of royal control. Furthermore, the age-regiments were kept in a state of permanent mobilisation.

By strengthening his internal power base Mswati was better positioned not only to withstand external pressures, but also to launch upon campaigns of expansion. Between 1856 and 1865 Swaziland acquired new territory as a result of several successful military expeditions. Some of these were directed towards the south-west, in areas where authority was disputed between the Swazi and the Zulu. Other campaigns were pursued in the north-east. Mswati re-established his authority over chiefdoms that had broken away from the Swazi state during the unstable years of his minority. He also encroached into areas that fell within the Portuguese sphere of influence in Mozambique. And in the early 1860s Mswati became embroiled in a succession dispute in the Gaza state. In 1861 the ruler of Gaza, Mawewe, was overthrown by his usurping half-brother, Mzila. Mswati gave his support to Mawewe, two of whose sisters were married to the Swazi king. After a protracted struggle, during which first one side and then the other would gain the upper hand, Mzila eventually won control of the Gaza state, forcing Mawewe to take refuge in Swaziland. But in order to secure his position Mzila had to move his capital further to the north. In doing so he abandoned much territory in the southern part of Gazaland. Mswati exploited this vacuum by sending expeditions to assert Swazi control in this vacated area.

During the mid-nineteenth century the Swazi state was thus becoming increasingly embroiled in the affairs of neighbouring societies. Dlamini diplomacy was based on considerations of both defence and expansion. Mswati had looked towards a group of Ohrigstad boers in the mid-1840s to strengthen his position against internal rebellion and Zulu aggression; and in 1855 he ceded an area of land to the boer community at Lydenburg, probably in return for a boer commitment to eliminate Mswati's rival, Somcuba, who had taken refuge at Lydenburg. A Zulu invasion of Swaziland in 1852 prompted Mswati to make overtures to the Natal government. This was even followed later by a Swazi proposal for a marriage between Mswati's sister and a member of the Shepstone family. While these overtures had been dictated by defensive considerations, it was Mswati's expansionist ambitions that led him to exploit internal divisions within the ruling family of the Gaza state.

During the last decade of his reign Mswati was thus able both to achieve virtual immunity from Zulu attack and to expand Swazi territory. He had also succeeded in securing his internal position. Several more princely rivals were eliminated; and the local autonomy of subordinate chiefdoms was further undermined. So at Mswati's death in 1865 the Swazi state was firmly established and authority firmly vested in the royal family. But, as Bonner has observed, Mswati's legacy was 'notably ambiguous'. The problem was that Mswati died leaving behind no acknowledged heir. The ensuing internal crisis was to leave the Swazi state ill-equipped to withstand the increasingly intrusive and powerful forces of colonialism.

There were two main contenders for the succession to Mswati. One was Mbilini, who was old enough to exercise power immediately, but being the son of Mswati's first wife was constitutionally debarred from the kingship. The other was Ludvonga, who was still a minor but had a strong claim based on the senior status of his mother. Before the end of 1865 the succession was settled on Ludvonga. But Mbilini's kingly aspirations remained alive, and he pursued his ambition by attaching himself to the Lydenburg boers in the way that Somcuba had done before him. Mbilini's cause, although it was to revive later, soon lost momentum. His following was not large; and one camp among the Lydenburg boers was opposed to harbouring him.[10]

Increasingly more pressing for the Swazi rulers was the need to cope with the expansive tendencies of white colonists from the Transvaal. In the 1840s and 1850s internal divisions within the Swazi royal family had prompted Mswati to seek boer support. In 1846 Mswati had ceded to the Ohrigstad boers a large area of land between the Crocodile and Olifants Rivers at a time when he was under a joint threat from Malambule and Mpande. In 1855 the Swazi ceded to the Lydenburg boers a 10-mile wide corridor along the northern bank of the Pongola River. This was a short-term strategic manoeuvre on the part of Mswati who wanted the boers to cooperate in eliminating Somcuba, who, while in exile in the eastern Transvaal, had long been a thorn in Mswati's side. It seems that Somcuba was disposed of, but the boers failed to fulfil some of the other terms of this agreement, which Mswati was soon treating as lapsed.

It was only in the 1860s that pressure on Swazi-claimed land became more serious, as the white population density in the eastern Transvaal was growing and more areas were being occupied by boers. In 1866, within a year of Mswati's death, boer-initiated negotiations resulted in an agreement that demarcated in detail a boundary between the Transvaal and Swaziland. The agreement represented, in Bonner's words, 'a decisive limiting of Swaziland's territorial jurisdiction'. A growing sense of insecurity and a need for territorial definition had probably persuaded the Swazi regents to agree to the treaty.

More exact territorial demarcation did not put an end to white pressure on Swaziland. In 1868 the South African Republic annexed Swaziland by proclamation. But as it turned out, the Republic was unable to put this paper annexation into effect. The early 1870s also saw an influx of concession-hunters and missionaries into Swaziland, although neither set of infiltrators made much progress at first. In 1875 an expedition from the South African Republic coerced the Swazi into signing a treaty that, among other things, imposed subject status on the Swazi and granted the Republic the right to construct a railway through Swaziland. On top of this the Swazi again found themselves under threat from the Zulu in the mid-1870s. Cetshwayo was keen to replenish depleted Zulu herds and to reassert hegemony in the Delagoa Bay hinterland, a crucial area for the trading and tributary interests of the Zulu state. Swaziland was thus an obvious target if these needs were to be fulfilled. It is known that Cetshwayo was anxious to launch attacks on Swaziland at various times between 1875 and 1877, but on each occasion he was restrained by his own advisers and by the threat of intervention from Natal or the Transvaal.

Most of these external threats in the 1870s did not materialise. This was fortunate for the Swazi state, because they occurred at a time when it was again troubled by internal crises. Since the death of Mswati in 1865 regents had been exercising power for over eight years during the minority of Ludvonga, Mswati's successor. Ludvonga was nearing the end of his minority when, in 1874, he became ill and died in suspicious circumstances. Ludvonga's death was followed by another lengthy period of crisis and uncertainty. There was a brief struggle for the succession before Mbandzeni was installed. Mbandzeni was a timid, ineffectual figure, and for some years he played a secondary role, as effective power rested with Ludvonga's mother, Sisile, backed by a 'regency junta'. But from the late 1870s Mbandzeni began to assert himself, and he showed increasing resentment towards Sisile, the queen regent, who had for long been wielding effective power. Early in 1881 open hostilities broke out between the two camps, culminating in Sisile's death.

It is against this background that the tide of white encroachment into Swaziland must be viewed. The encroachment took two main forms: one was an invasion of concessionaires, the other was a more formal type of colonial expropriation or annexation. Concession-hunters had begun to show a special interest in Swaziland after the discovery of gold in the eastern Transvaal in 1873. A host of prospectors flocked into Swaziland in search of gold. From much the same time numerous grazing, hunting and wood-cutting concessions were being granted away. In 1876 Mbandzeni, who was allowed considerable latitude by the regents to dispense concessions, granted a grazing concession of 36 000 acres in southern Swaziland to Joachim Ferreira and Ignatius Maritz. In the mid-1880s there was a further escalation of concession-hunting in Swaziland, as fortune-seekers flooded into the country. For assistance in coping with this invasion Mbandzeni in 1886 called in Offy Shepstone, the son of Sir Theophilus. Offy Shepstone was given the task of controlling concessions, much to the annoyance of boer graziers in Swaziland who had hoped to convert their grazing concessions into freehold tenure. It seems that Shepstone was able to exert some short-term control over the concessionaires, while apparently lining his own pocket in the process. But the control was short-lived. In 1888 Mbandzeni curbed the overmighty Shepstone by restricting his authority. And early in 1889, as Mbandzeni's health rapidly declined, 'the concessionaires', in Bonner's words, 'entered into a final frenzied scramble to secure what resources were left.... [Concessions] of every conceivable description were wheedled out of the king, and the economic assets of the kingdom progressively stripped.' In addition to the more usual grazing and mineral concessions, a new set of grants were made in this last phase. These included revenue concessions, which alienated the king's revenue, and a customs concession, which granted away customs dues.

The second form of white encroachment involved the gradual erosion of Swazi independence and the whittling away of territory through boundary delimitations. In 1879 the British, who had recently annexed the Transvaal, appointed a commission to delimit the Transvaal–Swazi boundary. Although the Swazi rulers were consulted and even reluctantly acquiesced in the commission's recommendations, the effect of the 1880 boundary demarcation was to excise permanently from Swaziland areas to the north-west and north-east that were populated by Swazi homesteads.

The Pretoria Convention of 1881 formally recognised Swaziland's independence. But within four years the South African Republic was trying to gain control of the territory. In 1885 a mission, led by Vice-President Joubert and Landdrost Krogh, attempted to secure a Republican protectorate over Swaziland. This attempt failed, but the South African Republic, intent on acquiring an outlet to the sea, would continue to strive for control of Swaziland.

Swaziland's ability to evade the Republic's grasping hand was undermined by internal dissension and weakness. Late in 1888 a number of leading councillors in Swaziland were executed for plotting to overthrow the king. Factions increasingly warred with each other; and there were numerous killings. In the meantime Mbandzeni's health had been deteriorating rapidly, and in 1889 he died.

Mbandzeni was succeeded by Ngwane V, who was only 14. His young age prevented him from exercising authority; but the future of Swaziland was, in any case, to be decided over the next few years, not by the Swazi themselves, but by the Britsh and the South African Republic. Between 1890 and 1894 three Swaziland Conventions were held, involving discussions between President Kruger of the South African Republic and Sir Henry Loch, the British High Commissioner. The British saw Swaziland as falling within the Republic's sphere of influence; at the first Swaziland Convention of 1890 this was formally recognised in return for the Republic's agreeing to refrain from any further interference in the British sphere north of the Limpopo. The second Convention of 1893 attempted to bring Swaziland under the Republic's authority. But the Swazi queen regent refused to give her consent to this arrangement; and in 1894 a Swazi deputation went to England to request that a British rather than a Transvaal protectorate be established over Swaziland. The deputation was brushed aside and Swazi protests were ignored. Within two months the third Swaziland Convention had been signed. Under this Swaziland became a protectorate of the South African Republic, which had full powers of legislation, jurisdiction and administration. Again the Swazi refused to consent to this loss of sovereignty. But the third Convention, unlike the second, was not conditional upon Swazi consent; so a proclamation was issued in Pretoria declaring that Swaziland was a protectorate under the South African Republic.

The Republic's protectorate over Swaziland came into being in 1895. But it was a short-lived affair, which was brought to an end by the Anglo–Boer War. Although the subsequent imposition of British protection may have been more preferable to the Swazi than Transvaal overlordship, the essential point is that by the 1890s the Swazi state had effectively lost its independence. It had not been subjugated by a direct process of colonial conquest, but it had become the victim of a more subtle process of 'conquest by concessions'. The discovery of gold in the Transvaal had sparked off a search for minerals in other adjacent areas throughout southern Africa, including Swaziland. In the 1880s the Swazi state lacked the internal stability and cohesion that was necessary to cope with this invasion of fortune-seekers. The British were fully prepared to sacrifice Swaziland as a pawn to win diplomatic concessions from the South African Republic. And the Republic itself saw Swaziland as a geographical obstruction to its ambitions for gaining access to the sea. The Swazi state lacked the resilience or cohesion to resist capitalist encroachment, as well as the diplomatic manoeuvring of Britain and the Transvaal. By the end of the nineteenth century her independence was lost.[11]

The southern Nguni

The southern Nguni were the first Bantu-speaking people south of the Limpopo to come into contact with white communities. They were also the first to be brought under direct colonial rule in southern Africa. The British annexation of British Kaffraria in 1847 marked the beginning of the formal colonial subjugation of the southern Nguni, a process which was to take almost fifty years to complete. The gradual loss of political independence did not, however, entail the immediate erosion of the southern Nguni's economic independence. There is substantial evidence to suggest that a thriving peasantry existed among the southern Nguni for a large part of the nineteenth century. But by the end of the century the southern Nguni economy was experiencing the stresses and strains brought about by natural disasters and by fundamental changes in the political economy of southern Africa.

The southern Nguni largely escaped the traumas and turmoil wrought by the *difaqane*. Only a few repercussions were experienced south of the Mzimkhulu. In 1827 Matiwane, the Ngwane chief, moved southwards across the Orange River to escape Moshoeshoe's expanding sphere of authority. The Ngwane encroached into Thembu territory, prompting the Thembu paramount chief, Ngubencuka, to request the assistance of the Cape colonial authorities. The latter responded by dispatching a force under Henry Somerset who, after mistaking the Ngwane for the Zulu, routed Matiwane at the battle of Mbholompo in 1828.

The other main consequence of the *difaqane* to have an impact on the southern Nguni was the arrival of numerous bands of refugees from the north. These refugees, who came to be called the Mfengu, were largely drawn from the ranks of the Bhele, Hlubi and Zizi chiefdoms; and their numbers were augmented by groups of Ngwane after their defeat in 1828. Moyer estimates that as many as 50 000 Mfengu may have arrived in the Transkei and Ciskei before 1835. Initially they were welcomed by the local chiefs. Many Mfengu became fully absorbed into southern Nguni communities; other Mfengu groups remained in a semi-independent, tributary relationship to local chiefs. But in time the servility and exactions demanded of these Mfengu caused resentment, and increasingly large numbers of Mfengu began to look to collaboration with the Cape colonial authorities as a more promising road for advancement.

In 1830, apart from the Mfengu, there were three main groupings, loosely defined, among the southern Nguni. In the south-west were the Xhosa, who maintained a friendly alliance with the Bomvana. In the north-east the Mpondo chiefdom under Faku was dominant. The Thembu occupied the central region, albeit somewhat uneasily. They had fallen out with the Gcaleka over the division of the spoils after the defeat of Matiwane in 1828; and

Thembu–Gcaleka relations remained strained over the following decades. Moreover, Moshoeshoe looked upon Thembuland as ideal cattle-raiding territory. In these circumstances, it was not surprising that the Thembu, like the Mfengu, should look towards the colonial authorities for protection.[12]

However, to suggest that there were three main power blocs among the southern Nguni at this time would be misleading. As we have seen in an earlier chapter, southern Nguni society was politically fragmented. On top of this, a tendency on the part of some groups towards collaboration with the colonial authorities was to create new divisions and tensions among the southern Nguni. In their turn the colonial authorities were able to exploit these divisions to facilitate the process of subjugation.

While the northernmost communities, most notably the Mpondo, had experienced some of the turmoil wrought by the *difaqane*, it was the south-western Xhosa communities that bore the brunt of the colonial presence in the first half of the nineteenth century. The early 1830s was a time of simmering discontent for the Xhosa. A severe drought occurred in 1829. Its effect was exacerbated by the decision of the colonial authorities in that year to expel Maqoma, brother of Sandile, Ngqika's successor, from a well-watered area in the Kat River valley. The action was taken against Maqoma on the grounds that he had attacked certain Thembu chiefs. After his expulsion the expropriated land became a reserved area for Khoi and 'Bastards', known as the Kat River Settlement.

In addition to this loss of land the Xhosa also had to suffer the effects of the reprisal system. This system was designed by the colonial authorities to counter cattle-raiding by the Xhosa. It permitted a commando to follow the spoor of stolen cattle to the nearest homestead and demand restitution or take Xhosa cattle as recompense. It was an arbitrary procedure which often resulted in injustice. Sometimes white-owned cattle which was thought to have been stolen had merely strayed; at other times innocent homesteads were punished.

In December 1834 the Xhosa invaded the Colony, determined, in Peires's words, 'to avenge their chiefs, their lands, their losses at the hands of the commandos'. For the first few weeks of the war the Colony was forced onto the defensive, as the settlers abandoned almost the whole country east of Algoa Bay, excepting Grahamstown and Fort Beaufort. On the Xhosa side the initiative for war belonged to the Rharhabe; but Hintsa, the Gcaleka chief, gave his approval and support to the campaign. The Xhosa could not, however, count on the support of the Mfengu, who, towards the end of the war, openly collaborated with the colonial forces.

The Sixth Frontier War of 1834–5 was a bitter, brutal struggle that lasted for nine months. Mortality figures vary, but at least 1 400 Xhosa and about 100 on the colonial side were killed. Among the Xhosa dead was Hintsa. He had voluntarily entered the British camp in April 1835, having been assured of his personal safety. He was then ordered to raise a ransom of 25 000 cattle and 500 horses for his release. In trying to escape, Hintsa was tragically and treacherously killed. Peires has described the incident:

He was pulled off his horse, shot through the back and through the leg. Desperately he scrambled down the river bank and collapsed into the water-course. A scout named George Southey, coming up fast behind him, blew off the top of his head. Then some soldiers cut off his ears as keepsakes to show around the military camps. Others tried to dig out his teeth with bayonets.

In September 1835 the Xhosa agreed to end the war. In the meantime the Cape Governor, D'Urban, had already in May annexed the belt of territory between the Keiskamma and Kei Rivers, and had proposed to expel the Xhosa east of the Kei to open up a new area for white settlement. In the event the British Colonial Secretary, Lord Glenelg, intervened to disallow the expropriation. So the colonial boundary reverted to the Fish River. While part of D'Urban's plan fell through, another part was carried out. At his invitation about 17 000 Mfengu in May 1835 moved out of Gcalekaland across the Kei into the Cape Colony. They were settled around Fort Peddie as a human barrier between the white settlers and the Xhosa. In responding to the invitation the Mfengu alienated both major sections of the Xhosa. They settled on land belonging to the Ngqika; and in the process of moving they took with them 20 000 head of Gcaleka cattle. The Mfengu were thus committed to a future course of colonial collaboration.

For almost a decade after the 1834–5 war relations between the Xhosa and the Colony were regulated on a more promising basis. This was largely due to the efforts of Andries Stockenström, who was appointed Lieutenant-Governor of the Eastern Cape in 1836. Stockenström's frontier policy rested on a process of making treaties and defining jurisdictional rights. Diplomatic agents were appointed to mediate between the chiefs and the colonial authorities. And the reprisal system was abolished in favour of a more complex but just procedure for recovering stolen cattle.

Although the treaty system was resented by the colonists, it worked fairly well for a few years. But in the early 1840s it came under stress. A severe drought in 1842 killed large numbers of cattle and duly placed a strain on the working of the treaties. And in 1844 the new Cape Governor, Sir Peregrine Maitland, responded to settler pressure by abandoning the treaty system. Farmers were again to be allowed to follow up stolen cattle; and if their animals were not found, compensation could be demanded. Earlier the decision of Lieutenant-Governor Hare to place troops east of the Fish, following the murder of a white farmer, had led the Xhosa to believe that their land was to be expropriated. Sandile, who had succeeded Tyhali as chief of the Ngqika in 1842, demanded the removal of these troops. The War of the Axe that broke out in 1846 took its name from an incident in which a Xhosa stole an axe from a colonist. This, though, was a mere spark, as essentially the war was fought over the struggle for land.

The war began with a strike by colonial forces into Xhosa territory. But for the invaders the campaign was not to be an easy one. An effective counter-offensive was launched by the Xhosa; and at one time the Gqunukhwebe threatened Port Elizabeth. Xhosa guerrilla tactics harassed colonial supply lines. The Colony's Khoi mercenaries were on occasions mutinous. Added problems of dysentery among the troops and horse sickness prevented the Colony from achieving military dominance. But the Xhosa position was no better. They were facing starvation, as their grain stores had been destroyed by colonial troops, and their cattle had been herded out for safe-keeping. By September it was vital for them to cultivate their fields to ensure a food supply. So in that month they laid down their arms, not because they had suffered military defeat but out of the dictates of the seasons. Even then the war was not over, as Phato, the Gqunukhwebe chief, and some Ndlambe chiefs continued an intermittent, harassing style of resistance into 1847. And although Sandile had discontinued fighting, he too refused to submit to colonial demands. The colonial response was to mete out scorched-earth treatment on Xhosa settlements, and to take Sandile captive.[13]

The first half of the nineteenth century had seen the gradual loss of Xhosa territory and the destabilising of the Xhosa polity. As Peires has observed, 'In 1800 the Xhosa nation was expanding, aggressive and self-confident.... By 1847 things were different. The Xhosa kingdom had shrunk and in shrinking, it had lost vast tracts of its most fertile territory.' But in the mid-nineteenth century the process of direct colonial subjugation was only just beginning. It started with sections of the Xhosa and continued until almost the end of the century when the last of the southern Nguni chiefdoms, the Mpondo, was brought under colonial rule. Why, one might ask, did the subjugation of the southern Nguni take so long? Part of the answer to this lies in the resistance offered by Africans to colonial expansion. The other part lies in the nature of imperial policy. The British government was generally unwilling to take direct responsibility for annexing and governing new territories; but nor was it willing to allow the Cape a free hand in conducting its own expansion into the lands of the southern Nguni.

The formal colonial subjugation of the southern Nguni began in 1847 when the new Governor and High Commissioner, Sir Harry Smith, proclaimed the annexation to Britain of the territory between the Keiskamma and Kei Rivers. British Kaffraria, as this new colony was called, was to be administered by the High Commissioner, assisted by civil commissioners who would advise the African chiefs and review their judicial actions. Smith, an arrogant and brow-beating military figure, also established a Mfengu settlement in the newly annexed territory, an action that was bound further to provoke the Xhosa.

Peires suggests that the annexation of British Kaffraria may have 'finally sealed the division of the Xhosa kingdom between the Gcaleka and the Rharhabe'; but it did not weaken the Xhosa resolve to resist colonialism. In 1850, a year of severe drought, there was growing unrest among the Xhosa in British Kaffraria. Smith responded typically to the situation by deposing the Ngqika chief, Sandile, and appointing Charles Brownlee, a white civil commissioner, in his place. Before the end of 1850 another frontier war had broken out. An expedition sent to arrest Sandile was attacked; and the military villages that Smith had set up in British Kaffraria were annihilated. The war lasted over two years and was finally brought to an end by Smith's successor,

Cathcart. More conciliatory than Smith, Cathcart restored Sandile to the Ngqika chiefship; but he also aggravated the land issue by handing over more Xhosa territory to white farmers, and by assigning captured land to the Mfengu, who had again collaborated with the colonial forces during the war.

The Gcaleka had not been major protagonists in the wars of 1846–7 and 1850–3. But they had supported the war effort of the western Xhosa, and in both wars were subjected to punitive raids by colonial forces. While the impact of these raids was limited, within a few years the Gcaleka were to be at the centre of a devastating catastrophe. A young girl, Nongqawuse, prophesied on the strength of a vision that if the Xhosa slaughtered their cattle and destroyed their crops, their ancestors would rise up to drive the whites into the sea, and food would be supplied from heaven. Sarhili, the Gcaleka chief, ordered his people to act upon the prophecy. In 1857 this massive act of self-destruction was accordingly carried out. Instead of the expected consequences, the cattle-killing brought on a disastrous famine. Thousands of people died of starvation, and thousands more flooded into the Colony in search of food. While the government provided some relief, it also took advantage of the depopulation to open up a large area of British Kaffraria to German settlers. An expedition of Cape Mounted Police was despatched to drive Sarhili beyond the Mbashe River.

The cattle-killing paved the way for Cape expansion into southern Nguni territory. In 1866 the British handed over British Kaffraria to the Colony. And the Cape was soon considering the possibility of annexing land beyond the Kei. As it turned out direct annexation of the Transkeian territories was preceded by the extension of Cape control into these areas. The latter process, which involved essentially the introduction of magistrates, was carried on fairly rapidly after the Cape achieved responsible government in 1872. In 1873 the Mpondomise were brought under white rule. Magisterial rule was introduced into Thembuland three years later. And the conclusion of the last frontier war saw Gcalekaland and Bomvanaland coming under Cape control.

The war of 1877–8 grew out of the long-standing hostility between the Gcaleka and the Mfengu. The initial spark was an incident in which two Gcaleka headmen were attacked by Mfengu at a beer-drinking party in Fingoland. The ensuing war was attributed, in colonial circles, to Gcaleka aggression. Sir Bartle Frere, who had become High Commissioner early in 1877, perceived the conflict as part of a greater anti-white pan-Africanist conspiracy that was spreading through southern Africa. But land was the real root of the war. The Gcaleka, along with the Ngqika and some Thembu factions, were striving to regain land from which they had been ejected and which had subsequently been handed over to the Mfengu. In its turn the Colony was determined to protect its Mfengu collaborators. Soon after the outbreak of hostilities Frere issued a proclamation deposing Sarhili and forfeiting his country. Colonial forces advanced across Gcalekaland, destroying Sarhili's great place and forcing him to retreat across the Mbashe River. Late in 1877 the Colony was confident that it had won the war. But Sarhili recovered, and Sandile's Ngqika and sections of the Thembu joined the struggle against the

Colony. The colonial victory was not achieved until May 1878, once the Gcaleka had been decisively beaten in battle.[14]

After the war Cape officials were stationed in Xesibe country and at Port St Johns. So by the end of 1878 all of the Transkei except Pondoland had come under Cape magisterial rule, before the process of formal annexation had even begun. Direct incorporation was delayed further by the Transkeian Rebellion of 1880–1. The rebels, who were mainly drawn from the Mpondomise, Thembu and Griqua, may have been inspired by the Sotho rebellion that had just broken out. Certainly a similar resentment towards Cape colonial control had brought on the Transkeian Rebellion. The Cape's policy of disarming Africans aroused particular antagonism; and chiefs were dismayed to see their powers being undermined by magisterial rule. Seemingly unaware of this discontent, the magistrate at Qumbu, Hamilton Hope, tried to obtain Mpondomise military assistance for the Colony in suppressing the Sotho rebellion. In his quest Hope, along with two other whites, was murdered. Much of Thembuland joined the Mpondomise in the effort to throw off white control. Magistracies were abandoned; public buildings, trading stores and churches were sacked. Rebel anger was also directed against the Mfengu. So it was hardly surprising that the Mfengu, along with the Bhaca, should again adopt a collaborative role in helping colonial forces to suppress the rebellion. Had the Gcaleka and Mpondo joined the rebellion its suppression would have been extremely difficult. In the event they stayed out, and by April 1881 the resistance was over. While the rebellion shattered white confidence, it also involved considerable loss of life and, for the rebels, loss of land and cattle, as white farmers moved in to take over land from which the rebels were driven.

After the rebellion the delayed business of annexation was finally carried through. By 1886 almost the whole of the Transkei, except Pondoland, had been formally incorporated into the Cape. A northern region of Pondoland had been annexed to Natal in 1866 as Alfred County; and in the late 1870s Frere was keen to subjugate the Mpondo. But the fear of Mpondo resistance prevented the immediate assertion of colonial control over the territory. In 1885 the British declared an imperial protectorate over the Pondoland coastline to forestall German designs in the area. External pressures on the Mpondo continued to build up. The Cape attempted unsuccessfully to introduce a resident commissioner into Pondoland in 1887; and several concession-hunters tried their luck in the territory. A period of internal instability followed the death of Mqikela, the Mpondo paramount, in 1887. Sigcau succeeded him early in 1888, but soon came into conflict with Mhlangaso, who had been Mqikela's leading councillor. While Sigcau was more conciliatory towards the Cape, Mhlangaso was determined that the Mpondo should not be subordinated. The debilitating conflict between the two of them undermined the capacity of the Mpondo to retain their independence. So when Rhodes, the Cape premier, decided that Pondoland should be annexed, the Mpondo were in no position to resist. In 1894, with Cape Mounted Riflemen lurking a few miles away, Sigcau was forced to accept annexation to the Cape.

And so the last of the independent southern Nguni chiefdoms was brought under colonial rule.[15]

Long before the process of subjugating the Transkei was completed the Cape government had been considering ways of administering its newly acquired territories. It was soon recognised that the Transkei should be governed in a distinctive way. This was partly because of white fears of being 'swamped', not least in the long term electorally, by an African majority. It was also seen that the Transkei could more readily serve as a labour reservoir if it was administered as a separate entity.

Concerned to break the power of the southern Nguni chiefs, the Cape government established a system of direct, magisterial rule. The Transkei was divided into twenty-seven districts, each to be headed by a white magistrate who served as both a judicial and an administrative officer. Headed by a chief magistrate, the district magistrates were responsible for collecting taxes, dispensing justice, and acting as links between the districts and the administrative authorities in Umtata. The districts were divided into locations, over each of which was placed a headman, appointed by the administration. These appointed headmen were mostly district chiefs or ward headmen or, in some cases, individuals who had no traditional authority. The effect of this system was to curtail drastically the powers of chiefs, especially in the judicial sphere. Their jurisdiction in criminal cases was taken away; and their official responsibility was to be reduced merely to arbitrating in civil cases according to customary law. Even in these cases ultimate jurisdiction lay with the magistrate. However, the chiefs did derive one negative advantage from this system. Their reputations among their own people were not tainted through having to act as agents of the colonial administration.

Alongside this administrative structure a council system was introduced into the Transkei in the 1890s. The objective was to curb African electoral power, which had been potentially enhanced by the incorporation of the Transkei into the Cape. From 1895 councils were gradually introduced into each magisterial district of the Transkei. They were not representative bodies, as four members of each council were nominated by the district headmen and two were appointed by the Governor. The quarterly meetings of the council were chaired by the district magistrate, whose presence inhibited free discussion. Moreover, the resolutions of the district councils had to be scrutinised by the magistrate. In effect the councils were powerless, serving as little more than forums for debate.

The objective of the council system was to provide an appearance of local self-government while at the same time effectively excluding black Transkeians from the Cape's non-racial franchise. The Cape constitution of 1853 had granted the vote to males of any race who either earned £50 a year or occupied property to the value of £25. The number of African voters was never large, and only a small proportion of the total African population at the Cape was enfranchised. But the number grew, and election candidates were increasingly forced to take the interests and views of black voters into account. The annexation of the Transkei considerably expanded the number of potential African voters. Measures were accordingly taken to restrict the growth of the African electorate. An Act passed by the Cape parliament in 1887 declared that land held under communal tenure was inadmissible as a property qualification for the franchise. This effectively disfranchised many Africans, who were further disadvantaged by the 1892 Franchise and Ballot Act, which raised the property qualification from £25 to £75.

African electoral power was further restricted by the Glen Grey Act of 1894. There were three main provisions to the Act. Firstly, it provided for the division of unalienated land in the district into allotments of about four morgen each. The allotments were to descend by primogeniture and were to be held in practice under individual tenure, but for the purpose of the franchise this was to count as communal tenure, thereby disfranchising the occupants. Secondly, a labour tax was imposed on African males who were unable to show that they had worked for three months out of twelve outside the district in which they resided. And thirdly, a council system was established in the district. Although the Act was first applied specifically to the Glen Grey district, its land tenure provisions were later extended to the southern Transkei, and it provided the basis for the council system that was to be introduced gradually into the Transkei. The Act also represented another stage in the process of African disfranchisement; and its strand of labour coercion was indicative of the changing character of the political economy of southern Africa.[16]

Labour coercion became necessary because of the resilient, independent character of the African rural economy in the nineteenth century. This resilience was manifested in the growth of an African peasantry; it was a characteristic of the northern Nguni, as we have already seen, and of the southern Nguni. The myth that precolonial African economies were entirely self-sufficient has long since been dispelled. Among the southern Nguni a propensity for surplus production existed before the arrival of whites. The Xhosa, for instance, participated in a regional trading network which brought them iron from Thembuland, Portuguese beads from Delagoa Bay, skins from Pondoland, and iron and copper from the Tswana. Among the commodities exported by the Xhosa were cattle, tobacco and dagga. As Peires has remarked, 'The Xhosa economy was neither static nor subsistence-orientated.'

The expanding settlement of white colonists in the eastern Cape both created new opportunities and introduced new pressures for the southern Nguni. Trade between the boers and the Xhosa had been carried on since the early nineteenth century, with the Xhosa trading cattle and ivory for copper, iron and beads. The arrival of the British settlers in 1820 added a new vigour to the exchange. Initially the colonial authorities frowned upon this trade. But, unable to curb it, they decided to regularise it. In 1824 the government instituted a regular fair at Fort Willshire near Ngqika's country. The fair rapidly developed into a major trading centre, as Peires shows:

The first seven months drew 50 441 pounds of ivory, 16 800 pounds of gum, about 15 000 hides and 137 trading licences. Xhosa from as far as the eastern side of the Kei and Thembuland attended the fairs, which seem to have attracted some two or three thousand at a time.

From 1830 the colonial government allowed traders to operate beyond the Keiskamma River. By 1835 there may have been as many as 200 traders active in Xhosa territory.

Further north colonial traders were also operating in Pondoland from the 1820s, albeit on a small scale. It was not until the 1860s that the Pondoland trade expanded, as the Mpondo began to barter large quantities of cattle to traders from Natal. They were exchanged for various items — blankets, firearms, horses, metal implements, beads, copper wire and trinkets. Textiles were imported to make more hides available for export; styles of dress changed accordingly. The horses and firearms strengthened the military capability of the Mpondo.

This early trade was double-edged in its effect on southern Nguni society. On the one hand the trade had a destructive impact. The export of cattle drained the region of a commodity that represented a major source of wealth and carried great social significance. Some of the imported items did not stimulate any new kinds of productive activity among the southern Nguni themselves. Indigenous crafts might be undermined, and a new dependence was created on imported manufactured goods, especially textiles and hardware. On the other hand the trade opened up new markets and created opportunities for producing a surplus. Moreover, some of the imported commodities, notably ploughs, did expand productive capacity and assisted the growth of a local peasantry.

One of the characteristics of this peasantry was its capacity for innovation and adaptation. The recent research of Bundy and Beinart has provided ample evidence for this. Southern Nguni peasant farmers, particularly among the Mfengu, Thembu, Xhosa and Mpondo, were quick to respond to new circumstances and opportunities. Imported ploughs were used in ever-increasing numbers, especially from the 1870s. By 1883 the plough and harrow had almost entirely replaced the pick and hoe in the Queenstown district. Many areas of African-occupied land were enclosed; and irrigation was increasingly practised. Crop diversification was another feature of peasant adaptation. Less emphasis was placed on subsistence crops, such as maize and sorghum, and instead there occurred a shift towards more marketable products, like wheat, barley, oats, vegetables and fruit. Similarly, sheep and wool came to play a prominent role in the peasant economy. There was a striking growth in African ownership of sheep in the 1860s and 1870s, as peasants came to appreciate the value of wool as a cash commodity. In the late 1870s and early 1880s, for instance, woolled sheep were introduced into Pondoland in significant numbers.

The capacity of peasants to produce a surplus depended considerably on their access to labour and land. It seems that peasants were generally able to utilise family labour to solve the one problem. And land could be purchased or rented. Many white landowners in the Cape found it profitable to lease tracts of land to African tenants. Some tenancy arrangements involved the rendering of labour service; other tenants might pay cash or a portion of their produce to the landowner as rent. In certain districts of the eastern Cape in the 1870s the renting of land by Africans was common. Bundy supplies some evidence:

> From Fort Beaufort it was reported that 'vast numbers of Kafirs have been allowed by landed proprietors in this district to hire ground from them'; in Bedford the majority of Africans living in the district were share-croppers ... and in Alexandra Africans could lease ground for agricultural purposes at very cheap rates.... The *Cape Commission on Laws and Customs* was told in 1883 that most Africans in Albany electoral division rented land from white farmers.

There were also opportunities for Africans to buy land. A Cape proclamation of 1858 permitted Africans to purchase Crown land at £1 an acre. By 1864 over 500 Africans had between them bought 16 200 acres. Moreover Crown land, as well as land at some mission stations, could be rented on the basis of individual tenure.

Access to land and labour provided some of the necessary means for peasant farming. But there were also other incentives and stimuli that came into play. One such stimulus was the missionary influence. Mission stations, as we have seen, provided access to land. Missionaries transmitted new skills and technologies. And they instilled an individualist ethic that broke some of the communal bonds of chiefly society. Bundy emphasises 'the role of the missionaries as torch-bearers of capitalist social norms and the market economy, as advocates of increased trade and commercial activity'. It would be a gross exaggeration, of course, to suggest that missionaries created the African peasantry; but their influence did serve to hasten the integration of many Africans, especially the Mfengu, into the colonial economy.

Another major stimulus to peasant activity was the enlargement of the market. The discovery of diamonds in the late 1860s, followed by the opening of the Rand mines in the 1880s, boosted considerably the demand for numerous products. The growing urban communities had to be fed; and the rising demand lifted the prices of meat, draught animals, grain, fruit and vegetables. White farming lacked the capacity to meet this demand; and there is substantial evidence that African peasant farmers over a wide area responded positively to these market opportunities.

Peasant activity seems to have been stronger in the Ciskei than the Transkei; the peasantry is more readily associated with the Mfengu than with any other section of the southern Nguni. In the 1840s and 1850s it was the Mfengu who showed themselves to be the most vigorous and enterprising peasant farmers. They sold tobacco, firewood, cattle and milk, as well as surplus grain. Many Mfengu in the Peddie district possessed wagons and oxen which they used to transport their products to towns. In the early 1860s at another Mfengu settlement near Alice 900 men out of a total population of 4 600 grew cereals and vegetables and exported 5 000 bags of grain and a little wool each year. In 1867 thousands of Mfengu moved across the Kei to a new settlement, when Governor Wodehouse allocated to them Fingoland and part of the Idutywa Reserve. There they continued to display their acumen and enterprise.

While the Mfengu may have predominated among the southern Nguni peasantry, there is also much evidence to show that other communities were producing a marketable surplus. Bundy tells us of some of the activities of the western Xhosa in the early 1860s:

> Amongst the Ngqika at Umgwali, some 500 peasants marketed their wares in neighbouring villages, selling especially wheat, butter and maize, while the Stutterheim Ngqika, short of cattle, were relying increasingly on agriculture and were keen to invest in woolled sheep. Near Kingwilliamstown over three hundred family heads had bought 1,675 acres of land from which they raised for sale as surplus 6,000 bags of grain and 2,000 bags of wool.

A large number of Ngqika and Ndlambe peasants sold their produce to storekeepers in Alice. The Thembu in the Queenstown district also earned a reputation for themselves as enterprising small farmers. Some Thembu came to be known as producers of wool. By the early 1870s it was reported that Thembu farming was improving: the plough was becoming widely used, and wagons were owned in increasing numbers. In 1876 the estimated exports from emigrant Thembuland were: 'wool worth £50,000, hides and skins worth £4,000, grain and timber worth £3,000 each; and about £70,000 of merchandise was sold locally.'

Surplus production among the Mpondo tended to centre on cattle during the middle decades of the nineteenth century. But from the 1880s the Mpondo peasant economy became more diversified. In the late 1870s and early 1880s woolled sheep were brought into Pondoland in significant numbers. Although pastoral production still predominated, there was also a shift towards cultivation. Maize, sorghum and tobacco were among the commodities exported by the Mpondo at this time.

The 1880s may have represented the zenith of the southern Nguni peasantry. By then it had become, in Bundy's words,

> geographically much more widespread and numerically far greater than before 1870; in all the predominantly African areas of the Cape, as well as in those districts of the Transkei over which the Cape exerted influence but not yet formal rule, a peasant class had emerged. Peasants still included a core of mission-based or mission-oriented peasants, but they were by now greatly outnumbered by non-mission peasants.

The growth of a peasantry wrought significant social and political changes in southern Nguni society. In this period chiefly authority came to be broken by colonial subjugation. It was further undermined by the changing political economy of the time. African tenancy and freehold arrangements weakened the chief's control over access to land. The shift to cultivation and the enlarged productive capacity resulting from the increased use of ploughs enabled homesteads to become more independent from chiefs in acquiring food. The chief's control over production was thus reduced.[17]

Peasantisation created new divisions and tensions within southern Nguni society. A process of incipient class stratification developed with the growth of what might be called a 'rural petty bourgeoisie'. As Bundy has observed, 'social antagonisms generated by the uneven spread of peasant practices could take violent forms. The 1880–81 uprisings saw a high incidence of attacks by rebels upon mission peasants and other innovators.' And in Pondoland the importation of firearms, a result of peasant activity, affected the struggle for power between chiefs.

While the southern Nguni peasantry may have reached its zenith in the 1880s, the seeds of its decline were also being sown in the last quarter of the nineteenth century. As was the case with Africans in Natal, the southern Nguni peasantry at this time was afflicted by ecological crises and by strains deriving from the changing political economy of southern Africa.

Between 1873 and 1896 the world's advanced capitalist economies were hit by a recession, the adverse effects of which were also felt in peripheral regions such as southern Africa, as farmers suffered from the falling price of their products. This was also a period when southern Africa felt the force of a series of natural disasters. In the late 1870s the Xhosa were afflicted by droughts, at a time when the people were suffering from the consequences of war and rebellion. In 1894 and 1895 Pondoland was struck by a severe drought, that was exacerbated by a series of locust plagues. And from 1896 southern Africa was ravaged by a rinderpest epidemic. It destroyed 80 to 90 per cent of the cattle in the Transkei, and almost as many in the Ciskei. It was 'an economic disaster', the effects of which Bundy has detailed:

> it liquidated much of the peasant's capital, adversely affected his credit-worthiness, made ploughing more difficult and transport facilities rarer and dearer. The immediate effect was to impoverish thousands of peasants and to force Africans onto the wage labour market in considerably greater numbers than before.

In spite of the devastation wrought by these crises, many African communities displayed remarkable powers of recovery. The Mpondo, for instance, were quick to replenish their herds in a few years after the rinderpest epidemic. Ultimately it was the wider structural changes occurring in the character of the southern African economy that were to have the more far-reaching effects on the peasant and subsistence economies of the southern Nguni.

The development of large-scale diamond-mining in the 1860s and gold-mining in the 1880s represented the most fundamental change. Both industries required large supplies of labour; and the imperative of cost minimisation demanded that this labour be cheap. Although there was a long history of participation by southern Nguni in the labour market, this had always tended to be discretionary rather than coerced. Moreover, the resilience of the rural economy in the third quarter of the nineteenth century made it unlikely that the required quantity of labour would be forthcoming. However, by the end of the nineteenth century southern Nguni were joining the flow of migrant labourers to the mines in ever-increasing numbers. The twin pressures of natural disaster and state intervention served over time to limit access to the means of production and undermined the southern Nguni rural economy. Access to land, for instance, was being curbed. The wars and rebellions in the years 1877 to 1881 had been followed by land expropriations. And from the 1890s the Cape began to legislate against African squatter peasants by restricting African tenancy arrangements on white-owned land. Not only was land becoming scarcer, its productive capacity was also declining as the southern Nguni population increased, bringing about overcultivation and overgrazing. In these circumstances the process of proletarianisation became marked, manifesting itself in a massive drift into wage labour. In 1893 some 27 511 people left the Transkei in search of work; by 1898 this figure had risen to 61 033.

While the trend towards proletarianisation was becoming more apparent, it was not until the twentieth century that it became entrenched on a large scale. As late as the 1890s there was still much evidence of peasant activity among the southern Nguni. African peasants, especially in Fingoland and Emigrant Tembuland, were still marketing surplus grain and wool. The Mpondo were largely able to resist the forces of proletarianisation until after the turn of the century. Only a small percentage of Mpondo became migrant labourers in the 1890s. As Beinart has noted, 'The crux of Mpondo economic independence ... was their wealth in cattle.' Other branches of peasant activity seem to have been thriving in Pondoland at a time when many southern Nguni communities were experiencing severe economic stress.[18]

It is difficult to trace exactly the course of the peasantry's decline. African rural impoverishment only assumed dire proportions in the twentieth century (and will thus form a prominent theme in Part Three). What is beyond question is that the nineteenth century saw the flowering of an African peasantry. Bundy's pioneering work has provided substantial documentation of its existence. As we have seen, the growth of the peasantry had socio-political as well as economic implications. The individualist ethic that lay beneath peasant activity broke some of the communal bonds of 'tribal' society. And in the late nineteenth century there were other movements and forces entering into play that reinforced this trend.

Just as mission stations had been catalysts of peasant activity, so the missionary influence permeated other areas of southern Nguni life. The economic individualism acquired by the peasantry was paralleled by an individualist ethos that spread into the political, social and intellectual lives of a growing number of Africans. New opportunities, that were not dependent on the will or authority of a chief, opened up in the fields of politics, journalism, education and the church. In response to these opportunities there emerged among the southern Nguni an elite group of educated Africans, a nascent petty bourgeois class. And just as the Mfengu had been a major element in the peasantry, so they were in the forefront of this new elite. Not tightly bound by a 'tribal' order or by chiefly authority, the Mfengu were particularly receptive to the individualist ethic; and having suffered the tribulation of displacement and dispossession during the *difaqane* they were eager to find new forms of security.

Some opportunities for African involvement in Cape electoral politics were provided by the Colony's non-racial qualified franchise. There was never to be a large number of African voters; and only a small proportion of the African population of the Cape came to be enfranchised. Admitted to the franchise were males of any race who either earned £50 a year or occupied property to the value of £25. This meant that African voters were drawn from what Trapido has called 'the new social class, consisting largely of ministers of religion, school-teachers, magistrate's clerks, interpreters, small traders, and peasant farmers'. Election candidates were compelled to take notice of their African voters. Some candidates tried to create African constituency organisations. They used influential Africans to assist their campaigns; and they relied more and more on African agents to win African electoral support.

African political activity in the late nineteenth century was not just confined to involvement in Cape elections. Efforts were made by Africans themselves to mobilise African opinion on a variety of issues affecting African interests. Petitions were sent to the colonial parliament or to London, usually on African initiative. African deputations were organised and mass meetings were held to protest against legislation that infringed African rights. In 1884 a weekly Xhosa newspaper, *Imvo Zabantsundu*, was founded. Edited initially by John Tengo Jabavu, a prominent Mfengu member of the educated elite, *Imvo* served as an organ for articulating grievances and mobilising opinion. Ngcongco has described its role:

> Between 1884 and 1890 Jabavu used his newspaper as a most effective weapon to hit at segregatory legislation, to expose politicians or political groups whose attitudes towards Africans were motivated by feelings or ideas of racism, as well as to speak generally on behalf of the down-trodden and other victims of injustice.

The growing African elite also made considerable efforts to organise itself. As early as 1879 the Native Educational Association was founded, and in 1883 the South African Native Political Association. Though the early organisation lacked scale and often permanence, a greater amount of continuous activity occurred at grassroots level and a greater measure of continuity existed between some of the earlier associations and later, more established bodies like the South African Native Congress than have previously been recognised.

The Christian church had much to do with the emergence of this African elite among the southern Nguni. As we have seen, mission-based Africans were prominent in the ranks of the peasantry. Education was obtained at church-linked institutions, pre-eminent among which was Lovedale College at Alice. Lovedale was opened in 1841, and it later produced, in Saunders's words, 'a new generation who were to engage actively in Cape politics and take up publicly political positions on matters of concern to the African community'. Generally though, the Christian influence made for the adoption of cautious, defensive stances by this elite. Confrontation was avoided, and the basic approach was accommodationist. The African independent churches that were beginning to emerge towards the end of the nineteenth century possibly represented an exception to this. One such church had been founded in 1883 by Nehemiah Tile among the Thembu in the Transkei. These churches did not just represent an assertion of African religious independence, but also an expression of protest against colonial rule.

The Christian influence may have infused caution and conservatism into the early African educated elite. In this way it set the tone for the early activities of the African National Congress (ANC). However, it also had more long-term implications for the growth of African opposition movements in South Africa in the twentieth century. The Christian influence broke down ethnic and tribal loyalties and therefore helped to lay the foundations for a broad-based nationalist movement.

The southern Nguni were the first Bantu-speaking people to resist the white advance in South Africa. We have seen here how this resistance was continued in the middle decades of the nineteenth century. We have also seen how new forms of opposition were beginning to emerge among the southern Nguni towards the end of the century. The eastern Cape frontier district has thus been an important formative arena in shaping the growth of African resistance and opposition to white domination.[19]

7
THE SOTHO AND VENDA: PEASANTISATION, RESISTANCE AND INCORPORATION

The southern Sotho

The area occupied by the southern Sotho west of the Drakensberg and north of the Orange in many ways bore the brunt of the upheavals of the *difaqane*. Yet in this area there also took place a remarkable regenerative process, in the shape of the emerging Basotho state. It was in a large measure owing to the shrewdness and resilience of Moshoeshoe that large numbers of southern Sotho and other refugee groups were able to survive under the protective umbrella of this state.

The greatest disruption and destruction experienced by the southern Sotho occurred during the height of the *difaqane* in the 1820s. But throughout the long period of Moshoeshoe's reign until his death in 1870 the southern Sotho continued to experience and survive a series of pressures and tensions. Some of these pressures were carried over from the *difaqane*. For instance, the tension that had developed in the 1820s between Moshoeshoe and his main southern Sotho rival, Sekonyela, the Tlokwa chief, remained unresolved for several years. The two managed to maintain an uneasy peace until their conflict revived in the late 1840s. A series of raids and counter-raids culminated in Moshoeshoe's launching a crushing and decisive attack against the Tlokwa in 1853, an attack that virtually destroyed the independent Tlokwa chiefdom.

To the west the *difaqane* continued to throw up large groups of refugees who came to press upon Moshoeshoe's state. In the years 1833–4 about 12 000 people migrated from this direction into Moshoeshoe's sphere of influence. These were mostly Tswana, but also included Kora, Griqua and 'Bastards'. A particularly large Tswana settlement, comprising about 7 000 members of the Rolong chiefdom, was established at Thaba Nchu under the leadership of Moroka. Moshoeshoe welcomed the newcomers, whose settlements he looked upon as buffers protecting him against potential aggressors from the west.

In a similar vein Moshoeshoe welcomed an entirely different kind of newcomer in the early 1830s. In 1833 he issued an invitation to three Frenchmen from the Paris Evangelical Missionary Society, and permitted them to start operating in his state. They were later followed by Roman Catholic, Anglican and Methodist missionaries. Moshoeshoe's welcoming attitude towards the missionaries was shaped largely by secular considerations. He saw mission stations, sited in peripheral regions, as further strengthening the protective cordon around his state. Not only did the missionaries perform a defensive function, but they also served as agents of expansion, moving into areas where Moshoeshoe's authority was doubtful or vulnerable. Moshoeshoe further valued missionaries as advisers. In particular, Casalis, one of the first three Paris Evangelicals to come to Lesotho, was accorded special status. He advised Moshoeshoe on his dealings with whites, and read and wrote his official correspondence.

In order to derive these benefits Moshoeshoe had to make concessions to the missionaries. He allowed their basic proselytising work to go ahead unimpeded. Moshoeshoe even agreed to review or abolish certain long-standing Basotho customs and practices that the missionaries considered incompatible with Christian values. In 1840, for instance, he repudiated the initiation rites that adolescent Basotho were expected to undergo; and in 1843 he took a stand against witch-killing. Generally, though, the missionary impact on the southern Sotho went further than this. They founded schools and taught literacy. And they strove to achieve a broader 'civilising' influence. As Judy Kimble has pointed out, 'The Paris Evangelical Mission Society ... explicitly tied the propagation of the gospel to their encouragement of commodity production, particularly wheat, the consumption of European goods, and labour for the white colonists.' Moshoeshoe himself rapidly acquired a taste for imported commodities; by the mid-1820s he was in possession of horses, saddles, European clothes, household utensils and other colonial products.

It would be a mistake, however, to exaggerate the missionary impact. While prepared to make some concessions, on other issues Moshoeshoe stood firm. For instance, he retained the practice of polygamy in Basotho society; and his own receptiveness to Christian teaching was little more than half-hearted or pragmatic. Among the wider southern Sotho population the missionary influence was tenuous and uneven. By the mid-nineteenth century the number of converts represented only a small fraction of Moshoeshoe's 80 000 followers; and most converts seem to have been concentrated in a few 'pockets' where missionary teaching had taken hold. While many southern Sotho adopted an equivocal or indifferent attitude, there was also a considerable degree of outright hostility. Several senior members of the royal family who did not share Moshoeshoe's tolerance towards the missionaries were openly hostile to Christian teaching. These differing responses created divisions within the court and among the wider populace. Moreover, further cleavages later arose out of sectarian rivalries between the various mission societies. There were tensions between the Wesleyans and Anglicans, and between the Wesleyans and the Paris Evangelicals; while the arrival of the Catholics divided the loyalties of the Basotho themselves.[20]

Within a few years of the missionaries' arrival, another more threatening pressure came to bear upon the southern Sotho. Since the 1820s trekboers from the Cape Colony had been steadily pushing the grazing frontier north of the Orange River. In the mid-1830s this process gave way to a large-scale boer migration; and by 1837 abut 5 000 Voortrekkers had moved across the Orange River. Initially relations between these newcomers and the southern

Sotho were friendly. Local chiefs looked upon them as sojourners, and were even prepared to grant the trekkers temporary grazing rights and a staging area. And Moshoeshoe, in his own shrewd way, saw the trekker presence as a possible counter to any threats that might emanate from the Ndebele or other hostile groups.

This easy relationship was short-lived, as wrangling over land rights soon developed. While Moshoeshoe and other chiefs reckoned to have granted only temporary access to land, the boer occupants within time came to claim permanent title. It was at this point that Moshoeshoe began to look towards the British for assistance. In 1843 he signed a treaty of friendship with the Cape Governor, Sir George Napier. The treaty also defined Moshoeshoe's territory as being limited by the Orange River and by a line running 25 to 30 miles west of the Caledon. The Napier Treaty failed to settle land disputes with the boers, and in 1844 Moshoeshoe announced that all land exchanges between his people and the trekkers were null and void. A year later Moshoeshoe reached a new agreement with Napier's successor, Maitland. This divided Moshoeshoe's territory into alienable and inalienable areas. Moshoeshoe agreed that a part of the Caledon–Orange triangle would form one such alienable area where boers could be granted occupancy, but not title, on a rent-paying basis. A portion of these rents were to help fund a British resident, who would act as an agent of the British government in Transorangia.

Moshoeshoe had hoped to find an ally in the British, but his hope was to be frustrated, as the potential ally became a temporary enemy. The British Resident, Major Warden, soon turned against Moshoeshoe. He made no attempt to remove boers from Moshoeshoe's inalienable land. What is more he looked upon Moshoeshoe as an overmighty chief who should be humbled. To carry out his objective Warden in 1851 assembled a combined force of troops, white farmers, Griqua, Kora and Rolong, and launched an attack on Moletsaṇe's Taung as the prelude to a move against Moshoeshoe. Moshoeshoe intervened and his followers repelled Warden's attack at the Battle of Viervoet. In 1852 the High Commissioner, Cathcart, made another attempt to use force to browbeat Moshoeshoe into submission. The southern Sotho again displayed their resilience in warding off this threat to their independence.

Under the Bloemfontein Convention of 1854 the British abandoned Transorangia. The Convention not only removed British authority from the Orange River Sovereignty, but also left undefined the disputed western boundary of Basutoland. It was thus hardly surprising that in this vacuum boer–Basotho tensions became heightened. As Thompson has noted, 'Conflict was inherent in the situation the British administrators left behind them when they evacuated the Orange River Sovereignty in 1854. Two communities were competing for control of the Caledon valley and the grasslands stretching northwards to the Vaal.'

Initially relations between Moshoeshoe and Hoffman, the first president of the Free State, were amicable. But in 1855 Hoffman was ousted, partly because he was considered to be pursuing too soft a line with Moshoeshoe; he was replaced by Boshof, a hard-liner. Much of the Free Staters' overt bitterness towards the Basotho seems to have centred on the issue of stock theft. This, though, was not the fundamental basis of the conflict. Stock theft was something that Moshoeshoe tried hard to curb; it was essentially a pretext used by the boers to further their claims to Basotho land. Moshoeshoe himself knew this: 'Believe me,' he wrote to the British High Commissioner, Grey, in 1857, 'the real cause of dispute is the ground. They wish to drive my people out.'

The Free State–Basotho war that broke out in 1858 'arose primarily', in Thompson's words, 'out of the situation in the lower Caledon valley, where black villages and white farms were interspersed between the boundary set by Maitland and claimed by Moshoeshoe, and the boundary set by Warden and claimed by the Free State.' The war was short-lived. The boers were not the first to be thoroughly daunted by the prospect of attacking Thaba Bosiu. They soon retreated, demoralised and in disarray, returning to the Free State, where in the meantime Basotho raiding parties had been attacking boer farms, seizing livestock and burning homesteads. Both sides in the conflict agreed to accept the arbitration of Sir George Grey. The imperial High Commissioner tried in effect to produce a compromise. Under the terms of the Treaty of Aliwal North of 1858 the disputed territory, claimed by both the Free State and the Basotho, was divided in half, the eastern portion being granted to Moshoeshoe, the western portion to the Free State.

After the war both Moshoeshoe's kingdom and the Free State experienced internal difficulties which may have contributed to the eventual outbreak of another war. It appears that the ageing Moshoeshoe, now over 70, was losing his grip on his state. His weakening authority set off a scramble for wealth and power among territorial chiefs and his own sons. The Free Staters were also internally divided and demoralised. And their economy was suffering from major setbacks — the trade cycle depression, lack of credit, and severe drought.

In this context both parties drifted towards a second war. Land once again formed the key issue. The Free State had for long coveted Moshoeshoe's fertile land across the Caledon: in 1857 *The Friend* had invidiously compared the inferior white-occupied land to the 'unsurpassed grazing grounds and cornfields' of the southern Sotho. Furthermore, the northern section of the 1858 boundary had not been delimited; and from 1860 Moshoeshoe's northern chiefs had begun to expand in this area, moving into territory which was loosely occupied but which theoretically belonged to the Free State.

In May 1865 the Free State declared war against the southern Sotho. In the early stages of the conflict the burghers again found Thaba Bosiu impregnable; Moshoeshoe's mountain fortress withstood two assaults. But gradually the Free Staters gained the ascendancy; boer commandos destroyed Basotho villages and captured vast quantities of stock. By April 1866 Moshoeshoe and other Basotho chiefs had been forced to accept unfavourable peace terms which severely truncated the Basotho kingdom, and gave the Free Staters much of the fertile land that they had coveted.

Scattered hostilities continued well into 1867 as the Free State forcibly took control of its newly won territory. This devastating process brought the Basotho close to disintegration. Moshoeshoe again pleaded for British imperial intervention and protection. Late in 1867 the British government was keen to adopt the sub-imperialist option, hoping that the Basotho state might be annexed to Natal. But in 1868 the High Commissioner, Wodehouse, went beyond his instructions and proclaimed the annexation of Basutoland to Britain. The annexation and the Convention of Aliwal North that followed it had the effect of sealing Basutoland's boundaries approximately to their present-day configuration, and reducing its agricultural lowlands to a third of what they had been in the 1850s. Then for a brief period of three years the British set about trying to establish a colonial administration, imposing a hut-tax and formulating regulations for magisterial rule. But the British government at the time was always more committed to the sub-imperialist option than to Basutoland itself, and in 1871 Britain handed over the territory to the Cape.[21]

In the meantime, Moshoeshoe had died in 1870. A few weeks before his death he had finally been converted to Christianity. His had been a remarkable career. He had presided over the growth of the Basotho state during a period of immense upheaval and turmoil. He had withstood enormous pressures during the *difaqane* and the period of boer expansion. A shrewd diplomat, he had even turned some of these pressures to his own advantage, playing off enemies or potential enemies against each other.

Since the 1820s Moshoeshoe had been the key figure in welding together the Basotho state. Its population had grown rapidly in size: by 1848 it was estimated to be about 80 000 people, by 1865 about 150 000. Moreover, it was a very diverse population, comprising peoples of different origins and cultures. Although predominantly composed of Sotho, many Nguni, San, Kora and Griqua groups also came to be incorporated. It thus became an enormous problem to maintain the integrity and cohesion of the polity. To secure this Moshoeshoe necessarily had to delegate and devolve power. While he maintained a firm grip on the core area of the state, he would delegate authority to his kinsmen in outlying areas, or allow considerable autonomy to immigrant communities that had been incorporated.

Moshoeshoe's own role was crucial in holding the state together. Firstly, he exploited the institution of marriage. As Burman has observed, 'To enhance his personal status and extend or strengthen his influence, Moshoeshoe married women from many different chiefly families; in 1833 he already had thirty wives, by 1864 about 150, some of whom were the daughters of his subordinate chiefs.' Secondly, he used his wealth for political advantage. Moshoeshoe was by far the wealthiest man in the state, being particularly rich in livestock. Through the judicious dispensation of gifts and loans he was able to do much to ensure the loyalty of his followers.

Although Moshoeshoe often relied upon advisers, especially his councillors, close kinsmen, and missionaries, he was the ultimate repository of power. So crucial was his central role it was widely believed that the state would disintegrate without Moshoeshoe at the helm. Indeed, signs of disintegration had begun to appear from the mid-1850s when illness and age were weakening Moshoeshoe's grip. Rivalry and jealousy came to develop among his sons and brothers. Moshoeshoe's four most senior sons were Letsie, Molapo, Masopha and Majara. Their prominent and favoured position aroused bitterness among Moshoeshoe's brothers, notably Posholi, Mopeli and Lesaoana, and among some of the sons of his other wives. Even among the four senior sons tensions existed. There was the likelihood that Molapo and Masopha would break away from Letsie, the heir-apparent, after Moshoeshoe's death. Furthermore, the chiefs of the allied Taung and Phuthi peoples, Moletsane and Moorosi, each with his own following and territorial base, were increasingly asserting their independence.

The annexation of Basutoland to the Cape in 1871 did little to halt this tendency towards disintegration, as the Cape adopted a divide-and-rule approach to the administration of the region. The territorial extent of chiefly authority was limited to specific districts. And the actual powers of chiefs were undermined by the imposition of direct magisterial rule. In particular, their judicial and military authority and their powers of land allocation were severely circumscribed.

Further divisions among the southern Sotho arose out of the varying responses of different chiefs to Cape rule. Some, like Masopha, adopted a defiant stance; others, like Letsie and Molapo, were diffident or even prepared to collaborate. In 1873, for instance, Molapo actually assisted the administration in the capture of the rebel Hlubi chief, Langalibalele, who had fled into Basutoland from Natal. However, by the late 1870s the southern Sotho were to offer more concerted resistance to the Cape administration.

The first to rebel was Moorosi, the Phuthi chief. The Phuthi, who were originally Nguni from Natal, had come to occupy land in the southern region of Moshoeshoe's state. There they enjoyed both a considerable degree of autonomy and the protection that adherence to Moshoeshoe provided. In 1877 an insensitive and high-handed magistrate, Hamilton Hope, was stationed among them. As Hope strove to assert his magisterial jurisdiction, so the ageing Moorosi clung to his chiefly authority. A series of crises culminated in the Lehana affair late in 1878. Although Hope had been removed from his magistracy, his successor, Austen, took it upon himself in November 1878 to arrest Lehana, Moorosi's son, for horse theft. It was a dubious charge, as the evidence against Lehana was thin. Moorosi much resented the treatment meted to his son, and on New Year's eve he organised a rescue party which enabled Lehana and some fellow-prisoners to make a successful escape from jail. In the deteriorating situation that followed, colonial reinforcements were brought in, and Austen abandoned his magistracy. By the end of February 1879 Moorosi was in open rebellion. He retreated to a mountain fortress with about 300 followers. There they held out for about eight months. They successfully withstood two colonial assaults, but succumbed to the third in November. Moorosi himself, along with most of his kin and councillors, was killed in this assault. Other rebel leaders were subsequently imprisoned; and many of Moorosi's former followers were sent as labourers to white farms in the Cape. The crushing of the rebellion marked the end of the Phuthi chiefdom.

Within a year a much larger, more widespread rebellion had broken out among the southern Sotho. The rebellion came to be called the Gun War because it was seemingly provoked by the Cape government's attempts to disarm the southern Basotho. Alarmed by the inflow of firearms brought into Basutoland by migrant labourers returning from thc diamond fields, the Cape parliament in 1878 passed the Peace Preservation Act, which provided for the disarmament of Africans who came under the Cape's authority. The following year Sprigg, the Cape premier, personally visited Basutoland to announce at a *pitso* that the southern Sotho were to be disarmed under the terms of the Act.

Letsie, the paramount chief, advised his people to submit to the demand. But Masopha, his powerful half-brother, adopted a more defiant attitude which gained wide adherence among the southern Sotho. Masopha fortified Thaba Bosiu and launched punitive raids against villages loyal to the administration. In September 1880 the rebellion erupted. Lerotholi, Letsie's son and heir, played a prominent part in the rebels' military operations. Joel, Molapo's son, was active in the north, while Masopha blockaded and twice attacked Maseru. Some southern Sotho, though, collaborated with the colonial forces — notably Jonathan, Joel's half-brother, and his followers. Early in 1881 a military stalemate developed as neither side could gain the ascendancy. So in April both parties accepted the arbitration of the High Commissioner, Sir Hercules Robinson. The terms laid down by Robinson reflected the Basotho's strong military position: there was to be a full amnesty, and permission was granted for guns to be licensed.

In military and political terms the Gun War represented one of the few successful acts of African resistance against colonial rule to occur in southern Africa. However, the southern Sotho were unable to capitalise on this, as internal divisions and tensions soon tore them apart. The Gun War temporarily subsumed the rivalry between Masopha, Letsie's half-brother, and Lerotholi, Letsie's son and heir. But after the war had ended the tension revived. It was marked by their differing attitudes to the colonial authorities: while Lerotholi became more accommodating, Masopha remained defiant, refusing to accept either a magistrate or the imposition of taxes. At the same time the conflict between Joel and Jonathan continued. In this worsening situation the Cape government lost control, and the British government reluctantly agreed to resume responsibility for Basutoland. (As a result of this transfer back to Britain in 1884, most of the southern Sotho came to escape eventual incorporation into South Africa's Bantustan structure; and their independence, attained in 1966, as a result received international recognition.)

One consequence of the reimposition of British rule was a shift away from the magisterial rule practised by the Cape administration to a more 'indirect' form of control. This was initiated by Marshal Clarke, Resident Commissioner from 1884 to 1894. He tried to strengthen the position of the paramount chief, who it was hoped would serve both as a focus of unity and as a partner in imperial government. This policy suited Letsie, who remained as paramount until his death in 1891, as well as his successor Lerotholi. It did not suit Masopha, who remained jealous and hostile towards his superiors. Finally in 1898 Lerotholi attacked Masopha's stronghold at Thaba Bosiu. After surrendering, Masopha was deprived of his chieftainship and forced to abandon Thaba Bosiu. A year later he died.[22]

The gradual political incorporation of the southern Sotho into Britain's southern African empire was paralleled by their growing integration into the colonial economic nexus. During the middle decades of the nineteenth century the southern Sotho economy was marked by three main characteristics or trends: increasing commercial penetration, resilient domestic rural production, and voluntary labour migration.

Traders from the Cape had been operating among the southern Sotho since the 1830s. They brought in clothing, hardware, firearms, horses, liquor, and other commodities. By the 1850s the possession of horses was widespread, and many Basotho had acquired firearms, mostly of an inferior, obsolete character. This trade stimulated local production. The traders mainly came in search of grain, cattle, wool and hides. It seems that the southern Sotho were largely able to meet this demand. In 1837 they had grain stored for four to eight years; in 1844 whites came in large numbers to buy grain. By the mid-1850s the southern Sotho were cultivating the land on both sides of the Caledon River; and they had, in Thompson's words, 'made LeSotho the granary of the southern high veld'. They had also built up their flocks of sheep and goats and their herds of cattle. Voluntary labour migration represented a third way in which the southern Sotho were becoming integrated into the colonial economy. As Kimble has pointed out, by the late 1860s, 'Basotho had been renowned for over four decades as good workers on white-owned farms, and in colonial towns and ports.'

The opening of the diamond mines enlarged the market for food and labour and so brought further prosperity to the southern Sotho. In 1873 they exported an estimated 100 000 bags of grain and 2 000 bales of wool. More trading stations were established. In 1878 Basutoland's grain exports were estimated to be worth £400 000 and her wool exports £75 000. The growth of diamond mining also increased the flow of migrant labour from Basutoland. By the end of the 1870s it was estimated that there were about 5 000 southern Sotho adult males employed on the diamond fields. This was in addition to another 5 000 employed on colonial railway works, and perhaps the same number again working on farms and in towns in the Free State and the Cape Colony. By the end of the century about 30 000 migrant workers were leaving Basutoland annually.

An interesting explanation for this increase in the flow of migrant labour has recently been put forward by Kimble. Avoiding simplistic models she has discerned three main pressures or stimuli in operation. Firstly, the royal Kwena lineage was concerned to acquire firearms as a means towards perpetuating its dominance. The flow of migrant labourers to the diamond fields was thus partly geared to the needs of this lineage. Secondly, missionaries often encouraged their converts to participate in temporary labour migration. It was seen as a way of breaking free from traditional obligations and chiefly authority, and of acquiring the economic individualism that formed part of the missionary ethic. And thirdly, from as early as the 1870s numerous homesteads were beginning to experience increasing impoverishment. Land expropriation, overpopulation, taxation, and intensified exploitation by chiefs all combined to force more and more adult males to resort to labour migration.

For the southern Sotho the last seven decades of the nineteenth century were a traumatic era. They had experienced the turmoil of the *difaqane*, the pressure of boer expansionism, British imperialism and Cape sub-imperialism, and the penetration of missionaries and traders. But, utilising the defensive potential of their terrain and assisted by Moshoeshoe's shrewd leadership, the southern Sotho displayed a remarkably resilient capacity for survival. They withstood the external invasions of the *difaqane*; and they were able to keep the boers at bay for several years. When in military difficulty they called in allies or played off one enemy against another. Although brought under colonial rule they engaged in one of those few acts of African resistance that could not be quelled by colonial military power. And the political and military determination of the southern Sotho was matched by their economic resilience, manifested in their energetic response to growing market opportunities. However, towards the end of the century there were warning signs that Basutoland was becoming a peripheral labour reservoir dependent on its links with South Africa's sub-metropoles. In the twentieth century it was increasingly to take on this character.[23]

The Tswana

The *difaqane* had brought great devastation and turmoil to the Tswana. Their relatively flat terrain did not provide them with any obvious defensive mountain strongholds. Moreover, the multiplicity of chiefdoms that characterised Tswana society persisted throughout the *difaqane*. There did not emerge any new centralised structures or dynamic leaders that might have welded the Tswana into a single more formidable polity. The Tswana were thus particularly vulnerable to the depredations of Mzilikazi's Ndebele and Sebetwane's Kololo. Some Tswana chiefdoms resisted these attacks; some fled; others accepted temporary Ndebele or Kololo overlordship.

The departure of the Ndebele in 1837 did not eliminate all external pressures on the Tswana. The Ndebele continued to pose a threat to the northern Tswana for many years. But what is more important, over the next few decades the Tswana were to become increasingly subjected to the forces of white expansionism, colonialism and capitalism. The missionaries steadily advanced along the road to the north, followed in their wake later in the century by Rhodes and his agents. Transvaal boers encroached upon Tswana territory in the east. In the middle decades of the nineteenth century the advent of traders represented the penetration of mercantile capital into Tswana society; in the last quarter of the century labour recruiters came as agents of mining capital.

The boer intrusion did bring some short-term relief for the Tswana. It was boers who, aided by groups of Hurutshe, Ngwaketse and Rolong, finally drove the Ndebele north of the Limpopo. The removal of this particular threat enabled many Tswana chiefdoms to reconstruct themselves. Some were able to reclaim their former lands, but others, like the Ngwaketse, struggled to do so in the face of boer competition and encroachment.

In the mid-nineteenth century the Kwena were the most powerful and prominent of the Tswana chiefdoms. During the late 1840s and early 1850s the chief Sechele, a convert of David Livingstone's, had built up Kwena power. He expanded his following by providing land for refugee Tswana communities. Furthermore, he accumulated firearms for his people by bartering with traders. From this power base Sechele tried to exercise influence over the neighbouring Ngwato and Ngwaketse chiefdoms. He intervened in successive internal Ngwato dynastic struggles. In the 1850s Sechele supported the claims of Macheng to the Ngwato chiefship, which was held by Sekgoma. In 1857 Macheng succeeded in overthrowing Sekgoma. But Sechele soon came to dislike Macheng's style of rule and his allegiance to Mzilikazi. So in 1859 Sechele's army organised the deposition of Macheng and the re-instatement of Sekgoma. In 1866 Macheng regained the chiefship by exploiting to his advantage a dispute between Sekgoma and Sekgoma's two Christian sons, Khama and Kgamane. Sechele was thus unable to bend the Ngwato to his will; and from the time of Khama's installation as Ngwato chief in 1875 it was the Ngwato who gradually assumed the most prominent position among the Tswana chiefdoms. Sechele also failed to extend his influence over the Ngwaketse to the south. The Ngwaketse had suffered heavily from Ndebele attacks, which had driven them into the Kalahari. But from the late 1850s they began to revive and consolidate once again under the leadership of Gaseitsiwe, who ruled from 1857 to 1889. Gaseitsiwe encouraged non-Ngwaketse immigrant groups to establish towns within his chiefdom; and he expanded Ngwaketse territory eastwards at the expense of the Hurutshe.

Of the more southerly Tswana chiefdoms the foremost were the Rolong and Tlhaping. Towards the end of the eighteenth century the Rolong had divided under four brothers, Rratlou, Seleka, Rrapulana and Tshidi, each group taking on the name of its leader. All four groups suffered disruption during the *difaqane*, when many Rolong took refuge at Thaba Nchu near the Caledon River in the south-eastern region of the present-day Orange Free State. After the *difaqane* the Seleka-Rolong remained at Thaba Nchu, but in the early 1840s the others returned north-westwards to their former territories south of the Molopo River.

In the 1850s the Tshidi-Rolong, under Chief Montshiwa, and the Rratlou-Rolong, under Gontse, came under pressure from the boers. So Montshiwa and his followers took refuge with the Ngwaketse until returning to their Molopo territory in 1877. The Rratlou-Rolong for their part found refuge with a group of Tlhaping. The Tlhaping had also broken up into a number of sections on the death of Chief Mothibi in 1838. The largest section came under the authority of Mothibi's brother, Mahura. Two smaller chiefdoms to the south were ruled by Mothibi's sons, Gasebone and Jantje.[24]

Throughout this post-*difaqane* reconstruction era missionaries continued to penetrate Tswana chiefdoms. Missionary expansion into this region had begun in 1816 when the London Missionary Society (LMS) opened a station in Tlhaping territory. They were followed by the Wesleyans, who began operating among the Rolong in 1823. From the early 1840s the LMS intensified their evangelising efforts among the Tswana. Within a decade of his arrival in South Africa in 1841 the leading light of the LMS, David Livingstone, had preached to the Ngwaketse, Ngwato and Tawana. Lutheran Hermannsburg missionaries began their work among the Kwena in the 1860s; and the Dutch Reformed Church established a mission among the Kgatla at Mochudi in 1877.

The Tswana chiefdoms were probably the most fertile field for missionary operations in the whole of southern Africa. Most Tswana chiefs accepted the missionary presence, while some even welcomed it. Chief Sechele was baptised by Livingstone in 1848. Khama, the Ngwato heir-apparent, was converted in 1860, to be followed by Lentswe, the Kgatla chief, in 1892, and Bathoen, the Ngwaketse chief, in 1894. Montshiwa, chief of the Tshidi-Rolong from 1849 to 1896, adopted a more ambivalent attitude. Initially he tolerated missionaries, but he also persecuted Rolong converts. From the 1880s he became more amenable to Christianity without ever taking the step to personal conversion.

It was probably a sense of vulnerability among the Tswana — arising from their *difaqane* experience, boer expansion, and the continuing Ndebele threat — that made them particularly receptive to missionary influence. Missionaries were welcomed as advisers and potential mediators; and their presence was seen as a form of protection against external aggression.

How do we assess the missionary influence on the Tswana? They introduced literacy and Western forms of education. Schools were built; religious and educational materials were translated and published in local dialects. The missionaries attacked various common Tswana practices, especially polygamy, the payment of bridewealth, circumcision and rainmaking. But only those chiefs who became converts, like Khama, Bathoen and Lentswe, were prepared to yield on any of these issues. Khama and Bathoen, for instance, abandoned rainmaking, while Lentswe turned it into a Christian ceremony.

Christianity and the missionary influence formed at times a source of division within Tswana communities. The Ngwato ruling elite in the mid-1860s was divided between adherents of Christianity and those whose response to Christianity was either lukewarm or hostile. Later Khama used Christian ideology to strengthen his own chiefly power and undermine the position of the *dikgosana* ('aristocracy'). In the mid-1890s Khama's tendency to consider himself 'in all things ecclesiastical and temporal supreme' (as one contemporary observer put it) brought him into a dispute with three of his half-brothers. Similar divisions occurred among the Ngwaketse. In 1887 a civil war was reported to be developing in Kanye, the Ngwaketse capital, between the adherents and opponents of Christianity.

Missionaries can also be seen as the forerunners of British imperialism in

Bechuanaland. As Dachs has written,

> Missionary prejudice favoured British rule, and the promotion of their own interests required British rule. So Mackenzie observed in 1876: 'On the whole, the old feudal power of the native chiefs is opposed to Christianity; and the people who are living under English law are in a far more advantageous position as to the reception of the Gospel than when they were living in their own heathen towns surrounded by all its thralls and sanctions.'

Thus missionaries like Mackenzie constantly called for the extension of British control, arguing that this was, in Dachs's words, 'essential to peace, to preserve order between the races, to maintain the road to the north from Transvaal control and to promote change'. In the 1880s missionary hopes were largely fulfilled. However, it would be a mistake to see British imperial intervention in Bechuanaland simply as a response to the missionary agitation. Rather the missionaries should be seen as one particular agency in the wider process of imperial expansion.

Explorers and traders represented another agency of expansion. They began to infiltrate Tswana society early in the nineteenth century. They came in search of ivory, cattle, ostrich feathers, and skins, introducing in exchange a variety of imported commodities, including beads, brass and copper wire, knives, and clothing. It is known that the Tswana made use of imported horses and firearms during the battles of the *difaqane*. From the 1860s Shoshong, the Ngwato capital, served as the major trading entrepot for Ngamiland, Matabeleland and the Zambezi Valley. This commerce seems to have been highly profitable for both parties involved in the exchange. Tlou provides some of the details:

> In the 1850s the ivory trade brought Cape merchants about 1,000 pounds sterling a year, from an outlay of 200 pounds sterling. In 1877 Khama's ivory sold for 3,000 pounds sterling. This was profitable since production costs were relatively low, with a substantial amount of the ivory coming from tribute. In the 1870s and 1880s, the Zambezi trade, most of which passed through the Ngwato capital, averaged 200,000 pounds sterling a year.

On the Tswana side the trade was particularly profitable for chiefs. To secure their share of the income, some chiefs issued decrees making the trade in feathers and ivory a chiefly monopoly.[25]

In the meantime the Tswana had been facing a more direct threat to their independence — from the Transvaal boers. Initially the boer presence on the highveld had been welcomed as a counter to the Ndebele; and many Tswana allied with the boers to drive the Ndebele across the Limpopo in 1837. But once the Ndebele had been removed, the boers themselves began to make grandiose claims to territory and sovereignty. By virtue of conquest they claimed almost all the land bounded by the Vaal, the Kalahari, the Limpopo and the Drakensberg. They also asserted their sovereignty over the Tswana on the grounds that they had displaced the Ndebele as the Tswana's overlords. While it is true that some Tswana chiefdoms had been subject to the Ndebele, notably the Hurutshe, Rratlou-Rolong and Kgatla, others like the Tlhaping, Ngwaketse, Kwena and Ngwato had not.

The boers interpreted the 1852 Sand River Convention to mean that the British had conceded to them undisputed ownership of all territory north of the Vaal, and had left them free to fix the western boundary of the Transvaal where they chose. With this confidence they soon proceeded to try to browbeat the Tswana into submission. In the same year as the Convention a boer commando attacked the Kwena town of Dimawe, trampled the inhabitants' fields, dispersed the defenders, and took away over 200 women and children to work on boer farms as 'apprentices'. In the same raid Livingstone's mission at Kolobeng was attacked and ransacked. And soon afterwards the Tshidi-Rolong were punished for failing to join the raid against the Kwena. In 1858 the boers attacked the Tlhaping and killed their chief, Gasebone, on the pretext of recovering stolen cattle. In 1868 the South African Republic proclaimed all territory west of the Transvaal up to Lake Ngami as part of its domain. In the following year the Kgatla chief, Kgamanyane, was publicly flogged in front of his people by a boer field cornet, said to have been Paul Kruger. Kgamanyane's crime was failing to provide labour for boer farms.

The boers were unable to assert their full authority over the Tswana, but they did succeed in encroaching steadily onto Tswana land. Either land was simply expropriated, or else loose tenancy arrangements with Tswana chiefs were arbitrarily converted into tenurial rights. The boers also tried to exploit divisions, actual or potential, within Tswana society, and to seek out Tswana collaborators. This was the particular strategy of President Burgers in the 1870s. As we shall see later, it was a strategy that brought turbulence to the Transvaal–Tswana frontier in the early 1880s.

Pressure on Tswana land was exacerbated by the discovery of diamonds in the late 1860s. The diamondiferous region near the Vaal River was claimed separately by the Orange Free State, the Transvaal, the Griqua, the Rolong and the Tlhaping. The dispute among the claimants was submitted to the arbitration of Keate, the Lieutenant-Governor of Natal, in 1871. Theoretically the Keate Award granted some recognition to the rights and claims of the Griqua and the Tswana, but in practice it turned out otherwise. The annexation of Griqualand West to Britain in 1871 hastened the process of Griqua proletarianisation. And in the mid-1870s a large area of Tlhaping land was surveyed into freehold farms by Frank Orpen, the Surveyor-General of Griqualand West. Much of this land was sold, and the Tlhaping displaced by these sales were herded into locations, which comprised only a small proportion of the lands they had previously occupied. At the same time boers from the Transvaal were steadily encroaching into Tlhaping and Rolong territory by signing bogus treaties with local chiefs. It was this loss of land and power that led some sections of the Tlhaping to join the Griqua Rebellion of 1878. Foremost among these was Botlasitse, a chief who had lost part of his land to the Transvaal. It was Botlasitse's family who led assaults against a local white trader and a white farmer. For a while he and his followers besieged Kuruman before the rebellion was put down late in 1878. Many Tlhaping stayed out of the rebellion, and some — notably Mankurwane and his followers — actively assisted the British in quelling it, along with the Rolong chief,

Montshiwa.

The legacy of this division between Tswana rebels and collaborators was to be carried over into the frontier disturbances of the early 1880s. After the British abandonment of the Transvaal in 1881, boers exploited internal Tswana divisions to pursue their expansionist ambitions. Some boers allied themselves with Botlasitse and the Kora chief, Massouw, against Mankurwane. The latter was forced to sue for peace and to cede to the boers much of his land, out of which they created the republic of Stellaland. At the same time the boers were allying with Moswete, a Rolong chief living in the Transvaal. This combination attacked Montshiwa who, like Mankurwane, was forced to surrender land, from which another boer mini-republic, Goshen, was carved.

In 1882 Mankurwane and Montshiwa appealed to the British for help. Initially the British government was unresponsive. However, by the end of 1885 vast tracts of Tswana territory had been brought under British overlordship. This development came about as a result of the convergence of three strands of imperialism — the missionary, capitalist and strategic imperatives. The first was represented by John Mackenzie, a missionary who campaigned vociferously for imperial protection of the Tswana. Cecil Rhodes, the chief agent of the capitalist imperialists, was for his part determined to keep open a route for imperial expansion into central Africa. And the strategic imperialists at the Colonial Office were concerned to prevent the Transvaal from linking up with the Germans, who in 1884 had declared a protectorate over southern South West Africa. So early in 1885 a British expedition under General Warren arrived in Bechuanaland. The boers were driven away, and a British protectorate, first established in Bechuanaland south of the Molopo River in 1884, was extended north of the Molopo to incorporate the Ngwaketse, Kwena and Ngwato chiefdoms, among others. Later in the year the region of the protectorate south of the Molopo was converted into a crown colony, to be known as British Bechuanaland until it was incorporated into the Cape in 1895.[26]

For the southern Tswana in British Bechuanaland the immediate impact of colonial rule was experienced in loss of land. The British recognised boer titles to land in Stellaland. And large tracts of land were alienated for white settlement, especially in the productive area east of Kuruman and along the Molopo River. The northern Tswana in the Bechuanaland Protectorate did not suffer so seriously from land alienation, although some chiefs granted concessions to individual adventurers. They might have suffered badly had the proposed transfer of the Protectorate to Rhodes's British South Africa Company been carried through in the mid-1890s, as the Company generally showed scant regard for African land rights. As it turned out, the transfer was shelved after the Jameson Raid, which thus had the indirect effect of preserving the northern Tswana's access to considerable areas of territory. In 1899 substantial reserves were demarcated by the British administration for the northern Tswana chiefdoms; only a relatively small strip of land on the Protectorate's eastern border was alienated for white settlement and for railway purposes.

The experience of falling under, first, direct British colonial rule and, later, Cape administration marked the demise of the southern Tswana's political independence. However, the protectorate status of the northern Tswana was less clear-cut. In theory the northern Tswana chiefs were entitled to retain control over the internal affairs of their chiefdoms. It is true that in practice the northern Tswana continued for the most part to remain directly subject to their own chiefs and courts; and their social relations continued to be governed primarily by their own laws and customs. On the other hand there was no doubt that the British administration exercised ultimate authority. From 1891 the High Commissioner was authorised to legislate by proclamation for Bechuanaland. Appeals against a chief's judgment could be heard jointly by the chief and a local magistrate. Then in 1899, in addition to the demarcation of the reserves, a hut-tax was imposed.

Although British 'protection' to some extent eroded the authority of northern Tswana chiefs, it also had the converse effect. Chiefs like Khama of the Ngwato and Sebele of the Kwena exploited the imperial presence to strengthen their own position against internal rivals and factions. The type of 'indirect rule' policy that the British adopted in the Bechuanaland Protectorate required strong chiefly authority. Khama, in particular, took advantage of this to build up an autocracy at the expense of the *dikgosana*, the Ngwato 'aristocratic class'. Sebele, too, strengthened the Kwena chiefship. When a dissident faction emerged in the early 1890s in opposition to Sebele, the imperial government arbitrated and upheld Sebele's chiefship.

A kind of symbiotic relationship developed between the British and the Tswana. The British needed Tswana cooperation in keeping open the route to the interior; and the Tswana needed British protection against the boers and the Ndebele. For this reason the colonial subjugation of the Tswana was a relatively peaceful process. However, Tswana acquiescence was not something that the British could take for granted. In the mid-1890s, for instance, the imperial government strove to offload the administrative responsibility for the Protectorate onto the British South Africa Company, which had its own reasons for wanting to acquire the territory. The Protectorate chiefs, aware of the Company's intentions and methods, protested vigorously against the proposed transfer, sending a delegation to England where a lively campaign was conducted in support of their cause. In the event the transfer fell through as the Company disgraced itself in the eyes of the imperial government because of its involvement in the Jameson Raid.

More overt resistance to colonial rule was offered by the southern Tswana late in 1896 and early in 1897, shortly after they had been brought under Cape administration. The trigger that precipitated the Langeberg Rebellion late in 1896 was the shooting of Tlhaping rinderpest-infested cattle that had strayed out of the Taung Reserve. There ensued hostile demonstrations by the followers of Galeshiwe, the chief of the Tlhaping in the Phokwani area. Attacked by a force of colonial police, Galeshiwe and his followers fled to the Langeberg mountains where they joined the Tlharo chief, Toto. There the rebels managed to sustain their resistance until the rebellion was suppressed in August 1897. The Langeberg Rebellion was an expression of deep discontent. The Tlhaping had lost vast areas of land through the 1884 London Convention and the 1886 Land Commission. They much resented the 10*s*. hut-tax imposed in 1896, and the 2*s*. 6*d*. wheel-tax introduced in 1894. In addition, authority had been steadily eroded under British and Cape rule. The rinderpest epidemic and the shooting of infected cattle finally drove them to rebellion.[27]

The Langeberg Rebellion occurred at a time when Tswana society was experiencing considerable strain, brought on partly by natural disaster and partly by the demands of an expanding and encroaching capitalist system. Three decades earlier the situation had been rather different. Then, the discovery of diamonds created new opportunities for the southern Tswana in particular. Shillington has shown how individual Tlhaping during the early period of the diamond discoveries in the late 1860s engaged in selling diamonds to white traders, prospectors and dealers. During the 1870s the growing demand for food and fuel at the diamond fields was partly met by Tlhaping producers and suppliers, who sold off 'the natural surplus of the rural economy'. However, Shillington goes on to point to some of the longer-term consequences of this activity. The 'self-reliant rural economy' of the Tlhaping suffered as production for the market was overemphasised; and the Tlhaping came to depend increasingly on imported commodities. Moreover an incipient process of class stratification within Tlhaping society became apparent, with the wealthier 'entrepreneurs' gaining at the expense of the lower strata of society.

Initially the Tswana tended not to enter the labour market at the diamond fields. It was only after 1876, when a special recruiting mission was sent through Bechuanaland, that more Tswana labour was forthcoming. By 1881 there were 2 571 Tswana working on the diamond mines. There was no significant migration of Tswana labour to the Rand gold mines in the late 1880s and early 1890s. Tswana workers were employed, though, in the construction of the railway and telegraph along the road to the north, and also by mining companies in Rhodesia.

By the end of the nineteenth century labour migration was becoming less of a discretionary option and more of a necessity for the Tswana. The process of proletarianisation gathered momentum in the 1890s as they were increasingly cut off from the means of production by a combination of colonial policy and ecological disaster. The rinderpest epidemic hit the Bechuanaland Protectorate with devastating impact early in 1896. An estimated 90 per cent of the cattle in the Protectorate either died or were destroyed. Sebele lost all but 77 of a herd of 10 000 cattle. The epidemic was followed by three years of drought and locusts. Many people died of famine and disease. By late 1896, some 2 000 Ngwaketse had died from sickness or starvation. All in all, the Tswana economy was devastated. Agriculture was damaged not only by the drought, but also by the loss of oxen that were used for ploughing. The transport business was also wrecked. According to one contemporary observer, 'hundreds of waggons were left abandoned, many with whole teams of sixteen bullocks lying dead and rotting in their yokes....'

Other factors militated against the economic independence of the Tswana in the 1890s. The completion of the Mafeking–Bulawayo railway in 1897 undermined local production, by bringing in cheaper imported commodities, and so finally destroyed the carrying trade. Although the demarcation of the Protectorate reserves in 1899 left the northern Tswana with extensive territory in the short term, it also deprived them of some of their most productive land in the east; and in the longer term the reserves would become overcrowded and overstocked. The hut-tax, introduced also in 1899, represented another link in the chain of coercion that undermined the northern Tswana's capacity for self-sustaining independent production. It was thus not surprising that from the 1890s the Bechuanaland Protectorate began to become a fertile field for labour recruiters from the Rand mines.[28]

In the last three-quarters of the nineteenth century the Tswana experienced a succession of pressures. They suffered the trauma of the *difaqane*; missionaries tried to attack their social structure, and boers tried to grab their land; the British undermined their political independence, and the emergent capitalist system subverted their economic independence. The Tswana also experienced various forms of incorporation in this period. Some were absorbed into the emergent Ndebele state, while others became attached to mission communities. Colonial subjugation involved various sections of the Tswana in differing forms of domination; some fell within a British crown colony, at least for a 10-year period, while others came under a British protectorate; some were incorporated into the Cape, others into the Transvaal and Free State. In spite of this the process of subjugation involved less violence and disruption for the Tswana than it did for the southern and northern Sotho or for the southern and northern Nguni.

The Pedi and Venda

During the 1820s the Pedi polity had almost disintegrated under the strain of internal division and the turmoil of the *difaqane*. But the Pedi revived from the late 1820s under the leadership of Sekwati, who used similar strategies to those of Moshoeshoe in ensuring the polity's survival and regeneration. Sekwati refrained from rash military confrontations. Rather he forged advantageous alliances and swelled the ranks of his followers by incorporating refugee groups. And, like Moshoeshoe, Sekwati avoided an excessive centralisation of authority. This point has been emphasised by Delius:

> Although the Maroteng chiefdom secured a formal dominance, its position in relationship to the more powerful of its subject chiefdoms could verge on that of *primus inter pares*. The latter exercised a regional hegemony within the polity and the paramountcy's authority over some notionally subject groups was in fact mediated through these regional foci of power.

But while local chiefs exercised considerable autonomy, there was no doubting the ultimate authority of the Maroteng paramount. This authority could be enforced or expressed in a number of ways: by force of arms, by dispensing wives to subordinates, by regulating access to land, by asserting ritual superiority, or by serving as a final court of appeal. Without this degree of centralisation the Pedi would not have been able to withstand external pressures for as long as they did throughout the middle decades of the nineteenth century.

The Pedi were situated uncomfortably close both to the Swazi state and to the trekker communities of the eastern Transvaal. The first major Swazi raid against the Pedi was launched, and repulsed, in the late 1830s. Thereafter there were constant rumours of further imminent Swazi raids against the Pedi polity, which had served as a haven for Swazi dissidents and refugees. But it was not until 1869 that another major Swazi attack was directed against the Pedi heartland, again unsuccessfully.

In the mid-1840s a trekker community settled east of the Steelpoort River, close to the Pedi domain. The presence of the boers was initially tolerated by Sekwati; and in 1845 the boer leader, Potgieter, negotiated an agreement with Sekwati whereby the Pedi supposedly granted land rights to the trekkers. Although the exact terms of the agreement are unknown, it seems likely that Potgieter interpreted it to mean that title to the land in question was transferred, while Sekwati saw himself as merely ceding usufructuary rights.

Relations between the boers, centred at Ohrigstad, and the Pedi were soon to deteriorate. Potgieter began to make increasingly onerous demands on the Pedi for tribute and labour. And the boers blamed the Pedi for cattle losses and labour desertion. In 1852 a boer commando under Potgieter attacked a Pedi stronghold at Phiring. The siege failed but the boers did capture a large quantity of Pedi cattle and goats. The following year Sekwati moved his capital to another mountain fortress, Thaba Mosego. There the ageing paramount managed to maintain an uneasy peace with his neighbours until his death in 1861.

Sekhukhune, Sekwati's eldest son, succeeded to the paramountcy. This succession was initially accepted by Mampuru, Sekhukhune's younger brother and rival claimant; and Sekhukhune's grip on power seemed to be firm. But in 1862 an open breach occurred between the two brothers, and thereafter Mampuru embarked on a strategy of exploiting and aggravating internal divisions within the Pedi polity and of building up external alliances. In these circumstances the 'confederal' character of the Pedi polity showed signs of weakening. Subject chiefdoms that had previously recognised the ultimate authority of the Pedi paramount began to assert their independence. Among these were the Kopa and the Ndzundza Ndebele to the south-west of the Pedi heartland, and the Masemola.

Further internal divisions among the Pedi arose out of missionary activity. Although Pedi migrant workers had already come under missionary influence in other parts of southern Africa, the first missionaries to begin operating within the Pedi domain were from the Berlin Missionary Society in the 1860s. Sekhukhune initially showed some goodwill towards the Berliners and their converts. But when these converts came to include members of his own family, including some of his wives and brothers, his tolerance weakened. In

1864 Sekhukhune began a campaign to halt the spread of Christianity, putting pressure on converts to recant. One of the Berlin missionaries, Merensky, decided to leave the Pedi heartland to found a new station at Botshabele to the south-west. It was Botshabele that for a few years provided a haven for Sekhukhune's converted half-brother, Dinkwanyane. The introduction of this division in the Pedi polity further weakened its capacity to withstand the growing pressure and demands emanating from the Transvaal.

In 1863 the Pedi and a boer commando had collaborated in a joint attack on the Ndzundza Ndebele. But by 1876 the Pedi and the Transvaal were at war with each other. This conflict must be viewed against the Transvaal's demands for land and labour and the consequent pressures exerted on the Pedi. By the late 1860s boers in the Lydenburg district were striving to acquire new unclaimed land. In this quest they encroached upon the Pedi domain, reviving old land claims and agreements dating back to the 1840s and 1850s.

In the 1870s the Transvaal's search for labour assumed a more coercive character. The Pedi had engaged in migrant labour on a voluntary basis since the 1840s. They migrated to areas as far-flung as Port Elizabeth, Natal and the diamond fields. Their quest for work seems to have been dictated primarily by a desire to accumulate cattle and guns. Moreover, migrancy was encouraged by Pedi chiefs, who welcomed the importation of firearms and exacted tribute payments from the migrants. By the 1870s the Transvaal was struggling to secure a labour supply in the face of competition from the diamond fields. Labour-coercive legislation was accordingly enacted: taxes and passes were introduced and measures were implemented to restrict African settlement on state or private land.[29]

It has long been the conventional view of historians that when President Burgers led an army of the South African Republic against the Pedi in July 1876, he was doing so to crush the expansionist ambitions of Sekhukhune. Delius has recently rejected this interpretation on the grounds that it fails to situate the war 'in the context of a changing regional and local political economy'. For Delius, the war has to be viewed against a shift in the balance of power in the region. The Pedi paramountcy, buoyed by recent victories over the Swazi, was regaining authority and power. In this situation many Pedi who lived in ill-defined frontier zones and had come loosely under the authority of the South African Republic now felt secure enough to return their allegiance to the paramountcy. This option became especially attractive at a time when boer demands for land, labour and tax were growing harsh and excessive. For the Republic this shifting allegiance exacerbated the shortage of land and labour, and underlined the necessity of destroying the independence of the Pedi. In these circumstances white fears were nurtured to provide justification for an attack on the Pedi. Rumours became rife that a Pedi invasion of the eastern Transvaal was imminent and that Sekhukhune was at the centre of a 'pan-Africanist' conspiracy.

The Republic's army which attacked the Pedi in 1876 included 2 400 Swazi warriors and 600 Transvaal Africans, in addition to 2 000 burghers. Both sides fared badly in the campaign. The morale of the burghers was low;

the Swazi soon withdrew their support; and assaults on Pedi mountain fortresses were generally unsuccessful. On their side the Pedi suffered heavy losses of cattle in commando raids; their plight was worsened by a drought which endangered the food supply; and a number of subordinate chiefdoms shifted their allegiance to the South African Republic. In this stalemate situation, peace negotiations began at the end of 1876. In February the following year a peace settlement was supposedly signed. It was, however, a dubious settlement, and Sekhukhune soon rejected the written terms, which were highly unfavourable to the Pedi. So when the British annexed the Transvaal in 1877 the Pedi still enjoyed their independence.

Continuing Pedi independence was to be as anathema to the new British administration as it had been to the Republic. Theophilus Shepstone, the British administrator of the Transvaal, initially tried to assert imperial hegemony over the Pedi. Although Sekhukhune would not allow himself to be browbeaten into accepting subject status, his own position as paramount was especially vulnerable in 1877 and 1878. There was the crisis of resources; and moreover, Sekhukhune was striving to reassert his authority over formerly subservient chiefdoms which had detached themselves from the Pedi polity.

In October 1878 an imperial force set out to attack the Pedi capital. But owing to drought and horse sickness it was forced to withdraw before even reaching Sekhukhune's base. The British authorities hoped that the defeat of the Zulu in 1879 would persuade Sekhukhune to accept imperial subjugation. The Pedi, though, were not to be so easily persuaded, and in November 1879 the British mobilised a massive invasion force that included 8 000 Swazi and 3 000 Transvaal Africans. This army inflicted a decisive defeat on the Pedi, with Sekhukhune surrendering early in December. Loss of life among the Pedi was enormous; and the major assault of the invaders was left to the Swazi, who lost between 500 and 600 men, as against 13 white soldiers killed.

Sekhukhune was captured and taken to Pretoria. The British appointed Mampuru, Sekhukhune's half-brother and rival, as paramount chief. In 1881 Sekhukhune was released, but within a year Mampuru organised his assassination. The Transvaal government, its independence recently regained, despatched a force against Mampuru, who had fled southwards and taken refuge with the Ndzundza Ndebele. After an eight-month siege Mampuru surrendered. He was hanged in November 1883. The Ndzundza Ndebele chiefdom was broken up and its people given over to boer farms as apprentice labour. The Pedi polity itself came to be divided into two parts by the Transvaal government during the 1890s, each section placed under a different chief. By the end of the century some Pedi acknowledged Sekhukhune II as chief, others looked to a son of Mampuru, and still others to a son of a former regent. As was the case with so many other independent polities throughout South Africa, the last two decades of the nineteenth century saw the end of Pedi independence.[30]

The Venda were largely able to withstand the impact of the two major population upheavals of the 1820s and 1830s, the *difaqane* and the great trek. They ensconced themselves in mountain strongholds in the Soutpansberg, and were thus in a position to avoid the brunt of the *difaqane*. As was the case elsewhere, refugee groups gravitated towards these strongholds, and many of them were absorbed by the Venda.

The presence of the tsetse fly and the mosquito to some extent deterred the trekkers from settling in areas of Venda occupation. Gradually, though, the Venda became drawn into the trekker orbit as labourers and traders. Some Venda worked for white farmers and hunters. Since horses and cattle could not survive the tsetse fly, Venda were also employed as porters. And boers in the nearby village of Schoemansdal traded with the Venda for ivory. The Venda would not, though, permit missionaries to operate in their territory.

The boers also became embroiled in internal Venda dynastic struggles. On the death of Chief Ravele in 1864 the boers opposed the succession of Makhado by supporting a rival claimant. But the boers were not strong enough to secure their candidate's claim. In 1867 boer reinforcements arrived, led by Paul Kruger, the Commandant-General of the South African Republic. Still the Venda held out in their mountain fortresses. The boers thereupon withdrew from the Soutpansberg, abandoning their settlements to the Venda; and Chief Makhado's followers proceeded to destroy Schoemansdal. The few boers who remained in the area paid tribute to the Venda chief to ensure their safety.

The Transvaal government continued to claim jurisdiction over land as far north as the Limpopo. And in the 1880s boers began to reoccupy the Soutpansberg. In the 1890s the Republic despatched a series of expeditions against the Venda, aiming at the piecemeal elimination of their strongholds. Chief Mphephu, who had succeeded Makhado in the mid-1890s, held out. He refused to pay taxes to the Republican government, and clung to Venda independence. Finally, in 1898, it took a force of about 4 000 boers, aided by African allies, to launch a successful assault against Mphephu's mountain fortress. Mphephu fled with about 10 000 followers across the Limpopo into Shona country. 'Thus', as Thompson has put it, 'the last of the traditional chiefdoms of South Africa was conquered just a year before the white people fell out among themselves.' The conquest of the Venda marked the end of the process of colonial subjugation in South Africa.[31]

* * *

The last seven decades of the nineteenth century represented an era of transition and trauma for most African societies in southern Africa. This era begins at the tail-end of the *difaqane* and concludes with all these societies under some form of colonial domination. A number of important processes can be identified in these decades: the consolidation and reconstruction of African states after the *difaqane*; their penetration by white missionaries, traders, concessionaires and land-grabbers; colonial conquest and subjugation, and African resistance thereto; as well as the processes of peasantisation, proletarianisation and incipient class stratification, all of which were stimulated by the mineral revolution.

It must be stressed that these processes took on a great variety of forms in different regions. Growing white penetration, for instance, gave rise to varying responses and a complex set of interactions. Some African societies, notably the Zulu state, restricted or obstructed the missionary presence; others tolerated or even welcomed missionaries, and in doing so often exploited or manipulated them for some political or material advantage. Moshoeshoe used missionaries as political advisers, as defensive buffers, and as agents of expansion; some Tswana chiefs saw missionaries as instruments for underpinning their own power.

It would be a mistake to view white encroachment in these years as a development in which powerful European colonies or republics expanded remorselessly at the expense of helpless African victims. The forms of interaction between black and white that occurred must be viewed against the internal backgrounds of both white and African polities. The Transvaal Republic, for instance, was for much of this period a highly vulnerable nascent state, suffering from internal divisions and lacking a sound economic base. In those circumstances the only way in which boer communities could fulfil their quest for more land was by exploiting divisions within neighbouring African polities. In the 1840s and 1850s they took advantage of tensions and rivalries within the Swazi royal family to wring land concessions from Mswati. In the early 1880s they aggravated internal divisions within Tswana chiefdoms to further their land-grabbing ends; and in the mid-1880s they intervened in the Zulu civil war to secure vast tracts of territory for themselves. These are just a few examples of the many black–white military alliances that were formed in this period. African rulers often exploited the white presence to strengthen their own position against rivals and dissidents, who in turn often resorted to the same strategy. Similarly, whites manipulated these internal divisions in African polities to their own ends.

The process of colonial subjugation also took different forms and met with varying African responses. It took a hundred years of intermittent warfare before the southern Nguni were subjugated. In the case of the Tswana the process of subjugation was relatively peaceful. Some African societies, notably the Zulu and the Pedi, fiercely resisted colonial efforts to destroy their independence. Others, like the southern Sotho, offered their strongest resistance after they had been brought under colonial rule.

While the political independence of African societies had virtually been destroyed by the end of the century, their economic independence had not. Access to the means of production was retained, albeit curtailed by loss of land through conquest and cession, and by ecological disaster. In the middle decades of the nineteenth century there is considerable evidence that a substantial African peasantry was engaged in producing a surplus for the growing market. The discovery of diamonds and gold presented an initial stimulus in the form of a further expanded market. But the advent of mining capitalism also set in motion the process of African proletarianisation. Colonial measures to tax Africans and restrict their access to land served to force an ever-increasing number of Africans to migrate to the labour-hungry mines. This growth of mining capitalism generated many new tensions and contradictions within the political economy of southern Africa. It is the state's attempt to cope with these contradictions that dominates much of the history of South Africa in the next century.

Part Three

THE TWENTIETH CENTURY PROLETARIANISATION, PARTITION, AND PROTEST

8
LAND, LABOUR AND AFRICAN POLITICS : 1900–1936

The southern Africanist historian, like all historians, is forever bedevilled by the twin methodological problems of periodisation and creating suitable categories of analysis. The demarcation of chapter divisions around major turning-points always blurs the continuities; and deciding what constitutes a turning-point hinges on the themes that are being explored. Similarly, when the historian tries to establish convenient analytical units he or she is at once snared in a trap. It is seemingly impossible to avoid the use of racial and ethnic categories in writing southern African history, but the use of such categories tends to imply that racial and ethnic divisions have been key determinants in the region's past. In this way other divisions, such as those of class, can be concealed.

Up until the present section this book has been largely constructed around ethnic and political categories. It has been done so on certain assumptions: firstly, that linguistic distinctions can be made between Nguni and Sotho societies; and secondly, that precapitalist African states and chiefdoms represent logical units of analysis. In this last section it does not make as much sense to use these categories. In an era of industrialisation, urbanisation and proletarianisation, ethnic categories take on less significance. It is true, of course, that African political and ethnic divisions have survived in the twentieth century. While these divisions may have survived partly because they have a life of their own, it could be argued that they owe their survival essentially to the policies of the South African government. This chapter will not, therefore, be organised around such categories, although regional variations and ethno-political divisions will be constantly examined.

Some might question whether the turn of the century represents any real turning-point in the African history of southern Africa. After all, was not the 'great event' of this time, the Anglo–Boer War, essentially a white man's war? It is argued here that the turn of the century does represent a suitable temporal divide. By the end of the nineteenth century all the Nguni and Sotho societies of southern Africa (excluding the Sotho communities of South West Africa) had lost their political independence. The Anglo–Boer War was not simply a white man's war; as we shall soon see, blacks were significantly involved in the struggle. One detects in the decade or so after the war certain economic and political trends that were to affect Africans for the rest of the century. The Peace of Vereeniging and the Act of Union placed severe checks on the political aspirations and rights of Africans. What is more, the labour policies of the mining industry and the commercialisation of white farming hastened the process of proletarianisation among blacks.

The South African War

The widely used label, 'Anglo–Boer War', has recently been rejected as misleading. Warwick has thoroughly examined the involvement of blacks in the war and has accordingly suggested it should be called the 'South African War'. Blacks were not only active participants in the struggle, they also endured much of its suffering and were greatly affected by its outcome.

Both contending sides used blacks in a variety of roles during the war. The British employed blacks to perform scouting and intelligence work, transport driving, portering, construction work and other duties at military camps. Black involvement on the British side was not restricted to non-combatant functions. When the British position was vulnerable late in 1899 various African contingents were called upon to assume defensive roles. Khama mobilised three to four thousand men to guard the Ngwato chiefdom against the boers; the defence of Zululand was entrusted to the Zululand Native Police; and African recruits, mainly Mfengu and Thembu, were called up to protect the Transkeian frontier against boer invasion. On the Republican side, too, blacks were conscripted as farm labourers, wagon-drivers, guides and scouts. And there is evidence that at times blacks fought alongside the boers.

Their involvement in the war brought enormous suffering to blacks. This was especially so when Mafeking and Kimberley were besieged by the boers early in the war. As food became more and more scarce at Mafeking the British officer in charge, Colonel Baden-Powell, drastically curtailed the food rations of the town's Rolong inhabitants. Some Africans in Mafeking were shot for stealing food from white households. Efforts were made to reduce the demand for food by forcing African refugees to attempt escape through the boer lines. This was what Pakenham has called the 'leave-here-or-starve-here policy' of the British. While it seems that many Africans did succeed in escaping, many others were shot by the boers. These casualties must be placed alongside the 1 000 or more other Africans who died during the siege of Mafeking. At Kimberley, too, about 1 500 people died in the siege, almost all of them black.

Historians have generally highlighted the horrendous suffering of boer women and children in the British concentration camps during the later phase of the war. Little attention, however, has been paid to the plight of blacks, thousands of whom were also herded into insanitary, disease-ridden camps. Over 14 000 blacks are recorded as having died in these camps.[1]

The South African War did not just bring death and suffering to Africans. It also created opportunities which many Africans exploited to their own advantage. For instance, the Pedi, who had fallen under the political domination of the South African Republic in the previous two decades, temporarily liberated themselves during the war when supporters of the Pedi paramountcy freed themselves from Transvaal control and re-established much of their former influence in Pedi affairs.

Perhaps of more significance were the opportunities for economic advancement that the war opened for Africans. The British military presence considerably enlarged the market for grain and livestock. It is known that the Ngwato, among others, responded positively to this demand and accordingly prospered during the war. Cattle were exported from the Transkei; and many Basotho profited from the sale of ponies. Black workers who had particular skills, notably drivers, leaders, scouts and blacksmiths, could earn high wages from the British army. As the British pursued their scorched-earth campaign there were opportunities for looting and picking up the spoils of war. And the evacuation of white farms in the Transvaal and Orange River Colony considerably increased the area of land open to African cultivation.

During the war many Africans had identified with the British cause in the expectation that a British victory would bring political and economic advancement for blacks. Their hopes were soon dashed. Under the terms of the Treaty of Vereeniging of 1902, the question of extending political rights to blacks was held over until self-government had been restored to the Transvaal and Orange River Colony. But when self-governing constitutions were granted to these two colonies in 1906 and 1907 blacks were still excluded from the franchise. Moreover, the Union constitution, which came into operation in 1910, while retaining the Cape's non-racial qualified franchise, continued to deny blacks political rights in the Transvaal, Orange Free State and Natal.

In the meantime other developments and trends dampened the hopes of those who had believed that a British regime would accord greater rights and opportunities to blacks. In 1903 Milner, the High Commissioner, appointed the South African Native Affairs Commission to devise a common policy for blacks in the whole region. When the Commission reported in 1905 it came out firmly in support of the principle of racial segregation: it recommended the territorial separation of black and white, urban segregation, and a political system based on racial separation. In the Transvaal the Milner regime had already been putting segregation into practice. Here the formal segregation of blacks in locations was authorised by municipalities; and the Municipalities Ordinance of 1903 denied blacks the municipal franchise.[2]

The African rural economy, 1902–1936

The decade after the war also saw the expectations and aspirations of Africans in the rural economy comprehensively dashed. The war had made land more accessible to Africans in some regions. But in the following years this accessibility rapidly diminished as the state intervened to assist the commercialisation of white farming. And so the decline of the African rural economy gradually set in, leading to dire rural impoverishment in the later decades of the century. Initially the process of decline was not uniform; and in order to draw out the variations over space we must examine the process as it was played out in different regions.

After the war boers in the Transvaal and Orange River Colony were given legal rights to their lands and military assistance to reoccupy their farms. In spite of this the post-war period offered short-term advantages to Africans in these areas. As Keegan has observed, 'In the aftermath of the war, the devastation of Boer farms and herds and the shortage of liquid capital in the settler economy contrasted sharply with the accumulation of stock and agricultural equipment in African hands.' Farms came onto the market because of losses or deaths during the war, and many were bought by Africans. White landowners often found that the best return could be obtained by renting land to African tenants. Alternatively sharecropping became a common practice in these years, especially in the arable districts of the Orange River Colony. 'The white farmers welcomed with open arms any black family with stock and equipment who could plough and sow. In return for a share of his crop, the African cultivator had opportunities that were closed to him in overcrowded Basutoland.' Keegan's research has shown that some sharecroppers could have been cultivating about 50 acres of land, with the more prosperous producing about 300 bags of maize in a season. It was a system that suited white landlords who lacked capital. It reached its peak in the decade after the South African War, and appears to have been 'the dominant relation of production in most of the arable districts of the white-settled highveld' during those years.

Although conditions immediately after the South African War did not favour the growth of large-scale white commercial farming in the Transvaal and Orange River Colony, it seems clear that the British administration envisaged such a development in the longer term. Within a few years a number of factors came into play that favoured the growth of rural settler capitalism. Firstly, new export markets for maize were opened up. Secondly, there was an injection of capital into white farming as new banks were established and the British paid compensation for war losses. And thirdly, the British administration intervened in other ways to subsidise and assist white, but not black, farmers. It extended the railway system and offered favourable rail rates to white farmers; it dispensed grants of equipment and seed; it supplied loans; and it took remedial action against pests and disease.

These advantages changed the outlook of white landowners in the Transvaal and Orange River Colony. It now became more profitable for them to use their land for direct production than to enter into cash tenancies or sharecropping arrangements with African peasants. Not surprisingly, therefore, African tenants and sharecroppers were soon under pressure as the state intervened in the interests of white commercial farmers. In the Transvaal the 1908 Natives Tax Act imposed a £2 levy on rent-paying tenants; and in the northern Transvaal some of these tenants were removed from white farms by direct government action. In the Orange River Colony an Act was passed in 1908 with the intention of prohibiting all forms of African tenancy other than labour tenancy. In the event it could not be implemented because of opposition from the British Colonial Office. But the important point is that the state was manifestly beginning to act against the independent African peasantry in the interests of both white commercial farmers and the mining industry. This intervention was to become even more forceful with the passing of the 1913

Land Act.[3]

In Natal and Zululand a similar picture took shape of African rural economies coming under stress early in the twentieth century. There, however, the South African War had not offered the same kinds of opportunity as in the Transvaal and the Orange River Colony. Furthermore, in Natal the drift towards large-scale white capitalist agriculture had begun earlier, in the late nineteenth century.

Between 1891 and 1908–9 the area cultivated by white farmers in Natal rose from 85 000 acres to 541 000 acres. The stimulus was derived partly from the expanding demand for farm produce in the mining centres, and partly from assistance provided by the Natal colonial state. Railway branch lines were constructed early in the twentieth century to serve white farming areas. The government provided a number of agricultural extension services, and promoted the white occupation and improvement of rural land. The result was that it became much more profitable for landowners to derive an income from their land through production rather than renting.

The main victims of this trend towards white commercial farming were African peasant farmers. Certainly it is true that many African peasants retained their access to land, especially those few wealthier peasants who owned land and were able to respond to the expanding market opportunities. By 1905 Africans in Natal either owned or were about to acquire over 238 000 acres of land. Generally, though, African rent-paying tenants were either evicted or called upon to enter into labour tenancy arrangements; and those who were able to retain their cash tenancies were faced with rising rents. White demand for land also resulted in a massive expropriation of African-occupied territory in Zululand. Consequent upon the recommendation of a delimitation commission, which reported in 1905, 2 613 000 acres of Zululand were thrown open to white settlement, leaving the remaining 3 887 000 acres to the Zulu.

This declining access to land was exacerbated by other pressures that came to bear on the African rural economy. Firstly, the tax burden on Africans in Natal was increased early in the century. Especially onerous was the poll tax that was introduced in 1905, aiming both to coerce labour onto white farms and into white towns, and extract an extra £76 000 of revenue from Natal's African population. Secondly, ecological disasters further worsened the plight of already disadvantaged African rural producers. The rinderpest epidemic of the late 1890s had been particularly devastating. 1903 was a year of drought, and it was followed by the spread of East coast fever over the next few years.

One effect of all this was an enormous increase in the number of Africans who entered into wage labour to earn or supplement their subsistence. According to Bundy, 'Over 200,000 Africans a year sought employment in Natal after the South African War, and about 25 000 left the area each year for work in the Transvaal.' This, though, was not the only response of Natal Africans who were feeling the combined effect of landlessness, taxation and ecological disaster. Within four years of the end of the South African War a major outburst of resistance was to occur in Natal.

The introduction and collection of the poll tax seem to have provided the spark and the occasion for resistance. Early in 1906 three chiefs in the Mapumulo district, supported by their followers, refused to pay the tax; and it seemed that they were prepared to back up their refusal by force. In February twenty-seven members of the Fuze chiefdom also adopted a defiant stance. A police detachment was sent to arrest the rebels. In an ensuing scuffle two of the policemen were killed. Within a few days martial law was declared over the whole of Natal. Those members of the Fuze chiefdom involved in the skirmish with the police were arrested. Of these, seventeen were eventually executed, some publicly. In the meantime colonial troops ranged through those areas where the poll tax was being resisted, using strong-arm tactics to overcome the defiance. The homestead of one chief in the Mapumulo district was bombarded with artillery fire. After surrendering he was punished with a massive stock fine and the confiscation of half of his land.

The poll tax also provoked the resistance of Bambatha, chief of the Zondi in the Umvoti district. In March Bambatha, who identified with those of his followers who resisted the tax, refused to present himself to the authorities in Pietermaritzburg when summoned. When a force was sent to arrest him he fled into Zululand. Bambatha returned to his chiefdom at the end of the month to discover that he had been deposed by the authorities, who had appointed his uncle, Magwababa, as regent in his place. Bambatha thereupon attacked and captured Magwababa. The police were sent in, and a small police party was ambushed by Bambatha, losing four men. As more colonial forces were mobilised to suppress the rebellion, Bambatha fled into the Nkandla forest on the border of Natal and Zululand. From there he was able to broaden his base of support as a number of other chiefs threw in their lot with him. In May the colonial forces began to engage the rebels. At the battle of Mome Gorge, early in June, Bambatha and his followers were routed; hundreds of rebels were killed in the clash, including Bambatha himself and other leaders. The Natal government was confident that this decisive blow had ended the rebellion. But within a few days another uprising began in the Mapumulo district, and this was not put down until the middle of July.

Three to four thousand Africans were killed during the disturbances; on the colonial side eighteen whites died in action, in addition to six white civilians who lost their lives. The scorched-earth strategy of the colonial forces rendered thousands more Africans homeless and destroyed their crops. One effect of this was to force an ever-increasing number of Africans into wage labour. There was also an aftermath of colonial retribution. Large numbers of rebels were tried in various parts of the Colony. Many death sentences were imposed, but all were commuted to life imprisonment.

Retribution was also directed at the person of Dinuzulu, Cetshwayo's son and successor as head of the Zulu royal family. Many whites claimed that Dinuzulu had masterminded the rebellion and should have been dealt with accordingly. At the end of 1907 he was arrested and later tried on twenty-three charges of high treason; Dinuzulu was alleged both to have incited

Bambatha to rebellion and to have harboured rebels. It was a weak case. While it is true that many rebels did take refuge with Dinuzulu, he was neither an organiser nor a participant in the rebellion; indeed, he had professed his loyalty to the colonial government. The greater part of the case against him did not stand up in the court proceedings. Dinuzulu was acquitted on most of the charges, but found guilty of harbouring rebels. He was sentenced to four years' imprisonment, but released by the first Union government.[4]

A survey of African rural economies in the decade after the South African War reveals varying patterns and responses in different regions. In the Transvaal and Orange River Colony the war created a specific set of conditions to which many Africans were able to offer a positive short-term response. In Natal the strain in the African rural economy, wrought by taxation, landlessness, and natural disaster, brought on rebellion in some areas. Among the southern Nguni there were further regional variations.

For the Ciskei and Transkei in this decade a general picture of rural deterioration emerges. As Bundy has remarked, 'Overcrowding and an annual deficiency in subsistence requirements had become the chronic, debilitating marks of the region's underdevelopment.' Symptoms of this deterioration were a growing dependence on imported food, and an increasing resort to migrant labour. By 1911 some 80 000 wage labourers were leaving the Transkei each year, about five-eighths of whom headed for the mines.

The deteriorating subsistence base of the southern Nguni had been brought about by two main factors. Firstly, a growing population had to be sustained by a diminishing land area. Colonial conquest and expropriation in the previous century had involved the southern Nguni in heavy loss of land. Moreover, the gradual commercialisation of white farming, backed by colonial legislation, was imposing pressure on cash tenancies and sharecropping arrangements, thereby forcing numerous African peasants off the land. Secondly, the rural economy was hit by a series of natural disasters. The rinderpest epidemic of the late 1890s was followed by droughts in 1900–1 and 1903; and the East coast fever of 1910–11 ravaged herds and brought on further impoverishment.

This pattern of accelerating rural impoverishment was not universal among the southern Nguni in the early twentieth century. There was a relatively small number of successful peasant farmers who were able to survive the hardships of these years, perhaps because they had a firmer capital base. Moreover, the Mpondo seem to have escaped or overcome this general trend towards the deterioration of the rural economy in the first decade of the twentieth century. Although they suffered heavy cattle losses during the rinderpest epidemic of the 1890s, they were able to display great resilience and adaptability in making a rapid recovery. As Beinart shows, an increasing number of migrant labourers left Pondoland at the turn of the century, earning enough money to enable them on their return to replenish their herds. Cultivation was intensified, as more ploughs were purchased, and it was extended over a wider area of land. Peasant farmers introduced sheep and goats in larger numbers. Some homesteads were able to sell surplus grain and wool to traders. By 1911 the rural economy of Pondoland was looking much healthier than in other southern Nguni regions. Herds had been replenished close to the pre-rinderpest level; and land was not too scarce, there being few signs of overcrowding. However, the year 1911 marked a turning-point, for it was then that Pondoland was hit simultaneously by drought and East coast fever. Again there was an increasing resort to migrant labour: by 1912 over 16 000 men were leaving Pondoland annually. This time the replenishment of cattle herds was a slower process, and it depended on the effective introduction of dipping facilities to counter the fever.[5]

Although there were short-term fluctuations and regional variations it is clear that African rural economies were under increasing strain by the time of Union. Their position was worsened when the Union government intervened to limit further African access to land. The 1913 Natives' Land Act laid down the principle of territorial segregation by setting aside the existing African reserves for African occupation and by prohibiting Africans from buying or leasing land outside these reserves, the extent of which would be fixed at a future date. The Act also sought to eliminate sharecropping in favour of labour tenancy in the Orange Free State province.

The 1913 Land Act was of greater significance in the long term than in the short term. Its immediate impact was limited, and varied from region to region. The Act could not be applied to the Cape because its provisions interfered with that province's non-racial franchise, which was entrenched in the constitution. Nor did the measure bring about a sudden transformation of productive relations. Neither African rent tenancy nor sharecropping was completely eliminated. However, if the African peasantry was not killed off, it was certainly stifled by the Act. Land would now be much more inaccessible. Opportunities for purchasing land were severely curtailed. Furthermore, a large number of African tenants were evicted from white-owned farms. As many observers have seen, the 1913 Act was probably as much concerned with the supply and distribution of labour as with territorial segregation. Thus the Act had the effect of transforming tenancies based on payment in cash or kind, into tenancies based on payment of labour service.

In the longer term the Act served to load the dice very much in favour of white capitalist farming and against African peasant farming. Without the Act there was still a possibility that a class of African capitalist farmers might have developed. Such a development was blocked by the 1913 legislation. However, it is also important to note that the measure, by safeguarding African access to a limited area of land, attempted, in Southall's words, 'to retard the process of complete proletarianization by maintaining the ties of migrant labourers to the land'. In this way the 1913 Act represents one of the foundations of the Bantustan policy that was to develop during the apartheid era.

During the two decades or so after the 1913 Land Act the rural economy of South Africa became increasingly dichotomised on racial lines. On the one hand, white capitalist farming developed rapidly; on the other, the African peasantry remained stunted and the rural subsistence sector continued to deteriorate. After 1910 the state increasingly intervened to assist and subsidise white farming. The establishment of the Land Bank in 1912 made special credit facilities available to white farmers. From the mid-1920s the government passed measures to promote agricultural exports and to protect the prices of farm produce. To stimulate local production the price of imported wheat came to be fixed above the international price, and export subsidies on maize were introduced.[6]

In stark contrast to this trend was the accelerating impoverishment of the African rural subsistence sector. As Bundy has pointed out,

> There exists a vast and depressing body of evidence as to the nature and extent of underdevelopment in the Reserves (and particularly the Ciskei and Transkei) in the forty years that followed the 1913 Act: the details abound of infant mortality, malnutrition, diseases and debility; of social dislocation expressed in divorce, illegitimacy, prostitution and crime; of the erosion, desiccation and falling fertility of the soil; and of the ubiquity of indebtedness and material insufficiency of the meanest kind.[7]

The report of the 1932 Native Economic Commission highlighted the extremely low level of productivity in the reserves. For example, the annual average production of maize in the reserves declined from 640 million lb in the 1921–30 period to 490 million in the years 1931–9.

The fundamental problem was overcrowding, arising out of population increase and land shortage. The 1913 Land Act allocated a mere 7,3 per cent of the total land area of South Africa to the African reserves. It was conceded that this allocation would be insufficient, and the Beaumont Commission was appointed to consider the release of additional areas for African occupation. In its report, issued in 1916, the Commission recommended that an extra eight million morgen of land be added to the reserves. In the event, though, the provision of extra land had to await the 1936 Native Trust and Land Act. This measure earmarked an area of 7 250 000 morgen — essentially based on the Beaumont Commission proposals — to be transferred to the reserves. The Act also exerted further pressure for the elimination of African cash tenancies on white-owned land; the idea was to ensure the labour supply for white farms by coercing cash tenants into labour tenancy.

The first three decades or so of the twentieth century had seen a steady transformation in the relations of production in the rural economy of South Africa. At the beginning of the century there had still been the possibility that capitalist farming could develop on non-racial lines. But the state intervened to assist the commercialisation of white farming and stunt the growth of the African peasantry. The result was to leave thousands of Africans in a state of semi-proletarianisation, either as labour tenants on white farms or as migrant labourers maintaining a partial dependence on the increasingly fragile rural subsistence sector.[8]

Migrant labour, proletarianisation and the urban experience till the 1930s

The growth of the mining industry on the Rand in the late nineteenth century had generated a seemingly insatiable demand for cheap labour. Between 1890 and 1899 the number of Africans employed on the gold mines rose from about 14 000 to 97 000. The South African War severely disrupted mining operations, but in the twentieth century the flow of migrant labourers to the Rand mines continued to increase dramatically. In 1904 there were 77 000 Africans employed in the Transvaal gold- and coal-mining industries. By 1913 this figure had more than doubled to 155 000 and by 1936 had more than redoubled to 318 000.

Explanations of this growing labour migration have tended to focus on push–pull factors. As we shall see, the gold-mining industry operated under certain constraints which could only be overcome by an adequate supply of cheap migrant labour. But this supply was not forthcoming simply because the mines demanded it. There was a major push factor at play, notably the deteriorating base of the African rural economy that forced more and more people to obtain their subsistence from wage labour. However, even when one takes into account pull and push factors the explanatory model remains too mechanistic. African rural impoverishment could not guarantee the labour supply. Accordingly the mines found that to secure sufficient quantities of labour a recruiting system had to be established. As Alan Jeeves's work has shown, recruiting itself was a profitable form of enterprise; and for many years it was a highly competitive business, in spite of the efforts of mine-owners to centralise and monopsonise the system.

Until recently the Rand mines have been heavily dependent on the supply of migrant labour from outside South Africa's political boundaries. Between 1904 and 1929 Mozambique was the main single source of African labour, always supplying at least 40 per cent of the Transvaal mines' total labour-force during those years. The British Protectorates of Basutoland, Bechuanaland and Swaziland between them provided about 10 per cent of the total in an average year from 1914 to 1930. The main South African source of migrant labour to the mines was the Cape, which always supplied at least 25 per cent of the total after 1915, and by the mid-1930s was supplying about 40 per cent; about three-quarters of the Cape's migrant labourers came from the Transkei.

Scholars disagree as to the impact that this manpower drain had on the economies of the reserves. Bundy points out that according to the 1936 census, about 54 per cent of the adult population of the reserves was absent (not only, of course, working on the mines, but also in other occupations and geographical areas). As a result, he argues: 'In all the Reserve areas, those who remained at home *and* were fit bore an added burden of dependency; those not fully able, but pressed into agricultural work, performed fitfully and feebly. Ploughing with cattle, in areas where the masculinity ratio was abnormally low, was neglected....' This view is shared by Southall, but not entirely by Beinart and Simkins. Beinart found that in Pondoland migrant labourers would often return to their homesteads when their labour was most needed in the crucial months of the agricultural cycle. And Simkins argues that the outflow of population reduced overcrowding in the reserves and thereby to some extent stabilised the reserve economies, at least until the 1950s.[9]

One of the main advantages of migrant labour to South African capital has been its cheapness. This factor was of particular importance in the gold-mining industry, which earlier in the century operated under certain severe constraints. Firstly, the average grade of the ore was low; secondly, the price of gold was fixed internationally, so increased production costs could not be passed on to consumers; and thirdly, expenditure on capital development was generally high, especially in the deep-level mines. These constraints necessitated the minimisation of production costs, which in turn required a minimisation of labour costs. But there were inherent difficulties in the way of achieving this. High wages had of necessity to be paid to attract the requisite supply of skilled labour. And the competitive demand for unskilled labour would tend to raise its cost. In the period after the South African War many African labourers were attracted towards more remunerative occupations on the roads, railways and reconstruction projects. Moreover, the state had to satisfy the needs of white farmers and take measures to secure the supply of farm labour.

In spite of these difficulties the gold mines were able to keep down the cost of their unskilled labour. In an effort to resuscitate the gold-mining industry after the South African War wages of unskilled workers were reduced from pre-war levels. In 1902 the Chamber of Mines tried to implement a 35*s*. a month wage, representing a massive downward revision from the 49*s*. level of 1899. But in the competitive post-war conditions it was impossible to sustain this reduction, and in 1903 wages were pushed back almost to the 1899 rate. However, over the next three decades the mines were able to keep down the wages of their unskilled labour to a remarkable degree. In 1913 the average monthly wage was 52s., still lower than the average wage paid in 1896. Between 1911 and 1936 the actual cash wage paid to African unskilled workers remained fairly static, rising only slightly; but in real terms the wage declined as buying power was eroded by inflation. It was not surprising, therefore, that low wages were the main grievance of African workers during this period.

Wages, though, did not represent the only cause of dissatisfaction. African mineworkers laboured under a range of disabilities. In particular they were subjected to a number of racially discriminatory measures. In the first place, employment colour bars restricted the upward mobility of African mineworkers. The 1911 Mines and Works Act prohibited the employment of black workers in many areas of skilled work on the mines; this colour bar was further strengthened by the 1926 Mines and Works Amendment Act. Secondly, African mineworkers were strictly controlled by a pass system that severely curtailed their freedom of movement from one area to another. The pass was mainly designed to check desertion, and it was closely tied to another provision of the 1911 Native Labour Regulation Act in terms of which breach of contract by an African worker was deemed a criminal offence. Thirdly, Africans were by law not allowed to strike. The 1924 Industrial Conciliation Act created machinery to deal with industrial disputes, but its procedures specifically excluded blacks.

Conditions on the mines for African workers were harsh and oppressive, especially during the earlier decades of the industry's existence. The vast majority of African mineworkers have been compelled in this century to reside in compounds. Only a minute proportion of the African work-force was accommodated in married quarters: in 1930 less than 1 per cent of almost 200 000 African mineworkers lived in such quarters. The compounds were densely packed with their worker residents. A single room in a compound, especially those built before the First World War, might contain between sixty and ninety men; from the 1930s the rooms were built to contain a smaller number of occupants. Conditions in the early compounds have been described by Moroney:

> As a result of overcrowding in most cases, workers were forced to sleep on earth floors which, because of poor drainage and leaking roofs, became muddy during rain. Heating facilities were seldom provided and workers installed their own *imbanla* or fire buckets which usually had no chimneys. Damp conditions combined with poor ventilation and the fumes of the fire buckets contributed towards the high incidence of respiratory disease rates on the mines.

The compounds were tightly controlled. Each fell under the authority of a white compound manager who maintained discipline and kept pressure on workers to carry out their shifts. The manager was assisted by African 'police' whose alleged excesses drew many complaints from workers. The compounds were not only controlled, they also served as instruments of control. They inhibited absenteeism and desertion. Being easily accessible to the police, they served to constrain worker unrest. And the use of compounds as a mechanism to reinforce tribal divisions limited the potential for worker solidarity and organisation.

Working and living conditions for African mineworkers on the Rand gave rise to a horrendous mortality rate, particularly during the earlier decades of the century. In 1903 over 5 000 African workers were officially reported to have died on the Rand mines. Most of the deaths were due to pneumonia, to which workers were especially vulnerable during the winter months when they worked in high temperatures underground but experienced very cold temperatures out of working hours above the ground. Death and disease were also brought on by poor diet. The mining industry's drive to minimise costs meant that the workers' diet was generally deficient. And the overcrowded living conditions in the compounds made it hard to check the spread of infectious diseases.[10]

Mineworkers did not accept their plight passively. At times they adopted various responses and strategies which revealed a strong consciousness of their oppressed situation. Moroney points out how workers were able to differentiate between the various mines: 'Through an extensive oral reportage system potential workers rapidly developed an awareness, not only of the range of employment and wage rates available, but also of the variety of living and working conditions on each of the mines.' The recruiting system, however, did not permit African migrants to choose their own mines. So various defensive mechanisms were adopted by workers to express their grievances. Some tried to operate through the legal system to obtain redress.

Others took more drastic action. Desertion was a common strategy for those who found working conditions unbearable. There is evidence, at least for the early years of the century, that the mines that offered the worst working and living conditions had the highest desertion rates.

There were also instances of strike activity, belying the notion that migrant workers lacked a capacity for collective organisation. A number of strikes took place just after the South African War. The first major strike occurred in 1913, involving about 13 000 African mineworkers. Although the strike was suppressed by the army and police, it did prompt the government to appoint a commission to investigate worker grievances; and following the commission's report a number of improvements in the living and working conditions of mineworkers were introduced. However, nothing was done about the low level of wages, which continued to be reduced in real terms by rising prices during the second decade of the century. It was this particular hardship that provoked a massive, widespread strike by African mineworkers on the Rand in 1920. Over the twelve days that the strike lasted some 71 000 African miners went on strike, and twenty-one mines had to stop production. According to the president of the Chamber of Mines the strike had 'practically paralysed the industry'. The strike also had the effect of forcing the mining industry to take greater cognisance of its black labour-force. Although wages were not raised, there was some improvement in working conditions and the mineowners began to think in terms of relaxing the job colour bar — a move that was to provoke the 1922 revolt by white miners. Moreover, in the mid-1920s Hertzog's Pact government blocked any possible move away from job discrimination in the mining industry by strengthening the colour bar. And it was not until the mid-1940s that African mineworkers were able again to flex their muscles and confront their employers in a major strike.[11]

Participation in the migrant labour market represented a state of partial proletarianisation. However, in the early decades of the twentieth century an increasing number of Africans moved into urban centres and became fully proletarianised. Between 1904 and 1936 the number of Africans in urban areas in South Africa rose from 336 800 to 1 146 700; whereas the former figure represented 10,4 per cent of the total African population of South Africa in 1904, the latter figure represented 19 per cent of the total in 1936. These figures blur the distinction between migrants and non-migrants; and it is well known that a centre like Durban, for instance, contained a high proportion of migrants among its African population. But there are indications that the process of full African proletarianisation was accelerating in the first three decades of the century. Firstly, secondary industry began to expand in the major centres, particularly in the years between 1915 and 1923. Between 1915/16 and 1921/2 the number of industrial establishments on the Rand more than doubled from 862 to 1 763; and there was a similar expansion in the Durban area. The imperatives of secondary industry were towards a more skilled, permanent labour force. One can safely assume, therefore, that a growing proportion of urbanised Africans were constituting such a labour-force. A second indication of growing permanence comes from the changing sex ratio of the urban African population. Between 1911 and 1921 there was a 5 per cent increase in the number of African males in Johannesburg, as against a 180 per cent increase in the number of African females over the same period. The trend was the same in Durban where the 1921 sex ratio of 6,6 African males to every African female had changed to 3,4:1 by 1936.[12]

This growing African population in the towns had to be accommodated in some form of urban shelter. The responsibility for providing this was generally avoided or neglected by both the central government and local authorities. By the mid-1930s only a few formal, municipally controlled townships for Africans had been built in the major urban centres. In Johannesburg the first such township was opened at Klipspruit in 1906; and work on a second, Western Native Township, began in 1918. Ndabeni was opened in Cape Town in 1902 and existed till 1927 when its inhabitants were moved to the new township at Langa. In Durban a small township, called Baumannville, was opened in 1916 to accommodate African families. But apart from this no other such housing for Africans was available in Durban until the opening of Lamont in 1934.

These formal townships housed only a small proportion of the African population in these centres. By 1923 less than 6 000 of the 70 000 Africans (excluding mineworkers) living in the Johannesburg municipal area were accommodated in townships. The proportion in Durban was similarly low. Moreover, the townships represented a living environment that was far from satisfactory. Swanson has noted one particularly bizarre feature of the siting of these early townships:

> With the advent of the plague, the 'sanitation syndrome' advanced the cause of urban segregation with the panacea of locations. Was there more than coincidence in the tendency for locations to be established or proposed in the vicinity of rubbish depots and sewerage farms, for example at Uitvlugt (Ndabeni) near Cape Town, Klipspruit for Johannesburg, and 'on the Umgeni [River] side of the rubbish depot' at Durban?

Both Western Native Township and Langa, too, were sited next to sewerage works.

Townships served as instruments for controlling urban Africans. Ndabeni, for instance, took on the character of a gaol, being surrounded by a 6-foot high barbed wire fence and patrolled by guards; visitors were severely restricted and no liquor was allowed. Even tighter control was exercised in the municipal 'hostels' and private industrial compounds that accommodated single male workers. These compounds suited employers who liked to have their workers close at hand, thereby avoiding the necessity of subsidising their transport costs in the form of higher wages. They were also useful mechanisms of control. In Durban hostels and compounds were generally referred to as 'barracks'; and hostel occupants were called 'inmates'. At the Bell Street hostel the lights were put out at 9 p.m., and no talking was permitted 'after lights out'.

Thousands of urban Africans, though, lived in communities that were subjected to minimal control by the local authorities. Early in the century a few leasehold or freehold townships were developed in Johannesburg outside of municipal control. These were the townships of Sophiatown, Martindale, Newclare and Alexandra. In the 1930s in the Durban area African freehold communities developed at Chateau and Good Hope Estates and at Clermont.

Another type of uncontrolled living zone was the urban slum yard. These were particularly prevalent in Johannesburg in the early decades of this century. According to Koch it was mainly during the First World War when 'a belt of slum yards developed stretching from western suburbs through the city centre to the suburbs on the eastern side of Johannesburg. These areas included Fordsburg, Ferreirastown, Marshalltown, City and Suburban, old and new Doornfontein, Jeppe, Ophirton, Prospect Township and Vrededorp.' A significant feature of both the leasehold townships and the slum yards was their non-racial character. For instance, in 1921 Martindale and Sophiatown housed 1 457 Africans and 557 whites in addition to over 900 coloureds and Asiatics. Similarly the population of the slum yards cut across ethnic lines.[13]

This relative absence of control in certain living zones had important implications for the way in which urban Africans earned their subsistence. In the early decades of the century opportunities for formal employment were limited. Manufacturing industry only began to develop significantly from the First World War onwards; and when it did expand Africans were barred from many skilled jobs by the colour bar. But openings existed for petty entrepreneurs at the turn of the century. Van Onselen describes, for instance, how Zulu washermen operated on the Rand until they were gradually forced out of business in the early 1900s by the growth of steam laundries.

While job opportunities in these urban centres were limited, so were wages low. Africans thus had to engage in other activities either to earn or to supplement their incomes. Many entered domestic service, which tended to be dominated by African men, the so-called 'houseboys', in these early years of the century. Others engaged in informal sector activity, legal and illegal. The chief form of enterprise was the concoction and sale of home-brewed liquor. Ellen Hellmann has shown how Rooiyard, an early Johannesburg slum yard, was a centre of the liquor trade. Rooiyard's central location enabled the liquor-dealers to tap the market generated by domestic servants. Hellmann described the liquor trade as an industry without which Rooiyard's residents would have been unable to earn a subsistence. It was also 'big business' in Durban. According to La Hausse, as early as 1906 there were liquor-dealers, including African women and 'low-class whites' in over 100 houses and dens: 'Alcohol was the thread which held together the environment of the insanitary shacks, sheds and back-yards, where women sold beer or more potent alcohol such as methylated spirits and *isitshimiyane* to African workers, temporarily free from the discipline of the work place.'

Liquor formed a central part of a wider African working-class urban culture, often known as *marabi*. It was linked to prostitution — another source of informal sector income — and to the shebeen parties. There is evidence, too, that organised groups, such as *amalaita* gangs, became involved in the liquor traffic. Van Onselen has depicted some of these gangs on the Rand in the early twentieth century. *Amalaita* gangs began to operate in the eastern suburbs of Johannesburg from 1906. They drew many of their recruits from among young male domestic workers — Van Onselen calls the gangs 'the 'houseboys' liberation army' — and they engaged in petty crime and pass forging, among other activities. A prominent gang leader at this time was Jan Note, whose criminal career began in the 1890s; he came to lead an organisation known as the Ninevites. They included vagrants and petty criminals who operated from disused mine shafts and old quarries. At the height of his career Note had almost 1 000 followers. Their activities were concentrated on breaking into stores and houses; from these forays large quantities of loot flowed into the compounds. The Ninevites became 'a well organised lumpen-worker alliance that held criminal control in the very heart of industrialised South Africa'.[14]

That these organisations were able to operate at all is an indication of the relative absence of control over urban Africans in the early years of the century. Although the compounds were tightly controlled, as we have seen, even there the Ninevites were able to obtain a foothold. By the mid-1930s, however, the state, both at the central and local levels, was gradually assuming stricter control over the daily lives of urban Africans. In the forefront of this movement was the Durban municipality, which developed its own system for administering the local African population early in the century. A key measure was the Native Beer Act, passed by the Natal Parliament in 1908. On the strength of this, the Durban authorities established a municipal monopoly of the manufacture and supply of beer to local Africans. The profits from this monopoly were to be channelled into a newly created 'native revenue account'. Such was the extent of these profits that in 1916 they were sufficient to finance the establishment of a municipal Native Affairs Department to manage African administration.

The passing of the 1923 Natives (Urban Areas) Act marked the first major intervention by the central state in the sphere of African urbanisation. The Act made a number of key provisions, though these were not binding on local authorities. Municipalities were empowered to set aside segregated areas for African occupation, to establish native revenue accounts, to restrict the domestic manufacture and consumption of liquor by Africans, and to apply some control over the influx of blacks into urban areas.

Various local authorities responded in an individual, haphazard way to the Act. Successive proclamations were promulgated, introducing racial segregation into specific urban areas. Cape Town was proclaimed in 1926, and Johannesburg and Durban in the early 1930s. Cape Town also took advantage of the Act to tighten up influx control in 1926. Durban and Johannesburg followed suit in the early 1930s, using the tougher provisions of the 1930 amendment to the 1923 Act.

Perhaps the most that can be said about the 1923 Act is that it set a pattern for the future. It did not centralise or regularise the administration of urban Africans. It established the principle of urban segregation, but non-racial communities continued to exist. This was because, in terms of the 1923 Act, proclaimed 'white' areas could only be cleared if alternative accommodation was available for persons being displaced — and generally local authorities were unable or unwilling to provide this. Similarly influx control could not be too rigidly enforced, partly because of inadequate administrative machinery, and partly from a fear of interrupting the labour supply. As will be shown later, the tightening of state control over the mobility and daily lives of urban Africans had to await the 1937 Native Laws Amendment Act.[15]

African opposition movements until the 1930s

Up until the 1970s there was a tendency on the part of many scholars to rely on a pluralist model which employed racial categories as the key units of analysis in the South African situation. The major theoretical and interpretative shifts that have occurred since the 1970s have highlighted the weakness of this approach. A rigid racial categorisation obscures those groupings and alliances that transcended alignments of race. But more significantly, it blurs the important class differences that existed within racial groups. One therefore has to be particularly careful to avoid a monolithic view of the 'African' experience in South African history. In turning our attention to African opposition to white supremacy, it is above all the class dimension of this opposition that we must try to elucidate.

It is not easy, however, to establish a clear delineation of African class groupings in twentieth-century South Africa. The notion of an African working-class is problematic. It is difficult to define such a class in terms of class consciousness because the extent of such consciousness is often not easily measurable. And there is a problem in defining the African working-class in South Africa in terms of its relationship to the means of production, because African migrants retained access to land and so were not fully proletarianised. Moreover, as Marks and Rathbone have observed:

> The very nature of conquest and colonisation, of racial as well as class subjection, has made it impossible to consider African working-class culture and consciousness as in any sense watertight or closed off from the rest of the black population. Not only were the connections between workers and peasants intimate and continuous; they were also frequently the same people at different but often closely juxtaposed periods of their lives.

In spite of these difficulties it is possible to establish an approximate categorisation of an African petty bourgeoisie in twentieth-century South Africa. It is, moreover, necessary to do this because the existence of such a class has an important bearing on the different forms of opposition displayed by Africans in this period.

Members of the African petty bourgeoisie have generally been small-scale entrepreneurs or holders of professional or clerical positions. But economic status is not necessarily the most useful criterion for differentiating between the petty bourgeoisie and the working-class. For, as Bonner has pointed out, the wages of an African clerk in many cases would have been little more than those of a mineworker. More important differentiating criteria have been shared values and self-identification. Members of the African petty bourgeoisie often professed Christianity and displayed a strong attachment to a self-help, self-advancement ethic; and the keys to this advancement were deemed to be education and capital accumulation. The acquisition of land on a free-hold basis was commonly a major aspiration. This was one way for the petty bourgeoisie to set themselves apart from the working-class. For instance, when proposals for a 'native village' (Lamont) in Durban were being put forward in the late 1920s and early 1930s there were strong calls from some Africans that plots be sold on a freehold basis, since this would effectively exclude unruly elements and eliminate illicit liquor, immorality and slums. As a member of the Durban Native Advisory Board, Rev. Mtimkulu, explained in 1933, there 'was a class of Native who could not be expected to live side by side with other Natives of the class of Ricksha boys'.

However, the African petty bourgeoisie and working-class cannot be too rigidly differentiated. Bonner has noted, 'the petty bourgeoisie as a class stands between the dominant relations of production of capitalism — that is to say, the capital/labour relation — and as such is pulled two ways.' One could phrase this differently by saying that the petty bourgeoisie had upward aspirations, but structural constraints and their actual experience pulled them downwards. Their opportunities for advancement or capital accumulation were strictly limited; and they shared with the working-class the grievances of low wages, inadequate housing, and the pass system. [16]

Thus we can identify contradictory tendencies that have both pulled apart and pushed together the African petty bourgeoisie and working-class. Those tendencies are very apparent when one examines African opposition movements in twentieth-century South Africa. At some moments this opposition seems to take on a clear petty bourgeois character; at other times it is more obviously inspired by the working-class; and then there are those instances when protest arises from a merging of these two class interests.

In the late nineteenth and early twentieth century a number of African political organisations were formed in southern Africa. The initiative behind these lay with members of the mission-educated African elite. Emerging from the mission schools was a group of Africans who were strongly attached to Christianity and who shared a vision of a non-racial, 'civilised' society in South Africa, in which merit counted for more than colour. Several members of this elite group went abroad to pursue studies in higher education. Walshe estimates that by the first few years of the century there were 'somewhere between 100 and 400' such students abroad. Many of these went to the United States where they became inspired by black American leaders like Booker T. Washington and W. E. B. DuBois who were calling for equal opportunity and the extension of civil liberties, but also demanding that blacks strive for self-improvement. Typical of those to be influenced was John Dube who returned to Natal from the United States to set up the Ohlange Institute near Durban. Ohlange, an industrial school run by Africans, was modelled on Booker T. Washington's Tuskegee Institute where industrial education and self-improvement formed the predominant emphases.

A host of African organisations sprang up in the last years of the nineteenth and early years of the twentieth century. These have been neatly catalogued by Odendaal:

In the Cape the most important bodies were the South African Native Congress, the Cape Native Convention ..., the Cape Peninsula Native Association, the Transkei Native Vigilance Association and the Transkeian Territories African Union. In the Orange Free State there were the Orange River Colony Native Vigilance Association (later Orange Free State Native Congress) and the Becoana Mutual Improvement Association. The Transvaal produced such groups as the Transvaal Native Vigilance Association, the Transvaal Native Congress, the Transvaal Basotho Committee, the *Iliso Lomzi*, the African National Political Union, and later the umbrella Transvaal Native Union and Transvaal Native Organisation. The Natal Native Congress and the *Iliso Lesizwe Esimnyama* were founded in Natal.

The chief significance of these organisations was that they offered a forum for the expression of petty bourgeois African opinion. In terms of direct action or protest they achieved little. The South African Native Congress, founded in 1898, held annual conferences to discuss social and political issues, and had the backing of a newspaper organ, *Izwi Labantu*. The Natal Native Congress, established in 1901, aimed to inform Africans of their rights and provide an outlet for the articulation of their grievances. Its essential conservatism was highlighted in the views of its first president, Martin Lutuli, who held that Africans should be represented in parliament by sympathetic whites. By 1903 Native Vigilance Associations had been founded in both the Transvaal and the Orange River Colony. They too served as a forum for the African elite, who used the Associations to voice their demands for equal rights for all 'civilised' men irrespective of race.

The business of constitution-making in South Africa in the first decade of the century gave these nascent opposition movements a specific focus. In 1907 a conference was held at Queenstown. It brought together over eighty delegates from various black organisations in the Cape to discuss the feared erosion or denial of black political rights in a unified South African constitution. The conference had intended to resolve upon a plan of action, but in the event it decided little more than to support Progressive candidates in the forthcoming Cape election against the Afrikaner Bond-dominated South African Party. The following year various African organisations sent an assortment of petitions or submissions to the National Convention sitting in Durban to draft the terms for South African unification. More concerted African opposition would be voiced when the draft South Africa Act was released. In 1909 a counter-convention of African leaders from all the South African colonies met in Bloemfontein under the auspices of the South African Native Convention. The main resolutions of this counter-convention accepted the principle of Union, but demanded that the new constitution provide equal rights for all South Africans, regardless of colour. However, the draft South Africa Act was passed by all four colonial parliaments fundamentally unchanged. In a last effort a multi-racial six-man delegation, including two African and three coloured leaders and a former Cape premier (W. P. Schreiner), visited Britain to appeal to the imperial parliament to amend the

Act in favour of blacks. The appeal was rejected and the South Africa Act was passed unaltered. Virtually the only concession to blacks built into the Act was the preservation of the Cape's non-racial franchise. This gave Africans a small amount of electoral leverage in the Cape, and enabled Dr Walter Rubusana to stand for and win a seat in the Cape provincial council in the first Union election of 1910.[17]

Within two years of Union a national African political organisation had been formed. Much of the initiative for this came from Pixley Seme, who had recently returned to South Africa after completing his legal studies in England. It was Seme's idea to summon a national meeting of African leaders for the express purpose of establishing a new organisation. And so in January 1912 numerous delegates, including both leading members of the African elite and traditional chiefs, assembled at Bloemfontein. At this conference the South African Native National Congress (SANNC, known from 1923 as the African National Congress or ANC) was formally established. John Dube was elected its first president; Pixley Seme was chosen as treasurer; and Solomon Plaatje as secretary-general.

The SANNC soon formulated a set of broad objectives. The organisation aimed to promote cooperation and communication between the government and Africans; to further the educational, social, economic and political advancement of Africans towards a level of equal opportunity with whites; to represent and educate African opinion; and to strive for the redress of grievances. In its early years the SANNC came to concern itself with three major grievances — exclusion from the franchise, the inequitable distribution of land, and growing racial discrimination in the job market. This sense of grievance among African leaders became particularly acute in the aftermath of the First World War. Participation in the war had falsely aroused African hopes that they would be rewarded with a reformed and more just social order after the war. Moreover, Africans had experienced war-time economic hardship and wages had lagged far behind rising prices.

Just as the early objectives of the SANNC were mild and moderate, so were its methods and strategies. Militant action was disavowed: Congress's constitution stipulated that the organisation would operate 'by means of resolutions, protests and a constitutional and peaceful propaganda'. One of its main strategies was to mobilise opinion and enlist support from potential sympathisers in different quarters. Soon after its formation the SANNC started a newspaper, *Abantu Batho*, to serve as its official mouthpiece. *Abantu Batho* contained articles in different Nguni and Sotho languages, as well as in English. This was an indication of the SANNC's concern not only to build African solidarity but also to enlist non-African support. Although it became a divisive issue in later years, the early nationalist movement was prepared to enlist the support of white sympathisers. Another key strategy in these early years was to appeal to the British government to pressure the South African government into making reforms.

Much of the early activity of the SANNC centred around peaceful campaigning on specific issues. The 1913 Land Act provided the first focus of attention. The SANNC issued declarations of protest against the Act, and organised a deputation and petition to the South African government. Finally Congress resolved to send a delegation to England to appeal to the imperial government on the issue. In Britain the delegation earned sympathy in some quarters, particularly from sections of the press, and certain humanitarian and religious bodies, but not from the government, which was unresponsive to their pleas.

It is interesting to note that this early African opposition was directed not so much against the principle of territorial segregation embodied in the Land Act, but more against the Act's inequitable distribution of land. However, in the 1920s and 1930s the ANC (as it was known from 1923) committed itself to oppose the principle of segregation. The particular focus of its opposition was a set of segregation bills that were presented to parliament by Hertzog's government in 1926. These four bills were interdependent. Their overall objective was to provide a new direction in 'native policy' based firmly on the segregation principle. African voters in the Cape were to be disfranchised; instead Africans were to be represented by seven white MPs and were to realise their political aspirations through a proposed council comprising fifty Africans, about one-third of whom would be elected. Moreover, the principle of territorial segregation was to be further entrenched, although the land areas reserved for Africans would be enlarged.

Hertzog could not muster the necessary two-thirds parliamentary majority to effect the amendment to the constitution. So the passage of the bills had to wait another ten years. In the meantime the ANC voiced its opposition to the proposed measures. But in doing so it stopped short of non-constitutional methods. Little action was taken other than to adopt resolutions at annual conferences and submit these resolutions to the government authorities through deputations.

This mild, non-militant form of opposition was typical of the SANNC/ANC in the first two or three decades of its existence. However, there had been a few occasions when the movement adopted or endorsed a strategy of passive resistance. In 1913 the Orange Free State provincial council empowered municipalities in the province to issue passes to African women. In July of that year about 600 women gathered in central Bloemfontein and handed a bag of passes to the municipal authorities. Although the SANNC was not responsible for organising the campaign, its leaders did take up the case of women imprisoned for their defiance.

Similarly there is evidence of a shift towards a more militant stance on the part of the Transvaal branch of Congress between 1918 and 1920. In 1918 it supported a strike by municipal sanitary workers. The following year it organised a passive resistance campaign against the pass laws. Thousands of passes were handed in on the Rand and over 700 Africans were arrested during the campaign. In 1920 some Congress organisers came out in open support of the African mineworkers' strike.

This departure from the more typical, constitutional strategy of the SANNC at the time was not endorsed by the movement's leadership. Figures like Sol Plaatje and D. D. T. Jabavu expressed misgivings about the radical direction being taken. This group in the movement was to persist for several years. In the late 1920s one faction in the ANC displayed leanings towards the Communist Party. This group was headed by Josiah Gumede, who was elected ANC president in 1927. Communist influence was particularly strong in the ANC's western Cape branch, in which Elliot Tonjeni and Bransby Ndobe, two militant leaders, strove for closer cooperation with the communists. The Communist Party of South Africa had been formed in 1921. After initially taking up the cause of white mineworkers, the party strove to enlarge its black following from the mid-1920s. By 1928 it had a membership of about 1 750, of whom 1 600 were black. It set about organising black trade unions, and it produced a newspaper, the *South African Worker*, in which more than half the articles were written in an African language.

Another influence, that cut across the radical–moderate divide, filtered into the ANC in the 1920s. This was Garveyism — the imported version of the ideas of Marcus Garvey, the black American leader. Garveyism, with its millennial undertones, foresaw the day of Africa's liberation and freedom from white government. Although Garveyism was vague as to how this could be achieved, it emphasised the importance of African initiative and self-help and attacked white paternalism. Gumede seems to have been influenced by Garvey; so too was one of Gumede's ideological opponents, James Thaele, who conducted a vigorous campaign against the radicals in the western Cape ANC in the late 1920s.

Some of these divisions came to a head in 1930 when the more conservative Pixley Seme was elected to the presidency of the ANC in place of Gumede. Over the next few years the ANC faded from the political scene. It may be that the divisions of the 1920s had taken their toll on the movement. More significant, though, was the continued focus of the ANC's petty bourgeois leaders on those aspects of government policy that barred their own progress and advancement. Given this emphasis the movement's potential for the mobilisation of mass support was extremely limited.[18]

In the task of mass mobilisation the ANC was less successful than the other major black opposition movement of the time, the ICU. The original Industrial and Commercial Union had been founded in Cape Town in 1919 by Clements Kadalie, a Tonga, who had recently moved to South Africa from Nyasaland. Within a few months of its founding the ICU was organising a strike of Cape Town dockworkers. The following year delegates from various black trade unions met in Bloemfontein to form a larger trade union federation, called the Industrial and Commercial Workers' Union of Africa. Selby Msimang became president of the new body; but Kadalie was passed over for the post of general secretary, and out of resentment withdrew his Cape Town delegates from the conference. For the first two years of its existence Msimang's ICU (by which the Industrial and Commercial Workers' Union of Africa had come to be known) operated mainly in the Free State and eastern Cape, while Kadalie worked independently in Cape Town. In 1922 Kadalie managed to convene a conference of Msimang's larger federation at Cape

Town, and at the conference succeeded in taking over the machinery of the ICU from Msimang.

The ICU was in the forefront of black opposition in the 1920s. But the movement was characterised by ambiguities that have made it a subject of some controversy among historians. In its search for external support the ICU revealed some of its ambiguities and contradictions. In 1923 it invited Tom Mann, the British communist trade union leader, to open an ICU conference; and in 1924 James La Guma, the assistant general secretary of the ICU, joined the Communist Party of South Africa. And yet at about the same time the ICU leadership was lured into a strange alliance with Hertzog's Nationalist–Labour pact. The ICU agreed to support the pact in the 1924 general election. It is hard to comprehend how the ICU could have allowed itself to be identified with Hertzog, unless his segregation policies were deemed to offer a fairer division of the country. Later Kadalie looked for support from white liberals, further illustrating the ambivalent and changing character of the movement. This point has been made well by Sheridan Johns:

> In terms of its own operations the ICU never resolved whether it was primarily a bona fide trade union or whether it was a political pressure group. At times it also took on the character of a mass movement of protest. Its efforts to further its programs vacillated between respectful representations to governmental authorities and threats of mass strikes. It alternated between hopes of reform with the aid of sympathetic whites in South Africa and reliance upon international pressures to bring about change within South Africa.

The ICU reached its peak in the years 1923–8 when its claim to be a mass movement assumed some justification. In those years its membership soared and new branches were opened. In 1925 the ICU had just over 30 000 members; in 1928 this had risen, by the ICU's own reckoning, to about 200 000. Much of the movement's growth had been in the rural areas. This development has usually been attributed to the rising support from African labour tenants and squatters, mainly in the Free State and Natal, seeking the ICU's assistance in the face of impending eviction from their lands. But recently Helen Bradford has shown how farm workers also became involved, particularly in the eastern Transvaal: 'a surge of protest broke out on eastern Transvaal farms in the period 1926–1928. There were strikes by recruited workers, wage demands by hired labourers, and farm workers and tenants alike became "insolent".'

Having reached its zenith in the years 1926–8 the ICU thereafter rapidly lost momentum, so much so that by the early 1930s it was a dying organisation. The problem was that its internal contradictions and paradoxes had increasingly manifested themselves in divisions and secession. One division centred around the growing influence of communists in the ICU. By 1926 communists had come to occupy a number of key positions in the ICU and they were beginning to criticise ICU leaders for neglecting the proletarian cause in favour of their own petty bourgeois interests. Kadalie retaliated by successfully purging the ICU of its communist membership: by 1927 it had been ruled that no ICU member could also be a member of the Communist

Party.

Even within the ICU's leadership itself there were growing divisions. The most damaging was that between Kadalie and A. W. G. Champion, the head of the flourishing Durban branch. In 1928 Kadalie suspended Champion from office in the ICU on the grounds that Champion had allegedly misused ICU funds for personal ends. Thereupon Champion and his followers broke away to form their own secessionist organisation, the ICU *yase* Natal.

Another leadership feud soon developed between Kadalie and W. G. Ballinger, a trade unionist who had been brought to South Africa to act as the ICU's adviser. Ballinger accused Kadalie of financial extravagance and drunkenness. Kadalie soon resigned and in 1929 formed the Independent ICU, at the same time trying to regain the support of those communists whom he had purged two or three years before. A number of local branches of the Independent ICU were established, but few of them took root. By the early 1930s both the original ICU, led by Ballinger, and the Independent ICU were losing the battle to create a national black worker organisation.

Regionalism had always been a major problem for the ICU. In its early years, until 1923, it had largely been a Cape-centred body. For a period in the mid-to-late 1920s, as we have seen, Natal was the major growth area. While the ICU seems to have gained a considerable foothold in the rural areas of the eastern Transvaal, it is significant that it made little impact on the Rand; in particular it failed to achieve any influence among mineworkers. Indeed, this is symptomatic of a wider strategic failure on the part of the ICU. Bonner argues that only at 'a superficial level' can the ultimate breakdown of the ICU 'be traced to financial instability, personal conflicts, weakness of central organisation and so on.' Rather he emphasises the ICU's crucial failure to attempt a concerted mobilisation and organisation of urban workers. And this failure, in turn, Bonner partly attributes to the 'elite or petit-bourgeois background' of the ICU's leadership:

> From the outset ... the movement was characterised by the cult of the personality, and by contradictory bourgeois aims. Both Champion ... and Kadalie bear this stamp. Each relied more on charisma than on organisation, and each saw the standing of the Union as being synonymous with his own.

Bonner's view of the ICU has recently been questioned by Bradford. She argues that the ICU, in contrast to the elitist ANC, did become 'a mass movement for national liberation' in the 1920s. One cannot, she continues, simply characterise the leadership of the ICU as being petty bourgeois. Most ICU organisers in the later 1920s were drawn from the ranks of the black lower middle class whose position, in terms of status and earnings, was closely linked to the under-classes. Some ICU officials were drawn directly from the ranks of the working-class. Moreover, the ICU was able to build a constituency around groups such as mission-trained craftsmen, small-scale producers and property-holders. These groups were becoming increasingly proletarianised as a result of the Pact government's civilised labour policy and its assault on the position of the African middle class.

Bradford also offers a corrective to the view that the ICU failed as a movement. She stresses that 'it is equally important to recognize the achievements of the ICU'. The circumstances of the time made mobilisation of black workers 'a Herculean task'. She goes on to conclude: 'In this context, the ICU had an astounding impact on consciousness and resistance in the countryside. It articulated popular grievances and fuelled protest to an unprecedented degree....' Equally we should not underestimate the ICU's achievement in some of the major urban areas, like Cape Town, Durban and East London.[19]

We have seen that the ICU, although on occasions identifying with strike action, rarely played a significant role in organising working-class resistance. In the absence of a centralised coordinating body, African working-class action therefore tended to be localised and sporadic. It has already been noted that the two years after the First World War represented a high point of African working-class resistance. In 1917 the Industrial Workers of Africa (IWA), a socialist organisation of African workers, was founded on the Rand. Although the extent of its influence is difficult to gauge, the IWA was almost certainly involved in the upsurge of worker activity on the Rand at that time. In 1918 a strike by African sanitary workers virtually crippled Johannesburg's sanitary service. Widespread demands for increased wages on the Rand culminated in the African mineworkers' strike of 1920. Worker militancy was not confined to the Rand. In Cape Town in 1919 about 2 000 workers were involved in a two-week dock strike. In the same year there were strikes in the Natal collieries and the Messina copper mine in the northern Transvaal. Durban's ricksha-pullers went on strike in 1918; and demands by the city's dockworkers for wage increases were backed by strike action in 1918 and 1919. Similar wage demands were made by African workers in Bloemfontein and Port Elizabeth. In Port Elizabeth in 1920 a crowd of workers marched on a police station where their leader, Masabalala, was being held. The police opened fire and twenty-one people were killed.

From 1927 the first African industrial unions began to be formed: these included the Native Laundry Workers' Union, the Native Bakers' Union, the Native Clothing Workers' Union, and the Native Mattress and Furniture Workers' Union. In 1928 the South African Federation of Non-European Trade Unions was established as an umbrella body; and over the next two years the number of African unions continued to increase. This growth in formal organisation was matched by an upsurge in worker action during the late 1920s, much of which was centred in Natal. In June 1927 about 4 500 African coal-miners in Natal went on strike for higher wages. In the same month there was a one-hour strike by 1 500 African dockworkers in Durban in support of colleagues who had been arrested for tax offences. It was also the dockworkers who led the boycott of Durban's municipal beer-halls in 1929. So effective was this boycott that for several weeks the municipality derived almost no revenue from its beer-halls. The boycott was a protest not only against the beer monopoly but also against the 'Durban system' of African administration which was largely financed by revenue from the sale of beer. The following year the leader of the Communist Party in Durban, Johannes Nkosi, organised a Dingane's Day pass-burning campaign. Over 2 000 passes and tax receipts were burnt; in a clash between demonstrators and the police Nkosi was killed. In 1930 there was a general strike of African railway and harbour workers in East London. For a short period over 80 per cent of the African workers joined the strike. An interesting feature of this strike was the key organisational role played by Kadalie and his recently formed Independent ICU. As we have seen, the attitude of the ICU's leadership to militant worker action was often vacillating and ambivalent. On occasions it had supported strike action, as in Cape Town in 1919. At other times it had identified with worker resistance, but had stopped short of significant active participation; during the 1929 Durban beer boycott, for instance, Champion had been keen to associate himself with the protest, but the main momentum and drive had come from the dockworkers.

It can be argued that some forms of African opposition in these early decades of the century took on a character that reflected the interests of a petty bourgeois leadership, while the more militant forms of activism were generally worker-inspired. However, a rigid class-based analysis of opposition and resistance would be misleading. As Bonner has argued, the petty bourgeoisie was often 'pulled two ways', and this tendency is reflected in the vacillating stance of both the ICU and the ANC towards militant action between 1918 and 1930. Moreover, there were some efforts to transcend the class divide. In 1929 the League of African Rights was launched, including in its leadership black radicals, like Gumede and Albert Nzula, and white communists, like Bunting and Roux. Although the League never gained much prominence it did try to serve as a bridge between the Communist Party, the ICU and the militant wing of the ANC.[20]

Another form of African opposition that cannot easily be analysed in class terms was Ethiopianism. African independent churches in South Africa date back to the 1880s when the Thembu Church was founded in the Transkei by a Wesleyan minister, Nehemiah Tile. Another Wesleyan breakaway group, led by Mangena Mokone, established the Ethiopian Church in Pretoria in 1892. This soon affiliated to the African Methodist Episcopal (AME) Church based in the United States. The AME Church grew rapidly throughout the Cape, Natal, the Orange Free State and the South African Republic, and by 1898 it could claim a total membership of over 10 000. But the following year it was affected by a secession when one of its leaders, James Dwane, broke away to form the Order of Ethiopia, which came to be loosely affiliated to the Anglican Church. Other independent churches were also forming in the late 1890s. In 1897 the Presbyterian Church of Africa, led by Pambani J. Mzimba, seceded from the United Free Churches of Scotland. The following year Simungu Shibe broke away from the American Board's Zulu mission to form the Zulu Congregational Church. As Parsons has shown, a number of independent church movements also emerged among the Tswana in the late nineteenth and early twentieth centuries.

An analysis of African independency at this time would suggest that the movement had strong political undertones. Independency was partly a reaction to the practice of those missionaries who tended either to frustrate African ambitions by closing off opportunities for African leadership within the mission churches, or to cause more general offence by denouncing African culture and custom. But independency was also a wider expression of opposition to colonialism, and proved particularly attractive in the context of taxation and land expropriation. Here it is worth noting that some of the early independent church leaders, like Mzimba, Dwane and others, were also involved in political activity.

At times independency took on a millenarian character. This can be illustrated by a glance at two well-known movements: the Israelites and the 'American Movement'. The Israelite Sect was founded in 1918 by Enoch Mgijima, who lived in the Bulhoek location near Queenstown in the eastern Cape. Each year its members gathered at Bulhoek commonage to celebrate the passover. In 1920 they set up a more permanent encampment on the commonage in order to await the end of the world. They ignored government orders and the urging of SANNC leaders to return to their homes. In May 1921 a strong force of police was called in. Armed with home-made weapons the Israelites confronted the police, who opened fire, killing 163 Israelites and wounding 129.

Another millenarian movement was founded in the Transkei in the mid-1920s by a colourful, if bogus, figure called Dr Wellington Butelezi. Among his brazen claims were the award of degrees from Rush Medical University in the United States and from Oxford and Cambridge Universities. Influenced by Garveyism, he infused it with a millenarian strain. From about 1925 Wellington began preaching widely in the Transkei. He told his followers that on the day of judgment black Americans would fly over in aeroplanes and drop balls of burning charcoal to liberate Africans from their oppressors. Those wanting salvation were called to paint their houses black and kill their pigs. His message took hold at a time when Transkeians were experiencing growing hardship as a result of drought, increased taxation, and the payment of fees for cattle-dipping. Moreover, as Edgar has observed, Wellington's 'meteoric rise to prominence came at a time when traditional leadership was losing its legitimacy in the eyes of the people and had been serving as instruments of government control.' To his followers, most of whom had little or no formal education, Wellington offered a message of hope. To the South African government, however, he emerged as a threatening figure. So in 1927 Wellington was banished from the Transkei. His followers sustained the movement for a few more years; and in 1929 there were high expectations that the American aeroplanes were about to arrive. Thereafter the millennial expectations subsided and the movement faded.[21]

The emergence of black opposition movements in the first few decades of the twentieth century did not pose any major threat to the South African state. The various movements failed to combine with the result that opposition was often uncoordinated and unconcerted. Different movements espoused different strategies and acted with varying degrees of militancy. Generally the more organised groupings, like the ANC and the ICU, adopted cautious, moderate methods, while the militant acts of protest tended to be isolated and sporadic.

In these circumstances the state did not require then (as it does today) massive machinery to suppress opposition. It needed to do little more than simply ignore the petitions, delegations and pleadings of organisations like the SANNC/ANC. For those more isolated acts of militant resistance the state could display a short, sharp show of force, as in Port Elizabeth in 1920 and at Bulhoek in 1921. However, as the ICU appeared to be gaining mass support in the later 1920s, so the state began to develop machinery to curb the activities of black leaders. Kadalie was prosecuted for defiance of the pass laws in 1926, but this resulted in no more than a £3 fine being imposed on the ICU leader. So the following year a restrictive clause was woven into the new Native Administration Act: in terms of this clause anybody deemed to be fomenting hostility between black and white would be liable to a £100 fine or a possible one-year prison term or both. The clause was directed against black and white radicals, a number of whom were arrested; but the police found it difficult to secure convictions. In 1929 a government amendment to the Riotous Assemblies Act gave the Minister of Justice power to banish any individual from any region where that individual's presence was deemed liable to create hostility between black and white. Oswald Pirow, the Minister of Justice at the time, used this legislation to ban meetings and restrict the movements of ANC, ICU and Communist Party leaders.

Compared to present-day South African standards the machinery of repression in the early part of this century was relatively mild. However, at this time the state was becoming increasingly concerned to devise political structures and arrangements that would serve to control the country's African population. The drift was towards a policy of segregation. As Shula Marks has noted, 'certainly by the end of World War I, segregation in some form or other had become the accepted convention within which solutions or resolutions of class conflict in South Africa were sought.'

There was a temporary departure from this trend with the passing of the Native Affairs Act in 1920. This provided for the establishment of a Native Affairs Commission, headed by the Minister of Native Affairs, to consider and make recommendations on 'any matter relating to the general conduct of the administration of Native affairs.' The Act also provided for the possible extension of the Transkeian council system to the rest of the country. More significant was the proposal to establish a national Native Conference, an umbrella advisory body of Africans that transcended tribal divisions.

If the 1920 Act seemed to abandon segregation principles, the 1927 Native Administration Act soon restored them. Lacey regards this latter measure as 'the first link in a chain of measures leading to the refurbishing of African traditionalism, with the emphasis on ethnic and cultural separatism'. The Act vested in the Governor-General the powers of 'Supreme Chief' over all Africans in the Transvaal, Free State and Natal. These powers included the right to alter tribal boundaries, divide communities, and order their removal from one area to another. Moreover, these powers could be exercised in practice by the Minister of Native Affairs. The Act also gave the Governor-General and the Minister authority to proclaim new laws or legislative amendments in many matters of African administration. To quote Lacey again: 'The 1927 Act was a definitive step by the National Party towards separate development, as the State ideology is known today.'

The 1927 Act marked a shift in state policy. During the nineteenth century the African chiefly order had in some areas led the resistance to colonial conquest and subjugation. In the early twentieth century the memory of this resistance was still strong enough for the chiefs to represent an apparent threat to colonial domination. In the course of this century, however, the state has increasingly coopted chiefs into structures of domination as agents for controlling the African population.

This shift can be exemplified by examining the changing nature of administration and control in the Transkei. We have seen in a previous chapter how the Cape government in the late nineteenth century established in the Transkei a system of direct magisterial rule that drastically undermined the powers of chiefs. In the business of administration the magistrates tended to bypass the chiefs, preferring to devolve administrative tasks upon headmen. In some ways, though, this was to the advantage of chiefs, as they were thereby, in Southall's words, 'to some extent shielded from popular disaffection and did not suffer the same disrepute as the bureaucratically appointed headmen, for they were less identified with white authority'. In terms of their popular support, therefore, Transkeian chiefs retained a considerable degree of political muscle. Consequently the state began to modify its stance towards the chiefs. Beinart has shown how this process worked in Pondoland: 'having accepted that chiefs would not be displaced, officials were concerned to remould the institution of chieftaincy and to incorporate chiefs into the bureaucratic structure. This was achieved in Pondoland partly by allowing royal and chiefly families to dominate many of the headmanships, and partly by giving certain powers, such as those over immigration and the local Council system, to the paramounts.' The 1927 Native Administration Act was an expression of this growing recognition of the chiefs' position.

The council system itself fitted neatly into the emerging pattern of segregated political and administrative structures. The system of general and local councils had been introduced into the Transkei from 1895. The local councils, which were gradually introduced into various Transkeian districts up till the 1920s, comprised the magistrate as chairman, and four elected and two nominated African members. The resolutions and recommendations of the local councils were forwarded to the general council. For a time Pondoland and the rest of the Transkei had separate general councils. In 1931 the two merged to form the United Transkeian Territories General Council, often known as the Bunga. Chaired by the chief magistrate, the Bunga's members consisted of the twenty-six district magistrates, three paramount chiefs, and three representatives from each district council. The Bunga was entitled to discuss wider social and economic issues affecting Africans, but only in an advisory capacity. It had the power to raise taxes, and the revenue that was raised helped to finance hospital care, road-building, and soil and water conservation schemes.

Outside the Transkei the council system was scarcely implemented. Only five local councils had been set up in the Transvaal by the 1940s; reserve boards of management, which were similar bodies to the local councils, were set up in two districts in the Free State; and in Natal only three local councils were established, and none of these contained elected members. However, in Natal an important development was occurring at an ideological level. In response to the process of African proletarianisation and the growth of the ICU, elements of Natal colonial opinion, epitomised by Heaton Nicholls, the MP for Zululand, were looking to a policy of retribalisation as a means of offsetting a potential class war. As Shula Marks has remarked:

Whereas in the 1870s and 1880s, the Zulu royal family had to be destroyed if Zululand was to be 'opened up' for white exploitation, now that the real powers of the Zulu kings had been removed, their regiments dismantled and their economic position undermined, the residual hold they had at an ideological level was to be used to make Zululand safe for the sugar planters!

In Natal perhaps more than anywhere else, the African chiefly order had symbolised African resistance to colonialism. A number of Zulu kings — notably Dingane, Cetshwayo and Dinuzulu — had clashed with white settlers, and with imperial or colonial armies. And yet by the 1920s the Zulu royal family was looked upon as a potential instrument of control, as a bastion against the challenges of an emergent African working-class. But this shift in perception was not a simple change in ideology. Rather it reflected transformations that were occurring simultaneously in the wider political economy of South Africa. In the second half of the nineteenth century the continued economic and political independence of African societies represented a barrier to capitalist development. However, as we have seen, by the early twentieth century African economic independence was being rapidly undermined as peasant and subsistence economies fell into decline. In this situation African political independence that was not based on firm economic independence posed less of a threat to the South African state. Indeed, the converse was true, and in this changing political economy the state increasingly began to look to the resurrection of a quasi-independent chiefly order as a means of sustaining the subjugation of the country's African population. As Lacey has noted, the government's strategy was 'to elevate chiefs as a class and then coopt them as agents of the State to rule, administer and control Africans in their areas. This was the process that began with the 1927 Act.' It was a process that was to reach its apogee in the Bantustan system evolved by successive Nationalist governments after 1948.[22]

9
CONTROL AND CONFRONTATION 1936–1976

The political economy of apartheid, 1936–1976

The periodisation of South African history has always been problematic. Landmarks in political history may be of less significance to the economic historian. And significant developments that have primarily affected whites may have had little impact on the experience of blacks. In this survey of twentieth-century African history in South Africa the mid-1930s seem to represent a watershed. One should not blur the continuities that run through the twentieth century, but in the mid-1930s certain measures were passed that set a clear direction for the following four decades. The principle of territorial segregation became firmly entrenched; the possibility that Africans might retain or even enlarge their place in the South African Westminster-style constitution was lost; and the policies of urban segregation and influx control were tightened. But in spite of these policies the mid-1930s also marked the beginning of an era of accelerating African urbanisation, as more and more Africans converged on the major urban centres. And it was the mid-1930s that saw the onset of greater militancy in African politics. As the lull of the early 1930s came to an end a more radical African political activism began to emerge.

The principle of territorial segregation, embodied in the 1913 Natives' Land Act, was confirmed and strengthened by the Native Trust and Land Act of 1936. This latter measure had two main provisions. Firstly, it set aside an extra 7 250 000 morgen of land to be added in the course of time to the African reserves. Secondly, the Act tried to remove rent-paying African tenants from white-owned land by penalising landowners who kept such tenants, and to tie the number of labour tenants on white farms more closely to the labour requirements of these farmers.

The 1936 Act must be viewed as part of a wider body of measures that were being passed contemporaneously to tighten segregation in the rural, urban and political spheres. Just as the 1936 Land Act abolished the right of Africans in the Cape to buy land outside the reserves, so the Representation of Natives Act of the same year deprived Cape African males of the franchise. This measure excluded all future Cape African voters from the common roll, while allowing existing African voters to remain there. Instead, Africans throughout South Africa were to elect four white senators by an indirect process. In addition, the Act provided for the creation of a Natives' Representative Council (NRC), on which twelve indirectly elected Africans would sit with four Africans nominated by the government, and with white native commissioners. Chaired by the Secretary for Native Affairs, the new body would be purely advisory in function. In practice the NRC turned out to be little more than a forum for the expression of African opinion and the articulation of African grievances. Its resolutions were constantly ignored by the government. The NRC's impotence was most starkly revealed in 1946 when the government refused to allow it even to discuss the African miners' strike. Thereupon the NRC adjourned itself indefinitely and faded into near oblivion before its final abolition in 1951. Perhaps the chief significance of the NRC was that it transcended ethnic divisions: as Butler, Rotberg and Adams have noted, 'It was the first and last official body that recognized that Africans had interests in common.'

The NRC was abolished by the 1951 Bantu Authorities Act, a key measure in the creation of the Nationalist government's Bantustan system. This Act provided for the abolition of existing tribal councils and for the gradual implementation of a three-tier system. The bottom tier was to comprise a Tribal Authority consisting of local chiefs and headmen. In the middle was the Regional Authority, which overlay two or more Tribal Authorities and drew upon the membership of the latter. At the top, the Territorial Authority would be responsible for the whole area of a reserve. The Act was to be implemented gradually, with different tribal groups 'advancing' to the various levels of government at different stages. In 1953 the first three tribal authorities were established in the Transvaal. But it was in the Transkei that the structure was implemented most rapidly. In 1957 the Transkeian Territorial Authority replaced the Bunga and took on limited governmental responsibilities.

According to the apartheid 'ideal' the road towards Bantustan self-government was to be matched by the growing economic independence of the Bantustans. The report of the Tomlinson Commission in 1955 called for a massive job creation programme in the reserves. Such a strategy would, it was held, curb the flow of Africans to white urban areas. But in the following years the government generally neglected to implement the Commission's recommendations, being unwilling to make the necessary financial commitment.

If little was done to render the reserves economically viable, successive Nationalist governments continued to legislate a framework for Bantustan self-government. A key piece of legislation was the Promotion of Bantu Self-Government Act of 1959. This measure proclaimed the existence of eight African 'national units', based on assumed linguistic and cultural diversity, but not on territoriality. A white commissioner-general was to be appointed to each unit as the South African government's official representative. Provision was also made for the gradual transfer of powers of self-government to the separate units. Although no definite timetable was laid down it was explicitly recognised that full independence represented a legitimate goal for these territories. There was no rush to implement the measure; and once again the Transkei was the first territory to fall under its provision with the passing of the Transkei Self-Government Act and the Transkei Constitution Act in 1963.

Further impetus to the Bantustan system was provided by new legislation in the early 1970s. The Bantu Homelands Citizenship Act of 1970 stipulated that all Africans would become citizens of one of the Bantustans; this was to apply even to persons who had never set foot in a Bantustan. The Bantu Homelands Constitution Act of 1971 enabled the government to bypass parliament in granting the various stages of self-government to each Bantustan.

As has already been noted, the Transkei was always the first homeland to pass through these stages. It would therefore seem useful to examine the process of constitutional change in the Transkei in some detail. For over twenty years since its inception in 1932, the United Transkeian Territories General Council (or Bunga) had acted as little more than a debating forum for its members. In its debates and resolutions it had repeatedly called for a non-racial common roll franchise. It was perhaps ironical, therefore, that when the Bunga voted itself out of existence in 1955, to be replaced by a Territorial Authority, it was entrenching the Transkei in the apartheid system and weakening the claims of Transkeians to the common roll franchise. The decision, in Southall's words, 'set the Transkei on the path which led to its becoming the first politically "independent" bantustan in 1976'. In 1957 the first Transkeian Territorial Authority was formally opened. It was composed of chiefs and nominated and elected councillors; and all its members were Africans, including the chairman. Its powers and responsibilities were limited and ill-defined.

The next step towards the Transkei's 'independence' was taken in 1963 with the passing of the Transkei Constitution Act. In terms of this Act the Transkei became a self-governing territory in name; and there was provision for some of the trappings, such as a flag and a national anthem. A six-man cabinet, presided over by a chief minister, was to be established, as was a Legislative Assembly, comprising sixty-four chiefs and forty-five elected representatives. The responsibilities of the new Transkei government included education, direct taxation and a number of other local matters, all of which combined to give it greater power than a provincial administration. The South African government hoped to make the Transkeian experiment work by nurturing two groups with a vested interest in it. The first was the old chiefly order, which dominated the Legislative Assembly. The second was the African petty bourgeoisie, which would gain materially from its control and membership of the burgeoning bureaucracy.

The Transkeian general election of 1963 represented a contest between two paramount chiefs to secure the election of followers who adhered to their respective policies and ideals. Chief Poto's campaign was based on a rejection both of apartheid and of the Transkei's new separate constitution. Chief Matanzima, on the other hand, supported the government's 'separate development' policy. It seems that most of the forty-five members elected in the 1963 election were supporters of Poto, but Matanzima had the support of the majority of chiefs, who outnumbered the elected representatives in the Assembly. It was thus Matanzima who was elected by the Assembly to the chief ministership by 54 votes to 49.

Once in power Matanzima's Transkei National Independence Party (TNIP) rapidly began to secure its position against Poto's opposition Democratic Party (DP). Successive general elections enabled the TNIP to take firm control of the Legislative Assembly, which, after the 1976 election, contained only seven opposition members. This trend is best explained not in terms of rising popular support for the TNIP, but rather in terms of the TNIP's ability to dispense patronage and manipulate chiefly influence to its own electoral advantage.

The South African government's constitutional framework of 'separate development' allowed Matanzima's government the opportunity to exercise only a limited degree of independence. Matanzima did contravene Nationalist education policy by introducing English-medium instruction, rather than Afrikaans or Xhosa, from Standard 3; and in 1964 the Transkeian government called on the authorities to relax influx control regulations. But generally Matanzima was too financially dependent on Pretoria to step very far out of line. One is in this regard struck by the continued existence in Transkei, at least until 'independence' in 1976, of many of South Africa's repressive and discriminatory laws.

In 1968 the Transkei Legislative Assembly asked the South African government to prepare the Transkei for 'independence' in the shortest possible time. During the early 1970s, Matanzima, realising that the South African government was intent on making Transkei 'independent' tried to use the 'independence' issue as a lever to gain additional land from South Africa. But Pretoria's refusal to offer any more than a few such concessions did not stop Matanzima from presenting a formal request for 'independence' in March 1974. And so the process of quasi-decolonisation got under way in October 1976 when Transkei became an 'independent' state, at least in South Africa's eyes if not in the eyes of the rest of the world.

Other 'homelands' gradually followed along the path taken by the Transkei. In Bophuthatswana tribal and regional authorities were established by the mid-1950s, and in 1961 a Territorial Authority was set up. In 1968 this Territorial Authority chose Chief Lucas Mangope as its first chief councillor; and it was he who led the Bophuthatswana National Party into Bophuthatswana's first general election in 1972, the year when self-government was formally declared in the territory. Mangope's party won twenty of the twenty-four seats up for election, the remaining four going to Chief Pilane's Seoposengwe Party. The other forty-eight members in the seventy-two-member Legislative Assembly were nominees, primarily chiefs and headmen designated by the regional and tribal authorities. At the first session of the Legislative Assembly Mangope was elected as chief minister by an overwhelming majority. And it was he who was to become president of Bophuthatswana when it too received its quasi-independence in 1977.

Zulu leaders have generally been less cooperative in implementing the government's Bantustan policy. Throughout the 1960s, Chief Gatsha Buthelezi, a member of the family that traditionally provided Zulu chief councillors, consistently rejected the government's plans to establish 'homeland' authority structures. But he did yield to pressure in 1970 when the Zululand Territorial Authority began to function, with Buthelezi himself unanimously elected as its chief executive officer. In 1972 KwaZulu moved towards self-government status when an Assembly was created, including nominated and indirectly elected members; again there was to be a heavy preponderance of nominated members, who were primarily chiefs. It was to be some years, though, before an election was held in KwaZulu because Buthelezi objected to the use of reference books, which were seen as symbols of oppression, as identifying documents for voters. In 1975 Buthelezi founded the Inkatha organisation, which was to take on the character both of a Zulu cultural movement and a political party. And when KwaZulu elections were eventually held in 1976 Inkatha swept the board. Buthelezi's political stance has left him walking a tightrope. On the one hand, he has spoken out against the government's apartheid policy more strongly than any other homeland leader, and has accordingly incurred the disapproval of those upon whom he depends for his survival. On the other hand, Buthelezi has compromised himself by operating within the Bantustan system, and over the years has displayed increasing intolerance towards those black groupings that oppose his views or strategies. In this way he has become increasingly alienated from left-wing political movements.

In 1971 legislative assemblies were established in five other Bantustans — Ciskei, Lebowa, Venda, Gazankulu and QwaQwa. The following year Ciskei and Lebowa received self-government, while Venda, Gazankulu, QwaQwa, Kangwane and South Ndebele were to be granted theirs over the next few years. And so over a period of three decades since the mid-1950s the government's Bantustan policy, probably the crucial element in the whole apartheid system, has taken shape. It remains for us to examine the key functions that the Bantustans have fulfilled in the South African political economy.[23]

The official ideology of the Nationalist government has been based on the theory of 'separate development', a theory that seems to have crystallised among leading Afrikaner nationalist thinkers during the late 1940s. In terms of this theory South Africa's population is not comprised of a white minority and a black majority, but rather of a whole set of ethnic minorities. The African people of South Africa can accordingly be divided into ten groups, each with its own distinctive culture and traditions. Therefore, the theory proceeds, out of respect for these differences, each African group should be allocated its own 'homeland' where it can develop culturally, politically and economically along its own lines. 'Separate development' theorists claimed that the implementation of this policy would reproduce the decolonisation process that occurred throughout Africa in the 1960s.

The critique of this theory is well known. Critics argue that the theory overlooks the many areas of homogeneity and the high degree of intermingling between African ethnic groups. Moreover, there is an inherent inconsistency in that Africans are treated as ethnically heterogeneous, while whites are assumed to be homogeneous. In addition, the idea of African nationhood is not matched by territoriality. The 'homelands' are highly fragmented; and they comprise only 13 per cent of the South African land area, whereas Africans make up over 70 per cent of the total South African population.

The critics of 'separate development' theory have proceeded to examine the political and economic functions that the policy fulfils in sustaining white supremacy and capitalist development. At a political level the Bantustan strategy has two main purposes. Firstly, it is a divide-and-rule mechanism. Through its policy of dividing Africans into ten different politico-cultural entities the Nationalist government seeks to claim that there no longer exists an African majority in South Africa. Moreover, the fostering of ethnic divisions between Africans is aimed at countering a trend towards greater African unity, a trend that has manifested itself both in African nationalism or black consciousness, and in African working-class movements.

Secondly, the Nationalist government has, through its Bantustan policy, co-opted two elements in African society to carry out the task of controlling the African population in the 'homelands' — traditional authorities and members of the petty bourgeoisie. As Frank Molteno has put it, 'What the Bantustan strategy involved was the reincorporation of a modified form of the tribal authority structure into the overall structure of domination.' In the classic style of indirect rule, chiefs have been called upon to act as agents of the South African state. For their services they have been rewarded with the trappings of power and the material comforts of high office. But the government could not rely on the chiefs alone to perform this role. As Southall has argued, 'The development of the Transkei as a projected neo-colony of South Africa demanded the creation of a dependent African petty-bourgeoisie whose material interests would be so structured as to induce it to be supportive of separate development....' Southall is referring to the politicians, bureaucrats and teachers who could profit from participation in the system by reaping higher material rewards than could be obtained in other sectors of the Bantustan economies. It is thus not surprising to find that the 'homeland' governments have tended to indulge in a massive expenditure on both bureaucratic expansion and on the trappings of independence — presidential palaces, airports, and stadiums. While all of these may give the appearance of genuine independence to uninformed outsiders, they conceal the failure to inject much-needed capital into the development of the impoverished rural areas of the Bantustans.

As many writers have observed in the past fifteen years the reserves/Bantustans have also functioned in a way that has furthered the development of white-dominated capitalism in South Africa. Initially the reserves served as labour reservoirs from which the mining industry in particular could draw its requisite supply of migrant labour. The existence of the reserves also kept down the wages of migrant workers, who were paid a single man's wage on the grounds that the migrant's family could obtain their subsistence in the reserves. Moreover, because migrants remained in a semi-proletarianised state, retaining access to land and cattle in the reserves, their potential for working-class organisation and action was (supposedly) stunted. Finally, in more recent years the Bantustans have increasingly become dumping-grounds or reception depots for the millions of Africans who have been uprooted from their urban or rural communities and removed to a 'homeland' under the government's resettlement programme.

According to the 'separate development' policy the 'homelands' were to become viable polities both politically and economically, so much so that Africans would increasingly identify with and gravitate towards them. The reality, however, has been harshly different. The 'homelands' have become more and more impoverished, and for their inhabitants escape to South African urban centres has come to offer the best hope of survival. According to Simkins the period from 1918 till the mid-1950s was one of 'fragile productivity maintenance' in the reserves. In this period 'the proportion of reserve subsistence requirements met by reserve agricultural production remained roughly constant' — made possible largely by the high rate of emigration from the reserves. Since the mid-1950s, with the refinement of influx control machinery making emigration more difficult, there has been a rapid decline in the productivity of the reserves. Simkins details this decline:

> Average population density rose from 60 persons per square mile in 1955 to 110 in 1969. Production per head plummeted, production as a proportion of subsistence requirements in the late sixties being less than two-thirds of the 1955 level. And the private industry wage/agricultural product ratio rose from 5 in 1955 to 11 in 1965 ushering in the contemporary disequilibrium between urban and rural African incomes. Increasing dependency of the reserves on remittances from the modern sector was the inevitable result.

The example of the Transkei well illustrates this trend. In the Transkei an increasing population density has brought about greater pressure on the land. Overcultivation and overgrazing have led to soil exhaustion. Outside of the subsistence economy few alternative employment opportunities have existed in the Transkei. As late as 1962 only 20 592 out of the total 1 400 000 Africans in the Transkei had paid jobs within the 'homeland'; and of these more than 8 000 were in domestic service. It is not surprising, therefore, that the Transkei's per capita income has been extremely low. According to Southall, 'careful perusal of offical data shows that the *per capita* annual income of the *de facto* population of the Transkei (including migrants) was only as little as R55 in 1973' – a figure that rates the Transkei below some of Africa's most poverty-stricken countries. A detailed survey carried out in the late 1960s showed that in some areas of the Transkei 85 per cent of households received an income below the poverty datum line. This massive poverty is marked by widespread malnutrition and a horrifying level of child mortality: almost 30 per cent of children in Transkei's rural districts die before they reach the age of 2, and 40 per cent before the age of 10.

A general feature of an underdeveloped economy, such as the Transkei's, is its dependence upon external links with a more developed capitalist economy. In the Transkei this dependence has manifested itself in two main ways. Firstly, an ever-increasing proportion of the Transkei's able-bodied males have had to resort to migrant labour to enable them to subsist. In 1936 53 per cent of Transkeian males between the ages of 18 and 54 years were absent from the Transkei for the whole part of the year. By 1974, some 257 000 Transkeians — or 83 per cent of the region's male labour potential — were employed as migrant labourers outside the Transkei. One effect of this was to overburden Transkeian women, who had not only to perform the tasks of household maintenance and child-rearing, but also to take on the main responsibility for agricultural production.

The second form of dependency has involved the Transkei's reliance upon financial grants from South Africa. Since the mid-1960s at least 50 per cent of Transkeian government revenue has always been derived from South African grants. Moreover, this proportion has mostly risen above 60 per cent; and between 1974 and 1975 it almost reached 80 per cent.

As Southall has remarked, 'the defining characteristics of the "Transkeian" state is that it has no independent base in the "national" economy (as indicated by its gross financial subordination to the Republic) and that its external dependence is incontrovertibly and irreversibly increasing year by year.' This lack of independence has formed a general characteristic of 'homeland' economies. And it is because of this lack of economic independence that the South African government is willing, indeed keen, to grant political 'independence' to the 'homelands'. The government knows well that economic dependence prohibits 'homeland' governments from asserting any genuinely independent line of policy that might threaten white supremacy or the overall dominance of the South African government.[24]

Over the past few decades an ever more fragile material base has had to support an increasing population in the 'homelands'. Apart from the natural population increase, the policies of the South African government have forced more and more Africans to live in the 'homelands'. Influx control has restricted African access to the urban areas; and there have been various forces at play reducing the number of Africans living on white-owned land in rural areas.

Earlier in the century the state had used the 1913 Land Act to launch an assault against African sharecroppers and rent-paying tenants ('squatters'). After 1936, when another Land Act was passed, a further assault was directed against African labour tenants on white farms and African squatters and landowners in white rural areas. One object of the 1936 Act was to eliminate from white-owned land all Africans not in the service of the owners of the land. Thus landowners had to pay a special tax on all their rent-paying African tenants who did not render labour service. The Act also provided for the establishment of labour tenant control boards which would have the power to limit the number of labour tenants on any farm according to the estimated labour requirements of that farm. It was not, though, until the 1950s and 1960s that further legislation provided the extra muscle necessary to carry through the intentions of the 1936 Act by converting labour tenants into wage labourers on farms. The Bantu Laws Amendment Act of 1964 allowed the government to prohibit labour tenancy within any area, and this prohibition was gradually enforced district by district. In 1936 it was estimated that there had been about one million African labour tenants on white farms. By 1973 there remained only about 16 000 labour tenants, almost entirely in Natal.

An obvious concomitant of this trend has been a major shift to the employment of full-time African wage labourers by white farmers. This shift has released more land, previously occupied by labour tenants and squatters, for white commercial farming. And it has reduced the number of Africans living on white-owned land, a reduction that has been in keeping ideologically with government policy. At the same time the increasing mechanisation of white farming in recent decades has lowered labour requirements, thereby enabling a further reduction in the African population in white rural areas. Figures are supplied by Greenberg:

> Between 1955 and 1962 the number of Africans in the white rural areas, after a century of almost continuous growth, remained steady and, after that, began an historic decline. Between 1960 and 1971, by one estimate, 438,000 Africans abandoned agricultural employment; between 1971 and 1973, an additional 248,000 made their exodus.

The ultimate intention of government policy has been to remove from 'white' rural and urban areas all Africans who were surplus to labour requirements. As one government spokesman, G. F. Froneman, remarked in 1965, African workers could only be present in white areas to supply the commodity of labour: 'it is labour that we are importing and not labourers as individuals.' In its effort to realise this intention the government has implemented, particularly in the last two or three decades, a massive programme of human removals and resettlement involving Africans in both rural and urban areas. The objectives of the removals policy were clearly spelt out in a government circular of 1967. This document classified various categories of non-productive Africans who would have to be removed from white areas. These categories included the aged, the unfit, widows, women with dependent children, and families who did not qualify for accommodation in white urban areas; also included were Africans on white farms who became 'superfluous as a result of age, disability or the application of ... the Bantu Trust and Land Act, No.18 of 1936....'

In the white rural areas two main categories of people have been the victims of removals; firstly, the labour tenants and squatters, and secondly, the inhabitants of so-called 'black spots'. As we have seen, labour tenancy and squatting had been largely phased out by the early 1970s. This elimination involved a massive uprooting of Africans from white-owned land. According to a report issued by the South African Institute of Race Relations in 1972, between 1960 and 1970 about 340 000 people were removed as a result of the abolition of labour tenancies on white farms, and a further 656 000 people were removed by laws preventing squatters from living on white farms.

'Black spots' are those African freehold areas falling in territory that has been designated as white. Most of these private holdings had been purchased during the forty years before the passing of the 1913 Land Act. Although long since outlawed, 'black spots' have only been eliminated on a large scale since about 1960. Some 'black spot' communities have been persuaded by government officials to move. Those who have resisted resettlement have had their lands expropriated and have themselves been charged with illegal squatting. The Institute of Race Relations has estimated that 97 000 people were removed beween 1960 and 1970 as a result of 'black spot' elimination; and Maré makes a further rough estimate that another 161 000 people were relocated from black spots between 1970 and 1976.

Recent research has provided us with a clearer picture of both the extent and the nature of resettlement in South Africa. The Surplus People Project has estimated that between 1960 and 1982 over three and a half million people have been relocated under the government's resettlement policy. Of this total, between 75 and 80 per cent were Africans. The single largest category of relocation has involved those removed from white farms; urban removals under the Group Areas Act have been the second largest category.

The implementation of relocation has depended primarily on coercion. This has been emphasised by the Surplus People Project:

> The force has been both structural — coercion is built into the web of discriminatory and oppressive laws and institutions restricting black freedom of movement and access to land — and specific to the particular instances of relocation. Sometimes the violence with which people are removed is direct — police and guns, bulldozers, demolished houses, arrests. Some-times the violence is less overt — intimidation, rumour, cooption of community leaders, the pressure of shops and schools being closed and building restrictions imposed in areas due for removal.

It is in the context of this policy of forced removals that the 'homelands' have in more recent years come to serve as human dumping-grounds, because it has been in the 'homelands' that the labour tenants, squatters and 'black spot' inhabitants have been resettled.

The consequences of forced removals have been devastating for their victims. The familiar pattern has been for resettled communities to be placed in camps in remote, arid areas with only the most rudimentary facilities being provided. One of the most notorious of these reception camps — Limehill in Natal — was investigated by Cosmas Desmond in the late 1960s. Africans were removed to Limehill in 1967 and 1968 from 'black spots' in the Dundee district. Once at Limehill each family was allocated a tiny plot, 50 yards square. There was no land for ploughing; and no livestock, except chickens, were allowed. There were neither shops nor medical services. And there were no wage-earning opportunities in the immediate vicinity. In these conditions Desmond found disease and death to be rife at the camp.

The short-term experience of relocation has generally been harsh and traumatic. The Surplus People Project notes 'the damaging social and pyschological effects inflicted on communities and individuals', since for most people the relocation process is one 'that only serves to emphasise their lack of personal control over their lives, over their families' lives'. The greatest problem for relocated communities is one of sheer survival. The material base of their

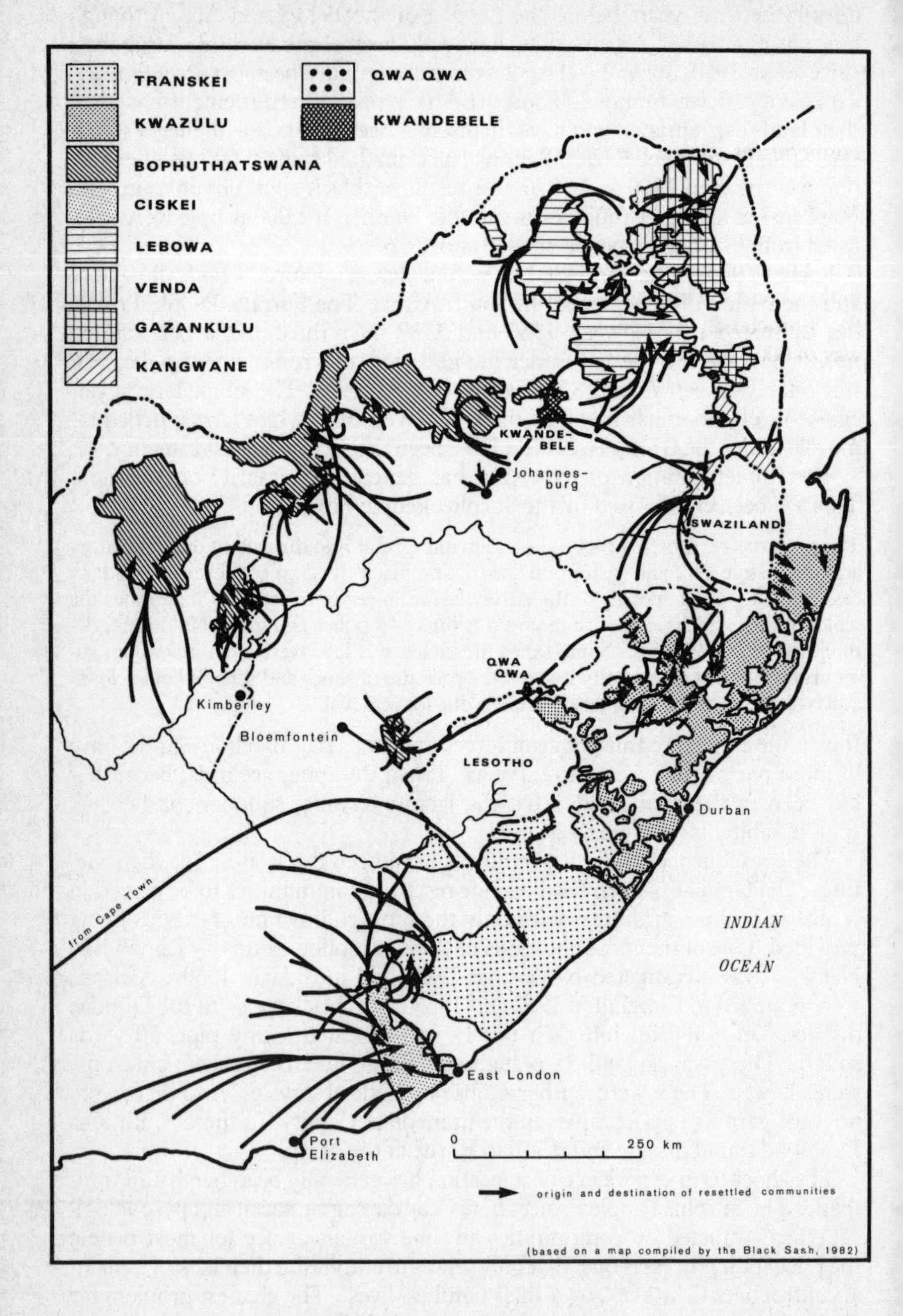

Resettlement to the Bantustans.

existence is often stripped bare. Opportunities for local employment are generally minimal. In relocation areas there has been an extremely heavy dependence on income derived from migrant labour. The findings of the Surplus People Project's fieldwork show 'that those families in closer settlements who have migrant workers are privileged members of their communities in economic terms. Given the lack of agricultural land and the dearth of local employment, having migrant workers in the household in most cases makes the difference between mere poverty and absolute destitution.'

The longer-term consequences of resettlement have been equally devastating. The problem of 'homeland' overpopulation has been greatly exacerbated in the process. This can be illustrated by the case of QwaQwa, the small Basotho 'homeland'. According to the 1970 census figures QwaQwa's population was 24 000. Ten years later the *de facto* population of QwaQwa was estimated at 300 000. It is therefore not surprising that the inhabitants of QwaQwa and other impoverished 'homelands' have had to seek some kind of access or link to the urban centres of South Africa, either through migrant labour or through 'illegal' urban migration.[25]

Since the mid-1930s the urban African population of South Africa has grown enormously. In 1936 an estimated 1 146 700 Africans were living in the towns and cities, rising to 2 329 000 in 1951, and to 4 989 000 in 1970. The 1936 figure represented 19 per cent of the total African population of South Africa, and the 1951 figure 27,9 per cent; by 1970 almost one-third of the African population was living in an urban area.

This growth can be partly explained by the pull of labour demand, generated particularly by the expansion of secondary industry. Between 1921 and 1958/60 there was a doubling of the relative contribution of secondary industry to the national product. In the second half of the 1930s South Africa experienced a significant post-depression recovery and entered a period of exceptionally fast industrial growth. The Second World War provided a further dramatic stimulus to industrial expansion. In the Durban–Pinetown area, for instance, both net industrial output and African employment in manufacturing industry more than doubled. Moreover, the government's suspension of the pass laws during the Second World War further accelerated African migration to urban areas.

At the same time there were push factors that drove Africans to the urban areas in increasing numbers. The deepening impoverishment of the reserves/'homelands' compelled more and more of their inhabitants to seek some form of subsistence in the urban centres. And, as we have just seen, the developing commercialisation and mechanisation of white farming, accompanied by the assault on squatters and labour tenants, forced thousands of Africans out of white rural areas. Although the government intended the 'homelands' to be the destination of these displaced people, many found their way to the towns and cities.

One feature of this growing urban African population was its changing sex ratio. The increasing number of African females moving to urban areas suggested that the urban African population was taking on a more permanent character. Indeed, it seems that some government planners in the 1930s and 1940s were thinking in terms of giving recognition to this greater permanence. The reports of the Young–Barrett Committee in 1939, the Smit Committee in 1942, and the Fagan Committee in 1948, were all critical of the migrant labour system and the pass laws.

In practice, though, the thinking of these planners was ignored. Instead, from the mid-1930s there was a steady tightening of the legislative screws to control the presence of Africans in urban areas. The underlying rationale of the legislation remained constant: an intention to limit the African urban presence to labour requirements. In this respect a key piece of legislation was the 1937 Native Laws Amendment Act, a measure that heralded the systematisation of influx control. The Act required local authorities to submit biennial estimates of their labour requirements; Africans in excess of these requirements could be removed; newcomers to an urban area would be allowed 14 days to find work, before being expelled; and women had to get permission from their local magistrate before leaving a rural area.

The election of the Nationalist government in 1948 was followed by a further strengthening of controls. Two important measures were passed in 1952. One consolidated passes into a single reference book. The second, another Native Laws Amendment Act, designated all towns and cities as prescribed areas in which influx control would be automatically applicable. Moreover, no African could remain in these areas for more than 72 hours unless they met certain qualifications (the now well-known 'section 10 rights'). Morris has stressed the significance of this Act: 'This was the most important piece of legislation in the post-war era and laid the basis for all state intervention to control the "distribution of labour" between town and country and within the towns from 1952 until 1971.' Both the 1952 Acts were strictly enforced. In the decade up to 1962 about four million Africans were convicted under the pass laws. Convictions increased after 1956, from which time African women were required to carry passes. The state utilised the second Act to expel 'surplus' Africans — the unemployable and the undesirable — from urban areas. Between 1956 and 1963 about 465 000 people were 'endorsed out' from twenty-three urban areas. These people, and those later affected by the passing of even stiffer Bantu Laws Amendment Acts in 1964, 1971 and 1978, can be added to the categories of victims of forced removals and resettlement in South Africa.[26]

The pass laws and influx control legislation have brought severe hardship to their hundreds of thousands of African victims. However, it is also necessary to view this machinery of control in another light, for the measures were not always effective and were in fact often resisted by Africans. For instance, the 1937 Native Laws Amendment Act, intended to restrict African urban migration, was followed, as we have seen, by a decade during which such migration rapidly increased.

The 1940s were also an era when Africans in some of the major urban centres strove to free themselves from various forms of government and municipal control. This striving was particularly reflected in the massive growth of shack settlements in these centres during that decade. In Johannesburg between 1936 and 1946 the black population increased by two-thirds, from about 229 000 to about 384 000. In 1940 the city's five 'official' townships accommodated just over 101 000 people. Others lived in freehold areas, such as Sophiatown, Newclare and Martindale. But there was still insufficient accommodation to house the city's growing African population, and so during the second half of the 1940s between 63 000 and 92 500 Africans moved into squatter settlements in the Johannesburg area. Stadler has shown that these settlements did not just arise in response to a housing shortage. Rather they were autonomous communities, with their own leaders and their own administrative machinery; and for these communities squatting formed part of a wider working-class struggle against oppressive conditions — low wages, high transport costs, and socio-political disabilities.

Proximity to urban centres and industrial areas was often a crucial consideration for Africans seeking living space. Close proximity reduced the cost of transport to the workplace and opened up numerous informal sector opportunities. Thus the private freehold townships of Sophiatown, Martindale and Newclare in Johannesburg's Western Areas were popular residential zones, occupied mainly by Africans, but also by coloureds, Indians and Chinese. As Lodge has noted, 'Unlike locations, these townships were not fenced off, there was no superintendent, nobody had to ask permission to live there, and compared to the geometrically planned municipal location, these densely packed suburbs were very difficult to police.' Workers made up the greatest part of the population of these townships; at different extremes there were also petty bourgeois standholders, and lumpenproletarian elements engaged in illicit brewing, prostitution, gambling or gangsterism. It would be a mistake to romanticise places like Sophiatown, but they did take on a special character. This, again, has been well captured by Lodge: 'Certainly, the freehold townships were often uncomfortable and often violent places to live in, but they were also characterised by mutual aid, interdependence and solidarity which would extend to the most ordinary (and therefore the most important) details of everyday life.'

A similar picture could be painted for Durban and Cape Town. The African shack-dwelling population of Durban grew steadily from the 1930s, mostly concentrated in the Cato Manor area to the west of the city. In 1936 there were about 2 500 African shack-dwellers living in Cato Manor, a figure that had risen to about 50 000 by 1950. The high population density and absence of facilities made living conditions at Cato Manor extremely unhealthy. But for its inhabitants it offered advantages: it was largely free from official control, except for the occasional police raid, and it was relatively close both to places of work and to the market for which the informal sector produced. In particular, Cato Manor came to be a major centre of illicit liquor production. In Cape Town, too, there was a rapid growth of the African shack population during the Second World War and afterwards. By 1952 only one-third of greater Cape Town's African population was housed in officially recognised townships; the rest were either scattered through the city or living in peri-urban squatter camps at Cook's Bush, Hout Bay, Elsie's River, Kensington and Windermere.

Since the early 1950s government policy has striven to undermine any independent base that Africans might have built for themselves in urban areas. This policy has involved an extensive programme of urban segregation and relocation, a programme that has added enormously to the number of those Africans who have been victims of forced removals and resettlement.

The shack settlements were a prime target in terms of government policy. By the early 1950s Johannesburg's squatter camps had been destroyed and their occupants rehoused in municipal housing schemes to the south of Johannesburg. In Durban the municipality tried unsuccessfully to 'peg' the growth of shacks in the mid-1940s. A temporary site-and-service scheme was introduced in 1952 with the establishment of the Cato Manor Emergency Camp. But the proximity of Cato Manor to Durban's white areas was anathema to government policy, and from 1958 Cato Manor's residents were gradually removed to KwaMashu, a newly built township to the north of Durban. The Cato Manor removals were fiercely resisted by many of the shantytown's inhabitants. The lead was taken by women whose livelihood had depended on the illicit liquor trade. As their opposition grew, rioting broke out in Cato Manor in 1959.

The process of urban relocation had been given impetus by two measures in the early 1950s. Firstly, the Group Areas Act of 1950 made racial segregation in urban residential areas compulsory. This measure, the culmination of urban segregatory legislation first introduced in 1923, was to effect extensive removals during the course of its implementation. Secondly, the Native Resettlement Act of 1954 established a resettlement board which was empowered to buy, sell or expropriate property in a particular area, and to plan townships. It was in terms of this latter measure that Africans were removed from freehold properties in Johannesburg's Western Areas from the 1950s. In the face of an organised ANC resistance campaign, over 22 500 families and almost 6 500 single people were removed from the freehold areas of Sophiatown, Martindale, Newclare and Pageview between 1955 and 1968. They were resettled in the new municipal townships of Diepkloof and Meadowlands, both of which formed part of Soweto, the growing black 'metropolis' south of Johannesburg.

The implementation of segregation has been only one prong of the urban removals fork. Two other major concerns have dominated government policy towards urban Africans. One has been to enforce more effectively the measures for limiting the African urban presence in accordance with labour requirements. As the Deputy Minister of Bantu Administration, Punt Janson, put it in 1972, the aim was to remove from the urban areas to the Bantustans 'unproductive people — those who because of old age, weak health, unfitness, or other reasons are no longer able to work'. These unfortunates were the people who could be 'endorsed out' of urban areas for not possessing section 10 rights under the 1952 Native Laws Amendment Act (and its subsequent amendments). It has been estimated that between 1960 and 1970 some

400 000 people were endorsed out of the towns and cities.

The second concern of the Nationalist government has been to relocate in the Bantustans as many as possible of those African workers entitled to work in an urban area. Two mechanisms have been adopted in an effort to fulfil this objective, which has only been realised in those urban areas which are close to 'homelands'. Firstly, a number of black townships in white urban areas have been demolished and their occupants removed to new townships in 'homeland' border areas, from where Africans commute to their place of work. Secondly, the same effect has been achieved without any physical removal of people taking place. In these cases boundaries have simply been redrawn to place existing townships inside 'homelands'. For instance, in 1977 Durban's KwaMashu township was at the stroke of a pen incorporated into KwaZulu.[27]

In pursuit of its apartheid 'ideal' the government has disrupted urban African communities and broken up families. Wholesale relocation has involved the removal of entire communities from shack settlements, from freehold areas, or from established townships in white areas. At the same time individuals — the so-called 'appendages' who have been deemed surplus to labour needs — have been banished on a massive scale to the impoverished 'homelands'. But this policy, even in its own terms, has only been partially successful. Shack settlements have continued to mushroom in the peri-urban areas of such cities as Durban, Cape Town, East London and Port Elizabeth. Africans have defied influx control machinery and the bulldozer in their efforts to find subsistence and shelter in the urban areas, which offer the best opportunities for survival. No sooner have shack settlements been demolished than they have been re-erected in another area. Thus the urban areas have formed one of the major sites of the African struggle in South Africa. It is to an examination of this struggle and the various forms of African resistance since the mid-1930s that we must now proceed.

Opposition and resistance, 1936–1976

The four decades between the mid-1930s and mid-1970s were marked by a series of troughs and peaks in African opposition and resistance to the South African system of white domination and capitalist exploitation. The period began with a trough. In the early 1930s movements like the ANC and the Communist Party of South Africa were becoming increasingly ineffectual. The branch and provincial organisation of the ANC had been steadily deteriorating; the depression had aggravated its precarious financial position; and divisions between moderates and radicals were continuing to undermine ANC unity.

With the ANC in a near moribund state, a new body — the All-African Convention (AAC) — was formed late in 1935. Over 400 delegates, many of them ANC figures, came together at the AAC's inaugural meeting at Bloemfontein in December 1935. They did so to voice and plan their opposition to Hertzog's segregation bills which had been published a few months before. The meeting passed resolutions rejecting Hertzog's land bill and the proposed disfranchisement of the Cape's African voters; and it highlighted other African grievances. In trying to follow these resolutions the AAC adopted well-worn tactics that had always failed in the previous two decades: appeals to the British government and delegations to the South African government. The AAC's delegation to meet Hertzog in Cape Town in 1936 proved yet another unsuccessful attempt to work through official channels. One immediate issue that faced both the ANC and the AAC was whether to boycott or participate in the Natives' Representative Council (NRC), an elective, advisory body set up under the 1936 Representation of Natives Act. In the event some prominent African leaders, including figures in the ANC, the AAC and the Communist Party, decided to participate and stood in the first NRC election in 1937.

Although some ANC leaders were associated with the AAC, the former looked upon the latter as no more than a coordinating body. The ANC continued to regard itself as the sole mouthpiece of the African people. The AAC itself enjoyed only short-lived prominence. By the early 1940s its constituency had dwindled to include a few African and coloured Marxists drawn mainly from the teaching profession in the Transkei and western Cape.[28]

The early 1930s also represented a stagnant period for African trade unions. At the best of times the business of organising African workers was fraught with difficulties. African unions were not illegal in the earlier decades of the century, but, as Bonner has observed,

> their ability to act was severely curtailed by Masters and Servants legislation which laid down criminal penalties for the breaking of a contract, by pass laws which forced people to take work under unfavourable conditions and provided machinery for prosecuting and deporting those who would not work, and by the migrant labour system.

In spite of these obstacles communists managed to organise a number of African trade unions on the Rand betwen 1927 and 1929, by which time about 10 000 Africans had become trade union members. However, this burgeoning movement soon collapsed, and only two of these unions on the Rand — the African Laundry Workers' Union and the South African Clothing Workers' Union — survived the great depression.

As was the case with African opposition politics, so African trade unionism revived in the mid-1930s, in a period of rapid industrial growth. Much of the initiative came from Max Gordon, a Trotskyite, who from 1935 helped to establish a number of new African unions on the Rand. By 1940 Gordon and his aides had organised about 20 such unions, involving a total membership of between 23 000 and 26 000. Late in 1941 the Council for Non-European Trade Unions (CNETU) was formed, a coordinating body to which most African unions in the Transvaal became affiliated. Dominated by communists, CNETU grew into what Lodge calls 'the most powerful African trade union grouping ever to have existed in South Africa'. By 1945 it claimed to embrace nationwide 119 affiliated unions with a total membership of 158 000 African workers.

This development of African union organisation was at times matched by a growth in African worker militancy and activism. In a four-month period between September 1942 and January 1943 there was a spate of strikes, mainly on the Rand but also in Natal. Over 8 000 black workers came out on strike during that period. Among those involved were sweet workers, coal miners, dockers, dairy workers, brick workers, railway labourers, and municipal employees. In September 1942 some 400 Natal coal miners set fire to their company's buildings when management rejected complaints about working conditions. In December the Johannesburg City Council conceded a 60 per cent pay increase after a one-day strike by 2 000 African municipal workers.

It was also in the 1940s that African mineworkers on the Rand came to realise their organisational potential more fully. Communists had tried unsuccessfully to organise African mineworkers in the early 1930s. It was not until 1941 that the African Mineworkers' Union (AMU) was formed. By 1944 the AMU could claim a following of about 25 000 members. At the AMU's annual conference in 1946 it was decided that a minimum wage of 10*s*. a day and improved working conditions be demanded. The Chamber of Mines failed to respond, and in August over 60 000 African miners went on strike. The strike, which lasted for a week, had disastrous short-term consequences for the miners. It was ruthlessly suppressed by the police at a cost of 12 dead and 1 200 wounded; no wage increase was to be granted until 1949; and the AMU was effectively destroyed. However, the short-term failure should not blur the wider significance of the event. The 1946 strike was the largest yet in South Africa's history; and, significantly, it was carried through by migrant workers, who were supposedly less capable of organisation and militancy.[29]

The 1940s also saw a reawakening of the ANC, even though the movement became increasingly wrought by internal tensions and was often ambivalent in its stance on vital issues. That the ANC held together at this time may have had much to do with the pragmatism of A. B. Xuma, who was its president from 1940 to 1949. One of Xuma's achievements was to streamline the organisation of the ANC. The new ANC constitution of 1943 aimed to centralise authority in a five-member executive committee, to revive the branches, and to eliminate the entrenched position of chiefs in the organisation's constitutional structure.

More significant were Xuma's attempts both to draw bright young talent into the ANC and to broaden its base. As we shall see, these two initiatives had contradictory consequences. Xuma's pragmatism led him to foster links between the ANC and other opposition movements. As Karis and Carter have remarked, 'Xuma was both an Africanist, calling for African unity and self-reliance, and a multiracialist, welcoming cooperation by whites of goodwill but turning increasingly to cooperation with nonwhites.' For instance, in 1944 Xuma aligned the ANC to an anti-pass campaign that had been initiated the previous year by the Communist Party, a campaign that failed in its objective to obtain a million signatures for a petition against passes. This was a time when communists were working more and more within the ranks of the ANC: in 1945 three leading African communists, Moses Kotane, J. B.

Marks and Dan Thloome were on the national executive of the ANC. Xuma's non-racial strategy was further illustrated in 1947 when he aligned with G. M. Naicker and Yusuf Dadoo, two leaders in the South African Indian Congress, to sign a 'Joint Declaration of Cooperation'.

Xuma had been concerned to broaden the base of ANC support and build links with other opposition movements. It was a strategy, though, that was much resented by the growing Africanist element in the ANC. Africanism in the 1940s found its main institutional expression in the ANC's Youth League. Founded in 1944, the Youth League was led initially by Anton Lembede until his premature death at the age of 33 in 1947. Son of a Zulu farm labourer, Lembede was a charismatic figure who has taken on heroic stature in Africanist tradition. Other early leaders in the Youth League are familiar figures who rose to prominence in later phases of the African struggle —names like Walter Sisulu, Oliver Tambo and Nelson Mandela.

Africanists in the Youth League recognised the need to cultivate African pride, assertiveness and self-reliance. They firmly rejected any paternalist support from white liberals. Indeed, their self-reliant stance led them generally to rule out collaboration with non-African movements. The Africanist analysis was based on race: Africans were the victims of racial oppression; accordingly Africans should unite to wage their struggle against this oppression. This position clashed with the class analysis of the communists, who were concerned to unite the working-class against capitalist exploitation. It was this kind of fundamental division that generated tensions within the ANC in the 1940s. But the organisation held together, seemingly able to accommodate within its ranks persons with differing ideologies and strategies — communists (like Kotane), Africanists (like Lembede), moderates (like Z. K. Matthews), and pragmatists (like Xuma).[30]

The 1949 annual conference of the ANC marked a turning-point in the movement's history. In the first place, the executive largely changed hands. Xuma, who had been resisting a militant activist strategy, was replaced as president by Dr James Moroka. At the same time a number of prominent Youth Leaguers were elected to the executive, including Sisulu, Mandela and Tambo. Secondly, the conference adopted the Programme of Action, a document that had been drawn up by radicals and Africanists during the previous two years. The Programme reiterated the ANC's rejection of white supremacy and all forms of segregation. To further these ends a council of action would be set up to organise a boycott of 'all differential political institutions'. This was to be part of a wider campaign of strikes, civil disobedience and non-cooperation.

The ANC planned to inaugurate its campaign with a mass black 'stay-at-home' on 26 June 1950, which was to be a 'National Day of Protest and Mourning'. But before that day another mass work stoppage was organised on a broader front, which included the ANC, the Communist Party, and the Indian Congress, and was planned for 1 May. Africanists in the ANC resented the non-racial character of the Mayday stoppage, which they also saw as a diversion from the Programme of Action. However, large numbers of

Africans in the Johannesburg area observed the stoppage, which ended tragically in clashes between police and crowds in Alexandra, Sophiatown, Orlando and Benoni, leaving 18 dead.

In contrast, the 26 June day of protest evoked a poor response in the Transvaal. This particular campaign had its most impressive impact in Port Elizabeth and Durban. In Port Elizabeth a very high proportion of the African work-force stayed at home. Lodge has explained this vigorous response of Africans in Port Elizabeth:

> Great poverty, comparatively few restrictions and a sizeable African industrial work-force led to the development of a powerful African trade union movement which deliberately concerned itself with issues well outside the scope of conventional economistic trade unionism. By 1950 politics was in the hands of working-class leaders to a degree which clearly distinguished Port Elizabeth from any other centre.

For the next two years there was a lull in African protest activity. But in 1951 planning was begun for a mass campaign of defiance and civil disobedience. The planning was directed by the ANC, but the South African Indian Congress (SAIC) was also closely involved, and two of its leaders, Dadoo and Cachalia, were on the campaign's planning council.

In January 1952 an ultimatum, signed by Moroka and Sisulu, was sent to Prime Minister Malan. It demanded the repeal of certain laws, notably the pass laws, the Bantu Authorities Act, the Group Areas Act, the Representation of Natives Act, and the Suppression of Communism Act. If the demands were not met, demonstrations would be held on 6 April, a special day that whites were to celebrate as the tercentenary of Van Riebeeck's arrival at the Cape. Not surprisingly Malan rejected the ultimatum. So on 6 April mass black rallies took place in many centres. The spirit of the occasion was later characterised by Albert Luthuli in his autobiography:

> To put it simply, while they celebrated three hundred years of white domination, we looked back over three hundred years of black subjection. While the whites were jubilant over what they said God had given them, we contemplated what they had taken from us, and the land which they refuse to share with us though they cannot work it without us.

The main defiance campaign itself began on 26 June 1952. The campaign centred on the defiance of apartheid regulations — using facilities reserved for whites, and disobeying the pass laws and municipal curfews. The civil disobedience started in Johannesburg and Port Elizabeth, but soon spread to other centres in the Transvaal, eastern Cape and western Cape, and later to Durban and Bloemfontein. The campaign lasted for over four months, during which time more than 8 000 resisters were arrested. Again the main area of defiance was the eastern Cape, where about 70 per cent of the arrests occurred. Apart from arresting the participants, the police also launched a crackdown on the campaign's leadership in terms of the Suppression of Communism Act. Twenty leaders, including Moroka, Sisulu, Marks, Mandela, and seven Indians, went on trial in Johannesburg, and fifteen leaders in Port Elizabeth. All thirty-five were given suspended nine-month prison sentences.[31]

In Lodge's view, 'The main achievement of the Defiance Campaign lay in gaining widespread popular support for the African National Congress. By the end of the campaign ANC leaders claimed a following of 100 000.' The campaign also marked the beginning of a period in which passive resistance became the dominant strategy of black opposition movements. It was a period that lasted throughout the 1950s and culminated in the Sharpeville crisis of 1960.

African passive resistance in the 1950s was generally sporadic, isolated, and not always successful. For instance, between 1953 and 1955 the ANC tried to mobilise resistance to the government's destruction of black freehold communities in Johannesburg's Western Areas. Meetings were held to voice opposition to the removals; and the more militant leaders, like Robert Resha, talked of confrontation. But when the removals were eventually initiated in February 1955 there was virtually no resistance. On 9 February 2 000 armed police moved into Sophiatown to oversee the operation. It was this deployment of force by the state that more than anything else prevented an outburst of open resistance to the Western Areas removals.

Less than two months after the destruction of Sophiatown had begun, the government first implemented its Bantu Education system. The Bantu Education Act had been passed in 1953. The measure aimed to transfer control of black education from the provinces to the central government, and to undermine the independence of private mission or church schools by cutting their subsidies. This centralisation of control was clearly designed to mould black education in such a way that blacks could be conditioned to fill a subservient role in society.

The Act came into effect in April 1955. The new system met with widespread sporadic opposition. On 12 April scattered boycotts of black schools began. The main area of boycotting was the east Rand, but at one point it spread to Soweto and Sophiatown. The boycott movement also had some impact in the eastern Cape; but the response there was surprisingly weak, given the region's earlier prominence in the defiance campaign. Throughout this period of initial opposition to Bantu Education the ANC's leadership was hesitant and vacillating. This may well explain the isolated and sporadic character of the opposition.

The 1950s were also marked by African consumer boycotts of commodities and services. Bus boycotts were not new to South Africa. In the early 1940s residents of Alexandra had engaged in several such boycotts to protest against increased fares. For a ten-day period in 1943 over 20 000 boycotters from Alexandra walked to their work in Johannesburg. In the early 1950s bus boycotting centred on Evaton, an African township about 30 miles south of Johannesburg. The main Evaton boycott ran for several months in 1955 and 1956. On occasions tension within the community between those who supported and those who opposed the boycott tactic erupted into violence. By the time the boycott ended fifteen people had been killed, and the bus company had lost £25 000 in fares. In 1957 there occurred another major bus boycott in Johannesburg, again prompted by a fare increase. It began in January at Alexandra, which remained the centre of the boycott throughout, and soon not only spread to other Johannesburg townships and to Pretoria, but also evoked solidarity boycotts in the eastern Cape. This boycott, which lasted over three months, was massive in scale, involving over 60 000 participants. It also brought positive results for the boycotters. The government soon passed a bill requiring employers to make a monthly payment to subsidise thc transport costs of their African workers. As a contemporary observer wrote, 'It was the first act of parliament in the forty-seven years of the Union to have been passed as a direct result of African pressure.' And in July 1957 bus fares were brought down to their pre-boycott level.

The ANC had been strangely quiet during the Evaton boycott, but was to be more prominent in 1957. Indeed, it tried both to enlarge the latter boycott and to use it as a means of politicisation. In February the ANC in the Cape Province announced a £1-a-day wage campaign and a plan to boycott Afrikaner Nationalist-produced commodities and Nationalist-controlled finance houses. One target was Anton Rupert's Rembrandt company. And in 1959 the ANC organised a successful three-month consumer boycott of potatoes in protest against the oppressive treatment of African farm labourers.

African women also played a prominent role in passive resistance movements during the 1950s. The ANC Women's League had been founded in 1948; and in 1954 it affiliated to the Federation of South African Women, a non-racial body set up to fight for women's rights, while also committing itself to the national liberation struggle. In 1955 the government announced that African women would be required to carry passes from the start of the following year. The decision provoked massive rallies and demonstrations. During the first half of 1956 in many parts of the country women marched into town centres to deliver petitions or protests to official figures. In August 20 000 women gathered in Pretoria to hand in petitions to the prime minister's office. However, the protests were ignored and the state remorselessly pursued its task of imposing passes on women.

In Durban in 1959 women's resistance escalated into violence. In June Durban's authorities attempted to eradicate the illicit liquor trade in Cato Manor. For many women liquor manufacture was their major means of subsistence. So in retaliation a large group of women invaded the Cato Manor municipal beer hall, destroying equipment and overturning vats. For two weeks Durban was in a state of unrest as women picketed the beer halls and clashed with police.[32]

The ANC's role in the various passive resistance campaigns of the 1950s appears somewhat inconsistent. At times it was uninvolved, as during the Evaton bus boycott; on occasions its organisational role was hesitant, as in the campaign against Bantu Education; at other times it played a leading part, as was the case with the 1957 bus boycott. This inconsistency may have reflected the uncertain character of the ANC during the 1950s. As Lodge has observed, in the early 1950s 'the ANC did not have a clearly articulated ideological position'; and, he goes on to say, 'it did not have a carefully worked out long-term strategy.'

This uncertain character was probably a product of the diverse influences working upon and within the ANC. Broadly there were three main strands within the organisation during the 1950s: these can be loosely labelled as charterist, Africanist, and workerist. The charterist position represented a concern to build a broad-based movement to oppose apartheid. This would entail accommodating people of all races and of differing ideologies. In June 1955 this ideal gained some fulfilment when the Congress of the People met at Kliptown near Johannesburg. The Congress was attended by 3 000 delegates, including 320 Indians, 230 coloureds and 112 whites. The main purpose of the Congress was to debate and adopt the Freedom Charter, a document that had been prepared by a drafting committee in the weeks before the Congress. The committee incorporated into the Charter numerous suggestions that had emanated from various quarters. In its final form the Charter stood as a statement of equal rights and as a programme of social democracy. It reaffirmed the multi-racial character of South African society, in which people of all races should have equal opportunities and rights; it envisaged a welfare state with adequate provision for health, housing and education; and it called for limited nationalisation and for basic worker rights.

The Freedom Charter was not formally adopted by the ANC until March–April 1956. This delay was perhaps a reflection of the Charter's broad scope. It could be said that it tried to be all things to everybody, and thus opened itself to criticism from various quarters. To some liberals the Charter looked like a socialist programme; for some Marxists the Charter represented the ideals of bourgeois democracy; and for Africanists the Charter made dangerous concessions to multi-racialism.

Africanist dissent within the ANC continued to grow in the 1950s, having gained a foothold in the Youth League in the 1940s. At the forefront of this dissent in the 1950s were A. P. Mda, Potlake Leballo and Robert Sobukwe. They resented the way in which non-Africans were intruding into the liberation struggle. Africanism demanded a more self-reliant, self-assertive and spontaneous approach to the struggle. In November 1958 the Africanists seceded from the ANC, and the following year founded a new organisation, the Pan-Africanist Congress (PAC), to represent their views and strategies. At the PAC's inaugural conference at Orlando in 1959 Sobukwe was elected as the first PAC president. Later in the year the PAC's trade union wing, the Federation of Free African Trade Unions of South Africa (FOFATUSA), was founded, claiming to represent about 9 unions and 17 000 African workers. The PAC itself failed to fulfil its early hopes of acquiring a mass membership. It did not manage to penetrate ANC strongholds; the main base of PAC support lay in the western Cape.[33]

A third emphasis within the ANC was concerned to concentrate efforts on building up African working-class support. This strand came to be embodied in the South African Congress of Trade Unions (SACTU). SACTU was founded in 1955 against a background of government repression of black trade unions. The 1950 Suppression of Communism Act had been directed primarily against the trade unions; and the Bantu Labour Act of 1953 had made strikes by Africans illegal. SACTU's inaugural conference was held at Johannesburg in 1955, attended by delegates representing 33 unions and over 41 000 workers of all races.

SACTU's intention was, in Feit's words, 'to be a political trade union, to harness workers' demands for economic amelioration to a political cause'. It was to participate in the political struggle against the pass laws, Bantu Education, and other forms of oppression. But the main focus of SACTU activity centred on worker organisation. It sought the affiliation of existing unions or assisted the formation of new ones. Three unions formed the backbone of SACTU — the Food and Canning Workers' Union, the Textile Workers' Industrial Union, and the Laundry, Cleaning and Dyeing Workers' Union. SACTU soon obtained the affiliation of other existing unions. In 1956 it helped to establish new metal workers' unions in Port Elizabeth and Cape Town; and in 1961 SACTU formed a farm workers' union and a national organising committee for mineworkers.

The first few years of SACTU's existence belonged to a period of growing African worker organisation and militancy. SACTU's total affiliated membership rose from about 20 000 in 1956 to about 55 000 in 1962. Between 1955 and 1960 almost 35 000 African workers participated in 420 illegal strikes, only a few of which were initiated by SACTU. In 1957 SACTU resolved to embark upon a national campaign for a minimum wage of £1 a day. Some 100 000 leaflets were distributed at the launch of the campaign. On 26 June a one-day stay-at-home was widely observed by black workers in Johannesburg and Port Elizabeth. But a call for a national three-day strike to coincide with the white general election in April 1958 met with a much poorer response, workers only in Port Elizabeth and Durban staying away. In May 1961 SACTU played a prominent role in mobilising support for a three-day stay-at-home that brought considerable disruption to industry and commerce in major centres.[34]

SACTU was to be crushed in the government crackdown on African opposition movements in the early 1960s. Between 1960 and 1966 over 160 SACTU office holders were banned from taking part in SACTU or other trade union activities. The crackdown was largely prompted by the Sharpeville crisis of 1960, a crisis that can be regarded as a major turning-point in African opposition politics. As a result of government suppression the ANC and PAC were forced to operate either underground or in exile; and they shifted their strategies towards violent forms of struggle.

The Sharpeville crisis arose out of a PAC anti-pass campaign. At the end of 1959 both the PAC and ANC planned anti-pass activities. The ANC was proposing to hold a series of nationwide demonstrations against passes in the first half of 1960. The PAC's scheme involved bolder gestures of defiance. On an appointed day, 21 March, PAC supporters were to leave their passes at home, and court arrest by presenting themselves at police stations. The ultimate objective was to fill the prisons, bring industry and commerce to a standstill, and so force the government to abolish passes. The campaign was planned to be peaceful. On the day the only significant response to the PAC's call came in African townships around Vereeniging and Cape Town. At the Sharpeville township near Vereeniging a crowd of about 5 000 gathered near the police station on the morning of 21 March. After an incident near the main gate the crowd began to surge forward. The police panicked and opened fire, killing 69 people and wounding 180. The majority were shot in the back.

For the following two weeks the country remained in a state of high tension. During the night of 21 March there was rioting in the Cape Town township of Langa, another PAC stronghold. By the end of the week about half of Cape Town's African labour-force was out on strike. On 24 March the ANC president, Luthuli, called for workers throughout the country to observe Monday 28 March as a day of mourning by staying at home. The call received an enormous response in major centres such as Johannesburg, Port Elizabeth and Durban. On 31 March there were massive African marches in Cape Town and Durban. An estimated 30 000 marched into the centre of Cape Town; they were persuaded to disperse, and soon afterwards a police cordon was thrown around Langa. On the same day another column tried to march from Cato Manor into the centre of Durban. About 1 000 people got through a police cordon and marched to the central gaol where they demanded the release of ANC detainees.

For a moment during the crisis the government appeared to weaken when, on 26 March, it temporarily suspended the pass laws. But it soon resolved to suppress the resistance. On 30 March a state of emergency was declared. The police were already swooping to make wholesale arrests. Thousands of Africans were charged for minor offences; 2 000 other activists were detained under emergency regulations; and the pass laws were soon re-enforced. On 8 April the government banned the ANC and the PAC under the newly passed Unlawful Organizations Act.[35]

The Sharpeville crisis marked the end of a decade during which passive resistance had been the main tactic of African opposition. One effect of the post-Sharpeville crackdown was to break a commitment to non-violence that had been held dear by many African leaders. While some stuck to this commitment, others did not. The ANC did not officially abandon its non-violent strategy, but it did spawn a new organisation, *Umkonto we Sizwe* (The Spear of the Nation), which would engage in acts of sabotage without harm to life. The decision to found *Umkonto* was made, on Mandela's recommendation, at a meeting of the ANC national executive in June 1961. Its actual sabotage campaign was initiated in mid-December that year with the bombing of various installations and government offices. During a period of eighteen months over 200 isolated acts of sabotage occurred in many different centres. They caused limited damage and gained little publicity.

In July 1963 the police raided *Umkonto*'s headquarters, a farm in the white suburb of Rivonia, north of Johannesburg. In the ensuing trial three of the ANC's most prominent leaders, Mandela, Sisulu and Govan Mbeki, admitted responsibility for the sabotage campaign. All three, and others, were found guilty and sentenced to life imprisonment. The convictions virtually destroyed the ANC's organisational head and removed the political leadership outside the country. During the height of the Sharpeville crisis the ANC had anticipated government suppression and had accordingly chosen Oliver Tambo to leave the country and act as the ANC's chief representative abroad.

In the aftermath of Sharpeville the PAC also spawned a military offshoot, the *Poqo* movement. *Poqo*, which was mainly based in the western Cape, carried through its violent strategy more brutally and on a larger scale than *Umkonto*. There was no concern not to endanger human life. Indeed, the spilling of blood was seen as a necessary means for achieving liberation. Its targets were often suspected black informers or collaborators, but *Poqo* was also prepared to kill whites indiscriminately. *Poqo*'s strategy was based on the assumption that its acts of violence could escalate into a mass popular uprising that would overthrow white supremacy. In November 1962, for instance, *Poqo* tried to promote an insurrection in Paarl. Some 250 men carrying axes, pangas and other weapons marched on the town. They tried to stone the police station but were repulsed by police fire. A few local white residents were then attacked at random, two being killed. After less than three hours the uprising was quelled; five insurgents had been killed. Another *Poqo* uprising was planned, but not realised, for Pretoria in 1963. The movement was largely broken by mass arrests in mid-1963.[36]

Almost all the opposition groupings and resistance movements discussed so far were essentially urban-based. This should not be allowed to obscure the existence of African protest movements in the rural areas in the 1950s and 1960s. Historians have documented four main rural rebellions that occurred between 1950 and 1963. Of these, the first two arose out of specific grievances; the second two, both in the Transkei in the early 1960s, represented more generalised forms of resistance.

In 1950 a rebellion broke out in the Witzieshoek reserve on the northern border between Basutoland and the Orange Free State. The rebellion was the culmination of long-standing resentment, on the part of a section of the community, against betterment schemes which had involved grazing controls, cattle culling, and population removals from grazing areas. In the Bafarutshe reserve near Zeerust in the western Transvaal it was the issue of women's passes that provided at least the occasion for revolt in the late 1950s. Passes were either not taken up or else were destroyed; attacks were made on the property of collaborators; and the local chief refused to cooperate with the authorities, only to be stripped of his office.

Rural resistance in the Transkei in the early 1960s was directed more generally against the government's Bantustan policy. The Mpondo revolt of 1960 represented the most widespread and sustained episode of rural resistance in this period. In eastern Pondoland a leadership group, called *Intaba*, set itself up as an alternative authority to the government-appointed chiefs. A number of chiefs who rejected *Intaba*'s authority were killed. The rebellion against the system of Bantu Authorities gained mass support among the Mpondo. In suppressing the revolt early in 1961 government forces arrested nearly 5 000 dissidents. Southall has emphasised the rebels' achievement: 'The significance of the revolt lay in its genuinely mass basis, its duration and its discipline. It was, indeed, a major triumph for the unarmed people of East Pondoland to so rudely demonstrate to the world that they repudiated their renewed subservience to the chiefs.'

Disaffection with the Bantu Authorities system was also prevalent in Thembuland from the late 1950s. There was strong opposition to the government-appointed chiefs, particularly Matanzima, formerly a minor chief who gained considerably in status by participating in the system. In 1962 there were three attempts on Matanzima's life. It was at this time that popular disaffection was being harnessed to *Poqo* activity. In 1963 unrest in Thembuland reached a peak. Thereafter it declined in the face of police arrests and Matanzima's growing control of Transkeian government machinery.[37]

The ferocious suppression of black opposition movements in the early 1960s was followed by a lull in African politics. Leaders were imprisoned, banned or forced into exile. From 1962 to 1968 there was a period of industrial peace, during which time the number of Africans involved in officially reported strikes did not rise above 2 000 a year. The state machinery, backed by draconian legislation and a growing army of informers and spies, made the task of recovery awesome.

In the 1970s the lull came to an end. Two particular developments shaped the renewal of the struggle. One was a revival of trade union organisation and militancy; the other was the growth of the black consciousness movement. In the early 1970s Durban formed the centre of African worker activism and a catalyst for the later resurgence of black unionism. The high proportion of migrant workers in Durban's African labour-force, and the relative proximity of a reserve army of labour, had enabled employers to keep African wages at an extremely low level. The further erosion of real wages by inflation caused great hardship to African workers. Wages were, therefore, the fundamental issue. In 1972 the Durban dock workers came out on strike over a wage demand and brought the harbour to a standstill. But 1973 proved the crucial year. The initial strike in January took place at Durban's Coronation Brick and Tile Factory, where African workers demanded a 120 per cent increase in the minimum wage rate. The main arena of strike activity was to be the textile industry, especially the Frame Group, which paid notoriously low wages. Soon the strikes spread not only to other industries, including sugar mills, transport, rubber works, engineering, construction, food and plastics, but also to other parts of the country, notably the Transvaal and the eastern Cape. In the first three months of 1973 there were 160 strikes involving 61 000 workers.

The Durban strikes provided a stimulus to greater union organisation and worker activity. In the aftermath of the strikes African unions were established or revived. Branches of the Metal and Allied Workers' Union were organised in Pietermaritzburg and Durban; and the National Union of Textile Workers established, as was the Union of Clothing and Allied Workers. Strike activity continued unabated over the next three years. From April 1973 until mid-1976 about 140 000 black workers went on strike in South

Africa; the overwhelming majority of these were African, but coloureds and Indians were also extensively involved. African workers had clearly given a powerful display of strength. Considerable wage increases had been extracted from employers throughout the country. And it is significant that in Durban migrant workers, supposedly more docile and less capable of organisation and militancy, had led the way in what was to be a new era for African workers.[38]

The second main development of the early 1970s was the growth of the black consciousness movement. The first institutional expression of the movement originated among black university students, who in the late 1960s became disillusioned with the National Union of South African Students (NUSAS), a body dominated by liberal white students. In 1969 the black students founded their own breakaway organisation, the South African Students' Organization (SASO). By 1972 SASO claimed a membership of over 4 000. Two other black consciousness organisations were founded in 1972. One was the Black People's Convention (BPC). This was to focus much of its activity on community projects; it did little by way of organising workers or engaging in direct political action. The other was the South African Students' Movement (SASM), which was to play a role in the Soweto revolt.

The black consciousness movement shared some of the ideas and attitudes of the earlier Africanists in the Youth League and the PAC. Like the Africanists, the proponents of black consciousness were concerned to promote African self-awareness, pride and self-reliance, and to break dependence on whites in the liberation struggle. In other respects, though, black consciousness thinkers departed from the Africanist outlook. Whereas Africanism had tended to exclude Indians and coloureds, the black consciousness movement was keen to incorporate them as blacks. While the Africanists worked through more formal political organisations, the black consciousness movement operated through more informal channels.[39]

Although the revival of black worker organisation and militancy, and the growth of the black consciousness movement, were two important developments in the early 1970s, neither significantly shaped the major popular outburst of the decade — the Soweto revolt of 1976. The spark that occasioned this revolt was a government decree that Afrikaans had to be used as a medium of instruction in African secondary schools. It was this decree that brought together about 20 000 Soweto schoolchildren in a protest march on the morning of 16 June. Eyewitness accounts differ as to how the violence started. Kane-Berman has described the outbreak:

> Police vehicles raced to the scene. Many of the eyewitnesses quoted in the newspapers at the time said the violence began when the police tried to seize placards and stop the march. The students taunted them, and they responded with teargas. Some reports had it that stones were then thrown and shooting started, while others said the police opened fire before stones were thrown. In any event, apparently no order from the police to the marchers to disperse was heard, and a senior police officer admitted at the time that no warning shots had been fired either.

As the firing started a 13-year-old schoolboy, Hector Petersen, was shot dead. Soon several other young protesters had met the same fate or had been wounded.

From that time the peaceful protest march became transformed into a violent, popular outburst, that soon spread throughout Soweto and, in the following weeks, into many different, far-flung areas of the country. In Soweto the students gave immediate vent to their anger. They resorted to stoning and burning. Their targets were police vehicles, commercial vans, beer-halls, liquor stores and other shops, and the offices of the West Rand Administration Board, the government body that administered Soweto. Within a few days 143 vehicles and 139 buildings in Soweto had been destroyed or damaged by fire. From Soweto the revolt soon spread to other townships on the Rand and in Pretoria, and to isolated areas of the eastern and western Transvaal, the Orange Free State and the northern Cape.

In August the revolt took on new dimensions. On 4 August the Soweto students tried to organise a mass stay-at-home. They damaged a stretch of the railway to Johannesburg and stoned buses to prevent people from going to work. They then formed a large column, about 20 000 strong, and marched towards Johannesburg, intending to gather at police headquarters in John Vorster Square. Their way was blocked by a police cordon. In the ensuing clash three more students were shot dead.

On 11 August African townships in Cape Town erupted. On that day African pupils decided to march to express their solidarity with Sowetans. Again a peaceful march escalated into violence, brought on by a cycle of police bullets and teargas, and stoning and burning from the demonstrators. Thirty-three people were killed that day in the Cape Town area. Intermittent disturbances, involving coloureds and Africans, continued in the region until December. In mid-September a successful stay-at-home was organised in Cape Town.

Johannesburg and Cape Town were the major centres of the 1976 revolt, but there was also a lengthy and bitter struggle waged in the main townships of the eastern Cape. In all, according to Kane-Berman's estimate, at least 160 black communities throughout the country were involved in the disturbances within the four months after 16 June. Estimates of the total death-toll in the revolt vary. Kane-Berman reckons on a figure of 661, but suggests that it could have been higher. Soweto accounted for about three-quarters of the deaths. According to an estimate by the Institute of Race Relations, by the end of 1976 over 1 500 had been convicted on charges arising out of the disturbances.

In recent years there have been some useful accounts of the 1976 revolt, notably by Hirson and Kane-Berman. But a detailed and measured historical analysis is still awaited. Explanations for the reasons and forces behind the disturbances are at present largely conjectural. Kane-Berman claims that 'Black Consciousness ... was probably the single most important factor' behind the revolt. The spread of black consciousness ideas 'is likely to have contributed heavily to the spirit of determination and assertiveness so evident among younger blacks all over the country'. But Kane-Berman produces little evidence to support his view. Hirson offers a testing critique of the whole black consciousness movement and plays down its influence in 1976. He prefers to set the 1976 revolt against the backdrop of the rising worker militancy of the early 1970s, and argues that as the revolt proceeded, the school students became increasingly radicalised and more sensitive to worker interests.

The link drawn by Hirson between worker militancy and the 1976 disturbances appears rather tenuous. At this stage it seems one should rather stress two points. Firstly, the revolt was very much youth-centred, although adults inevitably became involved. According to one estimate almost two-thirds of those who died in the revolt were under the age of 26; and school pupils provided much of the leadership and organisation. Secondly, the revolt was directed to an overwhelming extent against oppressive or hostile symbols. The personnel and property of the police and the West Rand Administration Board represented one obvious target. The system of Bantu Education was another: at least 350 black schools were attacked countrywide. And the students attacked beer-halls and shebeens in an effort to strike at the source of a hated social evil.[40]

Less than ten years after the event it is still difficult to assess the wider impact of the 1976 disturbances. Certainly they ushered in an era of enhanced black activism and militancy, manifested in a resurgence of the ANC's popularity, the development of black worker organisation, and the revival of guerrilla activity. In the immediate aftermath of the revolt the government itself cracked down on opposition movements, banning various organisations and detaining leaders. However, whereas these strong-arm tactics had succeeded in seriously undermining black opposition in the aftermath of Sharpeville, they have not succeeded in the aftermath of Soweto.

10
COLONIALISM, DECOLONISATION AND NEO- COLONIALISM: THE BLS COUNTRIES

Until the late 1960s the British maintained a direct imperial administrative presence in the three protectorates of Swaziland, Basutoland and Bechuanaland. Britain had assumed responsibility for those territories rather reluctantly. That she had assumed responsibility at all was the result of particular historical events. Basutoland had been annexed to the Cape in 1871. But the Cape's administration of the territory became increasingly uncomfortable during and after the Basotho rebellion of 1880–1, and in 1884 the imperial government resumed authority. The Bechuanaland Protectorate, originally created in 1885, had been destined for inclusion into the British South Africa Company's sphere of influence. But the Company was disgraced by its involvement in the Jameson Raid, and it was that single event more than anything else that kept Bechuanaland directly in the imperial fold. In the mid-1890s Swaziland had come under the authority of the Transvaal government, and there it would probably have remained had it not been for the South African War.

From early in the twentieth century the British generally assumed that the protectorates would eventually be transferred to South Africa. The possibility of such a transfer was provided for in the South Africa Act of 1909. Indeed, successive South African prime ministers, from Botha to Verwoerd, all requested transfer on various occasions. Had Smuts's government not fallen in 1924 incorporation might have taken place. In the event all three territories remained outside the sphere of South African political authority, largely because of Britain's insistence that the territories could not be transferred without consultation with their inhabitants. Had they been transferred each territory would ultimately have been slotted into the South African government's Bantustan framework. As it turned out the three territories escaped this fate, and to-day each is recognised internationally as a legitimate independent state. However, while the three countries have remained free of direct South African political control, they have not managed to escape the consequences of South Africa's dominance in the wider economy of the subcontinent. It remains for us to examine the particular political and economic paths followed by each of the three territories in the twentieth century.[41]

Swaziland

During the last two decades of the nineteenth century Swaziland had experienced debilitating pressure and turmoil. Numerous concessions had been recklessly granted away, especially by King Mbandzeni during the 1880s, and white adventurers had acquired trading, mining, grazing and land rights in large areas of Swaziland. The territory had also become a pawn in the diplomatic wrangle then developing between the British and the Transvaal Republic. The Swazis' subjugation by the Transvaal was felt immediately with the imposition of burdensome taxes. The rinderpest epidemic of 1896–7 decimated Swazi herds. And in 1899 Bunu, the reigning king, died, leaving an heir, the future King Sobhuza II, who was only 1 year old.

Swaziland formally came under British authority in 1903 when the Swaziland Order-In-Council was issued in London. For the next three years it was administered as a district of the Transvaal. In 1906 it was disannexed from the Transvaal; from that time it became a British dependency, although its constitutional status was not exactly defined. A proclamation of 1907 provided for the appointment of Swaziland's first resident commissioner, who was to be the chief imperial representative in the territory.

The vague, undefined status of Swaziland in the colonial era has led scholars to disagree in their interpretation of the position of traditional authorities under colonial rule. How powerful constitutionally was Sobhuza II when he took over the kingship in 1921 after the 22-years' regency of his grandmother, Labotsibeni?

Vilakazi argues that the king's status was reduced to that of paramount chief, who was subordinate to the resident commissioner: 'Although British administrators often consulted with the Paramount Chief, the responsibilities of the traditional Swazi authorities were limited in practice to the collection of taxes and to matters that were strictly within the traditional sector, always providing that tradition was not "repugnant to natural justice".' From a materialist perspective Fransman argues differently. He contends that during the colonial period the dominance of the Swazi rulers was 'transformed' but also 'essentially conserved'. The main basis of their dominance was 'their continued control over the allocation of land', and their continued ability to exact the payment of tribute-labour. Fransman's view is disputed by Crush, who focuses largely on the first two decades of the twentieth century. During this time, Crush argues, the position of the Swazi chiefs became increasingly vulnerable. They were deprived of many chiefly prerogatives and were co-opted into the colonial structures of coercion. Their ability to allocate land to followers was severely circumscribed as the amount of land under their control was reduced; and over time the central Dlamini authorities were increasingly less able to extract surplus labour from commoners.

From the 1940s the British tried to define the king's powers more clearly. They first sought to reduce those powers: the Native Administration Proclamation of 1944 vested in the high commissioner the power to appoint and depose chiefs. But the Swazi rulers successfully opposed this measure, and in 1950 a new set of proclamations was issued. These gave the king the right to exercise wide-ranging powers, subject to the resident commissioner's approval. They included the authority to appoint or depose chiefs, to impose levies on the people, to establish courts, and to regulate the constitution and use of the newly established Swazi National Treasury. These measures considerably strengthened the hands of the Swazi rulers during the decolonisation period in the early 1960s.[42]

If the colonial state's intervention in the Swazi political sphere was somewhat indecisive, it acted speedily on major economic issues. And the way in which it acted made clear the intent of colonial economic policy. The British authorities were faced with the immediate, crucial task of regulating access to land and resources in Swaziland by sorting out the concessions issue. This meant deciding between the conflicting claims of the white concessionaires and the Swazi. Accordingly, Lord Milner, the High Commissioner, appointed a concessions commission in 1904. In its report of 1907 the commission recommended that in the case of recognised concessions (not all concessions were recognised by the commission) one-third of the land be taken away from the concessionaires and given to the Swazi; the remaining two-thirds would become the full property of the concessionaires. To implement the recommendations the new High Commissioner, Lord Selborne, issued a partition proclamation in 1907 and appointed a special commissioner to carry out the demarcation.

The effect of the partition was to deprive the Swazi of about 63 per cent of the land area of Swaziland and to leave about 42 per cent of the Swazi population stranded outside the reserved areas. Those so stranded could remain on concessionaire-owned land for five years from 1909. In 1913 a proclamation was issued providing for the removal of Swazi from such land, if the owner so desired; in 1914 landlords began to exercise their powers of eviction. As Fransman, Crush and Daniel have argued, the colonial state's land partition was a significant component of its wider policy of servicing the interests of capital accumulation in Swaziland. As Crush has put it:

> This was exemplified in the alienation of a disproportionate quantity of land for settler-estate production, the enshrinement in space of the hitherto unknown institution of private property, the provision of accessibility to Swazi labour and the ensuring of its release from the indigenous mode of production (through taxation), and, later, the sale of crown land to incoming settlers, at nominal prices.

The partition was not effected without opposition from the Swazi. In 1907 a Swazi deputation travelled to London to voice their disapproval to the Colonial Secretary, Lord Elgin, albeit to no avail. In 1922 Sobhuza II, recently enthroned, challenged the partition in the courts and fought the issue all the way to the Privy Council, again in vain. The land partition was to be a festering grievance, which provoked widespread opposition from Swazi chiefs. The grievance, though, was partly alleviated by an effort, initiated and furthered by the royal family, to buy back land from white owners for Swazi occupation. As a result of this effort the land area held by the Swazi had risen from 37 per cent at the time of partition to 51,6 per cent by 1960.

The land partition may have been designed to lay a foundation for settler capital accumulation, but the early optimistic expectations of the settlers were not to be fulfilled. Settler farm production expanded slowly, farmers being handicapped by the distance of the Rand market. Before 1920 cattle ranching was the only successful form of settler production; after 1920 tobacco and cotton became the other main branches. In the mining sphere tin was produced, and there was some success with gold-mining before 1916. But the total value of mineral production was insignificant until the 1960s.[43]

Few Swazi engaged in commodity production in Swaziland during the first half of the twentieth century. The vast majority either remained in the subsistence sector, or were forced onto the labour market. At the turn of the century there were two main pressures operating in the latter direction. One was ecological disaster: the rinderpest epidemic of 1896–7 and the outbreak of East coast fever in 1902 deprived many Swazi of an important means of subsistence. The other was colonial taxation: when the British resumed control of Swaziland in 1902 they immediately imposed a £2 per annnum poll tax on each adult male over 18, and a £2 hut tax for each wife.

Thus more and more Swazi were thrown onto the labour market, enlarging the labour supply, for which both local and foreign capital were competing. In time the relative failure of settler capitalist production limited the local demand for labour; and from 1914 settler labour needs were to some extent met by labour tenancy arrangements.

Before 1907 the Swazi generally shunned migrant labour on the Rand mines, largely because of the lengthy contracts, appalling working conditions and high mortality figures. But between late 1906 and the end of 1907 the number of Swazi workers on the Rand mines more than trebled, rising from 718 to 2 221; and there was another surge after 1910. According to De Vletter the number of Swazi recruited annually for the South African mines from the 1930s to the mid-1970s remained fairly constant, averaging between 7 000 and 8 000. But over the same period the total number of Swazi migrants in South Africa, male and female, working in all occupations, grew significantly. In 1921 about 6 000 Swazi were employed in South Africa; this figure rose to about 9 500 in 1936, and to about 25 600 in 1976. Many of these absentee workers were employed on farms in the eastern Transvaal and Natal.

How is this growing export of Swazi labour best explained? In the earlier years of the century human agency played an important role in generating a supply of Swazi migrant labour, whereas later it seems that structural factors came more prominently into play. The first independent labour recruiters entered Swaziland in 1907; from 1912 recruiting in the territory came to be dominated by the Native Recruiting Corporation (NRC). By paying cash advances to mineworkers and making use of black runners, the recruiters were increasingly able to secure labour. Recruiters were assisted by the cooperation not only of the colonial authorities but also of Swazi chiefs, who derived financial advantage either from levies imposed on migrants or through fees exacted from recruiters or companies demanding labour. There is evidence that the Swazi royal family supported labour recruiting operations, particularly those of the NRC, at least until the late 1940s.

Crush argues that the 1907 land partition was not a major factor in generating a supply of Swazi migrant labour, since the most significant period of growth in the export of such labour preceded the population removals that followed upon partition. However, it does seem that in the longer term the partition must have contributed significantly to the accelerating impoverishment of the Swazi rural economy in the twentieth century. The limited land area available to Swazi producers was increasingly unable to support a population that rose by 81 per cent between 1904 and 1936. At the same time Swazi cattle holdings were growing: by 1930 Swazi herds had risen 78 per cent above their 1897 level. The consequent overgrazing and soil erosion seriously undermined agricultural productivity. Escalating rural impoverishment forced more and more Swazi into wage labour. Colonial Office annual reports from 1908 onwards stressed the increasing Swazi dependence on money wages. And it is significant that the most impoverished regions of Swaziland, the south and west, came to be the major sources of labour outmigration.

Swaziland's impoverishment was exacerbated by British neglect of the territory. In 1931 the imperial government appointed Sir Alan Pim to investigate Swaziland's financial and economic position. The following year he issued a report in which he was highly critical of Britain's treatment of the territory. Little stimulus for economic development had been provided, and hardly anything had been done to promote African education. Another expert visitor in the early 1930s described Swaziland as the 'most neglected of British dependencies'. It may well have been that this neglect was a product of Britain's expectation that she could offload responsibility for the territory onto South Africa at an early date. As we have seen, this transfer never materialised; and, as we are about to see, the eventual offloading of responsibility had to await decolonisation in 1968.[44]

The early 1960s represented a crucial period in the decolonisation process in Swaziland. It was a time of bargaining and constitution-making, carried on against a background of class struggle and political regrouping in Swaziland. As the British prepared to devolve power in the early 1960s there were four main groups in Swaziland struggling for supremacy. Firstly, there were the Swazi rulers, whose main political organisations comprised the Swazi National Council and the Imbokodvo National Movement (INM). Secondly, there were the whites, who came to be divided into two political parties: the conservative United Swaziland Association (USA), and the more liberal Swaziland Independent Front.

The third main group was composed of the Swazi petty bourgeoisie, which found institutional expression in about five different political parties. The first of these was formed in 1960 — the Swaziland Progressive Party (SPP), led by J. J. Nquku. A breakaway group, led by Dr Ambrose Zwane, hived off from the SPP to form a more militant party, the Ngwane National Liberatory Congress (NNLC) in 1963. Other parties included the Swaziland Democratic Party (SDP), the Mbandzeni National Convention, and another Swaziland Progressive Party. Although there were variations between the programmes of each party, they all agreed that Swaziland should become a non-racial, democratic, independent state.

The Swazi working-class represented the fourth main group. They displayed their strength in 1962 and 1963, years when new trade unions were formed and workers organised a spate of strikes. The strikes severely disrupted both local and foreign capitalist operations, particularly affecting timber and sugar production, railway construction, and asbestos mining. At the height of the strikes in 1963 the British administration airlifted into Swaziland a battalion of Gordon Highlanders from Kenya to quell the workers.

Against this background the business of constitutional negotiation and change proceeded. In December 1963 the British government promulgated a new constitution for Swaziland. It vested executive power in Her Majesty's Commissioner, the chief imperial representative, backed by an executive council that was not responsible to the legislature. The legislature itself was to be made up of some official and nominated members, but the majority were to be elected; of the twenty-four elected members, eight were to be Swazi, eight white, and eight of any race.

In the early 1960s the position of the Swazi rulers appeared to be under threat from sections of an increasingly organised Swazi petty bourgeoisie and working-class. But from the middle years of the decade the rulers were able to secure their ascendancy, partly by forming an alliance of convenience with conservative whites. In the 1964 election, the first held under the new constitution, all but one of the twenty-four seats were won by supporters of either the INM or the USA.

The Swazi rulers continued to strengthen their position before the pre-independence election of 1967 by absorbing the SDP and a number of NNLC leaders. Early in 1967 Swaziland's independence constitution was promulgated. The constitution gave wide powers to the king, who could appoint one-fifth of the lower house's members and one-half of the senate's members; the existence of the monarchy and the king's prerogatives were entrenched in the constitution, and the king had the power to block changes in entrenched clauses. The remaining twenty-four members of the lower house of the legislature were to be elected on a non-racial common roll in eight three-member constituencies. In the ensuing election in April, the INM won all twenty-four seats and almost 80 per cent of the total vote.[45]

In September 1968 Britain formally granted independence to Swaziland. In the following years King Sobhuza and his supporters consolidated their position economically and politically. Sobhuza had a strong material base on which to build. The independence constitution vested in the king control over Swaziland's mineral wealth. In 1968 Sobhuza created the Tibiyo Fund into which all income derived from mineral royalties and the granting of land rights was to be deposited. In theory the Tibiyo Fund was a trust for the whole nation, but in practice it was strictly controlled by the king and served as a major vehicle for domestic capital accumulation, with its revenue accruing to the Swazi rulers rather than to the Swaziland Ministry of Finance.

Although politically secure Sobhuza resented the independence constitution's legalisation of opposition. He likened political parties to nations, 'each fighting a battle to be in power; each wanting to rule the other'. In his eyes the Westminster-style constitution introduced into Swaziland an illegitimate contest for power that rightfully belonged to the king and aristocracy. It was therefore not surprising that the independence constitution did not survive. A crisis arose after the 1972 general election. Although the king's Imbokodvo Party won an overwhelming majority, one constituency returned three members of the NNLC. The state retaliated by trying to deport one of these three members on the grounds that he was not a Swazi citizen, but the high court set aside the deportation order. In April 1973 Sobhuza suspended the constitution, thereby dissolving and banning 'all political parties and similar bodies that cultivate and bring about disturbances and ill-feelings'. These 'similar bodies' included trade unions, which were thereafter severely restricted. After the suspension of the constitution power came to be heavily centred upon Sobhuza who arrogated all executive, legislative and judicial authority to himself. For the next five years he ruled by decree.

Although Swaziland obtained political independence, its economy continued to display the characteristics of underdevelopment and dependency. It has also been characterised by the co-existence of an impoverished non-capitalist sector alongside an export-oriented capitalist sector. The former has been based on Swazi Nation Land, that area set aside for Swazi occupation. Productivity on this land has steadily diminished, so much so that a subsistence level of production has barely been achieved, let alone any commodity production.

Swaziland's capitalist sector serves to highlight the dependent character of the country's economy. This sector has increasingly come under the control of foreign capitalist interests, especially South African capital. A 1971 survey concluded that the 'foreign-owned ... sector now contributes about two-thirds of total GDP [gross domestic product], employs probably more than 75% of total wage-earners, and provides 90% of direct taxes and virtually all the exports.' The growing trend towards monoculture, with a heavy reliance on sugar for export earnings, has made Swaziland vulnerable to fluctuations in the world market price for the product. And, as Daniel has shown, 'Each year since independence has seen South Africa supplying Swaziland with more than 95 per cent of its imports by way of a freight haulage system operated by South African Railways which has a virtual transportation monopoly over Swaziland's import and export traffic.' Since achieving political independence Swaziland has thus remained locked in a situation of neo-colonial dependence.[46]

Basutoland/Lesotho

Writing in the mid-1960s Jack Halpern described Basutoland as

> the paradox of the High Commission Territories: economically their ugly sister, she is politically their Cinderella, at least to modern African eyes. Completely surrounded by South Africa, Basutoland is viewed as an island of freedom by those who oppose apartheid, and this view is shared, in varying degrees, by the Basuto themselves. But to hundreds of thousands of Basuto their homeland, of which they are intensely proud, is also an island of poverty from which they must go into the apartheid State if

they are to survive.

The first part of Halpern's characterisation no longer holds: politically, Lesotho is today certainly no 'island of freedom'. But the second part still stands: Lesotho remains an 'island of poverty', one of those regions situated on the underdeveloped periphery of South Africa.

In its experience of underdevelopment and dependency Lesotho has shared a similar fate to that of Swaziland. Moreover, in the twentieth century both territories have been the victims of British imperial neglect and the targets of South African imperial expansion. But there the similarities end: in many ways the historical experiences of Lesotho and Swaziland have been very different. Whereas a peasant class emerged in Basutoland in the nineteenth century, such a class was not prominent in Swaziland at that time. While a large area of Swaziland was alienated to white settlers, the Basotho retained access to their land. Swaziland was brought under colonial rule with minimal resistance, while the Basotho, as we have seen, fiercely resisted the imposition of Cape colonial control.

It was as an indirect result of the Basotho's relatively successful resistance in the Gun War of 1880–1 that Lesotho today enjoys an independence that is internationally recognised. As Murray has remarked,

> But for the Gun War one hundred years ago, in which the Basotho successfully resisted the Cape Government's attempt to disarm them, and which induced the British to resume direct responsibility for Basutoland, it is likely that the constitutional history of Lesotho would have been very different. It may well have joined the Transkei, Bophuthatswana and Venda in the track of ethnic nationalism and the achievement of an abortive 'independence'.

Even so, Lesotho has not been able to escape the consequences of its incorporation into the southern African regional economy. And notwithstanding its internationally recognised independence, Lesotho today bears some of the political hallmarks of South Africa's authoritarian, repressive Bantustan regimes.[47]

From the time that it resumed control of Basutoland in 1884 Britain strove as far as possible, for the next fifty years or more, to govern the territory through the chiefs. Basutoland's dual administrative structure left considerable authority in the hands of the Basotho royal house and the Kwena aristocracy. As Roger Leys has remarked, 'the British sought to consolidate a form of feudal aristocracy by vesting in the ruling house and the "sons of Moshoeshoe" the ideological and repressive functions of state power.' In practice this meant that wide executive and judicial authority was entrusted to the chiefs, who also retained control over land allocation. Chiefly power came to be institutionalised in the Basutoland National Council (BNC). This advisory body, which was given formal colonial recognition in 1910, was composed very largely of the paramount chief's nominees. Morover, the paramount chief could 'place' his relatives in district chiefships, a practice that led to an enormous growth in the number of chiefs. This in turn brought a proliferation of tribal courts, through which each chief exercised his judicial authority. According to Halpern, some chiefs abused this authority by transforming their courts 'into petty racketeering concerns'.

This parallel structure and its abuse were much resented by Basotho commoners and widely criticised in a report, written in 1935 by Sir Alan Pim, who had been commissioned by the British government to investigate the state of affairs in Basutoland. Following on the report, reforms were introduced in 1938. These had the effect of curbing the paramount's power to place his relatives in chiefships, reducing the number of chief's courts, and curtailing the judicial functions of chiefs. Further reforms were carried through in the 1940s. Provision was made for a small elective element in the BNC. District councils were established: these took over some of the chief's administrative powers, and were responsible for electing the new representative element in the BNC.

During the 1950s there were growing demands from various quarters in Basutoland for self-government. In 1955 the BNC resolved to request from the British government the power to legislate on internal matters. The Colonial Secretary was sympathetic and two constitution-making committees set to work. In 1960 the new constitution came into effect. The BNC now became a legislative council with competence over a wide range of domestic affairs. Half of its members were to be elected by universal adult male suffrage, with the district councils acting as electoral colleges. The other half of the membership was to comprise twenty-two chiefs, fourteen nominees of the paramount and four officials.[48]

Basutoland's first election under the new constitution was fought in 1960, but behind it lay a long history of parties and political movements. As early as 1904 the first modern political organisation, the Basutoland Progressive Association (BPA), had been established. It sought to eliminate the abuse of chiefly power, and it called for far greater elected representation in the decision-making process for its supporters, who were mostly drawn from the mission-educated elite. A more radical group, called Lekhotla la Bafo, was founded by Josiah Lefela just before the First World War. It was more commoner-oriented than the BPA, and was uncompromising in its rhetoric, rejecting colonial authority outright.

Lekhotla's successor was the Basutoland African Congress. This party, which changed its name to the Basutoland Congress Party (BCP) in 1959, was founded by Ntsu Mokhehle in 1952. Mokhehle had been involved in the Youth League in South Africa in the 1940s, and so modelled his party on the ANC. Later in the 1950s two parties with a more conservative stance were established. The Marema Tlou Party was set up in 1957 with a specific programme of support for the status of the paramount and other principal chiefs. The next year the Basutoland National Party (BNP) was founded by Chief Leabua Jonathan. Its main constituency lay among the lesser chiefs, traders and Catholics.

The BCP emerged from the 1960 election with a clear overall majority of seats in the National Council. The BCP won twenty-nine seats, while the Marema Tlou Party took five, independents another five, and the BNP only one seat. Mokhehle's hand was duly strengthened, and he was soon demanding that Basutoland be granted full independence. In 1962 the National Council authorised the creation of a constitutional commission. After two years of constitution-drafting and a conference in London in 1964, a new constitution was finally agreed upon, based on the Westminster model. The king was to be essentially a figurehead, though having the right to appoint eleven members to the upper house of the legislature. The lower house, the National Assembly, would comprise sixty members elected by universal suffrage. And the cabinet would be responsible to the legislature.

When an election was held in 1965 under the new constitution Basutoland's party formation had changed somewhat since the previous election. Mokhehle's authoritarian leadership had aroused resentment in some quarters of the BCP. In 1961 a breakaway group formed the Freedom Party, which in time merged with the conservative Marema Tlou Party. The merger, the Marema Tlou Freedom Party (MFP), represented what Spence has called 'a curious alliance between conservative elements and ex-B. C. P. radicals'. In addition a Communist Party was established in 1961, to become at the time the only legal communist party in Africa south of Nigeria.

Internal divisions, leadership struggles and secession seriously weakened the BCP in the early 1960s. It was not therefore a great surprise when the BCP lost the 1965 election, winning twenty-five seats, against the BNP's thirty-one and the MFP's four. Chief Jonathan, the BNP leader, was appointed prime minister, a position he still held in October 1966 when Basutoland was granted its independence by the British to become the Kingdom of Lesotho.[49]

In the early years of independence the power base of Jonathan's government proved fragile. The civil service was dominated by BCP supporters. King Moshoeshoe II, unhappy with his figurehead role, sought to win more substantial executive powers. What is more, the BNP's base of popular support was being steadily eroded, so much so that in the 1970 election the BNP lost its majority to the BCP. It was at this point that Jonathan resorted to authoritarian rule. He remained in power after the election defeat by suspending the constitution, placing the king under house arrest, and arresting opposition leaders. Jonathan then tried to disarm his opponents by attempting to build a government of national reconciliation. He drew the MFP into his coalition, and was soon able to split the BCP. In 1973 he created an interim National Assembly in place of the suspended elected legislature. Members of the new Assembly would not be elected, but in effect be Jonathan's nominees. Jonathan succeeded in drawing a BCP contingent into this interim body. The BCP was further weakened the following year when it failed in a clumsy coup attempt, as a result of which many BCP leaders, including Mokhehle, fled Lesotho, and others were jailed.

Relations between Jonathan's government and the South African government have gone through two main phases since independence. There was an early period of cooperation when Jonathan tried to bolster his internal position by courting South African support: at one time he even employed South African civil servants seconded to key government posts. But since the early

1970s the relationship has soured. Lesotho has pursued its historical claim to areas of land in the Orange Free State. Moreover, Jonathan has tried to undercut the BCP opposition by adopting a more overtly critical and rhetorical stance against South Africa's racial policies. However, while political relations between the two countries may have changed, Lesotho has remained locked in a state of economic dependence on South Africa.[50]

Murray has characterised Lesotho's economic history over the past hundred years as representing a transformation 'from granary to labour reserve'. The 'granary' era belongs to the late nineteenth century when a thriving Basotho peasantry responded to market opportunities by producing and selling a surplus. For most of the twentieth century, with the possible exception of a boom period during the First World War, the territory has more and more taken on the character of a labour reserve.

There are many symptoms of Lesotho's economic impoverishment. One is the state of the rural economy. As Murray has noted, 'productive activities on the land have long ceased to provide an adequate livelihood for the large majority of Basotho.... For the most part, individual land holdings today are small, fragmented, eroded and exhausted. An increasing proportion of the population has no lands at all.' Lesotho has become over the years a net importer of maize, the main staple food, whereas it was once a net exporter. The total production of maize in Lesotho was more than three times lower in 1970 than it had been in 1950. Individual families have increasingly had to rely on income from cash wages to survive. 'The population of Lesotho today', Murray remarks, 'is aptly described as a rural proletariat which scratches about on the land.' Only about 13 per cent of the total land area of this mountainous country is cultivable. A growing population has placed enormous pressure on this limited resource. Soil erosion, overgrazing and exhaustion have severely affected the productivity of land.

While Lesotho's inhabitants have had to rely more and more on cash wages for subsistence, there have been very few opportunities for wage-earning in Lesotho. The country possesses few employment-generating resources, and the level of domestic investment has been low. Since independence the government has tried to stimulate industrial development through the Lesotho National Development Corporation, which ploughed about R20 million into relatively small enterprises between 1967 and 1972. But it has had little impact on employment creation, and in 1976 there were still only about 27 500 Basotho employed in Lesotho. And yet during the 1970s there has been a quite considerable growth in Lesotho's gross national product. This apparent paradox is explained by the fact that a high proportion of this gross national product has been derived from the wage remittances of migrant labourers.

The hallmark of Lesotho's economic dependence has been the heavy reliance of its population on the earnings of migrant labourers in South Africa. Basotho labour migration to South Africa began in the last decades of the nineteenth century, and has grown significantly during the twentieth century. In 1911 there were over 24 600 such migrants, representing 5,8 per cent of Lesotho's *de jure* population. This had risen dramatically by 1960 to over

206 400 migrants, representing 23,2 per cent of the population. Such growth occurred in the first hundred years or so of Basotho labour migration, a period that Murray calls the 'phase of incorporation' in Basotho migration history. This was a time when Basotho labour was much needed in South Africa, and when migrants could move quite freely into South Africa to exploit wage-earning opportunities. The period since the 1960s, and more particularly the 1970s, has been a 'phase of relative alienation', during which time tighter control has been exercised by the South African state over the influx and employment of foreign migrants. There was a dramatic drop in the number of Basotho migrants in the early 1960s, the annual figure falling to about 117 200, or 12 per cent of the population, in 1966. However, in spite of tighter South African controls, the number of Basotho migrants in South Africa, at least those working on the mines, increased again from the late 1960s and through the 1970s. In 1977 Lesotho supplied more than a quarter of the South African mining industry's black labour complement.

Lesotho depends on the earnings of migrant labourers to a staggering degree. It is difficult to estimate exactly how much of these earnings find their way into Lesotho. Although an official record is kept of migrants' remittances and deferred pay, there is no way of establishing the amounts of money sent home through the post or brought back by returning migrants themselves. In spite of this uncertainty, Murray confidently estimates the degree of dependence: 'The earnings of these migrants far exceed Lesotho's Gross Domestic Product and, according to a recent survey ..., about 70 per cent of mean rural household income is derived from migrant earnings.' Migrant labour has therefore been a crucial means of survival for Lesotho's inhabitants. But the social costs of this survival have been just as enormous. Family survival has entailed family separation; and this separation has wrought social dislocation and breakdown. Murray's research has confirmed

> that a system in which large numbers of men spend long periods away at work, leaving their wives and children at home, generates economic insecurity, marital disharmony, material and emotional misery and problems relating to sexual morality and legitimacy of children irrespective of the cultural definition of these matters.

Murray has also suggested that various forms of ill-health in Lesotho can also be linked to 'the ravages of out-migration', particularly respiratory and sexually transmitted diseases carried by returning migrants.

Reliance on the earnings of migrants has not been the only symptom of Lesotho's economic dependence on external links. A landlocked enclave, Lesotho has depended on the South African transport system for its exports and imports. Its electricity has been supplied from South Africa; and its tourism industry has relied largely on an influx of visitors from South Africa. Membership of the Southern African Customs Union has also been vital to Lesotho: in the early 1970s the country's share of customs union receipts amounted to about two-thirds of total government revenue.

In recent years foreign aid to Lesotho has grown. This marks something of a change from the long period of British neglect in the colonial era. Britain had been obsessed with making her colonial territories self-sufficient: colonial budgets were to be balanced from sources of internal colonial revenue. The British therefore did very little to finance development in Basutoland or to provide for social welfare. Health and educational services were neglected. That primary education was relatively well developed in Basutoland was largely due to the work of missionaries. British financial input was minimal: between 1940 and 1960 a mere £250 000 was spent on education from the Colonial Development and Welfare Fund. Only in the 1960s did the British government start giving an annual grant-in-aid to the territory. In the 1970s Lesotho came to receive a growing amount of foreign aid, which rose from R5 million in 1973/4 to R30 million in 1975/6.

In spite of increasing foreign aid Lesotho has remained one of the poorest countries in the world. Although it is internationally recognised as an independent country, in its underdeveloped state Lesotho resembles South Africa's Bantustans. Like some of the Bantustans, Lesotho is completely surrounded by South African territory. A hundred years ago the Basotho displayed economic resilience and a potential for independent growth; but since the late nineteenth century their economy has become increasingly impoverished and dependent on external links. But the widespread impoverishment of the country should not be allowed to blur the process of class differentiation that has been occurring. Leys has argued that 'under colonial rule a type of chieftaincy emerged, taking on the characteristics of a petite bourgeoisie and consolidating a place in commodity production denied both to the emerging stratum of educated commoners and to the mass of commoners.' In Lesotho, as in the Bantustans, there have clearly been people who could profit from holding key positions in the machinery of state. They could inhabit islands of wealth in a sea of poverty.[51]

The Bechuanaland Protectorate/Botswana

The northern Tswana had been brought under British protection in the mid-1880s to drive a wedge between the Transvaal and the Germans in South West Africa, and so also to keep open the road to the north. The Bechuanaland Protectorate had originally been destined to become part of the British South Africa Company's sphere of operations, but it was spared that fate because of the Jameson Raid and the Company's subsequent disgrace. Britain's reluctant, half-hearted acceptance of responsibility for the territory was to have a bearing on its later history. Like Swaziland and Basutoland, the Protectorate was a target for South African imperial expansion for several decades; and Britain's keenness to offload the territory made it vulnerable to South Africa's grasp. Expecting or hoping that its imperial overlordship would be short-lived, Britain neglected the Protectorate, as it did Swaziland and Basutoland. And so for most of the twentieth century the Bechuanaland Protectorate has taken on the character of a labour reserve, another outpost in the underdeveloped periphery of South Africa.

In spite of these similarities, the history of the Protectorate in the twentieth century and that of its two counterparts also have points of difference. Today Botswana possesses the richest natural resources of the three, although ironically one of Lesotho's greatest assets — water — has probably been Botswana's scarcest resource. The political history of the Protectorate, and later Botswana, has also taken a rather different course. At the time of colonial subjugation both Swaziland and Basutoland had fairly strong, unifying, precolonial state structures; but Bechuanaland did not. At the time of independence in the 1960s all three territories were to be given Westminster-type constitutions; but only in Botswana has multi-party democracy survived. We must now examine the salient features of the territory's political history from the early years of British protection through to the first decade of Botswana's independence.

In the early years of the Protectorate the British established only a rudimentary administration. They adopted a form of parallel rule which left the eight main chiefs in the territory a considerable degree of autonomy. In 1920 a Native Advisory Council (renamed the African Advisory Council in 1940) was created. The Native Advisory Council ultimately came to comprise the eight main chiefs, a number of their nominees, and seven British officials. Although a powerless body, it served some purpose as a channel of communication between the chiefs and the administration. At various stages, for instance, the chiefs in the Council were able to voice their strong opposition to the possible incorporation of the Protectorate into South Africa.

In the 1930s Britain shifted from parallel rule to an indirect rule approach in the Protectorate. In 1934 two proclamations were issued, curtailing chiefly power and bringing the chiefs under the closer control of the British resident commissioner. Not surprisingly the measures aroused chiefly opposition. In the forefront of the opposition was Tshekedi Khama, who since 1925 had been acting as regent over the most prominent of the Protectorate chiefdoms, the Ngwato, pending the coming of age of the heir, Seretse Khama. Tshekedi had already been at loggerheads with the British authorities. In 1933 Tshekedi had been temporarily deposed from the regency by an autocratic acting high commissioner, Admiral Evans. Evans suspended Tshekedi for allegedly ordering the flogging of a white man who had assaulted an African woman. The British government was soon forced to overrule Evans and reinstate Tshekedi. So Tshekedi was neither prepared to accept passively the enactment of the 1934 proclamations. He and Chief Bathoen II of the Ngwaketse challenged in court, unsuccessfully as it turned out, the validity of the proclamations.

These events paled into insignificance against the dispute surrounding Seretse's marriage. In 1948, while studying law in England and still heir to the chiefship, Seretse married Ruth Williams, an English woman. Tshekedi and a section of the Ngwato tribe opposed the marriage, and therefore also Seretse's right of succession, on the grounds that a chief could not marry outside his tribe, let alone marry a white woman. In 1949 the Ngwato *kgotla* (public assembly) eventually voted in favour of Seretse's right to succeed to the chiefship. But this did not satisfy Tshekedi, who went into exile in Kwena territory. Nor did it satisfy the British government, which was seemingly afraid of upsetting South African sensitivities on the multi-racial marriage issue. The British government therefore resolved not to recognise Seretse as chief and to perpetuate Tshekedi's exile. Even though Tshekedi and Seretse were reconciled in 1952 Britain maintained its policy of non-recognition. Tshekedi was allowed back into the Protectorate in 1952, and Seretse in 1956. Although they renounced their claims to the Ngwato chiefship, both came to be actively involved in local politics.[52]

In the early 1960s the decolonisation process was set in motion. In 1960 a new constitution was introduced, providing for among other things a Legislative Council that would comprise a component of elected African members. But the first Legislative Council election of 1961 was held before a clear party structure had emerged in the Protectorate. The first significant party to be established was the Bechuanaland People's Party (BPP), formed at the end of 1960. Led initially by K. T. Motsete, the BPP was modelled along the lines of the ANC, and its programme and rhetoric were militantly anti-colonial. In its nationalist outlook it strove to transcend tribal differences. But it could not transcend individual divisions within its leadership. In 1962 Motsamai Mpho, the party's secretary-general, was expelled; he soon formed his own breakaway party, which came to be called the Botswana Independence Party (BIP). Two years later the BPP was riven by another split between its two main leaders, Motsete and Matante, who each formed their own BPP factions.

Another political force emerged in 1962 with the formation of the Bechuanaland Democratic Party (BDP). Founded by Seretse Khama, the BDP could draw upon a wider base of popular support than the BPP, not only among the Ngwato, but also in other tribal areas. It attracted the support of the chiefs who were frightened by the BPP's anti-tribalist rhetoric. And, although firmly committed to non-racialism, its anti-colonial stance was less militant than that adopted by the BPP.

In the mid-1960s the Protectorate was granted self-governing status and then full independence in rapid succession. Early in 1965 a new self-government constitution, the product of talks held in 1963, came into operation. It provided for a Legislative Assembly, the vast majority of whose members were to be elected by universal adult suffrage, and for a House of Chiefs, the role of which was purely advisory. The executive cabinet was to be presided over by the Queen's commissioner until full independence; otherwise the cabinet would be responsible to the legislature. In March 1965 there was a general election in which the BDP won twenty-eight of the thirty-one seats. Less than a year later a new independence constitution was being negotiated in London. Based on the 1965 model, the 1966 republican constitution dispensed with the Queen's commissioner and provided for an executive president who would, in effect, be elected by members of the Legislative Assembly. In September 1966 the independent state of Botswana was formally proclaimed; and Seretse Khama was duly chosen as the first president.

The political history of Botswana since independence has differed from that of Swaziland and Lesotho in two significant respects. Whereas in Swaziland, and to a lesser extent in Lesotho, the chiefly order has continued to represent a powerful force, in Botswana formal chiefly power has been almost totally destroyed. Secondly, in Botswana a multi-party political system has survived, while in Swaziland and Lesotho it has not. Both of these issues require examination.

The undermining of Tswana chiefly power had begun during the Protectorate era. Reforms in the 1930s weakened the chiefs' judicial authority and reduced their potential for personal accumulation. Immediately on the achievement of self-government in 1965, the new BDP government moved quickly to pass bills that further destroyed chiefly authority. One measure stripped chiefs of all their legislative powers and most of their executive authority. Later the Tribal Land Act of 1968 removed one of their last major prerogatives, the control over land allocation in tribal areas. The chiefs themselves have been largely unable to resist this erosion of their position. The House of Chiefs has proved to be a largely impotent and ineffectual body. However, many chiefs have managed to retain prestige and exercise informal influence at a local level. And some have looked to the Botswana National Front (BNF), formed in 1965, to further their interests. The BNF party represented, in the words of one commentator, 'an uncomfortable alliance between traditionalists, under the leadership of Bathoen, and more radical elements'.

Botswana is one of the very few countries in Africa that has continued to hold multi-party elections since independence. This seemingly atypical survival has been a subject of debate. Cynics have suggested that the multi-party system in Botswana has persisted only in name; the overwhelming dominance of the BDP makes Botswana a one-party state in practice. Others, like Colclough and McCarthy, reject this view, claiming that Botswana's leaders have held a strong sense of constitutionality and a genuine commitment to multi-partyism.

Explanations of this survival are more problematic. Wiseman argues that there have been within Botswana society a number of cleavages, the most significant of which has been that between the government and the chiefs. 'These cleaveages', suggests Wiseman, 'underpin the multi-party framework which in turn in part reflects them.' A different line of argument has been presented by Stevens and Speed. They claim that Wiseman's notion of a key cleavage between government and chiefs is flawed. More significant for Stevens and Speed has been the absence of such a cleavage. The government's supremacy over the chiefs has been secured; and the internal cleavages that do exist 'are relatively shallow and cross-cutting'. This, coupled with the country's economic advance since independence, has in their view made for the relative stability of the multi-party system in Botswana.[53]

This whole question requires deeper probing before satisfactory explanations can emerge. However, some would argue that political structures should not be the key issue in an analysis of Botswana's history. As Massey has maintained, 'the reality of the political economy of Botswana' belies any 'rosy portrayal' of a democratic country with a growing economy. It is to this 'reality' that we must now turn our attention.

The Tswana rural economy has for long been bedevilled by ecological hazards, the chief of which has been the scarcity and infrequency of rainfall. But this alone does not explain the rural economy's underdeveloped state, which needs to be viewed within the context of both British imperial policy and the territory's incorporation into the wider southern African regional economy.

The precarious state of arable farming among the Tswana has long been cause for concern. In 1941 Schapera found that 'the vast majority in each tribe reaped either too little or barely sufficient for their needs'. In the early 1960s Halpern found Tswana agriculture 'so underdeveloped that even in relatively good years maize, which is the country's staple food, has to be imported'. In drought years there was a heavy reliance on famine relief. By 1966, after some years of drought, over 100 000 people (one-fifth of the population) were depending on famine relief programmes for their food.

Cattle-raising has for long been the dominant branch of rural production. But this too has been vulnerable to cattle diseases, and to occasional droughts that have decimated Tswana herds. During the drought of the early 1960s about 400 000 cattle died, amounting to about one-third of the estimated cattle population in 1960. In spite of these severe setbacks, the overall cattle population of the territory grew approximately tenfold between 1911 and 1978, from 300 000 to 3 000 000 head.

During the colonial era internal productive activity in the Protectorate was very much cattle-centred. Cattle dominated the territory's export trade, and it came to form the basis of its major industry, meat-processing. An export abattoir was established at Lobatse in 1954. Up till that time cattle had had to be exported on the hoof, mainly to South Africa and central African colonies. Thereafter all beef exports in time went through the Lobatse abattoir; and from the late 1950s Britain came to form a major part of an expanding beef export market.

The discovery of gold in 1866 at Tati in the north-eastern region of present-day Botswana foreshadowed the later gold discoveries in southern Africa. In the late 1880s there was a rush of prospectors to the Protectorate. But in the colonial era mining was not a significant branch of the Protectorate's economy. Gold was mined at Tati on a small scale until 1964; and from the 1950s asbestos and manganese were mined in the south-eastern region of the Protectorate. Output, though, was generally low; and neither mining nor any other industry offered many wage-earning opportunities in the Protectorate. As late as 1960 there were only about 10 000 wage-earners working in the Protectorate, representing a mere 2 per cent of the resident population.

The fragile rural economy and the scarcity of local wage-earning opportunities forced increasing numbers of the Protectorate's inhabitants to join the flow of migrant labourers to South Africa. During the 1930s migrants from the Protectorate numbered about 10 000; by the mid-1960s the figure had risen to about 50 000. The Protectorate's inhabitants came to depend on the earnings of migrants to a staggering degree. Schapera found that between 1938 and 1942 some 47 per cent of the cash income of the Protectorate's African population was derived from wages earned outside the territory.

Migrants did not go to South Africa to obtain 'the social prestige attaching to a man who has experienced life in the outside world', as Sillery suggests they did. Rather it was the push of economic necessity, brought on by various constraints. One was ecological, but as Parson has pointed out: 'The natural environment of marginal soils and unpredictable rainfall did not alone cause labour migration.' The collaborative role of chiefs must also be noted. Some chiefs actively encouraged or even coerced labour migration. Chiefs often received commission for supplying labourers; and, at least until the 1930s, a part of a migrant's earnings could accrue to a chief in the form of levies and dues. The colonial state probably played the most crucial part in stimulating labour migration from the Protectorate. Colonial taxes were levied from 1899; and for those without cattle this necessitated the earning of a cash wage. The colonial demarcation of reserve boundaries limited African access to land; and some of the most fertile land on the Protectorate's eastern border was carved into white farming blocks.

The impoverishment of the Protectorate and the consequent growing dependence on migrant labour must also be viewed in the context of Britain's neglect of the territory. The Protectorate had been established in the 1880s at a time when Britain was exercising great financial stringency within her empire. As Colclough and McCarthy have remarked:

> In 1885 the High Commissioner had stated that Britain's intention with regard to the administration of Bechuanaland was to do as little as possible. Throughout most of the following eighty years of British rule this promise was kept — so much so that at independence Botswana was worse off in terms of both social and directly productive infrastructure than any other ex-British territory in Africa.

The British were determined that the colonial budget in the Protectorate should balance itself. The Protectorate was expected to be self-supporting, deriving its revenue from local sources, such as taxation, customs revenue, licences and dues. Given that more than 90 per cent of government expenditure in the Protectorate in the first quarter of the twentieth century was absorbed by basic administrative costs, it is hardly surprising that there was an almost total neglect of social services in the territory.

Some British financial assistance, in the form of small grants or loans, was occasionally forthcoming, and from the mid-1950s Britain began to render an annual grant-in-aid. Notwithstanding this aid, Britain continued to neglect infrastructural development and social services in the territory. In the early 1960s Bechuanaland schools were said to be worse housed and worse equipped than any in British Africa. And there were hardly any public medical services. The colonial administration appeared to be more concerned to eliminate cattle disease than human disease, realising perhaps that government revenue depended partly on the territory's cattle industry.[54]

At the time of independence Botswana was thus utterly impoverished, its per capita income level being one of the smallest in the world. However, since independence the Botswana economy has assumed a much brighter appearance. The figures seem to tell an amazing success story. The gross domestic product almost quadrupled in the first seven years of independence, and increased almost tenfold in the 1970s. In 1966 Botswana was one of the poorest countries in the world; by 1976 its per capita income was higher than the average for Africa and Asia (excluding Japan). Government revenue rose from 4,5 million pula (or rand, as the currency then was) to 72,7 million pula in 1975/6. Expenditure on public development increased sixfold to 30 million pula between 1965/6 and 1972/3.

The rise in government revenue, particularly that available for expenditure on development, can partly be accounted for by a massive inflow of foreign aid since independence. Also significant has been the renegotiation in 1969 of the Southern African Customs Union agreement. This renegotiation boosted government revenue by doubling Botswana's share of customs receipts.

A more significant contribution to Botswana's economic recovery has come from the growth in two principal productive sectors, the beef industry and mining. The first ten years after independence were highly favourable to Botswana's beef industry. The drought ended in 1966, and over the next twelve years the size of the country's cattle herd almost trebled. There was a strong export demand for Botswana's beef and a worldwide increase in the beef price over those ten years. Between 1966 and 1977 the net sales of the Botswana Meat Commission, a parastatal that processes all of Botswana's meat exports at the Lobatse abattoir, rose from 7 million to 42 million pula.

Since the late 1960s developments in mining have led the economic upswing. Diamond-mining began at Orapa in the early 1970s; later it was started at Letlhakane (and more recently at a very rich mine at Jwaneng). In the mid-1970s operations began at the Selebi-Phikwe copper–nickel mine and at the Morupule coal mine. The sales of the mining industry increased from 3,4 million pula in 1970/1 to nearly 95 million pula in 1976/7.

Rising revenue in the first decade of independence enabled the government to finance infrastructural development and to expand social services. New towns were built at Selebi-Phikwe and Orapa; and three new reservoirs were constructed. Educational facilities were rapidly enlarged, so that in ten years primary school enrolments doubled and the number of those being educated at secondary and tertiary levels rose seven times. Health services were improved, with a special emphasis on giving poorer people access to health care facilities. Infrastructural development, the expansion of the public sector, and industrial development also widened employment opportunities. Total formal sector employment in Botswana rose from about 20 000 in 1964 to about 71 000 in 1976. Between 1964 and 1975 the proportion of the total population employed in formal sector jobs doubled.[55]

This picture of Botswana's seemingly spectacular economic advance in the first decade of independence is deceptively rosy. It conceals the underdeveloped, dependent character of the economy; and it blurs the internal inequalities and the accelerating process of class differentiation. Generally Botswana's development programmes have been concentrated on urban areas, to the neglect of rural areas. But even within the rural areas growing inequalities have developed. A relatively small class of wealthy cattle-owners has emerged. Some of these have roots in the old chiefly hierarchy; others are drawn from the ranks of politicians and senior bureaucrats who have invested their income in cattle. Some members of this class have diversified into arable production. At the opposite end of the scale are those who own no cattle and suffer dire poverty. Colclough and McCarthy have recently estimated that the poorest 40 per cent of rural households receive 12 per cent of total rural incomes, while the richest 20 per cent control about 58 per cent of income. A similar differentiation has been occurring in the urban areas. Wages paid to the working-class have been extremely low. For instance, in recent years wages paid to mineworkers in Botswana were about one-third of the level paid for comparable work in South Africa. Urban workers have therefore found it necessary to maintain links with the fragile rural subsistence economy.

The decade of economic recovery after independence did not reduce the flow of migrant labourers to South Africa. According to the estimate of Colclough and McCarthy, the number of absentees from Botswana rose from about 50 000 in the mid-1960s to about 70 000 in the mid-1970s. Similarly the cash inflow to Botswana derived from migrant labour increased from about 2 million pula in the late 1960s to about 10 million in 1976.

Continuing migrancy has been just one sign of the dependent character of Botswana's economy. Another has been its reliance on exports. As Colclough and McCarthy have remarked: 'The pattern of development has been dominated by the enhanced production of raw materials for export, and the internal linkages of this export sector have been very small.' This production has in turn depended heavily upon the inflow of foreign capital investment and aid. This state of dependence has been summarised by Ochieng:

> Botswana fits into a fairly typical pattern — in her dependence on a few trading partners, on increasing inflows of capital to offset a growing trade deficit, on a few commodities for export and on increasing imports of staple foods. There are other crucial forms of dependence — on foreign skills and technology, and on international transit and transport rights, to give just two examples.[56]

Botswana, like Swaziland and Lesotho, was granted its independence after decades of British imperial neglect. In its first years after independence, though, Botswana seemed to follow a different path from its two counterparts — travelling along the road of liberal democracy and staging a remarkable economic recovery. But these differences should not be allowed to blur the essential similarity of their post-independence experiences. All three have remained part of the underdeveloped southern African periphery, dependent on external linkages and vulnerable to any break in those links. Although their political independence is internationally recognised, they have in other ways shared some of the characteristics of South Africa's 'homelands'. They have continued to function as labour reserves. And judging by her recent effort to transfer Kangwane to Swaziland, South Africa is obviously eyeing them as further potential dumping-grounds for her 'surplus' African population.

11
CONCLUSION

Had one twenty years ago wished to develop some understanding of the history of the African people of South Africa, one would have been hard pressed to amass much information from the historical literature available at that time. South African history was predominantly 'white' history. Our archaeological knowledge of the South African Iron Age was decidedly thin. To obtain a glimpse of the precolonial history of African societies one had to rely on writings of non-historians. One could look to sketchy historical introductions in the anthropological monographs; or one could draw on the writings of the early collectors of oral traditions — pre-eminently, Bryant, Soga and Ellenberger. Similarly, very little research had been been carried out either on African resistance to colonial conquest and subjugation, or on the growth of African opposition to white domination and exploitation in the twentieth century.

Today, of course, the historiographical picture is very different. There is a burgeoning literature that covers all these and other once neglected fields. Indeed it is such a body of literature that has made possible this present attempt at a synthesis. What is significant too is that our new insights into African history have been derived from a number of different disciplines: primarily from historians and archaeologists, but also from anthropologists, sociologists, economists, political scientists, and linguists.

Some of the greatest strides have been made in the field of Iron Age archaeology. One of the most significant of these advances has been to demolish once and for all the notion that 'migrating hordes of Bantu-speakers' arrived in southern Africa at much the same time as whites first settled in the Cape. Some people still cling to this obsolete notion, even though it is based on a chronology that is inaccurate to the extent of about 1 400 years. Indeed, serious scholars no longer bother with this 'dead horse'. Archaeologists are currently concerned with more crucial issues. They have been investigating the dynamic interaction between Iron Age communities and their environment; and changes over time in social experience have also been highlighted. In this regard, particular emphasis has been laid on the break between the Early and Late Iron Ages. This break is generally reckoned to have occurred at the end of the first millennium A.D. and to have been marked by a change in ceramic style, the colonisation of previously unoccupied highland areas, and a greater emphasis on herding in the mixed farming economy.

Archaeologists have also detailed regional variations on the Iron Age map of South Africa. For instance, they have pointed to a greater emphasis on cattle-keeping in the upland regions during the Later Iron Age than in the lowland regions, where cultivation seems to have predominated, especially during the Early Iron Age. It has also been conclusively demonstrated that some early African communities were mineral producers. There is substantial evidence of the early production of copper, tin and gold, in addition to iron, the major product; the Phalaborwa complex may have been South Africa's first mining metropolis. Some regions, though, were bereft of mineral resources. One obvious consequence of these regional variations and specialisations would have been exchange and trade. This is substantiated by archaeological research, which has unearthed extensive evidence of trade goods at Iron Age sites.

There are still, though, questions about the Iron Age that remain unanswered. We are uncertain as to why exactly a break occurred between the Early and Late Iron Ages. Was the break marked by an immigration of new peoples? Or was there an underlying continuity between the two phases? We also know little about Iron Age social and political structures that predate the oral and written record. The continuity within the Late Iron Age — from about the eleventh century to the early modern era — is less problematic. Maggs, in particular, has expertly detailed the interface between the archaeological and historical record in his work on the southern highveld. Yet there are specific regions that require more intensive archaeological investigation. Up till now much of the research into the Iron Age seems to have been concentrated in the north-eastern region of South Africa. It would seem that more work needs to be carried out on the south-east, the area of southern Nguni occupation, and in the north-western region, occupied today by the Tswana.

The advances in Iron Age archaeology have been matched by a growing literature on the history of African communities in the late precolonial phase. In the past few years a number of monographs have been published on the history of the Zulu, Swazi, Xhosa, Mpondo, Basotho and Pedi. Although there are variations in their temporal coverage, these studies focus mainly on the nineteenth century, spanning the later precapitalist era and the beginning of capitalist penetration and colonial subjugation. Together they share a number of broad concerns. Each has tried to dissect the particular society or community under investigation, to analyse its socio-political structure, and to relate that structure to its material base. And at the same time each has also been concerned to highlight the process of historical change in the societies under investigation, and to examine the impact on them of capitalist penetration and colonial domination.

These monographs have performed a number of invaluable functions. Firstly, they have filled an important empirical gap. We now know much more about the basic history of the Zulu, Swazi, Xhosa, Mpondo, Basotho and Pedi. Part of the task of the authors has been to tackle empirical problems — establishing a clear chronology, and correcting factual error in the light of new evidence. Indeed, there is still scope for further research of this kind. Various Tswana chiefdoms and the Venda still await a thorough historical examination.

Secondly, such detailed monographs have collectively served to highlight regional variations over space and time. Historians now recognise that the conventional tendency to distinguish sharply between states and stateless societies in Africa is oversimplified. But the dichotomy should not be discarded entirely. In this survey we have identified four nineteenth-century African societies for which the 'state' label would be appropriate — the Zulu, Swazi, Pedi and Basotho. In each case a single, dominant lineage expanded its power sufficiently for it to superimpose a state structure over a network of chiefdoms and homesteads. Using a more refined categorisation one might call these overall structures 'tributary states', since the payment of tribute was one of the main forms of subordination to the central authority.

On the other hand, we have observed that among the southern Nguni, Tswana and Venda, no overall state structure emerged. Among the Tswana there was a proliferation of independent chiefdoms, the number of which steadily increased over the years through a process of fission. Southern Nguni chiefdoms hung together in 'clusters' or loose 'confederations'.

Thirdly, a major achievement of the new African historiography has been to examine more closely the internal dynamic of particular African societies. Structural-functionalist anthropology had tended in the past to present these societies as harmonious, ordered systems in which people's status and roles were carefully defined and regulated in an ideological framework of kinship and authority. Revisionist historiography has pointed rather to the tensions and conflicts within these societies. Such conflicts could develop between central and subordinate chiefdoms, between chiefs and commoners, or between groups within the homestead. Some scholars have likened these conflicts to class struggles, arising out of relations of domination and exploitation. Peires, for instance, has contended that 'classes of chiefs and commoners did exist in Xhosa society and that the struggle between them was the motor force of Xhosa history'. He has also advanced 'the much more far-reaching suggestion that class relations were the central contradiction at the heart of every Nguni society, and that the differences between them reflected the varying state of the class struggle in each'.[1]

This new historiography has been marked by much conceptual creativity. Old assumptions about the nature of African society have been questioned. And, specifically, the links between material forces and the exercise of power have been drawn out and analysed. At the same time, though, the process of reconceptualisation has drifted somewhat into a logjam. In an earlier section we saw how the search for appropriate modes of production that could be applied to precolonial African societies has been largely inconclusive. Furthermore, the empirical substantiation of class struggles within precapitalist African societies is limited. While we do have extensive evidence of struggles waged at the centres of power, particularly over succession disputes, we have little firm evidence of commoner struggles against chiefly power.

The fourth main achievement of recent historical writing on southern African societies has been to detail more exactly and analyse more fully the course of change over time. The nineteenth century in particular was a period that spanned a number of significant watersheds and transitions — the evolution of the Zulu state, the *difaqane*, the intrusion of mercantile capital, the arrival of missionaries, colonial subjugation and African resistance, peasantisation and the beginnings of proletarianisation.

Recent studies of early nineteenth century Zulu state formation have viewed it essentially as an evolutionary rather than a revolutionary process. The Zulu state was not the creation of a single, dynamic individual — Shaka — but rather the culmination of a long process of socio-political consolidation among the northern Nguni. The new historiography has broken away from the old emphasis on individual agency as the chief motor of history, and has come to focus more on the material forces that either make possible or constrain human actions. Climatic variations and animal disease, for instance, can obviously have a far-reaching impact on societies whose material base is rooted in mixed farming. Thus among the northern Nguni in the early nineteenth century a crisis of resources may, in Guy's view, have been resolved by the creation of the Zulu state. For the Tswana, the uniform, arid expanse that made up their domain probably contributed to the shaping of their socio-political structure. If key resources were to be exploited rationally within a Tswana chiefdom, the chiefdom would necessarily have to exercise a high degree of centralised control over the economy at the expense of the ward's local autonomy.

Probably one of the most cataclysmic episodes in the history of southern Africa in the nineteenth century was the *difaqane*. Cobbing has rightly questioned many of the assumptions that lie beneath previous historical writing on the *difaqane*; and he has shown how some of these assumptions have played into the hands of apartheid's propagandists. What Cobbing's suggestive essay really does is to point to the need for further empirical research on the *difaqane*. In particular we require a better understanding of its demographic impact. To what extent were the fertile areas of the interior conveniently depopulated to make way for the Voortrekkers? Has the devastation wrought by the *difaqane* been exaggerated? Have later historians relied too much on the evidence of contemporaries who had an interest in exaggerating the devastation? These are important questions — and difficult ones to tackle, given the relative scarcity of evidence.

Another significant change occurring in the nineteenth century, highlighted by southern Africanist scholars and widely noted in the second part of this book, was a shift in the relations of production within some African communities. Certain groups, often those linked to mission stations, began to break free from the communal, redistributive economy and to engage in commodity production, producing a surplus for an expanding market. This trend towards peasantisation seems to have been most apparent in the middle and later decades of the nineteenth century. But it was by no means universal. Historians have observed the growth of a peasant class in parts of the Transkei and Ciskei, Natal, and Basutoland, and among sections of the

Tswana. There is no evidence as yet of such a class having emerged in Zululand or Swaziland in the nineteenth century.

By the end of the century this peasant class seems to have come under severe pressure. Its access to land was being curtailed, firstly by colonial conquest and subjugation, and secondly by the eviction of African rent-paying tenants and sharecroppers from white-owned land, as landowners increasingly turned from renting to more intensive commercial farming. The territorial segregation imposed by the 1913 Land Act further limited African land-holding opportunities outside the reserves. African farming has been further restricted in the twentieth century by South African state policy, which has effectively denied Africans easy access to the major arteries of the country's evolving transport network, to state subsidies, special credit facilities, and scientific aid, all of which have been made available to white farmers.

The evidence points to a decline in the peasantry that still needs to be more carefully detailed and analysed. The chronology of this decline, for instance, may be less clear-cut than Bundy at first implied. More recent research suggests that African peasants were continuing to produce a surplus for the market well into the twentieth century, albeit on severely disadvantageous terms. It may also be the case that scholars have too readily equated the growing proletarianisation of Africans — an undoubted fact at this time — with the decline of the peasantry. Figures clearly show a rapid growth in the number of African migrant labourers at the turn of the century, but they do not tell us what proportion of those labourers were former peasants.

Research on early labour migration in southern Africa demonstrates that this was by no means a uniform process. It is too simple a generalisation to suggest that migrant labourers were merely the hapless victims of various forms of coercion, although, of course, there were a number of forces at work. As Crush has remarked: 'From within particular societies, different types of migrants emerged, with varying needs and motives for participating in wage-labour, and dispatched by different "sending agencies".'[2] Some African societies, such as the Basotho, participated in labour migration from a relatively early date; others, like the Swazi, were later participants. Some, like the Mpondo, became migrants on a discretionary basis, at least for a while; others, like the Zulu, were subject to more coercive forces. Moreover, these forces varied over time and space. In some cases the coercion emanated from human agents, labour recruiters or collaborating chiefs. Other coercive forces were more impersonal: the demand for cash to pay taxes, or declining access to the means of production.

While new research is revealing these varying patterns of migrant labour, more work needs to be done on the impact of migrancy on African rural communities. Did the loss of able-bodied male labour seriously disrupt productive processes in African rural economies? Or did the exodus of migrants perhaps alleviate overpopulation in the reserves? In other words, was migrancy a symptom or a cause of rural impoverishment? The most likely answer to this last question is that migrancy has been a symptom of rural underdevelopment. The brief survey of African rural economies in Part Three bears out Murray's conclusion that 'capital accumulation has taken place in the core areas of southern Africa at the expense of the peripheral areas'.[3]

One of the fundamental objectives of state policy in the twentieth century has been that the reserves should provide subsistence for those Africans surplus to labour requirements in urban areas. Accordingly a massive resettlement programme has dumped millions of 'surplus people' in the 'homelands'. However, during the course of the twentieth century these increasingly impoverished rural peripheries have been less and less able to fulfil the functions required of them. The result has been a massive movement of Africans from these underdeveloped peripheries to urban areas in search of some means of subsistence, quite contrary to the intention of government policy-makers.

While many urban Africans have entered wage labour, opportunities were also present in urban areas for those who wished to pursue more independent economic activities. For a large part of this century a number of urban African communities were able to enjoy a relative degree of freedom from official control and regulation. These were the occupants of the private leasehold or freehold townships, and of shack settlements. In these uncontrolled living zones a thriving informal sector often operated, enabling people to supplement meagre wage incomes or to earn a subsistence in the complete absence of any wage income. But in this area, too, the South African state has repeatedly intervened, destroying these communities and their independent existence, forcing their occupants either to live in bleak, strictly controlled townships or to return to a 'homeland'.

The destruction of these urban communities in many ways parallels the erosion of the African rural peasantry. In both cases Africans were victims of coercion that deprived them of access to the means of production. This overall process of proletarianisation has been well captured by Van Onselen:

> during this transition to a modern industrial state, most black South Africans were systematically denied access to alternative means of earning an independent livelihood until the point was reached where they had only their labour to sell, and so came to form the largest part of the working class in the new society.[4]

In the nineteenth century all the African societies of South Africa lost their political independence. Over the past hundred years the economic independence of African communities and individuals has been steadily eroded. But they have not been passive victims of this destruction. A major theme of Parts Two and Three has been African resistance to colonialism and the growth of opposition to white domination. We have noted the many attempts on the part of independent African chiefdoms or states to resist colonial subjugation in the nineteenth century. In some cases this resistance was long and drawn-out. The southern Nguni fought against colonial domination intermittently over a hundred-year period. Protracted conflicts were also carried on between the Basotho and the Orange Free State boers, and between the Pedi and the Transvaal boers. In other cases resistance was brief but spectacular, as with the Zulu in 1879. Other African societies came under colonial domination without offering almost any resistance at all. The Tswana, for instance, seem to have accepted, or even welcomed, British overlordship in the 1880s.

Once subjugated a number of African communities continued to resist their colonial rulers. Such resistance was generally suppressed. But a successful rebellion was waged, for example, against Cape colonial rule by the Basotho in 1880–1. Colonial forces were unable to quell the rebellion. And in 1884 the Cape government, disillusioned with its sub-imperialist role, transferred the responsibility for Basutoland back to Britain. In the long term this transfer enabled the majority of Basotho to remain outside the orbit of South African political control.

The strongest motive behind all these acts of resistance was probably the desire to retain or regain independence from colonial rule. Had the Zulu state, for instance, accepted the terms of Frere's ultimatum in 1879 it would have been tantamount to a loss of independence. But despite their resistance, by the end of the nineteenth century all African chiefdoms and states in South Africa had been brought under some form of colonial rule.

In the twentieth century black opposition to white domination in South Africa has taken various forms. There has been mild political protest, with a reliance on delegations and petitions. This was characteristic of the early ANC. There has been widespread, coordinated passive resistance, epitomised by the defiance campaign of the early 1950s. There have been local community struggles: resistance to urban relocation, and bus, rent or consumer boycotts. Worker organisation and militant action have developed steadily over the past seventy years. One thinks particularly of the mineworkers' strikes of 1920 and 1946, and the widespread industrial strikes of 1973. There have been outbursts of popular resistance, as in 1976. And there has been the shift to a strategy of armed struggle by the ANC and the PAC since the 1960s.

A wide range of diverse elements has constituted the leadership and activists in different struggles. Some forms of opposition have been worker-inspired; others have been led by petty bourgeois figures; still others have taken a populist form, transcending class differences. Some struggles have had an Africanist or black consciousness orientation; others have been non-racial. Opposition has thus been made up of a number of strands, some interconnected, some cross-cutting. One point is clear, though: that ethnic categories have no real relevance to the study of opposition in twentieth-century South Africa. Class categories, on the other hand, do assume and disclose greater meaning in this context.

The two concepts of ethnicity and class are crucially significant to many themes covered in this survey. In the first two parts of this book the terms 'Nguni' and 'Sotho' have been used as organising categories. The limitations of these categories are patent. The labels say nothing about the self-identification of the people concerned; they are inapplicable to the Iron Age; and the categories have little relevance to twentieth-century history. In this book they are used primarily as linguistic labels, although they do also have some cultural connotations. Each of these generic terms embraces a number of different African polities that existed during the precolonial era. These polities rarely represented rigidly exclusive ethnic entities. We have seen how the early Swazi state incorporated existing Sotho communities and assimilated elements of Sotho culture. It was common for southern African states or chiefdoms to absorb groups of different ethnic origins. Moshoeshoe's Basotho state, for instance, represented an ethnic amalgam. So did the Mfengu, many of whom were themselves incorporated into southern Nguni chiefdoms.

Afrikaner Nationalist ideology today claims that there is no African majority in South Africa, but rather a whole set of minorities: more specifically, there are deemed to be some ten or so mutually exclusive, culturally and linguistically heterogeneous African ethnic entities, each with their own separate historical roots. This notion is a hollow sham. The present-day 'homelands' have shallow roots in history. The notion is also a denial of historical trends in the twentieth century. It is true that there exist some ethnically based organisations like Inkatha, and that ruling groups in the 'homelands' have tacitly acknowledged ethnic differentiation by participating in the system. However, the vast majority of African organisations and movements in the twentieth century have transcended and openly disavowed narrow ethnic differences. This is true of political movements like the ANC and PAC; it is true of trade unions and community-based movements.

What is clear is that ethnic differentiation, particularly in the twentieth century, has been imposed from above on the African people of South Africa. It has served a number of functions. In particular it has enabled the government to adopt a divide-and-rule strategy in curbing and controlling the African majority. This has not only been applied at the 'homeland' level, but also in workers' hostels where different 'tribal groups' have been kept apart from each other. This has often created tension where none might have existed. As one African writer, the late Can Themba, has put it: 'The situation has been aggravated, according to many people, by the policy of ethnic grouping, which has led the more tribal among us to think of other tribes as "foreigners", "enemies".We are not allowed to learn to live together in peace....'[5]

A more pertinent form of differentiation among Africans has been that of class stratification. We have seen how some scholars have tried to apply a class analysis to precapitalist African societies. But these analyses have tended to be theoretically hesitant, and their supporting evidence has often been insubstantial. However, from the later nineteenth century a process of class stratification within African societies becomes more clearly discernible. One begins to observe the emergence of something like an African petty bourgeoisie, a group who can be differentiated according to their economic position and lifestyle, their self-identification as an elite superior to the rank-and-file, and their values, one of which laid great stress on individual accumulation. During the twentieth century one can trace how this group has operated through structures and organisations, sometimes official, sometimes oppositional, in pursuit of their own interests. However, as some writers have shown, the concept of an African petty bourgeoisie can also be problematic. The group cannot always be clearly distinguished from the working-class, with whom they are the common victims of racial discrimination. Thus at times there has been a broad-based African opposition to white domination; at other times there have been popular struggles, with which the African petty bourgeoisie were conspicuously out of touch.

All this goes to show that the African history of South Africa is extremely complex. A fundamental characteristic of racism and racial ideology is the tendency to stereotype another racial group. Such stereotypes abound in South Africa. Racial stereotypes are always ahistorical. They miss any notion of change over time or variation over space. They encapsulate vast assumptions about the past into glib generalisations or aphorisms. They serve to legitimate an unjust social order. This book has tried to counter some of these stereotypes by pointing to the many diverse and complex strands that can be found in the history of the African people of South Africa.

REFERENCES

Part One: African society in the precolonial era: from the third century to *c.* 1830

1. R. R. Inskeep, *The Peopling of Southern Africa* (Cape Town, 1978), pp. 130–1; R. J. Mason, 'Background to the Transvaal Iron Age — new discoveries at Olifantspoort and Broederstroom', *Journal of the South African Institute of Mining and Metallurgy*, 74 (1974), 211; T. Maggs, 'Mzonjani and the beginning of the Iron Age in Natal', in *A Collection of Archaeological Papers*, from *Annals of the Natal Museum*, 24, 1 (1980), 71–6; M. Hall and J. C. Vogel, 'Enkwazini: fourth century Iron Age site on the Zululand coast', *South African Journal of Science*, 74 (February 1978), 70; T. Maggs, 'Msuluzi Confluence: a seventh century Early Iron Age site on the Tugela River', in *A Collection of Archaeological Papers*, from *Annals of the Natal Museum*, 24, 1 (1980); T. M. O'C. Maggs and M. A. Michael, 'Ntshekane: an Early Iron Age site in the Tugela Basin, Natal', *Annals of the Natal Museum*, 22 (1976), 737.

2. The site has been dated to the seventh–eighth century A.D. T. Maggs, 'The Iron Age sequence south of the Vaal and Pongola Rivers: some historical implications', *Journal of African History*, 21 (1980), 4; T. M. Evers, 'Recent progress in studies of the Early Iron Age in the eastern Transvaal, South Africa', *South African Journal of Science*, 73 (March 1977), 80; Maggs, 'Msuluzi Confluence', p. 139; Maggs, 'Mzonjani', p. 90; T. Maggs, 'The Iron Age south of the Zambezi', in R. G. Klein (ed.), *Southern African Prehistory and Paleoenvironments* (Boston, 1984), p. 336; J. M. Feely, 'Smelting in the Iron Age of Transkei', *South African Journal of Science*, 81 (January 1985), 10–11.

3. Inskeep, *Peopling*, pp. 124, 130–1; R. R. Inskeep and T. M. O'C. Maggs, 'Unique art objects in the Iron Age of the Transvaal, South Africa', *South African Archaeological Bulletin*, 30 (1975), 135; H. P. Prinsloo, 'Early Iron Age site at Klein Afrika near Wylliespoort, Soutpansberg Mountains, South Africa', *South African Journal of Science*, 70 (September 1974), 271; N. J. van der Merwe and R. T. K. Scully, 'The Phalaborwa story: archaeological and ethnographic investigation of a South African Iron Age group', *World Archaeology*, 3 (October 1971), 178; D. W. Phillipson, *The Later Prehistory of Eastern and Southern Africa* (London, 1977), p. 139; M. Hall and J. C. Vogel, 'Some recent radiocarbon dates from southern Africa', *Journal of African History*, 21 (1980), 441–3; Evers, 'Recent progress', p. 78; Maggs, 'Msuluzi Confluence', p. 135.

4. Maggs, 'Iron Age sequence', pp. 5–7; M. Hall, 'Early farming communities of southern Africa: a population discovered', *South African Historical Journal*, 15 (1983), 2–3; Maggs, 'Mzonjani', p. 87.

5. R. J. Mason, 'First Early Iron Age settlement in South Africa: Broederstroom 24/73, Brits district, Transvaal', *South African Journal of Science*, 69 (November 1973), 325; Maggs, 'Msuluzi Confluence', pp. 122, 143; Maggs and Michael, 'Ntshekane', p. 737; Maggs, 'Iron Age sequence', pp. 9–10.

6. Maggs, 'Mzonjani', p. 87; Maggs, 'Msuluzi Confluence', pp. 131–2, 136–8; Mason, 'Background to the Transvaal Iron Age', pp. 211–12; Van der Merwe and Scully, 'Phalaborwa', p. 181; Inskeep and Maggs, 'Unique art objects', pp. 135–6; Maggs, 'Iron Age south of Zambezi', p. 341.

7. Mason, 'Background to the Transvaal Iron Age', pp. 211, 213; Hall, 'Early farming communities', pp. 7–8; Maggs, 'Mzonjani', p. 93; M. Hall and A. Morris, 'Race and Iron Age human skeletal remains from southern Africa : an assessment', *Social Dynamics*, 9, 2 (1983), 34; Maggs, 'Iron Age south of the Zambezi', pp. 339–40.

8. Inskeep, *Peopling*, p. 124; Maggs, 'Iron Age sequence', pp. 11–13; Hall and Vogel, 'Recent radiocarbon dates', p. 451; R. J. Mason, 'Iron Age research in the western Transvaal, South Africa, 1971–72', *Current Anthropology*, 14 (1973), 485–6; T. M. Evers, 'Recent Iron Age research in the eastern Transvaal, South Africa', *South African Archaeological Bulletin*, 30 (1975), 71–83.

9. Hall and Vogel, 'Recent radiocarbon dates', p. 443; Phillipson, *Prehistory*, pp. 147, 206.

10. T. M. O'C. Maggs, *Iron Age Communities of the Southern Highveld* (Pietermaritzburg, 1976), pp. 285, 314–18; Evers, 'Recent Iron Age research', p. 76; Maggs, 'Iron Age sequence', p. 11; R. Mason, *Prehistory of the Transvaal* (Johannesburg, 1969), p. 400.

11. Hall, 'Early farming communities', pp. 4–5; Maggs, *Southern Highveld*, pp. 318–21; T. Robey, 'Mpambanyoni: a Late Iron Age site on the Natal south coast', in *A Collection of Archaeological Papers*, from *Annals of the Natal Museum*, 24, 1 (1980), 163.

12. Mason, *Prehistory of the Transvaal*, pp. 406, 415; Van der Merwe and Scully, 'Phalaborwa', pp. 179–83; G. St. J. Oxley Oxland and H. White, 'Ancient mining practices in the Rooiberg area', *Journal of the South African Institute of Mining and Metallurgy*, 74 (1974), 245; E. O. M. Hanisch, 'Copper working in the Messina district', *Journal of the South African Institute of Mining and Metallurgy*, 74 (1974), 250–1; T. M. Evers, 'Iron Age trade in the eastern Transvaal, South Africa', *South African Archaeological Bulletin*, 29 (1974), 35.

13. T. M. Evers and R. P. van den Berg, 'Ancient mining in southern Africa, with reference to a copper mine in the Harmony Block, north–eastern Transvaal', *Journal of the South African Institute of Mining and Metallurgy*, 74 (1974), 225–6; Maggs, *Southern Highveld*, p. 321; L. Fouché (ed.), *Mapungubwe: Ancient Bantu Civilization on the Limpopo* (Cambridge, 1937), p. 25; Evers, 'Iron Age trade', pp. 34–5.

14. Fouché, *Mapungubwe*, p. 162; G. P. Rightmire and N. J. van der Merwe, 'Two burials from Phalaborwa and the association of race and culture in the Iron Age of southern Africa', *South African Archaeological Bulletin*, 31 (1976), 147, 152; D. Birmingham and S. Marks, 'Southern Africa', in R. Oliver (ed.), *The Cambridge History of Africa* (Cambridge, 1977), vol. 3, p. 618.

15. Maggs, 'Iron Age sequence', pp. 13–14; Inskeep, *Peopling*, p. 134.

16. Mason, *Prehistory*, p. 379; Van der Merwe and Scully, 'Phalaborwa', pp. 184–5; Evers, 'Iron Age trade', p. 33; Maggs, *Southern Highveld*, pp. 314–18.

17. Hall, 'Early farming communities', p. 8; R. M. Derricourt, *Prehistoric Man in the Ciskei and Transkei* (Cape Town, 1977), pp. 178–9; S. Marks, 'South Africa: "The myth of the empty land"', *History Today*, 30 (January 1980), 7–12; T. M. Evers, 'Salt and soapstone bowl factories at Harmony, Letaba district, northeast Transvaal', *Goodwin Series*, 3 (1979), 106; Feely, 'Iron Age of Transkei', pp. 10–11.

18. S. Marks and A. Atmore, 'The problem of the Nguni: an examination of the ethnic and linguistic situation in South Africa before the Mfecane', in D. Dalby (ed.),

Language and History in Africa (New York, 1970), p. 125; S. Marks, 'The traditions of the Natal "Nguni": a second look at the work of A. T. Bryant', in L. Thompson *African Societies in Southern Africa* (London, 1969), pp. 129–31, 139–40; M. Wilson, 'Problems for research in Tswana history', *Botswana Notes and Records*, 3 (1971), 70; M. Wilson, 'Changes in social structure in southern Africa: the relevance of kinship studies to the historian', in Thompson (ed.), *African Societies*, pp. 80–3; J. Wright, 'Politics, ideology, and the invention of the "Nguni"' (unpublished paper, 1983); M. M. Fuze, *The Black People*, ed. A. T. Cope (Pietermaritzburg, 1979), p. 1; A. T. Bryant, *The Zulu People* (Pietermaritzburg, 1967), pp. 14–27; M. Legassick, 'The Sotho–Tswana peoples before 1800', in Thompson (ed.), *African Societies*, p. 93; C. Hamilton and J. Wright, 'The making of the Lala: ethnicity, ideology and class-formation in a precolonial context' (unpublished paper, University of the Witwatersrand History Workshop, 1984). The scope of this study is restricted to the Nguni south of the Limpopo and therefore excludes those groups, like the Ndebele and Ngoni, who dispersed northwards during the *difaqane*.

19. P. Bonner, *Kings, Commoners and Concessionaires* (Cambridge, 1983), pp. 9–26; D. W. Hedges, 'Trade and politics in southern Mozambique and Zululand in the eighteenth and early nineteenth centuries' (unpublished Ph. D. thesis, University of London, 1978), pp. 156–93; L. Thompson, 'Co-operation and conflict: the Zulu Kingdom and Natal', in M. Wilson and L. Thompson (eds.), *The Oxford History of South Africa* (Oxford, 1969), vol. 1, p. 341; A. Koopman, 'Dingiswayo rides again', *Journal of Natal and Zulu History*, II (1979), 1–12; J. Wright and A. Manson, *The Hlubi Chiefdom in Zululand–Natal: A History* (Ladysmith, 1983), pp. 12–13.

20. Hedges, 'Trade and politics', pp. 183, 202–17; Thompson, 'Zulu Kingdom and Natal', pp. 342–5; Wright and Manson, *Hlubi Chiefdom*, pp. 12–14; Hamilton and Wright, 'The making of the Lala', pp. 10–14; H. Slater, 'Transitions in the political economy of south–east Africa before 1840' (unpublished D. Phil. thesis, University of Sussex, 1976).

21. J. B. Wright, 'Pre-Shakan age-group formation among the northern Nguni', *Natalia*, 8 (1978), 22, 28; M. Gluckman, 'The individual in a social framework: the rise of King Shaka of Zululand', *Journal of African Studies*, 1, 2 (1974); E. V. Walter, *Terror and Resistance* (New York, 1972), pp. 110, 137–42, 249; Hedges, 'Trade and politics', pp. 6–7, 110, 119, 127–30, 194–9; A. Smith, 'The trade of Delagoa Bay as a factor in Nguni politics, 1750–1835', in Thompson (ed.), *African Societies*, pp. 173–84; M. Gluckman, 'The kingdom of the Zulu in South Africa', in M. Fortes and E. E. Evans-Pritchard, *African Political Systems* (London, 1970), p. 25; J. Guy, 'Ecological factors in the rise of Shaka and the Zulu kingdom', in S. Marks and A. Atmore (eds.), *Economy and Society in Pre-industrial South Africa* (London, 1980), pp. 102–18; Wright, 'Pre-Shakan age-group formation', p. 25; J. B. McI. Daniel, 'A geographical study of pre-Shakan Zululand', *South African Geographical Journal*, 55, 1 (1973), 23–31; Wilson, 'Changes in social structure', p. 73.

22. M. Wilson, 'The Nguni people', in Wilson and Thompson (eds.), *Oxford History of South Africa*, vol. 1, pp. 79–81, 87; Derricourt, *Prehistoric Man*, pp. 135, 185–91. The name 'Xhosa' requires some clarification. In a political sense the Xhosa represented only one of a number of groups among the southern Nguni. In a wider linguistic sense most southern Nguni peoples are classified as Xhosa-speaking. J. B. Peires, *The House of Phalo* (Johannesburg, 1981), p. ix.

23. Derricourt, *Prehistoric Man*, p. 210; G. Harinck, 'Interaction between Xhosa and Khoi: emphasis on the period 1620–1750', in Thompson (ed.), *African Societies*, pp. 150–7, 164; Peires, *House of Phalo*, pp. 22–4.

24. W. D. Hammond-Tooke, 'Segmentation and fission in Cape Nguni political units', *Africa*, 35 (1965), 145; Wilson, 'The Nguni people', pp. 91–5; R. Derricourt, 'Settlement in the Transkei and Ciskei before the Mfecane', in C. Saunders and R. Derricourt (eds.), *Beyond the Cape Frontier* (London, 1974), pp. 59–60; Peires, *House of Phalo*, pp. 84–5.

25. J. H. Soga, *The South-Eastern Bantu* (Johannesburg, 1930), pp. 101–2; Peires, *House of Phalo*, pp. 13–17, 46–52, 58–63, 82.

26. Hammond-Tooke, 'Segmentation and fission', pp. 149, 154–5, 157–9; Peires, *House of Phalo*, pp. 21–2, 27–31; J. B. Peires, 'Introduction', in J. B. Peires (ed.), *Before and After Shaka* (Grahamstown, 1981), pp. 8–9; J. B. Peires, 'Xhosa expansion before 1800', in *The Societies of Southern Africa in the 19th and 20th Centuries* (Institute of Commonwealth Studies, London), vol. 6 (1974–5), 7.

27. B. Sansom, 'Traditional economic systems' and 'Traditional rulers and their realms', in W. D. Hammond-Tooke (ed.), *The Bantu-speaking Peoples of Southern Africa* (London, 1974), pp. 135–76, 246–83; Maggs, *Southern Highveld*, pp. 140–3, 159, 295, 314–21; G. W. Stow, *The Native Races of South Africa* (London, 1905), p. 417; D. Birmingham and S. Marks, 'Southern Africa', in R. Oliver (ed.), *The Cambridge History of Africa* (Cambridge, 1977), vol. 3, pp. 611–14; M. Legassick, 'The Sotho-Tswana peoples before 1800', in Thompson (ed.), *African Societies*, p. 100; G. Y. Okihiro, 'Precolonial economic change among the Tlhaping, *c.* 1795–1817', *International Journal of African Historical Studies*, 17, 1 (1984), 66–78.

28. N. Parsons, *A New History of Southern Africa* (London, 1982), pp. 41–50; S. Marks and R. Gray, 'Southern Africa and Madagascar', in R. Gray (ed.), *The Cambridge History of Africa* (Cambridge, 1975), vol. 4, pp. 412–19; Stow, *Native Races*, pp. 420–4; W. F. Lye and C. Murray, *Transformations on the Highveld: The Tswana and Southern Sotho* (Cape Town, 1980), p. 26; Legassick, 'Sotho-Tswana peoples', pp. 102–4, 122; I. Schapera, 'A short history of the Bangwaketse', *African Studies*, 1 (1942); Q. N. Parsons, 'On the origins of the bamaNgwato', *Botswana Notes and Records*, 5 (1973), 92, 95–96.

29. T. Tlou, 'The nature of Batswana states: towards a theory of Batswana traditional government — the Batawana case', *Botswana Notes and Records*, 6 (1974), 66; Sansom, 'Traditional rulers', pp. 251ff, and 'Economic systems', pp. 142–7; I. Schapera, 'Kinship and politics in Tswana history', *Journal of the Royal Anthropological Institute*, 93 (1963).

30. Lye and Murray, *Transformations*, p. 27; Maggs, *Southern Highveld*, p. 226; L. Thompson, *Survival in Two Worlds* (Oxford, 1975), pp. 14–19; P. Sanders, *Moshoeshoe, Chief of the Sotho* (London, 1975), pp. 3–5; Parsons, *New History of Southern Africa*, pp. 47–8.

31. P. Delius, *The Land Belongs to Us* (Johannesburg, 1983), pp. 12–19, 48–52; Parsons, *New History of Southern Africa*, p. 38.

32. D. N. Beach, *The Shona and Zimbabwe 900–1850* (London, 1980), pp. 211–17, 260–3; Parsons, *New History of Southern Africa*, p. 38; M. Wilson, 'The Sotho, Venda and Tsonga', in Wilson and Thompson (eds.), *Oxford History of South Africa*, vol. 1, pp. 172–5; N. J. van Warmelo, 'The classification of cultural groups', in Hammond-Tooke (ed.), *Bantu-Speaking Peoples*, pp. 78–83; N. M. N. Ralushai and J. R. Gray, 'Ruins and traditions of the Ngona and Mbedzi', *Rhodesian History*, 8 (1977), 1–11; H. A. Stayt, 'Notes on the Balemba', *Journal of the Royal Anthropological Institute*, LXI (1931), 236.

33. J. D. Omer-Cooper, *The Zulu Aftermath* (London, 1966), pp. 57–93; L. Thompson, 'Cooperation and conflict: the High Veld', in Wilson and Thompson (eds.), *Oxford History of South Africa*, vol. 1, pp. 391–405; Lye and Murray, *Transfor-*

mations, pp. 31–3.

34. Maggs, *Southern Highveld*, p. 227; Thompson, 'High Veld', pp. 394–5; Lye and Murray, *Transformations*, pp. 35, 38–9, 47; Thompson, *Survival in Two Worlds*, p. 68.

35. Thompson, *Survival in Two Worlds*, pp. 1–69; Sanders, *Moshoeshoe*, pp. 19–59; Lye and Murray, *Transformations*, pp. 28–49.

36. Parsons, *New History of Southern Africa*, pp. 67–77; Lye and Murray, *Transformations*, pp. 35–9; Omer-Cooper, *Zulu Aftermath*, pp. 93–8; R. Kent Rasmussen, *Migrant Kingdom* (London, 1978); M. Kinsman, 'The impact of the *difaqane* on southern Tswana communities, with special reference to the Rolong' (University of the Witwatersrand History Workshop paper, 1984), pp. 1–27.

37. Delius, *The Land Belongs to Us*, pp. 19–30.

38. R. A. Moyer, 'A history of the Mfengu of the eastern Cape 1815–1865', (unpublished Ph. D. thesis, London University, 1976), pp. 72–166; W. Beinart, 'Production and the material basis of chieftainship : Pondoland *c.* 1830–80', in Marks and Atmore, *Economy and Society*, pp. 121–4; Kinsman, 'Impact of the *difaqane*', p. 1; Marks and Atmore, 'Introduction', in Marks and Atmore (eds.), *Economy and Society*, p. 16; Omer-Cooper, *Zulu Aftermath*, p. 180; J. Cobbing, 'The case against the *mfecane*', pp. 4–7, 10–12, 15–17.

39. C. Meillassoux, 'From reproduction to production: a Marxist approach to economic anthropology', in H. Wolpe (ed.), *The Articulation of Modes of Production* (London, 1980), p. 193; J. Lonsdale, 'States and social processes in Africa: a historiographical survey', *African Studies Review*, 24, 2/3 (1981), 139, 149, 172, 175; R. Law, 'In search of a Marxist perspective on pre-colonial tropical Africa', *Journal of African History*, 19, 3 (1978), 446; C. Coquery-Vidrovitch, 'Research on an African mode of production', in M. M. Klein and G. W. Johnson (eds.), *Perspectives on the African Past* (Boston, 1972), pp. 33–41; P. Bonner, 'Classes, the mode of production and the state in pre-colonial Swaziland', in Marks and Atmore, *Economy and Society*, pp. 81–4; S. Marks and A. Atmore, 'Introduction', in *ibid.*, p. 10; J. Crush, 'The struggle for Swazi labour, 1890–1920' (unpublished Ph. D. thesis, Queen's University, 1983), pp. 44–9.

Part Two: An era of transition *c.* 1830-1900

1. R. Mael, 'The problem of political integration in the Zulu empire' (unpublished Ph. D. thesis, University of California, Los Angeles, 1974), pp. 61–4; P. A. Kennedy, 'Mpande and the Zulu kingship', *Journal of Natal and Zulu History*, 4 (1981), 26; F. N. C. Okoye, 'Dingane: a reappraisal', *Journal of African History*, 10, 2 (1969), 222–5, 230–5.

2. J. Wright and R. Edgecombe, 'Mpande kaSenzangakhona *c.* 1798–1872', in C. Saunders (ed.), *Black Leaders in Southern African History* (London, 1979), pp. 45, 47, 55–9; Kennedy, 'Mpande', pp. 21, 26–7, 37; Mael, 'Political integration', pp. 85–93, 168–97, 209–12, 234–49, 296–313; J. Guy, *The Destruction of the Zulu Kingdom* (London, 1979), p. 13; C. Ballard, 'John Dunn and Cetshwayo : the material foundations of political power in the Zulu kingdom, 1857–1878', *Journal of African History*, 21, 1 (1980), 88–90.

3. J. Guy, 'Cetshwayo kaMpande *c.* 1832–84', in Saunders (ed.), *Black Leaders*, p. 77; Guy, *Destruction of the Zulu Kingdom*, pp. 15, 21–2, 39; Mael, 'Political integration', pp. 175–6; Kennedy, 'Mpande', p. 38; P. Colenbrander, 'The Zulu political economy on the eve of the war', in A. Duminy and C. Ballard (eds.), *The Anglo–Zulu War: New Perspectives* (Pietermaritzburg, 1981), pp. 81–6; N. Etherington, *Preach-*

ers, Peasants and Politics in Southeast Africa 1835–1880 (London, 1978), pp. 74–86.

4. N. Etherington, 'Anglo–Zulu relations 1856–1878', in Duminy and Ballard (eds.), *Anglo–Zulu War*, pp. 21–6, 36; C. de B. Webb and J. B. Wright (eds.), *A Zulu King Speaks* (Pietermaritzburg, 1978), p. 55; Guy, *Destruction of the Zulu Kingdom*, p. 59.

5. C. Ballard, 'The transfrontiersman: the career of John Dunn in Natal and Zululand 1834–1895', (unpublished Ph. D. thesis, University of Natal, 1980), ch. 6; Guy, 'Cetshwayo', pp. 89–91; Guy, *Destruction of the Zulu Kingdom*, pp. 83–7, 98–101, 124–41, 148–64, 183–209, 217–27, 231–9, 242; J. Guy, 'The destruction and reconstruction of Zulu society', in S. Marks and R. Rathbone (eds.), *Industrialisation and Social Change in South Africa* (London, 1982), pp. 174–90; R. Edgecombe, 'Sir Marshal Clarke and the abortive attempt to "Basutolandise" Zululand, 1893–97', *Journal of Natal and Zulu History*, 1 (1978), 43–53; E. Unterhalter, 'Migrant labour and the Nquthu district of Zululand, 1879–1910', (unpublished paper, n.d.), p. 3.

6. D. Welsh, *The Roots of Segregation* (Cape Town, 1971), pp. 2, 23; C. C. Ballard, 'Natal 1824–44: the frontier interregnum', *Journal of Natal and Zulu History*, 5 (1982), pp. 51–4, 58, 63; E. H. Brookes and C. de B. Webb, *A History of Natal* (Pietermaritzburg, 1965), pp. 49–50, 58–60; C. Bundy, *The Rise and Fall of the South African Peasantry* (London, 1979), p. 170; Etherington, *Preachers, Peasants and Politics*, pp. 11, 47–59, 67, 87–96.

7. H. Slater, 'Land, labour and capital in Natal: the Natal Land and Colonisation Company 1860–1948', *Journal of African History*, 16, 2 (1975), 260–1, 272; Welsh, *Roots of Segregation*, p. 47; H. Slater, 'The changing pattern of economic relationships in rural Natal, 1838–1914', in Marks and Atmore (eds.), *Economy and Society*, p. 163; Bundy, *South African Peasantry*, pp. 170–4, 179–82; S. Hindson, 'Peasant and petty-bourgeois: persistent tendencies in the emergence of social forms — Edendale, Natal 1850–1900' (unpublished paper, 1980); N. Etherington, 'Natal's first black capitalists', *Theoria*, 45 (1975), 31–5.

8. A. Manson, 'A people in transition: the Hlubi in Natal 1848–1877', *Journal of Natal and Zulu History*, 2 (1979), 13–20, 23; N. A. Etherington, 'Why Langalibalele ran away', *Journal of Natal and Zulu History*, 1 (1978), pp. 7–9; for more detailed treatment of the Langalibalele episode, see W. R. Guest, *Langalibalele: The Crisis in Natal 1873–1875* (Durban, 1976), and N. Herd, *The Bent Pine* (Johannesburg, 1966).

9. Bundy, *South African Peasantry*, pp. 183–92; Slater, 'Changing pattern of economic relationships', pp. 161–4.

10. Bonner, *Kings, Commoners and Concessionaires*, pp. 27–34, 37–41, 45–9, 52–60, 63–4, 74–5, 85–9, 103–9; P. Bonner, 'Factions and fissions: Transvaal/Swazi politics in the mid-nineteenth century', *Journal of African History*, 19, 2 (1978), 219–38; P. L. Bonner, 'Mswati II *c*. 1826–65', in Saunders (ed.), *Black Leaders*, pp. 70–2.

11. Bonner, *Kings, Commoners and Concessionaires*, pp. 54–5, 74–6, 109–12, 118–20, 123–9, 132–4, 145–6, 161–3, 171–2, 183–4, 189–95; J. S. M. Matsebula, *A History of Swaziland* (Cape Town, 1976), pp. 115–31.

12. Peires, *House of Phalo*, pp. 86–8; Moyer, 'History of the Mfengu', pp. 72–130.

13. Peires, *House of Phalo*, pp. 89–94, 109–15, 128–34, 145–59; C. C. Saunders, *The Annexation of the Transkeian Territories* (Archives Year Book, Pretoria, 1976), pp. 1–2.

14. Peires, *House of Phalo*, pp. 117, 161–2; Saunders, *Annexation of the Transkeian Territories*, pp. 59–67, 168–71; C. C. Saunders, 'The annexation of the Transkei', in C. Saunders and R. Derricourt (eds.), *Beyond the Cape Frontier* (London, 1974), pp. 186–8; J. S. Galbraith, *Reluctant Empire* (California, 1963), pp. 224, 247–8, 263–4; Moyer, 'History of the Mfengu', pp. 220–3.

15. C. C. Saunders, 'The Transkeian Rebellion of 1880–81: a case-study of

Transkeian resistance to white control', *South African Historical Journal*, 8 (1976), 32–9; Saunders, *Annexation of the Transkeian Territories*, pp. 21, 77, 148–9, 156–7, 161–7; W. Beinart, *The Political Economy of Pondoland 1860–1930* (Cambridge, 1982), pp. 31–5.

16. Saunders, 'The Annexation of the Transkei', pp. 193–5; W. D. Hammond-Tooke, *Command or Consensus* (Cape Town, 1975), pp. 78, 88–90; R. Southall, *South Africa's Transkei* (London, 1982), pp. 88–9; Saunders, *Annexation of the Transkeian Territories*, pp. 140–4; R. Edgecombe, 'The Glen Grey Act: local origins of an abortive "Bill for Africa", in J. A. Benyon *et al.* (eds.), *Studies in Local History* (Cape Town, 1976), pp. 89–98.

17. Peires, *House of Phalo*, pp. 97, 100–1; Beinart, *Pondoland*, pp. 22–8; Bundy, *South African Peasantry*, pp. 34, 37, 45, 52–5, 65–72, 75–9, 90; Moyer, 'History of the Mfengu', pp. 133–5, 413–16.

18. Bundy, *South African Peasantry*, pp. 83, 87, 95–9, 118–23, 127, 134–5; Beinart, *Pondoland*, pp. 28–9, 47–8, 55.

19. S. Trapido, 'African divisional politics in the Cape Colony, 1884–1910', *Journal of African History*, 9, 1 (1968), 80–1, 88–9; C. C. Saunders, 'The new African elite in the eastern Cape and some late nineteenth century origins of African nationalism', in *The Societies of Southern Africa in the 19th and 20th Centuries*, vol. 1, 1969–70, pp. 45, 47; L. D. Ngcongco, 'John Tengo Jabavu 1859–1921', in Saunders (ed.), *Black Leaders*, p. 146; C. C. Saunders, 'Tile and the Thembu Church: politics and independency on the Cape eastern frontier in the late nineteenth century', *Journal of African History*, 11, 4 (1970), 557, 569.

20. Sanders, *Moshoeshoe*, pp. 125–9, 134–5, 148, 154, 183–4, 196–7; Thompson, *Survival in Two Worlds*, pp. 71, 77, 90–5, 100–4, 110–14; J. Kimble, 'Lesotho and the outside world, 1840–1870 — prelude to imperialism' (unpublished paper, 1977), p. 9; Lye and Murray, *Transformations*, p. 69.

21. Thompson, *Survival in Two Worlds*, pp. 114, 122–5, 134–7, 148–64, 219, 237–52, 257–8, 261, 277–91; Sanders, *Moshoeshoe*, pp. 77–82, 89–94, 172–6, 186–95, 221; Kimble, 'Lesotho and the outside world', pp. 1, 13.

22. Thompson, *Survival in Two Worlds*, pp. 172–4, 211, 257–8; Sanders, *Moshoeshoe*, pp. 206–7, 279; L. Thompson, 'The subjection of the African chiefdoms, 1870–1898', in M. Wilson and L. Thompson (eds.), *The Oxford History of South Africa* (Oxford, 1971), vol. 2, p. 268, S. B. Burman, *Chiefdom Politics and Alien Law: Basutoland under Cape Rule, 1871–1884* (London, 1981), pp. 11, 141–70, 176–83; S. Burman, 'Masopha *c.* 1820–99', in Saunders (ed.), *Black Leaders*, pp. 104–11; A. Atmore, 'The Moorosi Rebellion: Lesotho, 1879', in R. I. Rotberg and A. A. Mazrui (eds.), *Protest and Power in Black Africa* (New York, 1970), pp. 3, 7–8, 20–35.

23. J. Kimble, 'Labour migration in Basutoland *c.* 1870–1885', in Marks and Rathbone (eds.), *Industrialisation and Social Change*, pp. 120, 128, 130–6; Thompson, *Survival in Two Worlds*, pp. 190–5; Sanders, *Moshoeshoe*, pp. 280–1; M. Wilson, 'The growth of peasant communities', in Wilson and Thompson (eds.), *Oxford History of South Africa*, vol. 2, p. 69; R. Leys, 'Lesotho: non-development or underdevelopment. Towards an analysis of the political economy of the labour reserve', in T. M. Shaw and K. A. Heard (eds.), *The Politics of Africa: Dependence and Development* (London, 1979), p. 120; Lye and Murray, *Transformations*, p. 73.

24. A. Sillery, *Botswana: A Short Political History* (London, 1974), pp. 32–6; Parsons, *New History*, pp. 129–33; L. W. Truschel, 'Accommodation under imperial rule: the Tswana of the Bechuanaland Protectorate, 1895–1910' (unpublished Ph. D. thesis, Northwestern University, 1970) pp. 140–1, 186; S. M. Molema, *Montshiwa* (Cape Town, 1966), pp. 30–2. Other Tswana chiefdoms at the time were the Lete and

the Tlokwa (who both paid allegiance to Sechele), and the Kgatla.

25. I. Schapera, *Tribal Innovators: Tswana Chiefs and Social Change 1795–1940* (London, 1970), pp. 119–30; Lye and Murray, *Transformations*, pp. 65–8; Truschel, 'Accommodation', pp. 43, 143–4; Molema, *Montshiwa*, p. 204; A. J. Dachs, 'Missionary imperialism — the case of Bechuanaland', *Journal of African History*, 12, 4 (1972), 650–2; N. Parsons, 'The economic history of Khama's country in Botswana, 1844–1930', in R. Palmer and N. Parsons (eds.), *The Roots of Rural Poverty in Central and Southern Africa* (London, 1977), pp. 118–20; T. Tlou, 'Khama III — great reformer and innovator', *Botswana Notes and Records*, 2 (1969–70), 102–3; J. M. Chirenje, *A History of Northern Botswana 1850–1910* (Madison, 1977), pp. 109–10.

26. Lye and Murray, *Transformations*, pp. 60–1, 72; Parsons, *New History*, pp. 129–30, 162–4; Sillery, *Botswana*, pp. 43–79; L. W. Truschel, 'Nation-building and the Kgatla; the role of the Anglo–Boer War', *Botswana Notes and Records*, 4 (1972), 185; Molema, *Montshiwa*, pp. 77–86; P. Kallaway, 'Tribesman, trader, peasant and proletarian', in P. Bonner (ed.), *Working Papers in Southern African Studies* (Johannesburg, 1981), vol. 2, pp. 20–1; K. Shillington, 'The impact of the diamond discoveries on the Kimberley hinterland: class formation, colonialism and resistance among the Tlhaping of Griqualand West in the 1870s', in Marks and Rathbone (eds.), *Industrialisation and Social Change*, pp. 110–12; P. Maylam, *Rhodes, the Tswana and the British* (Westport, 1980), pp. 17–19.

27. Parsons, *New History*, p. 164; Schapera, *Tribal Innovators*, pp. 51–5; Truschel, 'Accommodation', pp. 31–46, 190–4; Maylam, *Rhodes, the Tswana and the British*, pp. 161–70, 187–9; Sillery, *Botswana*, pp. 106–13; H. Saker and J. Aldridge, 'The origins of the Langeberg Rebellion', *Journal of African History*, 12, 2 (1971), 299–317.

28. Shillington, 'Kimberley hinterland', pp. 100–7; Maylam, *Rhodes, the Tswana and the British*, pp. 212–17; C. van Onselen, 'Reactions to rinderpest in southern Africa 1896–97', *Journal of African History*, 13, 4 (1972), 474–8; Truschel, 'Accommodation', p. 158; Chirenje, *Northern Botswana*, p. 252.

29. Delius, *The Land Belongs to Us*, pp. 26–8, 30–40, 53–9, 62–76, 83–4, 87–95, 97–101, 108–22, 133–4, 150–1, 158–78, 184–6.

30. *Ibid.*, pp. 181–202, 205–12, 224–46, 251–2; K. W. Smith, 'The fall of the Bapedi of the north-eastern Transvaal', *Journal of African History*, 10, 2 (1969), 246–52; Thompson, 'Subjection of the African chiefdoms', pp. 282–3.

31. Thompson, 'High Veld', pp. 424, 440–1; Thompson, 'Subjection of the African chiefdoms', pp. 281–3; Parsons, *New History*, pp. 122–3, 174; H. A. Stayt, *The Bavenda* (London, 1931), p. 19.

Part Three: The twentieth century: proletarianisation, partition and protest

1. P. Warwick, *Black People and the South African War 1899–1902* (Johannesburg, 1983), pp. 4, 21–3, 26, 33–8, 43–6, 75–87, 116–17, 129–31, 145–52; T. Pakenham, *The Boer War* (London, 1979), pp. 406–8; W. R. Nasson, 'Moving Lord Kitchener: black military transport and supply work in the South African War, 1899–1902, with particular reference to the Cape Colony', *Journal of Southern African Studies*, 11, 1 (1984), 25–51.

2. Warwick, *Black People*, pp. 47, 96–8, 137–8, 176; C. M. Tatz, *Shadow and Substance in South Africa* (Pietermaritzburg, 1962), pp. 6–11.

3. T. Keegan, 'The restructuring of agrarian class relations in a colonial economy: the Orange River Colony 1902–1910', *Journal of Southern African Studies*, 5, 2 (1979), 238, 242–5, 251–3; T. Keegan, 'The sharecropping economy, African class formation and the 1913 Natives' Land Act in the highveld maize belt', in Marks and Rathbone

(eds.), *Industrialisation and Social Change*, pp. 195–201; Bundy, *Peasantry*, pp. 209–12, 215.

4. Bundy, *Peasantry*, pp. 185–91; Slater, 'Economic relationships in rural Natal', pp. 163–4; S. Marks, *Reluctant Rebellion* (Oxford, 1970), pp. 127–30, 140–1, 180, 189–90, 198–213, 223–40, 251–303.

5. Bundy, *Peasantry*, pp. 122–7; Southall, *Transkei*, pp. 73–5; Beinart, *Pondoland*, pp. 48–51, 70–5.

6. Keegan, 'Sharecropping economy', pp. 203–5; Bundy, *Peasantry*, pp. 213, 230–3; Southall, *Transkei*, p. 85; M. L. Morris, 'The development of capitalism in South African agriculture: class struggle in the countryside', *Economy and Society*, 5 (1976), 293–5; see also P. L. Wickins, 'The Natives' Land Act of 1913: a cautionary essay on simple explanations of complex change', *South African Journal of Economics*, 49, 2 (1981), 105–29; F. Wilson, 'Farming, 1866–1966', in Wilson and Thompson (eds.), *Oxford History of South Africa*, vol. 2, pp. 136–9.

7. Bundy, *Peasantry*, p. 221. This picture has recently been modified by Simkins, who argues that although the reserves provided a fragile subsistence base by the second decade of the twentieth century, the rapid decline of the reserve economies only really began in the 1950s. C. Simkins, 'Agricultural production in the African reserves of South Africa, 1918–1969', *Journal of Southern African Studies*, 7, 2 (1981), 262, 264, 270.

8. E. Hellmann (ed.), *Handbook on Race Relations in South Africa* (London, 1949), pp. 172–4, 184; H. Wolpe, 'Capitalism and cheap labour-power in South Africa: from segregation to apartheid', *Economy and Society*, 1 (1972), 440.

9. S. T. van der Horst, *Native Labour in South Africa* (Cape Town, 1942), pp. 136, 216–17; A. H. Jeeves, 'Over-reach: the South African gold mines and the struggle for the labour of Zambesia, 1890–1920', *Canadian Journal of African Studies*, 17, 3 (1983), 393–410; Bundy, *Peasantry*, p. 225; Southall, *Transkei*, pp. 80–1; Beinart, *Pondoland*, p. 100; Simkins, 'Agricultural production', p. 270.

10. F. A. Johnstone, *Class, Race and Gold* (London, 1976), pp. 17–20, 36–7, 70, 185–8; N. Levy, *The Foundations of the South African Cheap Labour System* (London, 1982), pp. 143–6, 153–7; Van der Horst, *Native Labour*, pp. 164–7, 179–80, 186–7, 205–10; F. Wilson, *Labour in the South African Gold Mines 1911–1969* (Cambridge, 1972), pp. 11, 57, 64–6; S. Moroney, 'The development of the compound as a mechanism of worker control 1900–1912', *South African Labour Bulletin*, 4, 3 (1978), 30–42.

11. S. Moroney, 'Mine worker protest on the Witwatersrand, 1901–1912', in E. Webster (ed.), *Essays in Southern African Labour History* (Johannesburg, 1978), pp. 35–44; Johnstone, *Class, Race and Gold*, pp. 167–84; L. Callinicos, *Gold and Workers* (Johannesburg, 1980), pp. 90–6; P. L. Bonner, 'The 1920 black mineworkers' strike: a preliminary account', in B. Bozzoli (ed.), *Labour, Townships and Protest* (Johannesburg, 1979), pp. 273–89.

12. T. R. H. Davenport, 'African townsmen? South African Natives (Urban Areas) legislation through the years', *African Affairs*, 68, 271 (1969), 107; H. A. Shannon, 'Urbanization, 1904–1936', *South African Journal of Economics*, 5 (1937), 176–8; C. de Coning, 'Some economic aspects of urban problems', in H. L. Watts (ed.), *Focus on Cities* (Durban, 1970), p. 126; G. Maasdorp and A. S. B. Humphreys (eds.), *From Shantytown to Township* (Cape Town, 1975), p. 10; A. Proctor, 'Class struggle, segregation and the city: a history of Sophiatown, 1905–1940', in Bozzoli, *Labour, Townships and Protest*, pp. 53–4.

13. Proctor, 'Sophiatown', pp. 52–9; N. Kagan, 'African settlements in the Johannesburg area, 1903–1923' (unpublished M. A. thesis, University of the Witwatersrand, 1978), pp. 32–41, 55–65, 177–9; E. Koch, "Without visible means of subsis-

tence": slumyard culture in Johannesburg, 1918–1940', in B. Bozzoli (ed.), *Town and Countryside in the Transvaal* (Johannesburg, 1983); C. Saunders, 'Segregation in Cape Town: the creation of Ndabeni', in *Africa Seminar: Collected Papers* (University of Cape Town), 1 (1978), 48; C. Saunders, 'From Ndabeni to Langa, 1919–35', *Studies in the History of Cape Town*, 1 (1979); M. W. Swanson, 'The "Durban System" : roots of urban apartheid in colonial Natal', *African Studies*, 35 (1976), 172; P. Maylam, 'Aspects of African urbanization in the Durban area before 1940' (unpublished workshop paper, 1980).

14. C. van Onselen, *Studies in the Social and Economic History of the Witwatersrand 1886–1914: New Nineveh* (Johannesburg, 1982), vol. 2, pp. 54–60, 74–102, 171–95; Koch, 'Slumyard culture', pp. 12–15; E. Hellmann, *Rooiyard* (Cape Town, 1948), pp. 39–49; P. la Hausse, 'The struggle for the city: alcohol, the ematsheni and popular culture in Durban 1902–1936' (unpublished workshop paper, 1984), pp. 11–13.

15. Davenport, 'African townsmen?', pp. 96–101; Saunders, 'From Ndabeni to Langa', pp. 14–16; Proctor, 'Sophiatown', pp. 59–68; Swanson, 'Durban system', pp. 159–75.

16. S. Marks and R. Rathbone, 'Introduction', in Marks and Rathbone (eds.), *Industrialisation and Social Change*, p. 2; P. Bonner, 'The Transvaal Native Congress, 1917–1920: the radicalisation of the black petty bourgeoisie on the Rand', in *ibid.*, pp. 271–2, 276–9, 286; P. Maylam, 'Twentieth century Durban: thoughts on its regional specificity, and some reflections on a recent workshop' (unpublished workshop paper, 1984), p. 8.

17. A. Odendaal, *Vukani Bantu! The Beginnings of Black Protest Politics in South Africa to 1912* (Cape Town, 1984), pp. 40–4, 50–62, 97–105, 168–80, 197–207, 216–27, 246–51, 285; P. Walshe, *The Rise of African Nationalism in South Africa* (Los Angeles, 1970), pp. 7–9, 12–17.

18. Walshe, *African Nationalism*, pp. 31–9, 80, 109–26, 165–7, 252–4; Odendaal, *Vukani Bantu!*, pp. 258–9, 270–80; T. Karis and G. M. Carter (eds.), *From Protest to Challenge* (Stanford, 1972), vol. 1, pp. 61–8, 147–54; E. Roux, *Time Longer than Rope* (Wisconsin, 1964), pp. 111–21, 232–40; M. Benson, *The Struggle for a Birthright* (Harmondsworth, 1966), pp. 55–7; Bonner, 'Transvaal Native Congress', pp. 291–306; T. Lodge, 'Organised black political resistance, 1912–1950', *Reality* (March 1981), 17–19; P. Rich, 'African politics and the Cape African franchise, 1926–1936', in *The Societies of Southern Africa in the 19th and 20th Centuries*, vol. 9, 1977–8, p. 129.

19. P. L. Wickins, *The Industrial and Commercial Workers' Union of Africa* (Cape Town, 1978), pp. 23–8, 61–7, 77–80, 106–9, 113–17, 157–63, 176–82, 202–9; S. W. Johns III, 'Trade union, political pressure group, or mass movement? The Industrial and Commercial Workers' Union of Africa', in R. I. Rotberg and A. M. Mazrui (eds.), *Protest and Power in Black Africa* (New York, 1970), pp. 700–7, 719–31, 738–54; Roux, *Time Longer than Rope*, pp. 161–7, 176–7; P. Bonner, 'The decline and fall of the I.C.U. — a case of self destruction?', in Webster (ed.), *Essays*, pp. 115–19; H. Bradford, ' "A taste of freedom": capitalist development and response to the ICU in the Transvaal countryside', in Bozzoli (ed.), *Town and Countryside*, pp. 135–47; W. Beinart and C. Bundy, 'The union, the nation, and the talking crow: the language and tactics of the Independent ICU in East London', in *The Societies of Southern Africa in the 19th and 20th Centuries*, vol. 12, 1980–1, pp. 69–75; H. Bradford, 'Mass movements and the petty bourgeoisie: the social origins of ICU leadership, 1924–1929', *Journal of African History*, 25, 3 (1984), 295–310; H. Bradford, 'Lynch law and labourers; the ICU in Umvoti, 1927–1928', *Journal of Southern African Studies*, 11, 1 (1984), 128–49.

20. Wickins, *Industrial and Commercial Workers' Union*, pp. 29–34, 46–7, 145; Roux,

Time Longer than Rope, pp. 156–7, 173; D. Hemson, 'Class consciousness and migrant workers: dock workers of Durban' (unpublished Ph. D. thesis, University of Warwick, 1979), pp. 169–86, 205–23, 255–63; P. la Hausse, 'Drinking in a cage: the Durban system and the 1929 riots', *Africa Perspective*, 20 (1982), 63–74; Johns, 'Trade union or mass movement?', pp. 745–6; J. Lewis, 'The new unionism: industrialisation and industrial unions in S. A., 1925–1930', in Webster (ed.), *Essays*, pp. 133–6; F. A. Johnstone, 'The I. W. A. on the Rand: socialist organising among black workers on the Rand, 1917–1918', in Bozzoli (ed.), *Labour, Townships and Protest*, pp. 248, 263–4; R. Cohen, 'Albert Nzula: the road from Rouxville to Russia', in Bozzoli (ed.), *Labour, Townships and Protest*, pp. 331–2.

21. Odendaal, *Vukani Bantu!*, pp. 23–9; Karis and Carter, *From Protest to Challenge*, vol. 1, pp. 7–8; D. P. Collins, 'The origins and formation of the Zulu Congregational Church, 1896–1908' (unpublished M. A. thesis, University of Natal, Durban, 1978), pp. 5–22, 60–95; Q. N. Parsons, 'Independency and Ethiopianism among the Tswana in the late 19th and early 20th centuries', *The Societies of Southern Africa in the 19th and 20th Centuries*, vol. 1, 1969–70, pp. 56–65; R. Edgar, 'Garveyism in Africa: Dr Wellington and the "American Movement" in the Transkei, 1925–40', in *ibid.*, vol. 6, 1974–5, pp. 100–9; Roux, *Time Longer than Rope*, pp. 135–41.

22. Roux, *Time Longer than Rope*, pp. 156–7, 192–3, 203, 213–14, 228–9; M. Lacey, *Working for Boroko* (Johannesburg, 1981), pp. 85, 92–111, 118–19; H. Rogers, *Native Administration in the Union of South Africa* (Johannesburg, 1932), pp. 31–2, 79–84; Hellmann, *Handbook*, pp. 35–6; Hammond-Tooke, *Command or Consensus*, pp. 90–7; Southall, *Transkei*, pp. 88–92; Beinart, *Pondoland*, pp. 108–22; S. Marks, 'Natal, the Zulu royal family and the ideology of segregation', *Journal of Southern African Studies*, 4, 2 (1978), 172–94.

23. Southall, *Transkei*, pp. 36–8, 45, 52–6, 94–8, 114–35; Karis and Carter, *From Protest to Challenge*, vol. 2, pp. 92–7; G. M. Carter, T. Karis, and N. M. Stultz, *South Africa's Transkei* (Evanston, 1967), pp. 120–4, 161–3; J. Butler, R. I. Rotberg, and J. Adams, *The Black Homelands of South Africa* (California, 1977), pp. 27–30, 35–40, 50–6; M. Horrell, *The African Homelands of South Africa* (Johannesburg, 1973), pp. 40–63.

24. Southall, *Transkei*, pp. 20–1, 35–9, 77–81, 172–82, 195–8, 208–9, 219–20; Carter *et al.*, *Transkei*, p. 177; Simkins, 'Agricultural production', p. 270; F. Molteno, 'The historical significance of the Bantustan strategy', *Social Dynamics*, 3, 2 (1977), 22–5; M. Lipton, 'Independent Bantustans?', *International Affairs*, 48, 1 (1972), 1–2; D. Innes and D. O'Meara, 'Class formation and ideology: the Transkei region', *Review of African Political Economy*, 7 (1976), 71.

25. Hellmann, *Handbook*, p. 193; Bundy, *Peasantry*, pp. 234–5; S. B. Greenberg, *Race and State in Capitalist Development* (Johannesburg, 1980), p. 96; G. Maré, *African Population Relocation in South Africa* (Johannesburg, 1980), pp. 1–11; Bundy, *Peasantry*, pp. 235–6; C. Desmond, *The Discarded People* (London, 1971), pp. 1–12, 37; A. Baldwin, 'Mass removals and separate development', *Journal of Southern African Studies*, 1, 2 (1975), 216; Surplus People Project, *Forced Removals in South Africa: General Overview* (Cape Town, 1983), vol. 1, pp. 1–30.

26. P. Maylam, 'Strategies of control and evasion: African urban history in South Africa *c.* 1900–1950' (unpublished conference paper, 1981), pp. 2–3; R. Bloch and P. Wilkinson, 'Urban control and popular struggle: a survey of state urban policy 1920–1970', *Africa Perspective*, 20 (1982), 6–10; M. Morris, 'State intervention and the agricultural labour supply post–1948', in F. Wilson *et al.*, (eds.), *Farm Labour in South Africa* (Cape Town, 1977), p. 63.

27. A. W. Stadler, 'Birds in the cornfield: squatter movements in Johannesburg,

1944–1947', *Journal of Southern African Studies*, 6, 1 (1979), 93–123; T. Lodge, 'The destruction of Sophiatown', in Bozzoli (ed.), *Town and Countryside*, pp. 340–5; P. Maylam, 'The "black belt": African squatters in Durban 1935–1950', *Canadian Journal of African Studies*, 17 (1983), 413–25; M. Wilson and A. Mafeje, *Langa* (Cape Town, 1963), pp. 4–5; Bloch and Wilkinson, 'Urban control', p. 30; J. Kane-Berman, *Soweto: Black Revolt, White Reaction* (Johannesburg, 1978), pp. 60, 79–80; Baldwin, 'Mass removals', pp. 223–4; A. Manson, 'From Cato Manor to KwaMashu', *Reality* (March 1981), 11–12.

28. Walshe, *African Nationalism*, pp. 117–23, 128, 249, 254; Karis and Carter, *From Protest to Challenge*, vol. 2, pp. 6–8, 81–6, 109–10; T. Lodge, *Black Politics in South Africa since 1945* (Johannesburg, 1983), pp. 9–10, 86–7.

29. Roux, *Time Longer than Rope*, pp. 326–7, 331, 336–42; Lodge, *Black Politics*, pp. 18–20; E. Feit, *Workers Without Weapons* (Hamden, 1975), pp. 28, 38–9; K. Luckhardt and B. Wall, *Organize or Starve! The History of the South African Congress of Trade Unions* (London, 1980), pp. 51, 59–62; P. Bonner, 'Black trade unions in South Africa since World War II', in R. M. Price and C. G. Rosberg (eds.), *The Apartheid Regime* (Cape Town, 1980), pp. 175, 178; M. Stein, 'Black trade unionism during the Second World War — the Witwatersrand strikes of December 1942', in *The Societies of Southern Africa in the 19th and 20th Centuries*, vol. 10, 1981, pp. 95–6; D. O'Meara, 'The 1946 African mineworkers' strike', *Journal of Commonwealth and Comparative Politics*, 13, 2 (1975), 146–73.

30. Lodge, *Black Politics*, pp. 20–9; Karis and Carter, *From Protest to Challenge*, vol. 2, pp. 84–92, 98–101, 106–8; Walshe, *African Nationalism*, pp. 312–14, 361–9, 389–92; G. Gerhart, *Black Power in South Africa* (Berkeley, 1978), pp. 45–84.

31. Lodge, *Black Politics*, pp. 26–7, 33–6, 41–62; Karis and Carter, *From Protest to Challenge*, vol. 2, pp. 104–5, 405–21, 426–7; Walshe, *African Nationalism*, pp. 290–3, 399–401; A. Luthuli, *Let My People Go* (London, 1963), p. 104.

32. Lodge, *Black Politics*, pp. 13–14, 61–2, 103–10, 114–17, 123–8, 141–6, 158; Karis and Carter, *From Protest to Challenge*, vol. 3, pp. 29–35, 275–7, 292; Roux, *Time Longer than Rope*, pp. 394–8; Benson, *Birthright*, pp. 179–86, 193, 215–16.

33. Lodge, *Black Politics*, pp. 69–77, 80–6; Karis and Carter, *From Protest to Challenge*, vol. 3, pp. 16–18, 56–65, 307–20; Roux, *Time Longer than Rope*, pp. 404–5.

34. Luckhardt and Wall, *Organize or Starve!*, pp. 92, 97, 99, 104–10, 172–216; Lodge, *Black Politics*, pp. 191–7; Feit, *Workers Without Weapons*, pp. 31–3, 71, 81–110; Bonner, 'Black trade unions', pp. 180–6.

35. Lodge, *Black Politics*, pp. 201–10, 216–24; Karis and Carter, *From Protest to Challenge*, vol. 3, pp. 325–39.

36. Lodge, *Black Politics*, pp. 231–55.

37. *Ibid.*, pp. 261–83; Southall, *Transkei*, pp. 108–14; B. Hirson, 'Rural revolt in South Africa: 1937–1951', in *The Societies of Southern Africa in the 19th and 20th Centuries*, vol. 8, 1976–7, pp. 115–28.

38. B. Hirson, *Year of Fire, Year of Ash* (London, 1979), pp. 122–43; Lodge, *Black Politics*, pp. 321–2, 326–8; Institute for Industrial Education, *The Durban Strikes 1973* (Durban and Johannesburg, 1974); D. Hemson, 'Trade unionism and the struggle for liberation in South Africa', in M. J. Murray (ed.), *South African Capitalism and Black Political Opposition* (Cambridge, Mass., 1982), pp. 709–17.

39. Hirson, *Year of Fire*, pp. 68–73, 82–6; Lodge, *Black Politics*, pp. 322–4; J. Kane–Berman, *Soweto*, pp. 103–4.

40. Hirson, *Year of Fire*, pp. 175–90, 202–3, 210–12, 227–9, 244–6, 255–8, 264–7, 282–3, 288–94; Kane–Berman, *Soweto*, pp. 1–28, 48; Lodge, *Black Politics*, pp. 328–34.

41. J. Halpern, *South Africa's Hostages* (Harmondsworth, 1965), pp. 51–5; J. E. Spence, 'British policy towards the High Commission Territories', *Journal of Modern African Studies*, 2, 2 (1964), 235–44.

42. F. J. Mashasha, 'The Swazi and land partition (1902–1910)', in *The Societies of Southern Africa in the 19th and 20th Centuries*, vol. 4, 1972–3, pp. 87–8; J. S. M. Matsebula, *A History of Swaziland* (Cape Town, 1976), pp. 149–50, 165–6, 176–7; A. Vilakazi, 'Swaziland: from tradition to modernity', in G. M. Carter and P. O'Meara (eds.), *Southern Africa: The Continuing Crisis* (Bloomington, 1979), pp. 270–1; M. Fransman, 'The state and development in Swaziland' (unpublished D. Phil. thesis, University of Sussex, 1979), pp. 78, 100–2; J. Crush, 'Struggle for Swazi labour', pp. 454–60.

43. Fransman, 'The state and development in Swaziland', pp. 57–63, 76–7, 156; J. S. Crush, 'The genesis of colonial land policy in Swaziland', *South African Geographical Journal*, 62, 1 (1980), 73–86; C. P. Youe, 'Imperial land policy in Swaziland and the African response', *Journal of Imperial and Commonwealth History*, 7, 1 (1978), 59–65; Mashasha, 'Land partition', pp. 88–101; Matsebula, *Swaziland*, pp. 156–9; Halpern, *South Africa's Hostages*, pp. 334–8; Crush, 'Struggle for Swazi labour', pp. 313–17.

44. Crush, 'Struggle for Swazi labour', pp. 142–50, 227–53, 280, 286, 302–4, 365–72, 395–434; Fransman, 'The state and development in Swaziland', pp. 65–73, 109–10; A. Booth, 'The development of the Swazi labour market 1900–1968', *South African Labour Bulletin*, 7, 6 (1982), 39–45; F. de Vletter, 'Labour migration in Swaziland: recent trends and implications', *South African Labour Bulletin*, 7, 6 (1982), 118, 136–7; Halpern, *South Africa's Hostages*, pp. 335, 405–17.

45. Fransman, 'The state and development in Swaziland', pp. 145–54, 200–21, 239–48, 281–5; M. Fransman, 'Labour, capital and the state in Swaziland, 1962–1977', *South African Labour Bulletin*, 7, 6 (1982), 61–74; Halpern, *South Africa's Hostages*, pp. 341–56, 365–82.

46. Fransman, 'The state and development in Swaziland', pp. 89–92, 288–92, 313–17, 349–50; Fransman, 'Labour, capital and the state', pp. 76–85; J. Daniel, 'The political economy of colonial and post–colonial Swaziland', *South African Labour Bulletin*, 7, 6 (1982), 90–1, 99–110; Vilakazi, 'Swaziland', pp. 274, 287; H. Kuper, *Sobhuza II* (London, 1978), p. 319; J. S. Crush, 'The parameters of dependence in southern Africa: a case study of Swaziland', *Journal of Southern African Affairs*, 4, 1 (1979), 55–62.

47. Halpern, *South Africa's Hostages*, p. 135; C. Murray, *Families Divided* (Cambridge, 1981), pp. 176–7.

48. Halpern, *South Africa's Hostages*, pp. 117–30; J. E. Spence, *Lesotho: The Politics of Dependence* (London, 1968), pp. 15–21, 30–4; R. Leys, 'Some observations on class differentiation and class conflict within the labour reserve of Basutoland', in *The Societies of Southern Africa in the 19th and 20th Centuries*, vol. 11, 1979–80, pp. 90–1; Murray, *Families Divided*, pp. 66–7.

49. Leys, 'Observations', pp. 92–4; Halpern, *South Africa's Hostages*, pp. 139–71, 248–50, 255–60; Spence, *Lesotho*, pp. 34–6, 41–8.

50. R. Weisfelder, 'Lesotho: changing patterns of dependence', in Carter and O'Meara, *Continuing Crisis*, pp. 250–5, 261–3; Leys, 'Observations', pp. 115–16; Spence, *Lesotho*, pp. 52–4; Murray, *Families Divided*, pp. 5–6.

51. Murray, *Families Divided*, pp. 13–35, 65, 75–7, 171; C. Murray, 'The effects of migrant labour: a review of the evidence from Lesotho', *South African Labour Bulletin*, 6, 4 (1980), 37; R. Leys, 'Lesotho: non–development or underdevelopment. Towards an analysis of the political economy of the labour reserve', in T. M. Shaw and

K. A. Heard (eds.), *The Politics of Africa: Dependence and Development* (London, 1979), pp. 105–14; Weisfelder, 'Lesotho', pp. 256–8; Halpern, *South Africa's Hostages*, pp. 178, 209, 216, 474–5; Leys, 'Observations', pp. 89–92.

52. Schapera, *Tribal Innovators*, pp. 52–64, 77–8; Sillery, *Botswana*, pp. 127–34, 146–51; Halpern, *South Africa's Hostages*, pp. 273–83.

53. Sillery, *Botswana*, pp. 155–8, 182–6; Halpern, *South Africa's Hostages*, pp. 284–96; J. H. Proctor 'The house of chiefs and the political development of Botswana', *Journal of Modern African Studies*, 6, 1 (1968), 60–5; C. Colclough and S. McCarthy, *The Political Economy of Botswana* (Oxford, 1980), pp. 34–46; J. A. Wiseman, 'Multi–partyism in Africa: the case of Botswana', *African Affairs*, 76 (1977), 70–9; C. Stevens and J. Speed, 'Multi–partyism in Africa: the case of Botswana revisited', *ibid.*, pp. 381–6.

54. Colclough and McCarthy, *Political Economy of Botswana*, pp. 14–22, 27–33, 120, 139–40, 169–71; Sillery, *Botswana*, pp. 138–43, 151–2; Halpern, *South Africa's Hostages*, pp. 297–314; D. Massey, 'The changing political economy of migrant labour in Botswana', *South African Labour Bulletin*, 5, 5 (1980), 2, 4, 9–10; J. Parson, 'The working class, the state and social change in Botswana', *ibid.*, p. 45.

55. Colclough and McCarthy, *Political Economy of Botswana*, pp. 54–5, 74–81, 140, 146–9, 176–7, 212, 225; Parson, 'Working class', p. 46; H. E. Dahl, 'Economic and social development in Botswana 1966–78', in C. Harvey (ed.), *Papers on the Economy of Botswana* (London, 1981), pp. 6–10; M. Hubbard, 'Botswana's beef export industry: the issue of the proposed northern abattoir', in *ibid.*, p. 44; B. Gaolathe, 'Mining development: environment, social costs, retained value and shadow wage rates', in *ibid.*, pp. 95–6; M. Stevens, 'Aid management in Botswana: from one to many donors', in *ibid.*, pp. 159–76.

56. Colclough and McCarthy, *Political Economy of Botswana*, pp. 22, 69–70, 74, 171–2, 191; Massey, 'Changing political economy', pp. 16, 19–20; Parson, 'Working class', p. 47; E. O. Ochieng, 'Botswana's trade structure compared with those of other small countries', in Harvey (ed.), *Papers*, p. 129.

Conclusion

1. Peires, 'Introduction', in Peires (ed.), *Before and After Shaka*, p. 20.
2. Crush, 'Struggle for Swazi labour', p. 43.
3. Murray, *Families Divided*, p. 174.
4. Van Onselen, *New Nineveh*, p. 74.
5. Can Themba, *The Will to Die* (Cape Town, 1982), pp. 70–1.

BIBLIOGRAPHY

Books

Argyle, J. and E. Preston-Whyte (eds.), *Social System and Tradition in Southern Africa* (Cape Town, 1978)

Beach, D. N., *The Shona and Zimbabwe 900–1850* (London, 1980)

Beinart, W., *The Political Economy of Pondoland 1860–1930* (Cambridge, 1982)

Benson, M., *The Struggle for a Birthright* (Harmondsworth, 1966)

Benyon, J. A., C. W. Cook, T. R. H. Davenport, and K. S. Hunt (eds.), *Studies in Local History* (Cape Town, 1976)

Bonner, P. (ed.), *Working Papers in Southern African Studies* vol. 2 (Johannesburg, 1981)

Bonner, P., *Kings, Commoners and Concessionaires* (Cambridge, 1983)

Bozzoli, B. (ed.), *Labour, Townships and Protest* (Johannesburg, 1979)

Bozzoli, B. (ed.), *Town and Countryside in the Transvaal* (Johannesburg, 1983)

Brookes, E. H. and C. de B. Webb, *A History of Natal* (Pietermaritzburg, 1965)

Bryant, A. T., *The Zulu People* (Pietermaritzburg, 1967)

Bundy, C., *The Rise and Fall of the South African Peasantry* (London, 1979)

Burman, S. B., *Chiefdom Politics and Alien Law: Basutoland under Cape Rule, 1871–1884* (London, 1981)

Butler, J., R. I. Rotberg, and J. Adams, *The Black Homelands of South Africa* (California, 1977)

Callinicos, L., *Gold and Workers* (Johannesburg, 1980)

Carter, G. M., T. Karis, and N. M. Stultz, *South Africa's Transkei* (Evanston, 1967)

Carter, G. M. and P. O'Meara (eds.), *Southern Africa: The Continuing Crisis* (Bloomington, 1979)

Chirenje, J. M., *A History of Northern Botswana 1850–1910* (Madison, 1977)

Colclough, C. and S. McCarthy, *The Political Economy of Botswana* (Oxford, 1980)

Dalby, D. (ed.), *Language and History in Africa* (New York, 1970)

Davenport, T. R. H., *South Africa: A Modern History* (Johannesburg, 1977)

Davenport, T. R. H. and K. S. Hunt (eds.), *The Right to the Land* (Cape Town, 1974)

De Kiewiet, C. W., *A History of South Africa* (London, 1957)

Delius, P., *The Land Belongs to Us* (Johannesburg, 1983)

Derricourt, R. M., *Prehistoric Man in the Ciskei and Transkei* (Cape Town, 1977)

Desmond, C., *The Discarded People* (London, 1971)

Duminy, A. and C. C. Ballard (eds.), *The Anglo–Zulu War: New Perspectives* (Pietermaritzburg, 1981)

Elphick, R. and H. Giliomee (eds.), *The Shaping of South African Society 1652–1820* (Cape Town, 1979)

Etherington, N., *Preachers, Peasants and Politics in Southeast Africa 1835–1880*

(London, 1978)
Feit, E., *Workers Without Weapons* (Hamden, 1975)
Fortes, M., and E. E. Evans-Pritchard (eds.), *African Political Systems* (London, 1940)
Fouché, L. (ed.), *Mapungubwe: Ancient Bantu Civilization on the Limpopo* (Cambridge, 1937)
Fuze, M. M., *The Black People*, ed. A. T. Cope (Pietermaritzburg and Durban, 1979).
Galbraith, J. S., *Reluctant Empire* (California, 1963)
Gardner, G. A., *Mapungubwe* (Pretoria, 1963)
Gerhart, G., *Black Power in South Africa* (Berkeley, 1978)
Gray, R. (ed.), *The Cambridge History of Africa*, vol. 4 (Cambridge, 1975)
Greenberg, S. B., *Race and State in Capitalist Development* (Johannesburg, 1980)
Guest, W. R., *Langalibalele: The Crisis in Natal 1873–1875* (Durban, 1976)
Guy, J., *The Destruction of the Zulu Kingdom* (London, 1979)
Hall, M., *Settlement Patterns in the Iron Age of Zululand* (Cambridge, 1981)
Halpern, J., *South Africa's Hostages* (Harmondsworth, 1965)
Hammond-Tooke, W. D. (ed.), *The Bantu-speaking Peoples of Southern Africa* (London, 1974)
Hammond-Tooke, W. D., *Command or Consensus* (Cape Town, 1975)
Harvey, C. (ed.), *Papers on the Economy of Botswana* (London, 1981)
Hellmann, E. (ed.), *Handbook on Race Relations in South Africa* (London, 1949)
Herd, N., *The Bent Pine* (Johannesburg, 1966)
Hirson, B., *Year of Fire, Year of Ash* (London, 1979)
Horrell, M., *The African Homelands of South Africa* (Johannesburg, 1973)
Horrell, M., *Laws Affecting Race Relations in South Africa* (Johannesburg, 1978)
Inskeep, R. R., *The Peopling of Southern Africa* (Cape Town, 1978)
Institute for Industrial Education, *The Durban Strikes 1973* (Durban and Johannesburg, 1974)
Johnstone, F. A., *Class, Race and Gold* (London, 1976)
Kane-Berman, J., *Soweto: Black Revolt, White Reaction* (Johannesburg, 1978)
Karis, T. and G. M. Carter (eds.), *From Protest to Challenge*, 4 vols. (Stanford, 1972, 1973, 1977)
Keppel-Jones, A., *South Africa* (London, 1963)
Klein, M. M. and G. W. Johnson (eds.), *Perspectives on the African Past* (Boston, 1972)
Klein, R. G. (ed.), *Southern African Prehistory and Paleoenvironments* (Boston, 1984)
Krige, E. J., *The Social System of the Zulus* (Pietermaritzburg, 1974)
Kuper, H., *Sobhuza II* (London, 1978)
Lacey, M., *Working for Boroko* (Johannesburg, 1981)
Levy, N., *The Foundations of the South African Cheap Labour System* (London, 1982)
Lodge, T., *Black Politics in South Africa since 1945* (Johannesburg, 1983)
Luckhardt, K. and B. Wall, *Organize or Starve! The History of the South African Congress of Trade Unions* (London, 1980)
Luthuli, A., *Let My People Go* (London, 1963)
Lye, W. F. and C. Murray, *Transformations on the Highveld: The Tswana and Southern Sotho* (Cape Town, 1980)
Maasdorp, G. and A. S. B. Humphreys (eds.), *From Shantytown to Township* (Cape Town, 1975)
Maggs, T. M. O'C., *Iron Age Communities of the Southern Highveld* (Pietermaritz-

burg, 1976)
Maré, G., *African Population Relocation in South Africa* (Johannesburg, 1980)
Marks, S., *Reluctant Rebellion* (Oxford, 1970)
Marks, S. and A. Atmore (eds.), *Economy and Society in Pre- industrial South Africa* (London, 1980)
Marks, S. and R. Rathbone (eds.), *Industrialisation and Social Change in South Africa* (London, 1982)
Mason, R., *Prehistory of the Transvaal* (Johannesburg, 1969)
Matsebula, J. S. M., *A History of Swaziland* (Cape Town, 1976)
Maylam, P., *Rhodes, the Tswana and the British* (Westport, 1980)
Molema, S. M., *Montshiwa* (Cape Town, 1966)
Murray, C., *Families Divided* (Cambridge, 1981)
Murray, M. J. (ed.), *South African Capitalism and Black Political Opposition* (Cambridge, Mass., 1982)
Odendaal, A., *Vukani Bantu! The Beginnings of Black Protest Politics in South Africa to 1912* (Cape Town, 1984)
Oliver, R., (ed.), *The Cambridge History of Africa*, vol. 3 (Cambridge, 1977)
Omer-Cooper, J. D., *The Zulu Aftermath* (London, 1966)
Pakenham, T., *The Boer War* (London, 1979)
Palmer, R. and N. Parsons (eds.), *The Roots of Rural Poverty in Central and Southern Africa* (London, 1977)
Parsons, N., *A New History of Southern Africa* (London, 1982)
Peires, J. B., *The House of Phalo* (Johannesburg, 1981)
Peires, J. B. (ed.), *Before and After Shaka* (Grahamstown, 1981)
Phillipson, D. W., *The Later Prehistory of Eastern and Southern Africa* (London, 1977)
Price, R. M. and C. G. Rosberg (eds.), *The Apartheid Regime* (Cape Town, 1980)
Rasmussen, R. K., *Migrant Kingdom* (London, 1978)
Rogers, H., *Native Administration in the Union of South Africa* (Johannesburg, 1933)
Rotberg, R. I. and A. A. Mazrui (eds.), *Protest and Power in Black Africa* (New York, 1970)
Roux, E., *Time Longer than Rope* (Wisconsin, 1964)
Sanders, P., *Moshoeshoe, Chief of the Sotho* (London, 1975)
Saunders, C. and R. Derricourt (eds.), *Beyond the Cape Frontier* (London, 1974)
Saunders, C. C., *The Annexation of the Transkeian Territories* (Archives Year Book, Pretoria, 1976)
Saunders, C. (ed.), *Black Leaders in Southern African History* (London, 1979)
Schapera, I., *Tribal Innovators: Tswana Chiefs and Social Change 1795–1940* (London, 1970)
Shaw, T. M. and K. A. Heard (eds.), *The Politics of Africa: Dependence and Development* (London, 1979)
Sillery, A., *Botswana: A Short Political History* (London, 1974)
Soga, J. H., *The South–eastern Bantu* (Johannesburg, 1930)
Southall, R., *South Africa's Transkei* (London, 1982)
Spence, J. E., *Lesotho: The Politics of Dependence* (London, 1968)
Stayt, H. A., *The Bavenda* (London, 1931)
Stow, G. W., *The Native Races of South Africa* (London, 1905)
Surplus People Project, *Forced Removals in South Africa: General Overview*, vol. 1 (Cape Town, 1983)
Tatz, C. M., *Shadow and Substance in South Africa* (Pietermaritzburg, 1962)

Thompson, L. (ed.), *African Societies in Southern Africa* (London, 1969)
Thompson, L., *Survival in Two Worlds* (Oxford, 1975)
Van der Horst, S. T., *Native Labour in South Africa* (Cape Town, 1942)
Van Onselen, C., *Studies in the Social and Economic History of the Witwatersrand 1886–1914*, 2 vols. (Johannesburg, 1982)
Walker, E. A., *A History of Southern Africa* (London, 1965)
Walshe, P., *The Rise of African Nationalism in South Africa* (Los Angeles, 1970)
Walter, E. V., *Terror and Resistance* (New York, 1972)
Warwick, P., *Black People and the South African War 1899–1902* (Johannesburg, 1983)
Watts, H. L. (ed.), *Focus on Cities* (Durban, 1970)
Webb, C. de B. and J. B. Wright (eds.), *The James Stuart Archive*, 3 vols. (Pietermaritzburg, 1976, 1979, 1982)
Webb, C. de B. and J. B. Wright (eds.), *A Zulu King Speaks* (Pietermaritzburg, 1978)
Webster, E. (ed.), *Essays in Southern African Labour History* (Johannesburg, 1978)
Welsh, D., *The Roots of Segregation* (Cape Town, 1971)
Wickins, P. L., *The Industrial and Commercial Workers' Union of Africa* (CapeTown 1978)
Williams, D., *Umfundisi: A Biography of Tiyo Soga 1829–1871* (Lovedale, 1978)
Wilson, F., *Labour in the South African Gold Mines 1911–1969* (Cambridge, 1972)
Wilson, F., A. Kooy, and D. Hendrie (eds.), *Farm Labour in South Africa* (Cape Town, 1977)
Wilson, M. and A. Mafeje, *Langa* (Cape Town, 1963)
Wilson, M. and L. Thompson (eds.), *The Oxford History of South Africa*, 2 vols. (Oxford, 1969 and 1971)
Wolpe, H., (ed.), *The Articulation of Modes of Production* (London, 1980)
Wright, J. and A. Manson, *The Hlubi Chiefdom in Zululand–Natal* (Ladysmith, 1983)

Articles and papers

Baldwin, A., 'Mass removals and separate development', *Journal of Southern African Studies*, 1, 1975
Ballard, C., 'John Dunn and Cetshwayo: the material foundations of political power in the Zulu Kingdom, 1857–1878', *Journal of African History*, 21, 1980
Ballard, C. C., 'Natal 1824–44: the frontier interregnum', *Journal of Natal and Zulu History*, 5, 1982
Ballard, C., '"A year of scarcity". The 1896 locust plague in Natal and Zululand', *South African Historical Journal*, 15, 1983
Beinart, W. and C. Bundy, 'The Union, the nation, and the talking crow: the language and tactics of the Independent ICU in East London', *The Societies of Southern Africa in the 19th and 20th Centuries*, 12, 1980–1
Bloch, R. and P. Wilkinson, 'Urban control and popular struggle: a survey of state urban policy 1920–1970', *Africa Perspective*, 20, 1982
Bonner, P., 'Factions and fissions in Transvaal/Swazi politics in the mid-nineteenth century', *Journal of African History*, 19, 1978
Booth, A., 'The development of the Swazi labour market 1900–1968', *South African Labour Bulletin*, 7, 1982
Bradford, H., 'Mass movements and the petty bourgeoisie: the social origins of ICU leadership, 1924–1929', *Journal of African History*, 25, 3, 1984

Bradford, H., 'Lynch law and labourers: the ICU in Umvoti, 1927–1928', *Journal of Southern African Studies*, 11, 1, 1984

Cobbing, J., 'The case against the mfecane' (unpublished paper, 1984)

Crush, J. S., 'The parameters of dependence in southern Africa: a case study of Swaziland', *Journal of Southern African Affairs*, 4, 1979

Crush, J. S., 'The genesis of colonial land policy in Swaziland', *South African Geographical Journal*, 62, 1980

Dachs, A. J., 'Missionary imperialism — the case of Bechuanaland', *Journal of African History*, 12, 1972

Daniel, J. B. McI., 'A geographical study of pre–Shakan Zululand', *South African Geographical Journal*, 55, 1, 1973

Daniel, J., 'The political economy of colonial and post–colonial Swaziland', *South African Labour Bulletin*, 7, 1982

Davenport, T. R. H., 'African townsmen? South African Natives (Urban Areas) legislation through the years', *African Affairs*, 68, 1969

De Vletter, F., 'Labour migration in Swaziland: recent trends and implications', *South African Labour Bulletin*, 7, 1982

Edgar, R., 'Garveyism in Africa: Dr Wellington and the "American Movement" in the Transkei, 1925–40', *The Societies of Southern Africa in the 19th and 20th Centuries*, 6, 1974–5

Edgecombe, R., 'Sir Marshal Clarke and the abortive attempt to "Basutolandise" Zululand, 1893–97', *Journal of Natal and Zulu History*, 1, 1978

Etherington, N., 'Natal's first black capitalists', *Theoria*, 45, 1975

Etherington, N., 'Why Langalibalele ran away', *Journal of Natal and Zulu History* 1, 1978

Evers, T. M., 'Salt and soapstone bowl factories at Harmony, Letaba district, northeast Transvaal', *Goodwin Series*, 3

Evers, T. M. and R. P. van den Berg, 'Ancient mining in southern Africa, with reference to a copper mine in the Harmony Block, north–eastern Transvaal', *Journal of the South African Institute of Mining and Metallurgy*, 74, 1974

Evers, T. M., 'Iron Age trade in the eastern Transvaal, South Africa', *South African Archaeological Bulletin*, 29, 1974

Evers, T. M., 'Recent Iron Age research in the eastern Transvaal, South Africa', *South African Archaeological Bulletin*, 30, 1975

Evers, T. M., 'Recent progress in studies of the Early Iron Age in the eastern Transvaal, South Africa', *South African Journal of Science*, 73, March 1977

Feely, J. M., 'Smelting in the Iron Age of Transkei', *South African Journal of Science*, 81, January 1985

Fransman, M., 'Labour, capital and the state in Swaziland, 1962–1977', *South African Labour Bulletin*, 7, 1982

Gluckman, M., 'The individual in a social framework: the rise of King Shaka of Zululand', *Journal of African Studies*, 1, 1974

Hall, M. and J. C. Vogel, 'Enkwazini: fourth century Iron Age site on the Zululand Coast', *South African Journal of Science*, 74, February 1978

Hall, M. and J. C. Vogel, 'Some recent radiocarbon dates from southern Africa', *Journal of African History*, 21, 1980

Hall, M., 'Early farming communities of southern Africa: a population discovered', *South African Historical Journal*, 15, 1983

Hall, M. and A. Morris, 'Race and Iron Age human skeletal remains from southern Africa: an assessment', *Social Dynamics*, 9, 2, 1983

Hamilton, C. and J. Wright, 'The making of the Lala: ethnicity, ideology and class-formation in a precolonial context' (unpublished paper, University of the Witwatersrand History Workshop, 1984)

Hammond–Tooke, W. D., 'Segmentation and fission in Cape Nguni political units', *Africa*, 35, 1965

Hanisch, E. O. M., 'Copper working in the Messina district', *Journal of the South African Institute of Mining and Metallurgy*, 74, 1974

Hindson, S., 'Peasant and petty–bourgeois: persistent tendencies in the emergence of social forms — Edendale, Natal 1850–1900' (unpublished paper, 1980)

Hirson, B., 'Rural revolt in South Africa: 1937–1951', *The Societies of Southern Africa in the 19th and 20th Centuries*, 8, 1976–7

Innes, D. and D. O'Meara, 'Class formation and ideology: the Transkei region', *Review of African Political Economy*, 7, 1976

Inskeep, R. R. and T. M. O'C. Maggs, 'Unique art objects in the Iron Age of the Transvaal, South Africa', *South African Archaeological Bulletin*, 30, 1975

Jeeves, A. H., 'Over–reach: the South African gold mines and the struggle for the labour of Zambesia, 1890–1920', *Canadian Journal of African Studies*, 17, 1983

Keegan, T. 'The restructuring of agrarian class relations in a colonial economy: the Orange River Colony 1902–1910', *Journal of Southern African Studies*, 5, 1979

Keegan, T., 'White settlement and black subjugation on the South African highveld: the Tlokoa heartland in the north eastern Orange Free State, *ca*. 1850–1914' (unpublished History Workshop paper, University of the Witwatersrand, 1984)

Kennedy, P. A., 'Mpande and the Zulu kingship', *Journal of Natal and Zulu History*, 4, 1981

Kimble, J., 'Lesotho and the outside world, 1840–1870 — prelude to imperialism' (unpublished paper, 1977)

Kinsman, M., 'The impact of the *difaqane* on southern Tswana communities, with special reference to the Rolong' (unpublished paper, University of the Witwatersrand History Workshop, 1984)

Koopman, A., 'Dingiswayo rides again', *Journal of Natal and Zulu History*, 2, 1979

La Hausse, P., 'Drinking in a cage, the Durban system and the 1929 riots', *Africa Perspective*, 20, 1982

La Hausse, P., 'The struggle for the city: alcohol, the ematsheni and popular culture in Durban 1902–1936' (unpublished paper, 1984)

Law, R., 'In search of a Marxist perspective on pre–colonial Tropical Africa', *Journal of African History*, 19, 1978

Lenta, G., '"Reserved" land in South Africa: a century of declining productivity', *Perspectives in Economic History*, 2, 1983

Leys, R., 'Some observations on class differentiation and class conflict within the labour reserve of Basutoland', *The Societies of Southern Africa in the 19th and 20th Centuries*, 11, 1979–80

Lipton, M., 'Independent Bantustans?', *International Affairs*, 48, 1972

Lodge, T., 'Organized black political resistance, 1912–1950', *Reality*, March 1981

Lonsdale, J., 'States and social processes in Africa: a historiographical survey', *African Studies Review*, 24, 1981

Maggs, T. M. O'C. and M. A. Michael, 'Ntshekane: an Early Iron Age site in the Tugela Basin, Natal', *Annals of the Natal Museum*, 22, 1976

Maggs, T., 'The Iron Age sequence south of the Vaal and Pongola Rivers: some historical implications', *Journal of African History*, 21, 1980

Maggs, T., 'Msuluzi Confluence: a seventh century Early Iron Age site on the Tugela River', *A Collection of Archaeological Papers*, from *Annals of the Natal Museum*, 24, 1, 1980

Maggs, T., 'Mzonjani and the beginning of the Iron Age in Natal', *A Collection of Archaeological Papers*, from *Annals of the Natal Museum*, 24, 1, 1980

Manson, A., 'A people in transition: the Hlubi in Natal 1848–1877', *Journal of Natal and Zulu History*, 2, 1979

Manson, A., 'From Cato Manor to KwaMashu', *Reality*, March, 1981

Marks, S., 'Natal, the Zulu royal family and the ideology of segregation', *Journal of Southern African Studies*, 4, 1978

Marks, S., 'South Africa: "the myth of the empty land",' *History Today*, 30, January 1980

Mashasha, F. J., 'The Swazi and land partition (1902–1910)', *The Societies of Southern Africa in the 19th and 20th Centuries*, 4, 1972–3

Mason, R. J., 'Background to the Transvaal Iron Age — new discoveries at Olifantspoort and Broederstroom', *Journal of the South African Institute of Mining and Metallurgy*, 74, 1974

Mason, R. J., 'Iron Age research in the western Transvaal, South Africa, 1971–1972', *Current Anthropology*, 14, 1973

Mason, R. J., 'First Early Iron Age settlement in South Africa: Broederstroom 24/73, Brits district, Transvaal', *South African Journal of Science*, 69, November 1973

Massey, D., 'The changing political economy of migrant labour in Botswana', *South African Labour Bulletin*, 5, 1980

Maylam, P., 'Aspects of African urbanization in the Durban area before 1940' (unpublished paper, 1980)

Maylam, P., 'Strategies of control and evasion: African urban history in South Africa *c*. 1900–1950' (unpublished paper, 1981)

Maylam, P., 'The "black belt": African squatters in Durban 1935–1950', *Canadian Journal of African Studies*, 17, 1983

Maylam, P., 'Twentieth century Durban: thoughts on its regional specificity, and some reflections on a recent workshop' (unpublished paper, 1984)

Molteno, F., 'The historical significance of the Bantustan strategy', *Social Dynamics*, 3, 1977

Moroney, S., 'The development of the compound as a mechanism of worker control 1900–1912', *South African Labour Bulletin*, 4, 1978

Morris, M. L., 'The development of capitalism in South African agriculture: class struggle in the countryside', *Economy and Society*, 5, 1976

Murray, C., 'The effects of migrant labour: a review of the evidence from Lesotho', *South African Labour Bulletin*, 6, 1980

Nasson, W. R., '"Doing down their masters": Africans, boers, and treason in the Cape Colony during the South African War of 1899–1902', *Journal of Imperial and Commonwealth History*, 12, 1, 1983

Nasson, W. R., 'Moving Lord Kitchener: black military transport and supply work in the South African War, 1899–1902, with particular reference to the Cape Colony', *Journal of Southern African Studies*, 11, 1, 1984

Okihiro, G. Y., 'Precolonial economic change among the Tlhaping, *c*. 1795–1817', *International Journal of African Historical Studies*, 17, 1, 1984

Okoye, F. N. C., 'Dingane: a reappraisal', *Journal of African History*, 10, 1969

O'Meara, D., 'The 1946 African mineworkers' strike', *Journal of Commonwealth and Comparative Politics*, 13, 1975

Oxley, O. G. St. J. and H. White, 'Ancient mining practices in the Rooiberg area', *Journal of the South African Institute of Mining and Metallurgy*, 74, 1974

Parson, J., 'The working class, the state and social change in Botswana', *South African Labour Bulletin*, 5, 1980

Parsons, Q. N., 'Independency and Ethiopianism among the Tswana in the late 19th and early 20th centuries', *The Societies of Southern Africa in the 19th and 20th Centuries*, 1, 1969–70

Parsons, Q. N., 'On the origins of the bamaNgwato', *Botswana Notes and Records*, 5, 1973

Peires, J. B., 'Xhosa expansion before 1800', *The Societies of Southern Africa in the 19th and 20th Centuries*, 6, 1974–5

Prinsloo, H. P., 'Early Iron Age site at Klein Afrika near Wylliespoort, Soutpansberg mountains, South Africa', *South African Journal of Science*, 70, September 1974

Proctor, J. H., 'The House of Chiefs and political development of Botswana', *Journal of Modern African Studies*, 6, 1968

Ralushai, N. M. N., and J. R. Gray, 'Ruins and traditions of the Ngona and Mbedzi', *Rhodesian History*, 8, 1977

Rich, P., 'African politics and the Cape African franchise, 1926–1936', *The Societies of Southern Africa in the 19th and 20th Centuries*, 9, 1977–8

Rightmire, G. P. and N. J. van der Merwe, 'Two burials from Phalaborwa and the association of race and culture in the Iron Age of southern Africa', *South African Archaeological Bulletin*, 31, 1976

Robey, T., 'Mpambanyoni: a Late Iron Age site on the Natal south coast', *A Collection of Archaeological Papers*, from *Annals of the Natal Museum*, 24, 1, 1980

Roth, M., '"If you give us rights we will fight": black involvement in the Second World War', *South African Historical Journal*, 15, 1983

Saker, H. and J. Aldridge, 'The origins of the Langeberg Rebellion', *Journal of African History*, 12, 1971

Saunders, C. C., 'The new African elite in the eastern Cape and some late nineteenth century origins of African nationalism', *The Societies of Southern Africa in the 19th and 20th Centuries*, 1, 1969–70

Saunders, C. C., 'Tile and the Thembu Church: politics and independency on the Cape eastern frontier in the late nineteenth century', *Journal of African History*, 11, 1970

Saunders, C. C., 'The Transkeian Rebellion of 1880–81: a case-study of Transkeian resistance to white control', *South African Historical Journal*, 8, 1976

Saunders, C., 'Segregation in Cape Town: the creation of Ndabeni', *Africa Seminar: Collected Papers* (University of Cape Town), 1, 1978

Saunders, C., 'From Ndabeni to Langa, 1919–35', *Studies in the History of Cape Town*, 1, 1979

Schapera, I., 'A short history of the Bangwaketse', *African Studies*, 1, 1942

Schapera, I., 'Kinship and politics in Tswana history', *Journal of the Royal Anthropological Institute*, 93, 1963

Shannon, H. A., 'Urbanization, 1904–1936', *South African Journal of Economics*, 5, 1937

Simkins, C., 'Agricultural production in the African reserves of South Africa, 1918-1969', *Journal of Southern African Studies*, 7, 1981

Slater, H., 'Land, labour and capital in Natal: the Natal Land and Colonisation Company 1860–1948', *Journal of African History*, 16, 1975

Smith, K. W., 'The fall of the Bapedi of the north-eastern Transvaal', *Journal of African History*, 10, 1969

Spence, J. E., 'British policy towards the High Commission Territories', *Journal of Modern African Studies*, 2, 1964

Stadler, A. W., 'Birds in the cornfield: squatter movements in Johannesburg, 1944–1947', *Journal of Southern African Studies*, 6, 1979

Stayt, H. A., 'Notes on the Balemba', *Journal of the Royal Anthropological Institute*, 61, 1931

Stein, M., 'Black trade unionism during the Second World War — the Witwatersrand strikes of December 1942', *The Societies of Southern Africa in the 19th and 20th Centuries*, 10, 1981

Stevens, C. and J. Speed, 'Multi-partyism in Africa: the case of Botswana revisited', *African Affairs*, 76, 1977

Swanson, M. W., 'The "Durban System": roots of urban apartheid in colonial Natal', *African Studies*, 35, 1976

Tlou, T., 'Khama III — great reformer and innovator', *Botswana Notes and Records*, 2, 1969–70

Tlou, T., 'The nature of Batswana states: towards a theory of Batswana traditional government — the Batawana case', *Botswana Notes and Records*, 6, 1974

Trapido, S., 'African divisional politics in the Cape Colony, 1884–1910', *Journal of African History*, 9, 1968

Truschel, L. W., 'Nation-building and the Kgatla; the role of the Anglo–Boer War', *Botswana Notes and Records*, 4, 1972

Unterhalter, E., 'Migrant labour and the Nquthu district of Zululand, 1879–1910' (unpublished paper, n.d.)

Van der Merwe, N. J. and R. T. K. Scully, 'The Phalaborwa story: investigation of a South African Iron Age group', *World Archaeology*, 3, 1971

Van Onselen, C., 'Reactions to rinderpest in southern Africa 1896–97', *Journal of African History*, 13, 1972

Wickins, P. L., 'The Natives Land Act of 1913: A cautionary essay on simple explanations of complex change', *South African Journal of Economics*, 49, 1981

Wilson, M., 'Problems for research in Tswana history', *Botswana Notes and Records*, 3, 1971

Wiseman, J. A., 'Multi-partyism in Africa: the case of Botswana', *African Affairs*, 76, 1977

Wolpe, H., 'Capitalism and cheap labour-power in South Africa: from segregation to apartheid', *Economy and Society*, 1, 1972

Wright, J. B., 'Pre-Shakan age-group formation among the northern Nguni', *Natalia*, 8, 1978

Wright, J., 'Politics, ideology and the invention of the "Nguni"' (unpublished paper, 1983)

Youe, C. P., 'Imperial land policy in Swaziland and the African response', *Journal of Imperial and Commonwealth History*, 7, 1978

Theses and dissertations

Ballard, C., 'The transfrontiersman: the career of John Dunn in Natal and Zululand 1834-1895' (Ph. D. thesis, University of Natal, 1980)

Collins, D. P., 'The origins and formation of the Zulu Congregational Church, 1896–1908' (M. A. thesis, University of Natal, Durban, 1978)

Crush, J., 'The struggle for Swazi labour, 1890–1920' (Ph. D. thesis, Queen's University, 1983)

Fransman, M., 'The state and development in Swaziland' (D. Phil. thesis, University of Sussex, 1979)

Hedges, D. W., 'Trade and politics in southern Mozambique and Zululand in the eighteenth and early nineteenth centuries' (Ph. D. thesis, University of London,

1978)

Hemson, D., 'Class consciousness and migrant workers: dock workers of Durban' (Ph. D. thesis, University of Warwick, 1979)

Kagan, N., 'African settlements in the Johannesburg area, 1903–1923' (M. A. thesis, University of the Witwatersrand, 1978)

Mael, R., 'The problem of political integration in the Zulu Empire' (Ph. D. thesis, University of California, Los Angeles, 1974)

Moyer, R. A., 'A history of the Mfengu of the eastern Cape 1815–1865' (Ph. D. thesis, London University, 1976)

Slater, H., 'Transitions in the political economy of south-east Africa before 1840' (D.Phil. thesis, University of Sussex, 1976)

Truschel, L. W., 'Accommodation under imperial rule: the Tswana of the Bechuanaland Protectorate, 1895–1910' (Ph. D. thesis, Northwestern University, 1970)

INDEX

Abantu Batho, 155
Acts of Parliament: Bantu Authorities Act (1951), 167, 185; Bantu Education Act (1953), 186; Bantu Homelands Citizenship Act (1970), 168; Bantu Homelands Constitution Act (1971), 168; Bantu Labour Act (1953), 188; Bantu Laws Amendment Act (1964, 1971, 1978), 173, 178; Franchise and Ballot Act (Cape) (1892), 103; Glen Grey Act (Cape) (1894), 103; Group Areas Act (1950), 175, 180, 185; Industrial Conciliation Act (1924), 146; Mines and Works Act (1911), 146; Mines and Works Amendment Act (1926), 146; Native Administration Act (1927), 163, 164, 165; Native Affairs Act (1920), 163; Native Beer Act (Natal) (1908), 151; Native Labour Regulation Act (1911), 146; Native Laws Amendment Act (1937, 1952), 152, 178, 180; Native Resettlement Act (1954), 180; Native Trust and Land Act (1936), 144, 166, 173, 174; Natives Land Act (1913), 63, 139, 143, 144, 155–6, 166, 173, 175; Natives Tax Act (Transvaal) (1908), 139; Natives (Urban Areas) Act (1923, 1930), 151–2; Peace Preservation Act (Cape) (1878), 117; Promotion of Bantu Self-Government Act (1959), 167; Representation of Natives Act (1936), 166, 182, 185; Riotous Assemblies Amendment Act (1929), 163; South Africa Act (1909), 136, 154–5, 196; Suppression of Communism Act (1950), 185, 188; Transkei Constitution Act (1963), 168; Transkei Self-Government Act (1963), 168; Tribal Land Act (Botswana) (1968), 211; Unlawful Organizations Act (1960), 190
Advisory Boards, 153
African Methodist Episcopal Church, 161
African Mineworkers' Union, 183
African National Congress (ANC), 109, 161, 162, 163, 180, 195, 204, 210, 223; establishment of, 155; aims of, 155; methods and strategies of, 155–7, 222; opposition to segregation, 155–6; internal divisions, 156–7, 183; stagnation of, 181; boycott strategy, 182, 184, 186–7; revival of, 183–4; commitment to non-racialism, 183–4, 188; and communists, 183–4; Africanism and the Youth League, 184, 188; passive resistance, 184–7; diverse influences upon, 188–9; and the Freedom Charter, 188; and SACTU, 188–9; shift to armed struggle, 190–1, 222
African National Political Union, 154
Alexandra, 150, 185, 186, 187
Aliwal North, Convention of, 115
Aliwal North, Treaty of, 114
All-African Convention, 181–2
Allison, James, 86–7
amabutho, 29, 31, 32
amalaita gangs, 150–1
Amalinde, Battle of, 38
American Board Mission, 85, 87, 161
'American Movement', 162
Anglo–Zulu War, 78–9, 83
anthropology, 2, 65, 216, 218
apartheid, 167–8, 170–2, 180–1; *see also* segregation, 'homelands'
archaeology, 2, 16–17, 23, 216–17
Austen, J., 116
Baden-Powell, Col. R. S. S., 137
Badfontein, 15
Bafarutshe reserve, 191
Balala, 46
Ballinger, W. G., 159
Bambatha, Chief, 141–2
Basotho (or southern Sotho), 21, 42, 56, 138, 217–18; origins, 22–3, 45, 48–9; settlement patterns, 42–3, 48; compared to Tswana, 48; interaction with Khoisan, 49; social and political structure, 49–50, 223; and the *difaqane*, 57–8, 111; and missionaries, 111–12; conflict with Orange Free State, 112–15, 221; under British rule, 115, 203–4; state formation, 115; internal divisions, 115–18; under Cape rule, 115–18; rebellion of 1880–1, 116–17, 119, 132, 196, 203; trade, 118; peasantry, 118–19, 203, 206, 219; migrant labour, 145, 206–7, 220; 'homeland', 177; underdevelopment, 203, 206–8; path to independence, 203–5; political parties, 204–5; politics since independence, 205–6; relations with South Africa, 205–8; class stratification, 208; *see also* Sotho, Basutoland, Lesotho
'Bastards', 111

Basutoland, 62, 88, 113–19, 139, 145, 196, 202–8, 222; *see also* Basotho, Lesotho, Sotho
Basutoland Congress Party, 204–6
Basutoland National Council, 203–4, 205
Basutoland National Party, 204–5
Basutoland Progressive Association, 204
Bathoen, Chief, 121
Bathoen II, Chief, 209, 211
Baumannville, 149
Beaumont Commission, 144
Bechuanaland Democratic Party, 210, 211
Bechuanaland People's Party, 210
Bechuanaland Protectorate, 62, 122, 124–5, 126–7, 145, 196, 208–13; *see also* Tswana, Botswana, Sotho
Becoana Mutual Improvement Association, 154
Benoni, 185
Berlin Missionary Society, 128–9
Bhaca, 61, 101
Bhele, 61, 96
black consciousness movement, 171, 192, 193, 194–5, 222
'black spots', 86, 174–5
Bloemfontein, 155, 156, 157, 160, 181, 185
Bloemfontein Convention, 113
Blood River, Battle of, 73
boers, 37, 70, 71–4, 77, 78, 81, 82–4, 85, 91–3, 94, 103, 112–14, 119–21, 122–5, 127–30, 131, 132, 137, 138–9, 219, 221
Bomva, Chief, 36
Bomvana, 33, 35–6, 96, 100
Bonner, P., 159
Bophuthatswana, 169, 203
Bophuthatswana National Party, 169
Boshof, President J. N., 113
Botha, General Louis, 196
Botha Bothe, 57
Botlasitse, 123–4
Botswana, 3, 9, 42, 208–11, 213–15; *see also* Tswana, Bechuanaland Protectorate, Sotho
Botswana Independence Party, 210
Botswana National Front, 211
boycotts, 186–7, 222
Bradford, H., 159–60
British Bechuanaland, 124–5
British imperial government: confederation scheme, 78; and the Zulu, 78–9, 81–3; and Natal, 84, 89; and the Swazi, 95–6, 196, 197–202; and the southern Nguni, 96–102; and the Basotho, 113–15, 117, 119, 196, 202–8; and the Tswana, 122, 123–6, 127, 196, 208–11, 212–13; and the Pedi, 130; and Africans during the South African War, 137–8; and African rights, 138, 154–6, 182; and white farming, 139; and the protectorates, 196
British Kaffraria, 96, 99–100; *see also* Ciskei
British settlers, 103
British South Africa Company, 124–5, 196, 208
Broederstroom, 3, 5, 6, 7
Brownlee, C., 99
Bryant, A. T., 20, 22–3, 25, 216
Buispoort Culture, 10
Bulhoek massacre, 162, 163
Bundy, C., 108, 220
Bunga, 164, 167–8
Bunting, B., 161
Bunu, King, 197
Burgers, President T. F., 123, 129
Butelezi, Wellington, 162
Buthelezi, Chief Gatsha, 169–70
Buthelezi lineage, 26
Cachalia, Y., 185
Cape, 143, 145, 216; and the southern Nguni, 34, 38, 96, 97–9, 100–6, 164; colonists, 101, 103–5; franchise, 103–4, 108–9, 138, 143, 155, 156, 167; and the Basotho, 115, 116–17, 118, 119, 196, 203, 222; and the Tswana, 124, 125, 126, 127; African opposition, 153–5, 156–7, 159, 161, 182, 185–7, 188, 191, 194; worker action, 192
Cape Native Convention, 154
Cape Peninsula Native Association, 154
Cape Town, 80, 149, 151, 157, 160, 179, 181, 189–90, 194
Carnarvon, Lord, 77
Casalis, E., 112
Castle Cavern, 3
Cathcart, Sir George, 100, 113
cattle-killing, 100
Cato Manor, 180, 187, 190
Cele, 26, 27, 71
Cetshwayo, 75–81, 93, 141, 165
Chalumna River, 3, 6, 16
Chamber of Mines, 146, 148, 183
Chamberlain, J., 81
Champion, A. W. G., 159, 161
Chateau Estate, 150
Ciskei, 33, 37, 96; Iron Age, 10, 16; economy, 33–4; peasantry, 105–6, 219; rural impoverishment, 142, 144; and 'homeland' status, 170
City and Suburban, 150
Clarke, Sir Marshal, 81, 117
class: in precapitalist societies, 64, 65–6, 218, 223; incipient stratification in African societies, 106, 126, 131, 223; and African opposition movements, 152–3, 161, 222, 223; stratification among the Basotho, 208; stratification among the Tswana, 214–15; *see also* petty bourgeoisie, worker organisation and action
Clermont, 150
coal-mining, 89, 145
Cobbing, J. R. D., 62–3, 219
Colenso, Bishop, 80
Colenso, Harriette, 80
Colonial Development and Welfare Fund, 208
Colonial Office, 77, 78, 80, 81, 124, 139
colour bar, job, 146, 148, 150, 155
coloured people, 150, 179, 182, 188, 193

communists, 157, 158, 159, 160, 161, 163, 181, 182, 183–4, 188, 205
compounds, 147, 149, 151
concessionaires, 93–4, 101, 124, 131
Congress of the People, 188
Cook's Bush, 180
Coronation Brick and Tile, 192
Council for Non-European Trade Unions (CNETU), 182
Cowan, Dr, 29
Customs Union, Southern African, 207, 214
Dadoo, Y., 184, 185
Daniel, J., 31–2
De Buys, C., 37
defiance campaign, 185–6, 222
Delagoa Bay, 14, 22, 25, 26, 30–1, 51, 77, 93, 103
Delius, P., 50–1
Democratic Party (Transkei), 169
Desmond, C., 175
diamond-mining: impact of, 83, 105, 107, 123, 126, 132; labour, 87, 117, 118, 126, 129; in Botswana, 214
Diepkloof, 180
difaqane (or *mfecane*), 35, 42, 51–2, 90, 96, 97, 108, 111, 115, 119, 120, 121, 122, 127, 130–2, 219; overall impact of, 54, 55–7, 62–3, 119, 219; course of, 54–62
Dingane, 29, 55, 74, 83–4, 90, 91, 165; as Zulu king, 71–3; relations with whites, 73; downfall of, 73–4
Dingiswayo, 29–30, 54; in exile, 26, 29–30; gains power, 26; death of, 27; and Shaka, 27; as innovator, 29–30; and trade, 31
Dinkwanyane, 129
Dinuzulu, 81, 141–2, 165
Dithakong, 46, 58
Dlamini, 25, 90, 91, 92, 197
Dlamini III, 25
Doornfontein, 150
drought, 82, 97, 98, 99, 107, 126, 130, 140, 142–3, 162, 212, 214
Dube, J. L., 153, 155
DuBois, W. E. B., 153
Dunn, John, 75, 79
Durban, 4, 148, 149, 150, 153, 159, 160, 161, 177, 179–81, 185, 187, 189, 190, 192–3
D'Urban, Sir Benjamin, 98
Dwane, J., 161
Early Iron Age, 42, 52; distribution of sites, 3–4; pottery, 4–5, 9; eastern zone, 4–5; settlement patterns, 5, 15; farming, 5–6, 19, 217; mining and technology, 6, 19, 217; art, 6–7; interaction with Stone Age people, 7, 17; identity of people, 7; origins of, 9; continuity of, 9, 14–15; *see also* Iron Age, Late Iron Age
East coast fever, 140, 142–3, 199
East London, 160, 161, 181
eastern Cape frontier wars: first (1779–81), 37; fourth (1811–12), 38; fifth (1818–19), 38; sixth (1834–5), 97–8; seventh (1846–7), 98–9; eighth (1850–3), 99–100; ninth (1877–8), 100–1
ecology: and the Early Iron Age, 6; and state formation, 31–2, 51; and southern Nguni statelessness, 40; and settlement patterns, 43–4, 47–8; and political structures, 48, 67, 219
Edendale, 86–7
education, 108, 109, 112, 121, 153, 169, 186, 187, 189, 193, 195, 208, 213, 214
Eiland, 3, 5, 10
Elgin, Lord, 198
Ellenberger, D. F., 216
Elsie's River, 180
Enkwazini, 3
Ethiopian Church, 161
Ethiopianism: *see* independent churches
ethnicity, 19; problem of classification, 20, 136, 222–3; myth of ethnic exclusivism, 34, 50, 52, 170–1, 222–3; functions of, 223
Etshaneni, Battle of, 81
Evans, Admiral E., 209
Evaton, 186–7
Fagan Commission, 178
Faku, Chief, 35, 61, 96
Federation of Free African Trade Unions of South Africa, 188
Federation of South African Women, 187
Ferreira, J., 94
Ferreirastown, 150
First World War, 155
Fokeng, 42–3, 48, 51, 56, 59
Food and Canning Workers' Union, 189
Fordsburg, 150
franchise: Cape, 102–3, 108–9, 138, 143, 155, 156, 166; question of rights for Africans, 138; African struggle for, 155, 168, 182; Representation of Natives Act (1936), 166
Freedom Charter, 188
Frere, Sir Bartle, 78, 100, 101, 222
Froneman, G. F., 174
Fuze people, 141
Galeshiwe, Chief, 125
Garvey, Marcus, 157, 162
Gasebone, Chief, 120, 123
Gaseitsiwe, Chief, 120
Gaza, 26, 55, 92
Gazankulu, 170
Gcaleka, 35, 37, 61, 96–8, 100–1
Glenelg, Lord, 98
Gluckman, M., 30, 32
Gokomere, 5
gold-mining, 89, 94, 95, 199; impact of, 105, 107, 132; labour, 126, 127, 144–8, 171, 199; at Tati, 212
Gontse, Chief, 120
Good Hope Estate, 150
Gordon, M., 182
Goshen, 124
Gqugqu, 71, 74, 84
Gqunukhwebe, 37, 98, 99
Grey, Sir George, 114
Griqua, 56, 59

Griqualand West, 123
Grout, A., 87
Groutville, 87
Gumede, J., 157, 161
Guy, J., 32, 219
Hammond-Tooke, W. D., 38–9
Hamu, Chief, 79, 80, 81
Hare, J., 98
Harinck, G., 34
Harmony, 10
Hedges, D., 30–2
Hertzog, J. B. M., 148, 156, 158, 181
Hinsati, Chief, 35
Hintsa, Chief, 36, 37, 97
Hlakwana, 58, 59
Hlubi, Chief, 79
Hlubi people, 26, 31, 96; and the *difaqane*, 54–5, 57, 58–9, 61; and the colonial economy, 87–8; Langalibalele's rebellion, 88, 116
Hoffman, President J. P., 113
'homelands' (or Bantustans), 117, 143, 166, 177, 191, 196, 215, 221, 223; as government policy, 17, 166–72; economies of, 171–3; as dumping-grounds, 175–7, 180–1; *see also* Bophuthatswana, Ciskei, KwaZulu, Transkei
Hope, H., 101, 116
Hout Bay, 180
Hurutshe, 42, 44, 45, 58–9, 120, 122
Iliso Lesizwe Esimnyama, 154
Iliso Lomzi, 154
Imbokodvo National Movement, 200–2
imiDange, 37
Imvo Zabantsundu, 109
independent churches, African, 71, 109, 161–2
Independent ICU, 159, 161
Indians, 179, 188, 193
Industrial and Commercial Union, 157
Industrial and Commercial Workers' Union of Africa (ICU), 157-60, 161, 163
Industrial Workers of Africa, 160
influx control, 151–2, 166, 169, 172, 173, 178, 180; *see also* passes, urbanisation
informal sector, 150, 179
Inkatha, 170, 223
Inqua, 35
Intaba, 191
Iron Age, 2, 42, 49, 216–17, 222; break between early and late phases, 3, 4, 9–10, 14–15, 16, 216–17; *see also* Early Iron Age, Late Iron Age
Isandhlwana, Battle of, 78
isiGqoza, 75
Israelite sect, 162
Izwi Labantu, 154
Jabavu, D. D. T., 157
Jabavu, J. T., 109
Jameson Raid, 124, 125, 196, 208
Janson, P., 180
Jantje, Chief, 120
Jeppe, 150
Joalaboholo, 57
Jobe, Chief, 26
Joel, 117
Johannesburg, 82, 149, 150, 151, 160, 179, 183, 185, 186, 187, 189, 190, 194
Jonathan, 117
Jonathan, Chief Leabua, 204–6
Joubert, P. J., 95
Jwaneng, 214
Kadalie, C., 157–9, 161, 163
Kangwane, 170, 215
Kat River Settlement, 97
Keate, R. W., 123
Kensington, 180
Kgalagadi people, 42
Kgamane, 120
Kgamanyane, 123
Kgatla, 42, 45, 49, 50, 58, 59, 121, 122
Khama, Chief, 120, 121, 125, 137
Khama, Seretse, 209–10
Khama, Tshekedi, 209–10
Khawuta, Chief, 37
Khoikhoi, 34–5, 37, 39, 46, 98
Khoisan, 14, 17, 34, 49
kholwa, 85
Khumalo clan, 54
Kimberley, siege of, 137
Kimble, J., 118
Klein Afrika, 3, 4, 5
Klipspruit, 149
Kololo, 56, 59, 119; *see also* Fokeng
Koni, 50
Kopa, 128
Kora, 46, 58, 111, 113, 115, 124
Kotane, Moses, 183–4
Krogh, J. C., 95
Kruger, Paul, 95, 123, 131
Kutswe, 50
Kuzwayo, 26
KwaMashu, 180–1
KwaZulu, 170, 181
Kwena, 42–3, 45, 48–9, 50, 57, 58, 59, 118, 119, 122–5, 203, 209
labour, African: migrant, 77, 107–8, 117–19, 126, 129, 132, 142, 144–6, 148, 171, 172–3, 177, 178, 182, 183, 192–3, 199, 206–7, 212–13, 215, 220–1; reservoirs, 102, 119, 171, 206, 208, 215; coercion, 103, 129, 140–1, 143, 220; recruitment, 119, 126–7, 145, 199, 220; on the Rand mines, 126–7, 144–8, 171, 199, 207; tenancy, 139–40, 143–4, 158, 166, 173–4, 177, 199; stabilisation of, 148–9; *see also* worker organisation and action
La Guma, J., 158
Lala, 22–3
Lamont, 149, 153
land: African purchase and renting, 84, 85–7, 88–9, 104–5, 139–40; declining African access to, 107, 132, 138–40, 142–4, 166, 173–4, 220; Basotho–Orange Free State conflict over, 113–15, 206; expropriated from the Tswana, 123–4, 126, 127, 213;

Pedi loss of, 129; African protest over, 155–6, 162; Swaziland partition, 198–200, 202
Langa (Cape Town), 149, 190
Langalibalele, Chief, 88, 116
Langeberg Rebellion, 126
Langeni, 26
Late Iron Age: interaction with Stone Age people, 8, 14, 17; chronology of, 9–10; pottery, 10, 15; settlement patterns, 10–11, 15–16; building styles, 11; farming, 11–12, 15, 19, 216–17; mining and metal production, 12–14, 19, 217; trade, 14, 17; continuity of, 15–16, 217; *see also* Early Iron Age, Iron Age
Laundry, Cleaning and Dyeing Workers' Union, 189
League of African Rights, 161
Leballo, P., 188
Lebowa, 170
Lefela, J., 204
Lehana, 116
Lekhotla la Bafo, 204
Lemba, 52–3
Lembede, Anton, 184
Lentswe, Chief, 121
Lerotholi, Chief, 117–18
Lesaoana, 116
Lesotho, 21, 49, 57, 112, 118, 202–3, 205–8, 210–11, 215; *see also* Basotho, Basutoland, Sotho
Lesotho National Development Corporation, 206
Letaba, 17
Letsie, Chief, 116–17
liberals, 158, 184, 188, 193
Limehill, 175
linguistics, 2, 17, 23, 34, 216
liquor, 150–1, 153, 160–1, 179–80, 187
Livingstone, David, 120, 121, 123
Lobedu, 21, 50
Loch, Sir Henry, 95
locusts, 82, 107, 126
Lolwe Hill, 12–13
London Missionary Society, 121
Lovedale College, 109
Lozi, 56
Ludvonga, 92–4
Luthuli, A., 185, 190
Lutuli, M., 154
Lydenburg, 5, 6, 7
Macheng, Chief, 120
Mackenzie, J., 122, 124
Madikane, Chief, 61
Mafeking, siege of, 137
Magaye, Chief, 71
Maggs, T., 43, 217
Magwababa, 141
Mahura, Chief, 120
Maitland, Sir Peregrine, 98, 113, 114
Majara, 116
Makhado, Chief, 131
Malambule, 90–1, 93
Malan, D. F., 185
Malawi, 55
Malunge, 90
Malusi, 27
Mampuru, Chief, 128, 130
Mandela, Nelson, 184, 185, 190
Mandlakazi, 80–1
Mangope, Lucas, 169
Mankurwane, Chief, 123–4
Mann, T., 158
MaNthatisi, 55–7
Mapungubwe, 10, 14
Maputo, 26
Maqoma, 97
Marabeng, 57
marabi culture, 150
Marema Tlou Freedom Party, 204–5
Marema Tlou Party, 204–5
Maritz, I., 94
Marks, J. B., 183–4, 185
Marks, S., 22
Maroteng, 50–1, 60, 127
Marshalltown, 150
Martindale, 150, 179–80
Masabalala, S. M., 160
Masemola people, 128
Masilo, Chief, 45
Masopha, Chief, 116–18
Massouw, Chief, 124
Matabeleland, 122
Matante, P. G., 210
Matanzima, K., 168–9, 192
Mathiba, Chief, 45
Matiwane, Chief, 54–5, 57–8, 96
Matokomo, 5
Matshana, Chief, 88
Matthews, Z. K., 184
Mawa, 74
Mawewe, 27
Mawewe, Chief, 92
Mbandzeni, 94–5, 197
Mbandzeni National Convention, 200
Mbedzi, 52
Mbeki, G., 190
Mbholompo, Battle of, 96
Mbilini, 92
Mbo, 22, 25, 28
Mbuyazi, 75
Mda, A. P., 188
Meadowlands, 180
Melville Koppies, 10
Merensky, A., 129
Messina, 13, 14, 17, 54, 160
Metal and Allied Workers' Union, 192
Mfengu, 21, 54, 99, 109, 137, 223; and the *difaqane*, 61–2, 96, 108; as colonial collaborators, 97–8, 100, 101; peasantry, 104–6, 108; as educated elite, 108; *see also* southern Nguni
Mgijima, E., 162
Mgungundlovu, 73
Mhlangaso, 101
Middelburg, 13

millenarian movements, 162
Milner, Lord, 138, 198
missionaries, 70–1, 77–8, 85–7, 93, 105, 108, 111–12, 115, 119, 121–2, 124, 127, 128–9, 131–2, 162, 186, 208, 219
Mlandela, 28
Mlawu, 37
Mnyamana, 80
mode of production analysis, 65–6, 218
Mokgatla, Chief, 45
Mokhehle, N., 204–5
Mokone, M., 161
Mokoteli, 57
Molapo, 116–17
Moleta, Chief, 45
Moletsane, Chief, 56, 59, 113, 116
Mome Gorge, Battle of, 141
Montshiwa, Chief, 120–1, 123–4
Moorosi, Chief, 116
Mopeli, 116
Moroka, Chief, 111
Moroka, J., 184–5
Morolong, Chief, 45
Moshoeshoe I, 55, 56, 60, 90, 96–7, 116, 119, 127, 132, 203, 223; early life, 57; withstands the *difaqane*, 57–8; builds power, 58, 111–12; and missionaries, 111–12; and the Orange Free State, 113–15; and the British, 113–15; death of, 115; achievement, 115; as chief, 115–16
Moshoeshoe II, 205
Moswete, Chief, 124
Mothibi, Chief, 120
Motsete, K. T., 210
Mozambique, 55, 91, 92, 145
Mpambanyoni, 12
Mpame, 5
Mpande, 71, 77, 78, 84, 91, 93; allies with boers, 73–4; as Zulu king, 74–5, 82; as diplomat, 74
Mpangazita, Chief, 54–6
Mphephu, Chief, 131
Mpho, M., 210
Mpondo, 21, 33, 35, 61, 96–7, 99, 101, 107, 217; origins, 35–6; colonial subjugation, 101; trade, 104; peasantry, 104, 106, 108, 142–3; migrant labour, 142–3, 145, 220; revolt, 191–2; *see also* southern Nguni
Mpondomise, 21, 33, 35, 36, 100–1
Mqikela, Chief, 101
Msimang, S., 157
Msuluzi Confluence, 3, 5, 6, 7
Mswati, 90–3, 132
Mthethwa, 26–7, 29, 32, 54
Mtimkhulu, Chief, 54
myths, historical: the empty land, 17, 216; static African past, 17, 19, 20, 29; ethnic exclusivism, 34, 50, 52, 170–1, 222–3
Mzila, Chief, 92
Mzilikazi, Chief, 46, 54–5, 119–20
Mzimba, P J., 161
Mzonjani, 2, 3, 6
Naicker, G. M., 184
Nandi, 27
Napier, Sir George, 113
Natal, 91, 104, 115, 116, 129, 138, 174, 199; Iron Age, 3–4, 5, 9, 10, 11, 12; and the Zulu state, 71–4, 75–6, 77, 78–80, 81–3, 93; government, 75, 77, 79–80, 81, 82, 89–90, 92, 140, 141–2; colonists, 81, 85–9; white farming, 140; African rural impoverishment, 141; Bambatha rebellion, 141–2; African opposition, 153, 158, 159, 161; worker action, 160, 161, 183; 'native policy', 163, 165; resettlement, 175; *see also* Natal Nguni
Natal Native Congress, 154
Natal Nguni: refugees from Zululand, 83–4; access to land, 84, 85–7, 88–90, 140; colonial administration of, 84–5; and missionaries, 85; peasantry, 86–90, 140, 219; and wage labour, 140–1; rebellion (1906–8), 141–2
National Convention, 154
National Party, 158, 164, 165, 167, 170, 223
National Union of South African Students, 193
National Union of Textile Workers, 192
Native Administration Proclamation (Swaziland) (1944), 197
Native Advisory Council (Bechuanaland Protectorate), 209
Native Affairs Commission, 163
Native Bakers' Union, 160
Native Clothing Workers' Union (or South African Clothing Workers' Union), 160, 182
Native Conference, 163
Native Economic Commission, 144
Native Educational Association, 109
Native Laundry Workers' Union (or African Laundry Workers' Union), 160, 182
Native Mattress and Furniture Workers' Union, 160, 182
Native Recruiting Corporation, 199–200
Natives' Representative Council, 166–7, 182
Ncindise, Chief, 35
Ncwangeni–Jere, 26
Ncwini, Chief, 36
Ndabeni, 149
Ndabuko, 80
Ndebele (Transvaal), 46, 129, 130
Ndebele (Zimbabwe), 46, 113, 119–22, 125, 127; and the *difaqane*, 54–6, 58–60, 62
Ndlambe, Chief, 37–8
Ndlambe people, 99, 106
Ndobe, B., 157
Ndondakusuka, Battle of, 75
Ndondondwana, 5, 7
Ndwandwe, 55, 60, 90; growth and expansion, 26, 31; clashes with the Ngwane, 27, 32, 54; clashes with the Mthethwa and Zulu, 27; environment, 32
Newclare, 150, 179, 180
newspapers, 108–9, 154, 155, 157
Ngamiland, 45, 122

Ngcobo, 27
Ngcolosi, 27
Ngona, 52
Ngoni, 55
Ngqika, Chief, 37–8, 97, 103
Ngqika people, 98, 99, 100, 105–6
Ngubencuka, Chief, 96
Nguni, 39, 49, 52, 53–5, 57, 70, 90, 115, 116, 136, 155, 218; usage of the term, 20–1, 23, 222; culture, 14, 25; language, 14, 21; division between northern and southern, 21, 23, 25, 33; compared to Sotho, 21; economy, 21, 23; settlement patterns, 21, 44; kinship, 21; origins, 21–3; social and political structure, 25, 39–41; environment, 47–8; *see also* northern Nguni, southern Nguni, Natal Nguni, Zulu, Swazi, Xhosa
Ngwaketse, 45, 58, 59, 120–2, 124, 126, 209
Ngwane, 31, 90, 96; origins, 25; and Sotho culture, 25–6; clash with the Ndwandwe, 27, 32, 54; environment, 32, 67; and the *difaqane*, 54–5, 57–8, 61
Ngwane V, 95
Ngwane National Liberatory Congress, 200, 201, 202
Ngwato, 45, 59, 120, 121, 122, 124, 125, 137, 138, 209–10
Ngwe, 88
Nicholls, Heaton, 165
Ninevites, 151
Njanya, 36
Nkharahanye, Chief, 58
Nkosi, J., 161
Nongqawuse, 100
Note, Jan, 151
Nqetho, Chief, 71
Nquku, J. J., 200
Nquthu district, 82
Ntshekane, 6
Ntsuanatsatsi, 43
Ntungwa, 22
Nxaba, 55
Nxego, Chief, 36
Nyasaland, 157
Nzula, A., 161
Ohlange Institute, 153
Olifantspoort, 13
Ophirton, 150
opposition, African political, 110, 216, 221–2, 224; early organisations, 108–9, 153–5; class character of, 152–3, 161; ANC, 155–7; ICU, 157–60; Durban beerhall boycott and pass campaign, 160–1; and independent churches, 161–2; diverse character of, 162; state suppression of, 163, 189–90, 192, 195; growing militancy, 166; stagnation, 181–2; revival, 183–8; diverse strands, 188–9; Sharpeville crisis, 189–90; in rural areas, 191–2; black consciousness movement, 193, 194–5; Soweto revolt, 193–5; *see also* African National Congress, Pan-Africanist Congress, worker organisation and action
oral tradition, 2, 22, 23, 26, 35, 42, 45, 216
Orange Free State (and Orange River Colony), 124, 127, 143; Iron Age, 11; and the Basotho, 113–15, 118, 205, 221; after the South African War, 138–9, 142; African opposition, 154, 156, 157, 158, 161, 194; 'native policy', 163, 165
Orange River Colony Native Vigilance Association (and Orange Free State Native Congress), 154
Orapa, 214
Order of Ethiopia, 161
Orlando, 185
Orpen, F., 123
Osborn, M., 81
Paarl insurrection, 191
Pageview, 180
Pai, 50
Pan-Africanist Congress (PAC), 188, 189–91, 193, 222, 223
Paris Evangelical Missionary Society, 111
passes, pass laws, 146, 153, 156, 161, 163, 177–8, 182, 185, 187, 189–90, 191; *see also* influx control
passive resistance, 156, 184–7, 189–90, 222
peasantry, 70, 109, 132, 139, 143, 219–20, 221; southern Nguni, 62, 96, 103–8, 142–3; Natal, 85–90, 140; Basotho, 118, 119, 203, 206
Pedi, 21, 45–6, 53, 132, 217–18; culture, 15; ethnic heterogeneity, 50; state formation, 50–1; social and political structure, 51–2, 127–8; and the *difaqane*, 51–2, 60–1, 62; regeneration under Sekwati, 127; external pressures, 127–8; and missionaries, 128–9; and the Transvaal, 129–30; migrant labour, 128–9; and the South African War, 137; *see also* Sotho
Peires, J. B., 34, 38–40, 218
Petersen, Hector, 193
petty bourgeoisie, African, 108, 152–3, 154, 157, 158–9, 161, 168, 171, 179, 200–1, 208, 222–4
Phalaborwa, 6, 10, 12–13, 14, 17, 51, 217
Phalo, Chief, 36–7
Phato, Chief, 99
Phuthi, 116
Phuthing, 49, 58–9
Pilane, Chief, 169
Pilgrim's Rest, 13
Pim, Sir Alan, 200, 204
Pirow, O., 163
Plaatje, Sol, 155, 157
Plaston, 5
Pondoland, 101, 102, 103, 104, 106–8, 142–3, 145, 164, 191–2; *see also* Mpondo, southern Nguni
Poqo, 191–2
Port Elizabeth, 160, 163, 181, 185, 189, 190
Port Natal, 83
Portugal, 30–1, 55, 92, 103
Posholi, 116
Potgieter, A. H., 91, 128

Poto, Chief, 168–9
Presbyterian Church of Africa, 161
Pretoria, 161, 187, 191, 194
Pretoria Convention, 94
Prospect Township, 150
Pulana, 50
Qadi, 71
Qwabe, 26–7, 28, 71
QwaQwa, 170, 177
Queenstown conference (1907), 154
railways, 93, 118, 124, 127, 140
Ramabulana, Chief, 52
Rand revolt (1922), 148
Ratsebe, Chief, 58
Ravele, Chief, 131
reserves, African, 143–6, 166, 171–2, 177, 191, 221; *see also* 'homelands', land resettlement (and relocation, removals), 86, 172, 174–7, 178, 180–1, 186, 221, 222
Resha, R., 186
resistance, African, 132, 216, 219, 221–2; motives, 70–1; organisation, 70–1, 164; Zulu, 78, 83, 132; Langalibalele's rebellion, 88; southern Nguni, 97–102, 132, 221; Basotho, 112–15, 116–18, 119, 132, 221, 222; Griqua rebellion, 123; Langeberg rebellion, 125–6; Pedi, 129–30, 132; Bambatha rebellion, 141–2; *see also* opposition, passive resistance, worker organisation and action
Retief, Piet, 74
Rharhabe, Chief, 37
Rharhabe people, 37, 97, 99
Rhodes, C. J., 101, 119, 124
Rhodesia, 126
rinderpest, 82, 89–90, 107, 126, 140, 142–3, 197, 199
Rivonia, 190
Robben Island, 88
Robinson, Sir Hercules, 117
Roka, 50
Rolong, 43, 45–6, 59, 111, 120, 121, 123, 124, 137
Rooiberg, 13
Roossenekal, 13
Roux, E., 161
Rrapulana, Chief, 120
Rrapulana-Rolong, 46
Rratlou, Chief, 120
Rratlou-Rolong, 46, 120, 122
Rubusana, W., 155
Rupert, A., 187
rural impoverishment, African, 138, 143–5, 171–3, 175–7, 220–1; *see also* 'homelands', land, resettlement
San, 7, 14, 33, 35, 39, 115
Sandile, Chief, 97, 98, 99, 100
Sand River Convention, 123
Sansom, B., 47
Santo Alberto, 34, 36
Sarhili, Chief, 100
Schapera, I., 47
Schreiner, W. P., 154
Schreuder, Bishop, 77
Sebele, Chief, 125, 126
Sebetwane, Chief, 56, 59, 119
Sebilong, 44
Sechele, Chief, 120, 121
Second World War, 177
segregation, policy of, 138; territorial, 143, 156, 166, 220; urban, 149, 151–2, 166, 180; Hertzog's bills, 156, 158, 181–2; political and administrative, 163–5, 166–72
Sekgoma I, 120
Sekhukhune I, 128–30
Sekhukhune II, 130
Sekonyela, Chief, 55, 57, 73, 111
Sekwati, Chief, 60, 127–8
Selborne, Lord, 198
Selebi-Phikwe, 214
Seleka, Chief, 120
Seleka-Rolong, 46, 56, 58, 120
Seme, Pixley, 155, 157
Senzangakhona, 27, 74
Seoposengwe Party, 169
shack settlements, 179–81
Shaka, 46, 54, 55, 61, 83, 90, 219; early life, 27; builds power, 27–8; as king, 28–30; assassination of, 29, 71; as innovator, 29, 30; disturbed personality, 30; and population control, 32
sharecropping, 104–5, 139, 142–3, 173, 220
Sharpeville, 185, 190, 191, 195
Shepstone, John, 88
Shepstone, Offy, 94
Shepstone, Sir Theophilus, 75–7, 80, 82–4, 94, 130
Shibe, S., 161
Shona, 50, 52, 53
Shoshong, 45, 122
Sia, 49
Sigcau, Chief, 101
Sigujana, 27
Sihayo, Chief, 78
Sikunyana, Chief, 27
Silver Leaves, 2, 3, 5
Singo, 52–3
Sisile, 94
Sisulu, W., 184, 185, 190
slum yards, 150
smallpox, 82
Smit Committee, 178
Smith, A., 30–1
Smith, Sir Harry, 99–100
Smuts, Jan, 196
Sobhuza I, 27, 90
Sobhuza II, 197, 198, 201–2
Sobukwe, R., 188
Soga, J. H., 216
Somcuba, 91–3
Somerset, H., 96
Somerset, Lord, 38
Sophiatown, 150, 179, 180, 186
Soshangane, Chief, 26, 55
Sotho, 25, 50, 51–2, 53, 70, 90, 101, 111, 115, 127, 136, 155; usage of the term,

20–1, 41, 222; pottery, 15; settlement patterns, 15–16, 21, 42–4; trade, 17, 44; subdivisions, 21, 42; comparison with Nguni, 21; language, 21; economy, 21, 43–4; kinship, 21; origins, 21–3, 42; and the *difaqane*, 54, 55–61
South African Congress of Trade Unions (SACTU), 188–9
South African Federation of Non-European Trade Unions, 160
South African government, 136, 142, 143, 144, 148, 155, 156, 159, 162, 163, 165, 166–72, 173–5, 178, 180–2, 186–7, 189, 190, 192, 193, 195, 220, 223
South African Indian Congress, 184, 185
South African Institute of Race Relations, 174, 194
South African Native Affairs Commission, 138
South African Native Congress, 109, 154
South African Native Convention, 154
South African Native National Congress, *see* African National Congress
South African Native Political Association, 109
South African Party, 154
South African Republic, 93, 94–6, 123, 129–30, 131, 132, 137–8, 161; *see also* Transvaal
South African Students' Movement, 193
South African Students' Organization, 193
South African War, 95, 137–9, 145, 196
South African Worker, 157
Southey, G., 98
South West Africa, 124, 136, 208
Soweto, 180, 186, 193–5
Sprigg, Sir Gordon, 117
states, African: and stateless societies, 64–5, 218; formation of, 29–32, 66–7
Stavenisse, 36
Stellaland, 124
Sterkspruit, 3, 6
Stockenström, A., 98
strikes, 146, 158; on the mines, 148, 156, 160, 167, 182–3; Johannesburg sanitary workers, 156, 160; Cape Town dockworkers, 157, 160; 1918–20, 160; late 1920s, 160–1; 1940s, 182–3; 1950s, 188–9; 1960s, 190, 192; 1970s, 192–3; in Swaziland, 201; *see also* worker organisation and action
Surplus People Project, 175–7
Swazi, 21, 50, 62, 74, 128, 129, 130, 217, 218; and Sotho culture, 25, 223; state formation and expansion, 90, 91–2; external relations, 90–4; internal divisions, 90–1, 92–4, 95, 132; state structure, 91; white encroachment upon, 94–6, 197; migrant labour, 145, 199–200, 220; under Transvaal rule, 197; under British rule, 197–9; king's status, 197–8; colonial economy, 198–200; independence, 200–1; post-independence politics, 201–2; underdevelopment, 202; *see also* Swaziland, Nguni, northern Nguni
Swaziland, 3, 25, 62, 67, 86, 90–6, 145, 196, 197–202, 203, 208, 210, 211, 215, 220; *see also* Swazi
Swaziland Democratic Party, 200, 201
Swaziland Independent Front, 200
Swaziland Progressive Party, 200
Swazi National Council, 200
Tahle, Chief, 35
Tambo, Oliver, 184, 191
Tanzania, 55
Tau, Chief, 46
Tau people, 50–1
Taung, 46
Taung people, 43, 56, 59, 113, 116
Tawana, 45, 59, 121
taxation, 132, 140, 142, 162; hut-tax, 82, 87, 115; Glen Grey labour tax, 103; colonial taxes on the Tswana, 125, 126, 127, 213; taxes on the Pedi, 129; Natives Tax Act (Transvaal) (1908), 139; Natal poll tax, 140–1; taxes on the Swazi, 197, 199
Tembe, 25
Textile Workers' Industrial Union, 189
Thaba Bosiu, 57, 114, 117, 118
Thaba Mosego, 128
Thaba Nchu, 111, 120
Thaele, J., 157
Thandile, 90–1
Thembu (northern), 61
Thembu (southern), 21, 33, 35, 36, 37, 55, 96–7, 101–2, 103, 104, 106, 108, 109, 137, 161, 192; *see also* southern Nguni
Thloome, D., 184
Thovela, 52
Thulare, Chief, 50, 60
Thuli, 26, 28
Tibiyo Fund, 201
Tile, N., 109, 161
Tlhaping, 43, 44, 46, 59, 120, 121, 122–3, 125–6
Tlharo, 125
Tlokwa, 45, 49, 55, 56–8, 73, 79, 111
Togu, Chief, 35, 36
Tonjeni, E., 157
Toto, Chief, 125
townships, 138, 149–50, 178–9
trade: Iron Age, 14, 17, 217; and the Ndwandwe, 26; and the Mthethwa, 26; and state formation, 30–1, 51, 66–7; and the southern Nguni, 34–5, 40, 103–4; and the Sotho, 44; and the Venda, 52; in Zululand, 77; in Basutoland, 118; and the Tswana, 122
trade unions, *see* worker organisation and action
Transkei, 37, 96, 109, 137–8, 153, 161, 182, 203; Iron Age, 3, 5, 6, 9, 10, 16; early occupation of, 33; precolonial economy, 33; colonial subjugation of, 100–2; rebellion (1880–1), 101, 106; colonial administration of, 102, 164–5; council system, 102–3, 163–5; peasantry, 104–8, 142–3,

220; rural impoverishment, 142–4, 172–3; migrant labour, 142, 145, 173; 'American Movement', 162; self-government, 167–8; politics, 168–9; 'independence', 169–71; underdevelopment, 172–3; rural resistance, 191–2; *see also* southern Nguni, Xhosa, Mfengu, Mpondo
Transkeian Territorial Authority, 167–8
Transkeian Territories African Union, 154
Transkei National Independence Party, 169
Transkei Native Vigilance Association, 154
Transvaal, 132, 138, 140, 145, 208; Iron Age, 2–3, 5, 6, 7, 8, 9, 10, 11, 12, 13, 14, 17; and the Zulu, 77, 78, 82; and the Swazi, 93–6, 196, 197, 199; and the Tswana, 119, 122–4, 127; and the Pedi, 128, 129–30, 137, 222; and the Venda, 131; after the South African War, 138–9, 142; African opposition, 154, 156, 159, 185, 193–4; worker action, 156, 158, 160, 182–3, 192; 'native policy', 163, 165, 167; *see also* boers, South African Republic
Transvaal Basotho Committee, 154
Transvaal Native Congress, 154
Transvaal Native Organisation, 154
Transvaal Native Union, 154
Transvaal Native Vigilance Association, 154
Tshawe, Chief, 36
Tshidi, Chief, 120
Tshidi-Rolong, 46, 120, 121, 123
Tshivhase, Chief, 52
Tshwane, Chief, 58
Tsonga, 22, 55, 90
Tswana, 21, 42, 43, 103, 161, 217, 218, 220; settlement patterns, 16, 42–4; origins, 22, 45; economy, 44; as a classificatory term, 44–5; internal divisions among, 45–6, 48, 123–4, 132; interaction with Khoisan, 46; social and political structures, 46–8, 119, 219; environment, 47–8, 219; compared to Basotho, 48; and the *difaqane*, 52, 56, 58–60, 111, 119; and white encroachment, 119, 122–4; major nineteenth-century chiefdoms, 120; and missionaries, 119, 121–2, 131; and the establishment of colonial rule, 124–5, 126, 127, 133, 208, 222; loss of land, 122–4, 126, 127; resistance to colonialism, 125–6; economic independence undermined, 126–7; migrant labour, 126, 145, 212–13, 215; underdevelopment, 208, 211–15; under British rule, 209–10; path to independence, 210; political parties, 210; politics since independence, 210–11; economic resources, 212, 213–14; economy since independence, 213–15; class stratification, 214; *see also* Bechuanaland Protectorate, Botswana, Sotho
Tuskegee Institute, 153
Tyhali, 98
Uitkomst Culture, 9, 15
Ulundi, Battle of, 79, 83
Umkonto we Sizwe, 190–1
unification of South Africa, 154–5
Union of Clothing and Allied Workers, 192
United States, 153, 161
United Swaziland Association, 200–1
urbanisation, African, 166, 177, 221; extent of, 148–9, 177–8; accommodation and housing, 149–51, 178–80, 221; employment and informal sector, 150; crime, 150–1; control, 151; reasons for, 177; government response to, 178, 221; urban relocation, 180–1, 186, 222; segregation, 149, 151–2, 166, 180; *see also* shack settlements, townships, worker organisation
Usuthu, 75, 80, 81, 83
Venda, 52, 70, 203, 218; history, 52–3; mining, 53; and the *difaqane*, 130–1; and the boers, 131; as a 'homeland', 170
Vereeniging, Treaty of, 136, 138
Verwoerd, H. F., 196
Victoria, Queen, 80
Viervoet, Battle of, 113
Von Bezing, Dr L., 2
Vrededorp, 150
wages, African, 146, 148, 150, 152, 153, 155, 171, 172, 179, 192, 215
Walter, E. V., 30
Warden, H., 113, 114
Warren, General Charles, 124
Washington, Booker T., 153
Waterval-Onder, 13
Webb, C. de B., 32
West, Lieutenant-Governor, 84
Western Native Township, 149
West Rand Administration Board, 194, 195
white commercial farming, 138, 139–40, 142, 143–4, 173–4, 177, 198–9
Williams, Ruth, 209
Wilson, M., 21
Windermere, 180
Witzieshoek reserve, 191
Wodehouse, Sir Philip, 105, 115
Wolseley, Sir Garnet, 79, 80, 81, 83
women, African, 149, 150, 156, 173, 177–8, 180, 187, 191
worker organisation and action, 157, 171, 222–3; African mineworkers, 147–8, 182–3, 189, 222; ICU, 157–60; after World War One, 160–1; early industrial unions, 160–1, 182; obstacles to unionisation, 182; growth of unions in 1930 and 1940s, 183; FOFATUSA, 188; SACTU, 188–9; stayaways, 184–5, 189–90, 194; growth in 1970s, 192–3, 222; and the Soweto revolt, 195; in Swaziland, 201, 202; *see also* strikes
Wright, J. B., 20
Xesibe, 101
Xhosa, Chief, 36
Xhosa people, 21, 22, 33, 35, 96, 109, 217, 218; trade, 34, 35, 103–4; interaction with Khoisan, 34–5; language, 34; relations with Thembu, 36; origins, 36; internal divisions, 36–9, 99; social and political structure, 38–40; compared to Zulu, 39–40; and

the Mfengu, 61; colonial encroachment and subjugation, 97–101; cattle-killing, 100; peasantry, 104–5; *see also*, Ciskei, Nguni, southern Nguni, Transkei
Xuma, A. B., 183–4
Yaka, Chief, 26
Young–Barrett Committee, 178
Youth League, ANC, 184, 188, 193, 204
Zambia, 55, 56
Zibhebhu, Chief, 79–81
Zimbabwe, 14, 46, 52
Zizi, 44, 49, 61, 96
Zondi, 141
Zulu, 21, 22, 27, 48, 54, 55, 58, 59, 61, 62, 65, 66, 67, 84, 85, 90, 91–3, 96, 130, 132, 140, 141, 150, 161, 165, 217, 218; under the Mthethwa, 26; expansion 27–8; military organisation, 28; nationhood, 28; centralisation of authority, 28–9; delegation of authority, 28; state formation, 29–32, 219; compared to Xhosa, 39–40; compared to Western models, 40–1; internal divisions, 71–3, 75–6, 82; under Dingane, Mpande and Cetshwayo, 71–6; crisis of resources in 1870s, 76; external pressures, 77–8, 82–3; and war of 1879, 78–9, 83, 221–2; post-war settlement, 79; civil war, 79–81, 132; under British rule, 81–2; labour migration, 82, 220; natural disasters, 82; and 'homelands' policy, 169–70; *see also* Natal Nguni, Nguni, northern Nguni, Shaka
Zulu Congregational Church, 161
Zululand, 3, 11, 55, 71, 73, 74, 75, 77, 78, 79, 80–3, 85, 137, 140–2, 165, 169–70, 220; *see also* Zulu
Zululand Native Police, 137
Zululand Territorial Authority, 170
Zwane, A., 200
Zwangendaba, Chief, 26, 55
Zwide, Chief, 26, 27, 54, 55, 60, 90